SUPER BOWL BLUEPRINTS

SUPER BOWL BLUEPRINTS

Hall of Famers Reveal the Keys to Football's Greatest Dynasties

Bill Polian and Vic Carucci

TRIUMPH
BOOKS

No part of this publication may be reproduced, stored in a retrieval system, or transmitted in any form by any means, electronic, mechanical, photocopying, or otherwise, without the prior written permission of the publisher, Triumph Books LLC, 814 North Franklin Street, Chicago, Illinois 60610.

Library of Congress Cataloging in Publication Data available upon request.

This book is available in quantity at special discounts for your group or organization. For further information, contact:

Triumph Books LLC
814 North Franklin Street
Chicago, Illinois 60610
(312) 337-0747
www.triumphbooks.com

Printed in U.S.A.
ISBN: 978-1-62937-889-3
Design by Patricia Frey

To my wife, Eileen, and our children and grandchildren. Thanks for the sacrifice that allowed me to live a football life. I love you all. To Vic Carucci, my friend of over three decades, who did all the heavy lifting on this book. What a joy it is to work with you.

—Bill Polian

To the Carucci family's incredible collection of bright lights that bring a smile to Pop's face every day: Emma, Logan, Victor, and Oliver, who arrived just in time to be a part of this dedication. I love you with all my heart.

—Vic Carucci

Contents

Introduction

In planning this book, Vic and I thought we could do a wide-ranging look at the NFL's best teams. We soon found out that was impossible.

Too much ground to cover, too little space.

Two teams not included are the Don Shula ("Perfect") Miami Dolphins and the Bill Belichick New England Patriots. This is an oral history and the voices of Coach Shula, the driving force behind the Dolphins; their personnel director, George Young; and many key players, like Nick Buoniconti, are regrettably no longer with us. We couldn't do this great team justice without them.

The key Patriots of the dynasty, Coach Belichick and Tom Brady, are still looking to add to their incredible legacies and their story is a book unto itself. We will appropriately leave that to others.

The 1985 Chicago Bears, under Hall of Famer Mike Ditka and Buddy Ryan, and the 1998–99 Denver Broncos, under Bill Walsh–disciple Mike Shanahan and with Hall of Famer John Elway running essentially West Coast III, were also worthy subjects. Unfortunately, like in football, the publishing business doesn't allow you to cover everything you want.

We had no interest in ranking teams, so whoever your favorite team of all time might be—you're right! We have no wish to join that conversation.

As we dove more deeply into this project, a clear picture emerged. From 1975 through 1997, a small number of franchises—led by committed ownership, Hall of Fame general managers, and most importantly, charismatic coaches who created systems of football that had lasting effects on the NFL—controlled the league's landscape.

Bill Walsh and his West Coast offense, aided by his successor George Seifert, won five Super Bowls with San Francisco. Walsh's disciple, Mike Holmgren, brought West Coast II and a title to Green Bay.

The NFC East was dominant and incredibly competitive during this period. Joe Gibbs brought the one-back offense to the NFL and won three Super Bowls with Washington. Jerry Jones and Jimmy Johnson reinvented the Dallas Cowboys, and behind offensive triplets—Emmitt Smith, Troy Aikman, and Michael Irvin—won three Super Bowls as well. Bill Parcells brought the 3-4 power defense and a power run game to the New York Giants and garnered two Lombardi trophies.

In the AFC, Chuck Noll and the Steel Curtain Cover Two defense won four Super Bowls. Al Davis, Tom Flores, and the Raiders' long-ball offense won two. And Marv Levy's no-huddle attack went to an unprecedented four straight Super Bowls. They lost to the Giants, Washington, and then Dallas twice.

We decided to add the Tony Dungy–Peyton Manning Indianapolis Colts. They won 115 games from 2000 to 2009 and appeared in two Super Bowls, winning one. Former Giants quarterback Phil Simms pointed out that "Peyton changed how quarterback was played at every level" because he was totally in control of a no-huddle offense at the line of scrimmage.

All of these teams had outstanding GMs who put the personnel in place. Chuck Noll and Bill Walsh were essentially their own GMs. Al Davis, with a big assist from Ron Wolf, ruled the Raiders, and Wolf teamed up with Holmgren to resuscitate Green Bay.

Jimmy Johnson brought great personnel acumen to the Cowboys, while Jerry Jones did the wheeling and dealing. George Young and Bobby Beathard, as personnel directors, both played a major role in building Shula's Dolphins. They then went on to prominence as the architects of the Super Bowl Giants and Redskins, respectively. Charley Casserly succeeded Beathard in Washington and continued the run of excellence. I honed my craft with Marv Levy in Buffalo and later had the good fortune to team up with Tony Dungy in Indianapolis.

Davis, Flores, Noll, Walsh, Gibbs, Beathard, Parcells, Young, Jones, Johnson, Levy, Wolf, and yours truly are in the Pro Football Hall of Fame.

This oral history is told through the voices of those who participated. You will, as we did, hear things that astound you and things that will bring tears to your eyes. Most of all, you will hear the stories of these legendary teams from the inside.

History from those who made it.

We hope you enjoy reading it as much as we enjoyed its production.

—Bill Polian

CHAPTER 1

The Architect, Al Davis, and "The Greatness of the Raiders"

"I've always felt that the Oakland Raiders had a lot to do with the development of the Pittsburgh Steelers in the '70s, because they were a tough, physical football team. Every game was a war. If you were going to compete with them, you had to be better.

"And that didn't just go for us. If you look at the history, the Jets had to go through the Raiders to get to the Super Bowl, Kansas City had to go through the Raiders to get to the Super Bowl, the Baltimore Colts had to go through the Raiders to get to the Super Bowl.

"They were always the gatekeepers."

—Joe Greene, Pittsburgh Steelers Hall of Fame defensive end

BILL POLIAN: In 1963, a young and relatively unknown receivers coach for the American Football League champion San Diego Chargers became head coach (and de facto GM) of the downtrodden Oakland Raiders. His name, Al Davis, would become synonymous with the franchise. Al laid the foundation for what he termed "the greatness of the Raiders."

In 1966, he departed to become commissioner of the AFL. His audacious and aggressive tactics in signing NFL players to huge "futures" contracts soon forced the AFL-NFL merger. Al was bypassed as commissioner of the newly merged leagues in favor of NFL commissioner Pete Rozelle, a slight he never forgot. He returned to the Raiders as managing general partner and built the team into a three-time Super Bowl champion and one of the NFL's most iconic franchises.

In addition to drafting and signing many Hall of Fame players, Al hired Hall of Fame coaches John Madden and Tom Flores, as well as Hall of Fame talent evaluator and Super Bowl–winning GM Ron Wolf. He also made history by hiring the first African American head coach in the modern history of the NFL, Art Shell, a Hall of Fame offensive tackle for the Raiders.

Until the end of his life, Al was a force to be reckoned with on and off the field in the NFL. He moved the Raider franchise twice from Oakland to Los Angeles and back to Oakland, before their ultimate move to Las Vegas after his passing. He engaged in numerous court battles over those moves in the process, creating new law and new franchise-movement standards for the NFL.

Often portrayed as a renegade, Al was at heart a football man who believed in the preeminence of his franchise. He is, without question, one of the most celebrated and impactful drivers of professional football in history.

Wolf, Flores, and Hall of Fame cornerback Mike Haynes take you behind the scenes of Al Davis' Raiders.

RON WOLF: I went to work for the Raiders in May 1963, not long after I took my last final at the University of Oklahoma. In 1962, I worked briefly for *Pro Football Illustrated*, the forerunner to *Pro Football Weekly*, a publication based in Chicago. The editor, Ted Albert, happened to be in San Francisco when Al was named head coach and general manager of the Oakland Raiders. Ted was there to interview Al and Al mentioned he was looking for somebody in his personnel department who knew the names of college players. Ted recommended me.

It was a part-time job that paid $65 a week, which was more money than I could ever imagine making at that time. But the best part was I got to watch Al put the whole thing together.

It was an amazing situation. There was a director of player personnel, there were four assistant coaches, Al, and me. I was a gopher, running to get hot pastrami from the Doggie Diner for everybody. But I got to sit there and watch everybody else share thoughts on every player.

Al would start every meeting going through the American Football League rosters, position by position. Now, there were only eight teams, so that wasn't that difficult. Still, we would rate every guy. It was a marvelous introduction to identifying what it takes to play the game, because you could see who the outstanding players were at each position. I learned so much.

That year, the Raiders went 10–4, which was unbelievable. The big move that Al made was to sign a free-agent receiver named Art Powell. He was just a remarkable player. In those days, you carried 33 players and they had to play both ways in some situations and they certainly had to play special teams. Art was the highest-paid player on our team with a $25,000, no-cut contract. That was $5,000 a year more than our two quarterbacks, Tom Flores and Cotton Davidson, were making.

The Raiders kind of stumbled in '64, '65, and '66. During those times, Al made some excellent trades. First, he got foundational players in Tom Keating, a linebacker from the Buffalo Bills, and Hewritt Dixon, a tight end that he moved to fullback, from the Denver Broncos.

Al knew he needed somebody to cover Lance Alworth, the San Diego Chargers' great wide receiver, and in 1965 he traded with the Oilers for just the cornerback to do that, Kent McCloughan. Everybody wants to take credit for it, but McCloughan was the one who introduced bump-and-run coverage with the way he played Alworth so tight.

Then, in 1967, Al hit the jackpot. He traded again with Buffalo to get quarterback Daryle Lamonica and Al made a deal with the Houston Oilers to get George Blanda, a kicker and quarterback, and made yet another trade with Denver to get another cornerback, Willie Brown. Al loved corners and you don't get a pair like McCloughan and Brown very often.

What drove that love for corners was that Al believed one play could win a game or lose a game. He wanted to make sure that he was covered there, if you will, with guys that could play man-for-man because he always wanted a guy in the middle of the field and would tie all of that to the pass rush.

And you were going to hit that quarterback. You were going to try to hurt that guy. It was a different era, a different game. Some of these things those guys did would get them thrown out of the game today. Sometimes it worked, sometimes it didn't. We used to hit Joe Namath a lot. It didn't stop him.

MIKE HAYNES: Al felt if the corners could lock down the other team's top receivers, then you could do anything on defense. To me, defensive backs are just as valuable as a quarterback. Maybe, for Al, they were more valuable.

If you go zone, guys can just do their job and they know that you're going to go over to that flat no matter what, even if there's no reason to go over there. You're going to go over to that flat because that's your job. If you have man-to-man, then you're going to follow that guy and you're going to be closer to him than you are in zone.

Al believed defense wins games. So, if that offense can't get the ball to their great wide receiver, if that running back can't get through a hole because there's no hole there, you're going to have a great chance of winning. If you were to have said to Al, "If you could have the number one offense with the number three defense, or the number one defense with the number three offense, what would you prefer?" He would say, "I'd prefer the number one defense and the number three offense, because you can stop that offense."

I'd choose a great defense over a great offense every time, too.

BILL POLIAN: Tom Flores was an original Raider who actually predated Al Davis' arrival in Oakland. He beat out 10 other candidates to eventually become the Raiders' starting quarterback. In 1965, he had his best year, thriving under Al's tutelage.

True to Al's philosophy of wanting big-armed quarterbacks who could go deep in his beloved vertical passing game, Al traded Tom to the Buffalo Bills for Daryle "the Mad Bomber" Lamonica. Flores continued his playing career in Buffalo and Kansas City, two teams that, ironically, had been AFL champions prior to Al's arrival in Oakland.

After retiring as a player, Flores returned to Oakland, first as a receiver coach and then as quarterback coach under John Madden. He succeeded Madden as the Raider head coach in 1979. He was instrumental in drafting and developing Ken "The Snake" Stabler.

Under Tom's leadership, the Raiders won two Super Bowls. He is the only coach of Hispanic heritage to do so. Flores finished his career as head coach and then president of the Seattle Seahawks. He was inducted into the Pro Football Hall Fame in 2021.

TOM FLORES: I had heard of Al, good and bad, from when he was the offensive line coach at USC from 1957 to 1959. But I'd never met him face-to-face until he started as head coach of the Raiders in 1963. I had been with them since 1960 as one of 11 quarterbacks on the team. There were so many of us they couldn't even fit us all into the team photo.

Al was in town for less than a week when he called me into his office. We hadn't talked five minutes before he was up at the blackboard, going over plays and stuff. He was so energetic and so excited about the game that he was bringing the town. I saw right away that it was a deep-ball passing game.

Of course, Al had learned a lot of this stuff from Sid Gillman when Sid was head coach for the L.A./San Diego Chargers and Al was their wide receivers coach from 1960 to '62. I liked all the football parts that Al brought to the table because, for a quarterback, it was fun.

MIKE HAYNES: We all knew about Al's love for unbelievably fast players, such as Cliff Branch. All of us would see a fast player on the roster in preseason and say, "That guy is going to make the team because he's so fast."

So many guys made the team just because they were fast. They may not have been the smartest guy. They might not even have been a guy you could really count on. But if they could run, Al was going to give them a chance because most teams were built on not making any mental errors, on the concept that the team that makes the fewest errors is going to win.

Al said, "You know, the one thing you cannot coach is speed." He was going to keep that linebacker, because he runs 4.4, 4.5. He might get faked out all the time on running plays, but on passing plays, when you say, "You cover that back; wherever he goes, you go," that linebacker could do it.

That's what Al figured out.

RON WOLF: When I was with the Packers, Al would sit with me at the NFL Scouting Combine in Indianapolis and he'd say, "You know, that offense you're running, there must be a glass shield 18 yards up the field and you can't go past that shield because you dump the ball off all the time. Don't you ever just want to throw it as far as you can throw it? Don't you want to throw it up the field and see if anybody could catch it?"

TOM FLORES: Our training camp was in Santa Cruz, California, and we played our home games at Kezar Stadium in San Francisco. We had guys from all over the country in training camp, and they were asking, "Where's Oakland?" I tried to explain to them where it was in relationship to Santa Cruz.

Finally, in 1963, they were starting to build the Oakland Coliseum. Al said, "We're going to build this stadium and I want to have on it the finest team with the finest players."

Of course, a lot of that was PR stuff, but I could see the things that he was doing would help the team win. He brought in guys that could play and he gave guys that were marginal an opportunity. He also brought in talent from traditional Black colleges. He was always looking for a better way to do something.

I had just had my best year as a quarterback when I got traded to Buffalo. I didn't really want to go. The Raiders were my team. But I was traded for Daryle Lamonica. Daryle came in and had a marvelous career in Oakland because he was young, and he had a strong arm.

In that era of football, everybody was trying to play man-to-man. There weren't a lot of different types of zone combinations like they have now, zone blitzes and stuff like that. So, it was easy to read and Daryle could go back and he could play it. He had his heyday there for three or four years.

Then Ken "the Snake" Stabler come around and it took him a while before he became the starter. I've asked people, "How long do you think it was before Snake started?"

They'd say, "Oh, second, third year."

"No. Fifth year."

And even then, he didn't start right away. In fact, he went home the first year and he played for a minor league team. It wasn't all stardom for him.

In '72, my first year as an assistant coach in Oakland, Snake started his first game. He threw two or three interceptions in the first half, so he was benched. Lamonica played the rest of the year and we won our division. It wasn't until '73 when Snake finally became the starter. He went on to have seven, eight good and great years there.

RON WOLF: I'm going to pat myself on the back on drafting Kenny Stabler in the second round from Alabama in 1968. It was all Ron Wolf, because I did all the legwork. At that time, Paul Brown made the statement that there isn't any way in the world that a left-handed quarterback could ever play in the National Football League. We were bucking that.

We drafted Eldridge Dickey, a quarterback and receiver from Tennessee State, first and then in the second round, we drafted Ken Stabler. John Rauch, who was our head coach at the time, helped me with that. John was a legend in SEC football, having been a standout quarterback at Georgia, where he also was an assistant coach before joining the Raiders. He knew all the people down there and asked them how they worked with a left-handed quarterback. He went into the center snaps and all those various types of things.

They called Ken "the Snake" for a reason. He was a marvelous runner. Like Joe Namath, his Alabama predecessor at quarterback, he got hurt in college and you never really got to see that mobility in pro football. But Ken was so accurate. I wasn't there to witness this because I was working with the Tampa Bay Buccaneers at the time, but it was said that the ball never hit the ground in the Raiders' practice the Thursday before their Super Bowl win against the Vikings.

Ken just had unbelievable accuracy and touch and all those things. Plus, the ball was crisp, and he had the guts of a stock car driver.

MIKE HAYNES: Al Davis loved football. He loved what it took to be great. He was one of those guys who wanted to know everything he could about a player. Where's he from? What is he about? Where did he get this way of thinking? Al thought that those types of things could be discovered, and they could be duplicated on his team.

Al loved trying to figure out what made coaches and players great. Before games, he would go up to members of the opposing team and talk to guys and he would know where they went to high school, what their high school coach was like. He would say, "Yeah, I've been following you since high school. I know about your coach…."

In those days, all the great players in the league wanted to play for Al because he had an appreciation for them and shared his appreciation for them. He gave us first-class treatment.

As a Patriot, when the game was over, everybody would usually just go their own way. Sometimes we would go to this little restaurant on Route One in Foxborough, Massachusetts, and just hang out there. But Al had a party for us at a hotel. He rented a space and each player had his own table, so I could bring my family and my friends that I invited to the game and they could come and sit with me and my family. He treated us with class and respect. His real strong suit was his passion and affection for the game.

If somebody stopped, let's say, big Earl Campbell, and the guy who came up and hit him wasn't a big guy, Al would make a point of saying, "Wow! That was a good hit!" He made you feel like he was a guy that you could go to if something was going wrong or you wanted to talk about something. You had that kind of feeling for him.

When I first joined the Raiders, I was looking for a new contract, one that would pay me much more than I was making with the Patriots and one that would end up putting me at the top of the Raider payroll. Al said, "Mike, you don't understand the culture here. You haven't done anything for the Raiders—nothing. If I brought you in and made you the highest-paid player, I'd have 20 guys lined up outside my door, saying, 'Hey, what has he done for the Raiders?'"

I said, "You know what, Mr. Davis? I understand that, I get it."

He was being reasonable. He also was giving me everything that I needed to hear to motivate me.

TOM FLORES: Al brought in players that sometimes were considered trouble. He treated us all the same, but you also had to treat us as individuals and that's not easy to do, because you still had to be part of the team. John Matuszak had some issues. Lyle Alzado was a wild, crazy guy. Ken Stabler was a fun guy to be around. He wasn't a troublemaker, but he just drove Al crazy because he always was trying to do a new contract every time he went through a divorce, I guess. Al would just shake his head.

But at times you'd go down the list and just say, "Why in the hell is that guy here?" Then you'd realize why he was there and why he was staying there and why he was able to do certain things that he wasn't able to do elsewhere. It didn't always work, not all of them were successes.

But we created an atmosphere for them where they could succeed. You make the atmosphere where they can play well and win and have a good time. You don't take away their personality. Let them be. Let the Alzados be the Alzados, the Matuszaks be the Matuszaks.

Even with some of the interesting guys we had in our history, we always had a pretty darn good locker room. You know you have a good locker room when you have good players and some that are just average pros. But you need those average guys on your squad—special team guys, smart guys—and they need to be on the same page as you. They need to have the same passion to win and to play for you and for that team.

When you're drafting people, the question you always ask is, "Is he going to be a leader? And if so, what kind of leader will be?" Then, you say, "This guy is going to be a vocal leader," or, "This guy is going to be a quiet leader."

If you structure your team that way, you end up having a pretty strong locker room, because that's where those guys stand up and let themselves be heard. They won't do it in public, they won't do it in the press. But when you get in the locker room and you lock the door and it's just the team, that's when the leaders shine.

They have the strength to stand up when the locker room gets a little hectic or somebody comes in and you need someone to be able to take that person aside and say, "This is not the way it's done. This is the way we want to do it here."

You don't change a guy, but you've got to direct him a little bit.

RON WOLF: Al ran everything. There wasn't anything he didn't do. When it came to evaluating players, his basic thing was height, weight, speed.

The great thing about working for him was he let you do your job. My job was scouting. But when you were preparing for the draft, you'd better be ready, because Al was going to come after you.

He pulled out all your old reports and he would read them out loud. He'd say, "How could you miss this guy? How could you miss that guy?" When I'd go in to see him, I would prepare myself and, invariably, he'd ask the one question I hadn't thought about. I don't know how he knew to do that, but he did it.

I remember, we were in the 12th round in 1979, and Al wanted a guy from Norfolk State. I wanted a nose tackle from Oklahoma named Reggie Kinlaw. With that, I got, "He better be a good player or I'm going to fire you."

Now, Reggie was more than a good player. What he did to Jeff Bostic, the center for the Washington Redskins, in the Raiders' 38–9 victory in Super Bowl XVIII, was unbelievable.

Yet Al was saying, "This guy better be a good player." You're talking about a guy in the 12th round, for God's sake.

Believe it or not, that was such a contrast to when we made Tim Brown the sixth overall choice in 1988. It was the highest we had ever picked in my time with the Raiders. Al wanted Paul Gruber, an offensive tackle from Wisconsin. We were trying to work a deal to get him and couldn't. Tampa took him with the fourth pick.

Al then turned to me and said, "You run the draft," and he left the room. So, I'm sitting there and I'm looking at Tim Brown, Michael Irvin, and Sterling Sharpe. That's not a bad trio, huh?

I took Brown because of the return ability.

MIKE HAYNES: One day during the off-season, I was working out at the Raiders' facility in El Segundo, California. Al Davis opened the door. I was at the other end of the football field. He put his arm up and waved me over.

"Mike, I want to show you something," he said. "I want to get your thoughts on this."

He turned on a projector and said, "Tell me what you think of this."

It was a college game and the kicker's getting ready to attempt maybe a 35-yard field goal. He goes to kick it, the ball gets blocked, a guy picks up the ball, he pitches it to one of his teammates and that guy is running up the field. And then a cornerback from Tennessee named Terry McDaniel passes his own guy and gets a block. That block sends the ball-carrier all the way to the end zone.

Al said, "Did you see that?"

I'm going, "Well, wait a minute. Did I see the guy block the kick? Yes. Did I see the guy pick up the ball and run instead of just thinking about diving on the ball? I saw that, too. Or did I see the guy who ran and got that key block?"

"The key block."

"Yeah, I saw it."

"You can't coach that, Mike."

"What do you mean?"

"You can't coach people to do that. They just made a great play by blocking that field goal. That's when most people would start to celebrate. But not this kid. This kid wanted that to be a touchdown. And he ran past everybody to get to that one guy."

When you saw that film, he ran 20 yards past people. It was just unbelievable that he was that fast. Then I was thinking, "That's odd. He called me all the way over here to see that? I don't get it."

When we drafted Terry McDaniel in the first round, I said, "What the hell? We drafted Terry McDaniel on that play?"

Then, I started thinking, "Maybe Al is different from everybody." He was saying, "You can't coach that." I'm thinking, "Why can't you coach that?"

Then I started thinking, "Maybe there are things that I do that you can't coach, and the reason Al has liked me is because nobody else can do it. And I do it instinctively. I wonder if that's what everybody on this team is?"

So right away, I started looking at the team differently. Rather than seeing a guy and saying, "He's undersized, he can't do this, he can't do that," I began to say, "He might be on the team for one specific reason."

TOM FLORES: Al was not for everybody, but if you knew him really well, like I did, like John Madden knew him, you knew that he did have a heart. Some people thought otherwise. He always wanted to be the renegade, he always wanted to be the maverick. That's the way he led his life and his team.

But he would do nice, warm, fuzzy things. If you needed help and you called him, he would be there. When I was in Seattle and my wife, Barbara, got sick, Al was the first guy to call. He said, "What can we do? How can I help?"

I was pretty impressed with that, but I knew he would do something like that. He did that with a lot of people.

Al and the rest of the original AFL owners were a lot different than the NFL owners. They were easier to get along with. We actually liked our owners. We'd get guys who had gotten cut from the NFL and when they came to the Raiders, they'd say they hated their owners. I remember one of our assistant coaches, Earl Leggett, saying that when he played for the Chicago Bears, George Halas wanted to fight him over a $500 raise.

BILL POLIAN: John Madden's tenure ushered in a golden age for the Raiders. Over his 10 seasons, the team had a 103–32–7 record. His teams won the Western Division seven times and made the playoffs eight times. In '76, the Raiders were 13–1 in the regular season, 2–0 in the playoffs, and capped off Madden's greatest season with a 32–14 win over Minnesota in the Super Bowl.

Ironically, the game most remembered in Madden's career by NFL fans was a loss, the "Immaculate Reception" game versus the Pittsburgh Steelers in a divisional playoff on December 23, 1972. This game still sticks in every Raiders' craw. Many believe, to this day, that the ball hit the ground before Franco Harris of the Steelers controlled it and ran for the winning touchdown.

Madden coached some of the greatest players in pro football history. His Hall of Famers include Fred Biletnikoff, George Blanda, Willie Brown, Dave Casper, Ray Guy, Ted Hendricks, Jim Otto, Art Shell, Ken Stabler, and Gene Upshaw. Al Davis, of course, shares the credit with Madden in that regard.

A large majority of today's fans know John as the former analyst of each week's top NFL telecasts or the namesake of the popular Madden NFL video game. Long before those pursuits, he was a man who brought Al Davis' vision for a preeminent sports franchise to life.

RON WOLF: When we were getting ready to hire John Madden, Al had me call Chuck Noll, the head coach of the Pittsburgh Steelers, to find out what he thought of John. John and Chuck were tight. In fact, John had an opportunity to go to the Steelers as Chuck's defensive coordinator. But when Al fired John Rauch, John Madden had the chance to become head coach of the Raiders.

I knew Chuck would be a reliable source on Madden. I had spent a lot of time around Chuck. In those days, the draft was in November, so in the spring, there'd be coaches out scouting and, boy, did I learn a great deal from Chuck.

During a visit to a school, I would always sit next to Chuck when coaches would come in and start talking about their players and just listen to what he asked. Then, I'd go to dinner with him that night and find out why he asked this, why he asked that, all the nuances involved.

He taught me about the importance of physiques and movement. I remember there was a cornerback that everybody said was going to be a first- or second-round draft choice. I was having dinner with Chuck and he said, "There's no way that he'll ever play corner because he's long-waisted and short-legged."

I never thought about that. He didn't say the guy wouldn't play in the secondary, just not cornerback. And you know what? He was right. Just little things like that, Chuck could see when a lot of other people didn't.

So, it was quite an endorsement when Chuck said he thought John would be an exceptional head coach. They knew each other from when John was the defensive coordinator at San Diego State and Chuck was defensive coordinator of the Chargers.

John was very bright. He was more defensive oriented, but as he progressed, he became really good at managing the final two minutes of the game. He won a lot of games for the Raiders in those final two minutes.

I guess you'd have to say John Madden was a players' coach, because he really respected the players and the players respected him. But don't forget, you always had Al Davis standing on the sidelines. It was kind of like Darth Vader was standing over there.

To be a coach for Al Davis for one year was like 10 years at any other place because of all you had to go through. He was tough on those guys. Al would meet with the head coach and his staff Monday, Tuesday, Wednesday, and Thursday night for three hours to go over what they were planning to do and how they were going to do it. He covered it all—offense, defense, special teams, player moves. Al was always interested in player moves.

And on Sunday, you had the little slips coming down from the press box saying, "Run this play… Run that play." It wasn't easy, but John had great success. That was part and parcel of the job. If you were going to be the head coach with the Raiders, you were going to have that.

TOM FLORES: My relationship with the Raiders continued even after I was traded to Buffalo in 1967. I never lost contact with them. I spent my last couple of years as a player in Kansas City, which was a good thing for me as far as winning because I was able to be a part of the Super Bowl IV championship team.

When I got a chance to come back to the Raiders as receivers coach in 1972, they were a playoff team almost every year. John Madden was the head coach and I got a chance to become part of a team that I never wanted to leave in the first place.

I always had a different point of view than John because he was a defensive-minded coach. But he had an open mind to offense and he did spend most of his time with the offense. When I came in, I was in charge of the wide receivers and the tight ends and John used to take the quarterbacks. I think he had to gain trust in me before he turned the quarterbacks over to me.

Then, within a short period of time, I became the passing game coach. I would draw up the plan for the passing game and then the running back coach and the offensive line coach would draw up the plan for the running game. We would present it to John, and he would yay or nay it and then we'd discuss it.

John was really good on game day. He did a great job of implementing the game plan, orchestrating the timing of when to send in plays and when to not. It was great that he allowed me the freedom of doing certain things. But if I came up with a wacko play, he'd look at me like I was a little goofy and I'd say, "Okay, we won't try that one."

Once in a while, I'd come up with a play that we both knew came from Al Davis. His plays were always that you had to throw the ball 90 yards down the field. But we liked it. We had Cliff Branch, who could fly. He was a track guy that knew how to play football and we took advantage of that.

BILL POLIAN: The image most fans have of the Raiders is reflected by their logo: the fierce, marauding pirate with an eyepatch and a scowl. Over the years, Al Davis enhanced the image with a physical, intimidating style of play epitomized by defenders like Jack Tatum, John Matuszak, and Lyle Alzado. They were characterized by Steeler coach Chuck Noll as a "criminal element."

Al wasn't afraid to burnish his and the Raiders' persona as renegades by engaging in lawsuits against the league and his fellow owners. In defiance of NFL rules, Al moved the Raiders from Oakland to Los Angeles and back to Oakland.

He frequently spoke of the Raiders' "commitment to excellence" and of the "greatness of the Raiders." During the '70s, '80s, and early '90s, his team backed up those words, as well as his "Just win, baby!" mantra, on the field. Opponents, particularly in the AFC, took exception to the words and actions in big way.

Beloved in Oakland and L.A., the Raiders were public enemy No. 1 to fans of the rest of the teams in the NFL. They were "the Evil Empire" long before that title was bestowed upon the Yankees by Red Sox fans. Oakland fans adopted the reputation enthusiastically, dressing as movie villains in silver and black with Darth Vader, of Star Wars fame, the leading character. They sat in an end zone section of the Oakland Coliseum known as "the Black Hole."

Al Davis reveled in the image.

MIKE HAYNES: When I came to the Raiders, I realized that there was no in-between with fans. They either loved them, or they hated them. And they were hated more than any other team in the league. We would play charity basketball games and people would show up just to boo us. I couldn't believe it.

Once, a woman gave me a hat that said "Raider Haters" on it and asked me to sign it. I said, "I'm not going to put my name on a hat that says, 'Raider Haters.'"

"Please sign it!"

I warned her that if I signed it, I would scratch off the "Raider Haters" part. I don't know if she thought I was bluffing, but I scratched it off and signed the hat. She pitched a fit.

RON WOLF: We started out with a rivalry against the Chiefs. That dwindled. Then it became the Jets. That dwindled. Then came December 23, 1972. My feelings for the Steelers changed after our divisional round playoff game that day at Three Rivers Stadium. The Immaculate Reception—Franco

Harris scooping up the ricocheted pass after Jack Tatum collided with John "Frenchy" Fuqua—left me and everyone else in the Raider organization with such bitter feelings.

As the Steelers were preparing for whoever they were going to play in one of their Super Bowls, I remember telling Lionel Taylor, who was on their coaching staff, "I hope you lose." He couldn't believe that.

"You've got to root for the American League," he said.

"Bullshit! I'm not rooting for you guys."

There was real animosity there.

I remember going to University of Missouri, when Woody Widenhofer was the head football coach after he had spent 11 seasons with the Steelers coaching linebackers and then as their defensive coordinator. I was sitting with him in the locker room and I said to him, "Can you imagine? I'm sitting in a Pittsburgh Steeler's locker room. Can you imagine that?" He laughed.

After that Franco Harris thing, it was important to beat those guys.

TOM FLORES: I loved the old American Football League. When the merger turned it into the American Football Conference and the National Football Conference in the NFL, we lost our identity. I didn't really like that. I always thought they should have kept it AFL and NFL. And I always got the feeling the NFL didn't want the AFL to be a part of it.

But without the AFL, along with TV obviously, football wouldn't be what it is today. I think the AFL brought a lot of change in the game on the field, a lot of change to the way you scouted guys. It brought a lot of the Black players into football, because as historically Black colleges were being ignored by the NFL in the old days, the American Football League started scouting them a lot and realizing that there were a lot of good players at those schools.

The American Football League was like a family. The Raiders were like a family. We started in Santa Cruz, just a little tiny family, and then we got a little bigger. We didn't have a home, so we kind of moved around for a little bit. Then, we finally got a home and we got a little bigger.

The American Football League reached out and got more cousins and uncles, and pretty soon you've got these guys all over the world. The Raiders were a big part of that. Their fans looked like they were bad guys, but they're really not bad people. It was like Halloween every Sunday, but they had the great tailgate parties and it was like a giant family.

You had the Raider Nation. The Chiefs. The Buffalo Bills. All fans with so much passion.

MIKE HAYNES: I started realizing, because I was a Raider, our mindset is shaped by the success the franchise had had through the years. With the Patriots, we'd get to the playoffs and might even have the best record and have a bye the first week, but we never won a playoff game. When I got to the Raiders, I didn't want to even bring that up, because I didn't want to be the reason that the Raiders failed to win that playoff game.

We began the postseason against the Steelers, and we played them really hard. I covered John Stallworth, I got an interception and we won the game. I felt like, "Whew! I got that big bear off my back."

After the last practice before the AFC Championship Game against Seattle to get to the Super Bowl, I was expecting Tom Flores to talk to our team for like 15 minutes and have some of the veterans who have played in Super Bowls say a few words or something. But Tom treated it just like another game. He called us all up and he said, "Okay, guys, we've got a big game tomorrow, but we play a lot of big games. I'll see you at the hotel tonight at six."

I'm like, "What? That's it? I'm getting ready to play in the biggest game of my life and that's all he has to say about it? Be at the hotel by six?"

That's when I started to develop this philosophy that if you feel pressure, you will fail. It's the job of the coach to somehow get you to not think about the pressure, but just think about your job and let the game take care of itself. And when I adopted that philosophy, I started seeing it play out in basketball games, golf matches, you name it. If a guy has a little three-foot putt, something that he normally probably doesn't even read and just hits it to the back of the cup, but decides to read it and he acts like it's something more than it is, he's going to miss it.

I started realizing that all pressure is self-imposed, and all great coaches and all great players have a way of just making it seem like it's not the biggest thing in the world.

Another thing I learned about being a Raider was the mentality that if you mess with one of us, you mess with all of us. We were playing the Miami Dolphins at the L.A. Coliseum and this guy goes into half-motion and then he cracks back on our linebacker, Jack Squirek, and broke his jaw. And so everybody's on Lester Hayes, saying, "Lester, you've got to call out the crack! You've got to call out the crack, man!" Lester had a stuttering problem, and he said, "I-I-I-I couldn't g-g-g-get it out. I couldn't get it out."

The next time it was a short-yardage situation, the guy comes back in the game and he goes in that little short motion again. This time, Matt Millen is at linebacker in place of Jack. And this time, Lester yells at the top of his lungs, "C…c…rrr…a…aaaaack!"

When the guy goes in to hit Matt, Matt hits him, the guy falls on the ground, and Lester and Matt are just giving the guy the business. They're hitting him while he's on the ground and forgetting all about the running back with the ball. Fortunately, I caught him before he could score a touchdown. We held them and I don't even think they scored on that drive.

But that was the Raiders. You don't do what that guy did to Jack and get away with it. I started to understand that that's the way the Raiders were.

BILL POLIAN: John Madden became the Raiders' linebacker coach in 1967. He had been a junior college coach for two seasons and then defensive coordinator at San Diego State. After only two seasons with the club, Al Davis named John the head coach of the Raiders.

At 32 years of age, John was the youngest head coach in the AFL. Madden wasted no time putting his stamp on Al Davis' Raiders. Right away, he identified improved tackling as a priority.

"Al was all about offense," Madden said. "I felt we weren't tough enough on defense. I told Ron Wolf we needed to draft the two best tacklers in college football. We took safety Jack Tatum and linebacker Phil Villapiano and immediately became a better, tougher defense."

RON WOLF: It was Ken Herock, our personnel director, who recommended Jack Tatum when he was coming out of Ohio State. He was 5'10" and a quarter, 211 pounds, and ran a 4.4. Then, we got the film and started watching how he played and how remarkable he was as a player. Woody Hayes told

Al Davis that he was his best running back, but he didn't want to use him on offense because he was too valuable on defense.

Somebody can point to a player and say, "Yeah, that's my guy." That was very rare with the Raiders, because it was more of a general feeling within the room to take a guy. Of course, you had to fight through Al Davis, which was tough because he could intimidate the whole room, myself included.

Jack had an aura about him. It was kind of like, "Don't mess with me." And nobody did. He's the only rookie that I know, in my time with the Raiders, that didn't have to stand on the table at training camp and sing his alma mater. His older teammates were afraid to ask him to do it. When you saw him, he was not a physically imposing individual. But what a tremendous athlete.

John Madden said to me that Tatum changed the entire defense of the Oakland Raiders. People were afraid to go inside, because he was going to hunt you up and he would hit you. And that was something he could do. He was a heck of a tackler.

Once we got him, you could see what he meant to that team. His presence made everybody tougher, made everybody more aggressive because you knew you had this guy there that could back it up. He was quiet, didn't say much of anything. He was just one heck of a football player.

I wouldn't say we had household names on defense. Only a fan could name the members of that defensive line or, for that matter, the secondary other than the corners. Dan Conners was in the middle. He is a marvelous player. He never got his due. Gus Otto was one 'backer and Phil Villapiano was the other 'backer. You always look back and say to yourself, "Should we have done something different?"

We kind of lost sight of Jack Ham from Penn State. He and Villapiano came out the same year, 1971. We got hot on Villapiano and selected him in the second round, 45th overall. We couldn't have gotten Ham, who the Steelers took 11 picks earlier in the second, unless we took him in the first round, and we took Tatum in the first round.

TOM FLORES: When I became head coach of the Raiders in 1979, I knew the team quite well, because I had been there for seven years as an assistant to John. Prior to that, I'd been there as a player, but had grown a lot and a lot of things had changed with me over that period of time. Most of all, I knew how the operation worked and I knew Al Davis and how he worked. I felt we needed to change, but not a lot because the culture was still there, the work ethic was still there.

We just had to make sure we upgraded ourselves as far as our thinking was concerned. Not so much our plan, because our plan was still pretty darn good, but our thinking. You've got to think beyond what we had been doing because the game was starting to change a little bit.

What it has become today is more of a passing league. We were leaning towards that, because Al liked to do that. If the owner is happy, then I'm happy. When he was unhappy, watch out. What he liked, I liked. I think that helped everything. John was same way.

When I first took over, I'd sit in the meeting room and say, "Alright, who's going be our next leader in the locker room? Gene Upshaw's the leader right now. Who's going to take over when Uppy retires?"

We had a linebacker, Ted Hendricks, who was brilliant. He would know the game plan inside-out and then he was a pain in the ass in practice, because he got bored. Dave Casper, our great tight end, was the same way. They'd do something and then they'd say, "Do we have to repeat that again?"

I'd say, "Yes. If I have to do it again, you have to do it again."

MIKE HAYNES: As tall and skinny as Ted Hendricks was, you would think they'd just blow him right back, 10 yards off the ball. Never happened. I can't explain why or how, but he always played great.

He was the one guy on our defense that could stand up in the middle before the play was called and point to where the ball was going.

TOM FLORES: Ted really didn't want to be a leader, but we made him a leader. I said, "The guys elected you captain."

He said, "I don't want to be captain."

"Tough. You'd better go out there and be their leader."

Pretty soon, he and Jack Tatum were the two captains and neither one of them wanted to be captain, but they turned out to be strong captains, because when they talked, the other guys listened. That's what a leader has to be—somebody that doesn't talk a lot, but when he does, you listen and pay attention. Those guys were just strong, strong people.

Snake was our starting quarterback and Jim Plunkett, who we had picked up in 1978, was our backup. We always liked Jim. He was right across the Bay at Stanford, so we got the chance to know him pretty well. He and I also had a lot in common, background-wise, so when he was released by the Niners, he was a free agent. I watched him when we played them that year. I thought his arm was shot, there was something wrong, but I couldn't figure it out.

So, Ron Wolf brought him over and John Madden asked Lew Erber and I to work him out. We put him through all kinds of drills. I said, "There's nothing wrong with him physically. I have no idea what's wrong with him anywhere else, but physically, he's strong. Strong arm and can still move."

Jim never was a great scrambler, but he could still move in his own way. So, we signed him and just made him sit and learn the system. No pressure.

The next year, I became head coach and we traded the Snake to Houston for Dan Pastorini, another strong-armed quarterback. I really wasn't for that trade. I wasn't so sure that was going to work out. Dan had his own way of doing things. He was kind of set in his ways, whereas Jim had adjusted to our way.

We knew that Jim was still able and capable but how effective, we weren't sure. Then, during the draft, we took Marc Wilson. Now, all of a sudden, we had three quarterbacks, all number one draft choices.

Mark was going to learn things our way in the pros. Of course, in those days, you could keep these guys forever if you wanted. Free agency wasn't an issue, so we didn't have to worry about that part. In the pecking order, we put Pastorini first, which might have been a mistake because we were struggling a little bit.

Then, Dan broke his leg. Jim came in and we were still struggling. There were all kinds of rumors that I was going to be fired and that Sid Gillman was behind the scenes getting ready to come in and take over the team.

My first meeting with a team, I just told them, "We have some issues going on and this whole thing is very touchy right now. We're not doing anything wrong. We just need to do it better. So, we're going to jump on your ass a little bit more, and we're going to push a little bit more so we can do it right.

"Our philosophy isn't wrong, our thinking isn't wrong. We're just not doing it well enough. You guys read the papers, you hear the rumors going around, you know what's going on. So, we're not kidding anybody."

In other words, I was telling them, "My ass is on the line. But so is yours. But we need to push it as professionals, and without panic." And we did. And without panic. We worked and we didn't change anything dramatically. Because if you start making changes, the players will see it right away. All of a sudden, you're fragmented and you're reaching, grab-bag style, for another idea.

I'd say, "No, no, no. If that was a good idea last week, why is it not a good idea this week? Just because we lost the game? No. We have to do something to take advantage of the other team's weakness with what we have."

We also needed to rebuild it a little bit because we were getting old. Gene Upshaw and Art Shell had a year or two left. We picked up running back Kenny King, we picked up safety Burgess Owens as a veteran, we picked up defensive end Cedrick Hardman as a veteran, same with wide receiver Bobby Chandler.

I had coached Bobby my one year coaching in Buffalo, when he was a rookie. Al asked me, "What do you think of Bobby Chandler?" I really liked him. I said, "What do they want for him?" He said, "They want Phil Villapiano." At that point, Phil was hurt, so I was all for it.

From our '76 Super Bowl team to our '80 Super Bowl team, there were only 11 guys left on the roster. Strong guys. Good locker room guys. Burgess Owens was a great leader for us. Bobby Chandler was as well. The pieces fit. We took our kind of guys that could play and live and become teammates like we wanted, like we had before with those 11 guys from the 1976 team.

There were a lot of nuances we had to make work and we were able to do it. I think, when you look at some of the great dynasties, you can just put a guy in and he fits right away. One of the greatest of all time was the Yankees. You'd give a guy the pinstripe uniform and say, "Okay, you're playing right field. Don't worry about playing center field. Some guy named DiMaggio has that covered. You're going to play right field. Play it well."

In '83, we had a great team. We were loaded. We had Marcus Allen. Plunkett and Wilson were our quarterbacks. Cliff Branch was still able to run deep. Todd Christensen had a great year as a tight end. We had Hendricks,

Rod Martin. We had Lester Hayes, but we didn't have another corner. When we had a chance to get Mike Haynes that year in a trade with New England, I said, "Whoa!"

We made the deal right at the deadline. We were actually past the deadline, but we got away with it. That was another one of those Al Davis things.

MIKE HAYNES: When the trade happened, I was having contract problems with the Patriots. I was starting to feel like the Patriots really didn't want to win. They really didn't want to go to the Super Bowl when my life was dedicated every single year to winning the championship.

I wasn't playing football just to play football, just because I was good at it. I played because I wanted to win as many championships as I could. I wasn't sure the Patriots really wanted to do that. They were trading away our good players and things like that.

Pat Sullivan was the general manager and we had a great relationship. I said to Pat, "I don't know that I really want to be here anymore."

"Okay, we'll try to trade you."

A little while later, he came back and said, "Mike, there's no one interested."

"What?"

I then got a phone call from Al Davis. He said, "I want to talk to you about becoming a Raider. What do you think about that?"

That was kind of hard for me at the time. The Raiders were not really one of my favorite teams because we had a player named Darryl Stingley who became a quadriplegic on a vicious hit from Jack Tatum. That injury changed my life. But I thought about it and I justified becoming a Raider because it wasn't going to be the Oakland Raiders. It was going be the L.A. Raiders and I'm from L.A, so I saw it as an opportunity to go home. I saw the Raiders as a new team.

"Yeah, Mr. Davis," I said, "I'd love to come play for you in Los Angeles."

The next day, Pat Sullivan called and said, "Mike, I'm sorry. We were in discussions with the Raiders, but the trading deadline elapsed, and we didn't have a deal."

So, I yelled out to my wife, "Well, honey, it looks like I'm going to be retiring."

Al Davis called again and said, "Hey, Mike, congratulations. You're a Raider."

I said, "I just got off the phone with Pat Sullivan and he said you guys didn't have a deal before the trading deadline."

Al went, "Ah, shit!" And hung up.

I called my attorney, Howard Slusher, and told him about the conversations I had with Mr. Davis and Pat Sullivan. Howard said, "Let me call you back." He called me back and said, "I want you to fly out here to L.A."

I made the trip and stayed at his house. We went over to the Raiders' facility and signed a contract. The NFL then said the contract was null and void, so I was left with nothing else to do except sue and say that contract should be good, that the system is no good, and we need to change the system.

We went to court to see when or if my case should take up the time of the court. The NFL was there, Gene Upshaw was there for the NFL Players Association, Howard and another attorney named Joseph Alioto, who was a good friend of Al's and also the former mayor of San Francisco. The judge decided that he did want to hear the case. He said, "Gentlemen, get out your calendars and let me see what you're doing in January or February," which was after the season. I was pissed off like you would not believe, because I was going to miss a season. I had never missed a season.

But my attorneys all seemed like it didn't matter. The league attorneys basically said, "It'll be a cold day in hell before we go to court to talk about these issues."

The Patriots would have to show that they were a small-market team and they really couldn't afford me, and they'd have to open up their books to show that. Of course, that wasn't going to happen.

The league attorneys said, "Look, Mike, you go to the Raiders, we'll work out the trade details later. But we're not going to go to court with this."

TOM FLORES: Getting Mike Haynes completed our defense. We had Lester Hayes, but we always had to make up for a corner that opponents would pick on. When we got Mike, all of a sudden you just said, "Okay, you've got the receiver you're assigned to."

And that was it.

He was like Velcro on those guys. That just changed the whole dynamic of how we approached other teams because we could take away the two guys outside and then put extra guys in the box to shut down the run.

Mike Haynes was a marvelous football player, strong in the locker room and bright. We had a lot of bright players.

BILL POLIAN: Mike Haynes and Darryl Stingley were teammates and the best of friends with the New England Patriots. In a very famous encounter, with a technique that is outlawed today in the NFL (and would very likely draw a hefty fine and lengthy suspension), Tatum launched and led with the crown of his helmet to drill Stingley with a hit so explosive and violent that it caused paralysis.

Haynes never forgot, nor forgave Tatum for the hit that ended Stingley's career and permanently handicapped him.

MIKE HAYNES: After Jack Tatum retired, he lived in the Bay Area and I remember him coming with us to a road game. I think we were playing Kansas City and Al let him fly on our plane. I didn't like Jack Tatum. I could not get over the experience that I had as a Patriot playing the Raiders and what Jack did to Darryl Stingley and how he handled it. I almost quit playing football because of that.

When Jack came out with his book, *They Call Me Assassin*, saying that he was purposely trying to injure guys like that, that just bothered me. When I saw him sitting on the plane, my whole temperature just changed. I just was immediately pissed off.

Darryl was one of the guys that I absolutely loved. He and Raymond Hamilton and Prentice McCray were my neighbors, and every morning we would drive over to practice together all the time. Darryl was like a big brother to me and to see that happen and see how Jack dealt with it, I just wasn't really happy.

Before that happened, I used to get psyched up in front of my locker. I would just be deep breathing, eyes closed, rocking kind of back and forth, just working myself up into this fit. Because one of the things I learned at Arizona State, playing for coach Frank Kush, is that I couldn't just go into a game without working myself up.

That lesson came in my freshman year. We were playing Texas El Paso and I wasn't expecting to get on the field. We were killing them and because we were beating them so bad, the coaches put me in at free safety. I'm going, "Yeah, they're just going to be throwing. This is going to be great."

Well, they didn't throw. The first play I was in it was a running play, a draw or something, and I came up as the free safety to tackle the guy and I didn't even touch him. He just faked me out of my shoes, I just hit air. Coach Kush called me to the side and told me, "Get your ass on the bench and just sit down where you belong."

I sat down on the bench, I pulled my helmet over my face and started to cry, because I was thinking, "My college career is over. That was the chance I was looking for, and it's over. I'm not going to get to play anymore."

I didn't get to play anymore that game, but the next game, it was the same kind of thing. We were ahead and he put me in again, but this time, they did pass it and I got an interception. I started running the ball and I ran right into an offensive lineman. I bounced back up and then I took off again and I almost scored. Before that game, I had worked myself up and I realized I needed that to be good.

But after the Darryl Stingley play, it just changed me. I realized that I could have done that to a player. I would have hit a guy like that if I had the opportunity. I used to say, "I'm going to knock that guy's block off."

After that injury, I realized something was wrong with me to think that way. This guy will never walk again. I can't imagine doing that to somebody.

When I saw Jack Tatum on the plane, I just wanted to let him have it. I realized at that point that I had changed. I realized that he was kind of the guy that I could have become. But I didn't even know how to deal with it. I'm not used to running away from my problems. I'm used to facing them. I decided I would face this one, too.

Jack had an empty seat next to him, so I said, "Hey, Jack, you got a minute? Can I sit here?" He said, "Okay." I'm sure he could read my body language, and I think a lot of guys on the team were probably watching me. I don't know if Al did this on purpose, but he probably did. That's the kind of guy Al was.

I said, "Hey, Jack, man, we've just got to talk."

"Yeah, what do you want?"

"In your book, man, you said you and George Atkinson were trying to hurt guys like that."

"Yeah, yeah. But I never did, Mike."

"You know, I can relate to that, because I guess I kind of was the same way. But why didn't you go see Darryl in the hospital? Why did you say what you were saying? I mean, you were like condoning what happened and stuff like that. You were playing on it."

"Mike, look, I didn't want to put that stuff in a book. They told me that if I want to be in a book, I had to do that."

"Oh, okay, I get it. So, you were doing it because you needed the money."

We ended up talking a little more about it. I knew I could never be Jack's friend, but at least I got a little closure.

BILL POLIAN: In January 1981, amid an international crisis and a monumental intramural battle in the NFL, Tom Flores tried to climb out of the gargantuan shadow of his predecessor, John Madden, in Super Bowl XV.

A large number of U.S. citizens working at the U.S. Embassy in Tehran had been taken hostage by the Iranian government. The world, and of course America, was focused on this literal life-and-death struggle to free the captives. Yellow ribbons, in honor of the hostages, adorned the Super Dome in New Orleans and most of the fans in the building.

If the challenge of the hostage crisis was not enough, Al Davis was embroiled in a bitter court fight with commissioner Pete Rozelle and his fellow NFL owners over Davis' desire to move the Raiders from Oakland to Los Angeles without league approval.

Amid all this turmoil, Flores, in his calm, matter-of-fact, professional quarterback's way, kept his team focused clearly on the goal: A victory over the Philadelphia Eagles and the world championship for the Raiders. With a reconstituted Jim Plunkett—who had gone from the top overall pick of the 1971 draft by the Patriots to an oft-injured journeyman—at quarterback, Flores met that challenge.

And it was Plunkett, who Flores had worked out when Plunkett was a free agent and concluded he was worth signing, who was the game's MVP.

TOM FLORES: We were the wild card that year, so we had to go to the playoffs the hard way, with two games on the road after beating Houston in the wild-card round. We had to go to Cleveland in sub-zero weather. The championship game was in San Diego, and we won that as underdogs.

We started getting momentum going. We just had the feeling, everybody had the feeling, everything was starting to fit. Guys were getting healthy and we were starting to make big plays. By the time we got to New Orleans, we were a pretty well-oiled machine.

We had played the Eagles that year in Philadelphia and they beat us, 10–7. They had eight sacks. They more or less handled us pretty good, so we knew we had to make some adjustments, a few little things. We didn't think the Eagles would make too many adjustments because they had succeeded the first time, so why would they change?

One of the big stories that week was how Dick Vermeil, the Eagles' coach, kept his players away from Bourbon Street and set tight curfews while we didn't have as much in the way of restrictions. When Dick was told during a news conference of some of our players being out after curfew on Bourbon Street, he said he would "send their ass home."

We didn't handle it that way. For one thing, we had played in a Super Bowl before Super Bowl XI in Pasadena, when I was an assistant coach. For another, we thought it was important to make it as normal a week as we could within the abnormality of a Super Bowl week. That's pretty hard to do with all the hoopla going on.

New Orleans is a different town altogether, so when we got there, I said, "Okay, this is the way it is. We'll start curfew on Wednesday."

After that meeting, our captains came to me and said, "Coach, you better start the curfew on Tuesday." So, I moved it up.

Every fine for a violation of team rules started at $1,000. I didn't overemphasize it and I didn't police it any differently than usual. I said, "Just be on time, work hard." Every two players had use of a car. They had their per diem, so they could eat out on their own every night. It was as close as we could get to being at home.

We had a couple of guys that were late for meetings, because they had to drive to another building in New Orleans. And then John Matuszak was caught out late, so I brought him in. I was standing there, looking way up at him, and I said, "You're 6'7", 310 pounds. Did you really think you're not going to be not seen on Bourbon Street? How stupid are you?"

"Well, Coach, I was just out there making sure that everybody else was in before curfew."

I was trying to keep from laughing. Finally, I said, "Get the hell out of here! Go to your meeting. Go!" He said, "I'm sorry, Coach."

What was I going to say? I fined him. Nobody else got caught. I won't say they weren't out, but nobody else got caught.

In a way, I knew how Dick would react because Dick was Dick. He wasn't going to change, and I love him for it because he was a great coach and a good person. We were the way we were. We weren't going to change, either. It was an important game, everybody knew that. If they didn't know it by then, something was wrong.

We made very few mistakes in the game. We had no turnovers. Jim Plunkett threw for 261 yards and three touchdowns. Their quarterback, Ron Jaworski, threw three interceptions, all to linebacker Rod Martin, and had a fumble. Their players were uptight. Their coaches were uptight.

We were loose. And we had a great party afterwards.

BILL POLIAN: Tom Flores' second Super Bowl, XVIII, ironically, matched him against another future Hall of Fame coach, Joe Gibbs.

The Redskins had won their regular-season meeting, with the Raiders at far less than full strength. Once again, Flores demonstrated his usual calm, professional demeanor, and led his team to an overwhelming victory.

MIKE HAYNES: We had played the Washington Redskins during the season and the Redskins won, 37–35. I didn't play in that game. I was still out in limbo land; I wasn't even a Raider yet. Marcus Allen didn't play in that game, either, because he was injured.

But that Super Bowl was the first time I had been on the field as a Raider against an opponent that didn't seem to respect the Raiders. The Redskins came out and they were happy and jumping around and looking forward to playing the game. I hadn't seen anything like that from any other team the Raiders had played. The only reason I think they felt they were able to do that was because they had already beaten us earlier in the year and they thought that they were the better team.

We knew, from watching film, that in their biggest offensive games, the other team played zone. We played man-to-man almost the whole game and they weren't used to that. The only time they would see zone was probably in the red area or blitzing situations or whatever.

Our strategy was to go bump-and-run, go man-to-man, and disguise all of our defenses. When we played Cover Three, we wanted to make it look like Cover One. Sometimes we'd get up and play bump-and-run, but actually I'd have deep-third responsibility.

We were really dialed in. Our defensive coordinator, Charlie Sumner, seemed to have their playbook or something. He would say, "Watch for the screen! Watch for the screen!" And that was the play that one of our linebackers, Jack Squirek, got the interception when they were trying to go to Joe Washington. Jack took it in for a five-yard touchdown to give us a 21–3 lead right before halftime.

Charlie just seemed to know what was going to happen. He would put in a linebacker at the right time, so he could cover the back. Or we'd take Matt Millen out, because Charlie knew Matt wasn't going to be able to run with the personnel they were using, and we'd put in Jeff Barnes.

I can't say that everyone we had was good at everything. But they were good at whatever role when they came into the game. If opponents really studied us, they would have been able to say, "Every time that guy comes in, they're in this defense."

If they were really smart knowing that, it would have been easy to tell what we were going to do. But even so, you've still got to run the play effectively to make it work.

In a lot of ways, I felt like we were undersized against those guys, but we played really great and we matched up really well.

BILL POLIAN: In March of 1989, at the NFL owners meeting in Palm Desert, California, Pete Rozelle floored the owners and GMs by announcing his retirement as commissioner. The Competition Committee had just finished its presentation on proposed playing rules changes. As was the custom, Dallas Cowboys president and Competition Committee chairman

Tex Schramm was presiding over the meeting. Commissioner Rozelle walked in from the wings, sat down next to Tex, and turned on his microphone. He announced, with little fanfare or emotion, that he would be retiring effective upon the selection of his successor.

The room was shocked into stunned silence, followed by snippets of verbiage like, "Oh, my God!... What the hell?... Oh, no!" My boss, Buffalo Bills owner Ralph Wilson, was seated next to me and said, "This can't be."

After the room settled down, Rozelle announced that the respective conference chairmen, Kansas City Chiefs owner Lamar Hunt for the AFC and New York Giants owner Wellington Mara for the NFC, would appoint a search committee to seek his successor.

There was probably another sentence or two to conclude the meeting, but truthfully, I was so shocked I can't remember what it was. I do remember that Pete left the room quickly to a standing ovation.

Obviously, the secret had been closely held because it seemed that only Mr. Hunt and Mr. Mara were privy to what had happened. It's also likely that Tex, who had spent a lifetime as Pete's closest confidant, was aware. It's also likely, given the "strained relations" between the two, that Al Davis was not aware of what was coming.

Before the 1980 season, the league turned down the Raiders' proposed relocation from the Oakland Coliseum to the Los Angeles Memorial Coliseum. Davis responded by suing the NFL for violation of antitrust laws, creating bad blood between Davis and Rozelle, along with other NFL club owners. The Raiders eventually won the lawsuit, clearing the way before the 1982 season for the move to Los Angeles.

That court fight, plus a decade of terrible labor strife, had worn Commissioner Rozelle down. He concluded it was time for him to go.

TOM FLORES: Before Super Bowl XV, there was a lot of talk about, if we won, would Pete Rozelle hand the Vince Lombardi Trophy to Al? Would he have someone else do it? I was even asked by a reporter, "Do you think Al will accept the trophy?"

"Listen, Al Davis is a tough guy," I said. "He's not in everybody's playbook as a best friend. But he's not going to do anything to hurt this game. The game's too important to him. And I don't think Pete Rozelle would, either, because he loves the game as well. So, they're not going to downgrade the game by their own personal feelings and their own competitive spirits."

And they didn't. The trophy presentation was short. Pete left right away. But they didn't denigrate the honor.

Eight years later, at the league meeting, we were all coming off of a lunch break. I was sitting next to Al. Rozelle started talking and nobody was really listening to anything. All of a sudden, he started to cry.

I looked up and then people all over the room were saying, "What's going on?" He told us that he was retiring. Then, he turned the meeting over to Lamar Hunt and Wellington Mara.

As Rozelle started walking out of the room, the first guy who came up to hug him was Al Davis. I still get a lump when I think about that moment in time. Here were two guys who were head-to-head all the time, but two guys who loved the game. And Al knew that Rozelle was a great commissioner, but it was time for him to move on. I'll never forget that.

BILL POLIAN: During my 19 years on the NFL Competition Committee, we dealt with many thorny issues. In the early 2000s, the Raiders were scheduled to open the season on a Thursday night in New England. Because the Raiders were traveling cross-country, this necessitated a special rule regarding the date on which the Raiders had to formalize their opening-day roster. Rather than make a unilateral decision, committee chairman Rich McKay designated me to ask Al to give us his preference. We would then ratify it and present the rule to the owners.

Over years of attending league meetings, I had become friends with then-Raider president Amy Trask and developed a cordial relationship with Al, our competitive circumstances notwithstanding. I put the question to Al, and he responded with a familiar complaint that the league office and the commissioner were biased against the Raiders. I listened politely and explained that the committee wanted to do the right thing by the Raiders and that the choice was his.

His demeanor softened and he replied, "Okay, thanks. We'll do it on Thursday."

He then patted me on the back and said: "Look around the room, Billy. You and me are the only football men here. What's happened to our league?"

I was so surprised I couldn't reply. Looking back, it was a rare poignant moment with an NFL legend reflecting on the game he loved as it used to be. A simpler time when winning games and commitment to excellence were all that mattered.

RON WOLF: Al was totally involved in the latter years. In fact, even at the end, he had a room at the Hilton, which is right down from the Raiders' complex in Oakland.

When I was with the Packers, he always called me to make a trade with him during the draft. I always would make the trade.

He'd say, "You owe me, you owe me." And I'd do it, just like a Pavlov's dog.

MIKE HAYNES: Al Davis was the guy who I ended up learning the most from, because he enjoyed talking the most. He loved getting to know the guys on the team and having a relationship with them. On the field, on the airplane, in a hotel, in the off-season, a lot of different ways.

I didn't treat him like he was just my boss and I didn't want to have anything to do with him. I treated him like he was my boss and he's been doing this a long time and I'd like to know more about this game.

CHAPTER 2

The "Steel Curtain" Descends on the NFL

BILL POLIAN: There are many who believe that the '70s Steelers are among the best teams of all time. Yes, I know the undefeated '72 Dolphins and my friend, the late Don Shula, would argue with that and they would have a good case. So do the Bill Walsh 49ers. Beauty is always in the eye of the beholder.

But for sheer defensive dominance and ferocity, only the '85 Bears compare, and the '70s Steelers won four Super Bowls to the Bears' one.

Before the ascendance of Dan Rooney as top advisor to his beloved father, Art Rooney, the Steelers were a perennial loser. They had no big-league practice facilities, no real home stadium, and a revolving door through which a series of failed head coaches passed. Dan Rooney spearheaded the hiring of Chuck Noll. Dan also empowered his brother, Art Jr., to set up a modern scouting department and, along with his father and brother, stayed with Noll through three start-up losing seasons.

In '72, great drafting and Noll's coaching began to pay off. That season, one of football's most iconic plays, Franco Harris' "Immaculate Reception," helped the Steelers to reach the AFC Championship Game, where they lost to the undefeated Dolphins. The Steeler Dynasty had begun.

Soon, the Steel Curtain—populated by Joe Greene, L.C. Greenwood, Ernie "Fats" Holmes, Dwight White, Jack Lambert, Jack Ham, Mel Blount, and Donnie Shell—became household names among NFL fans. That defensive mentality remains the Steelers' identity to this day. The offense—featuring

Harris, Terry Bradshaw, Lynn Swann, John Stallworth, Mike Webster, and Rocky Bleier—was equally dominant and physical. From '72 through '79, the Steelers won seven division championships and four Lombardi trophies.

In this chapter, you will hear from Hall of Fame players Greene, Bradshaw, and Blount, as well as Hall of Fame coach Tony Dungy, who played and coached for Chuck Noll for 10 years. Tony imparted Noll's philosophy directly to our Super Bowl–winning Indianapolis Colts. You will also hear from legendary Super Bowl–winning assistant coach Tom Moore and the third-generation leader of the franchise, Art Rooney II.

ART ROONEY II: To understand the '70s and, really, what they meant to all of us—my family, the team, the city, our fans—you have to understand the pre-'70s a little bit. We had come through almost 40 years of frustration and not much success.

In particular, I always think about the early '70s. The reaction of our fans and the city to our success was just really remarkable and probably something I'll never experience again. All of a sudden, we have this team that just becomes dominant. It was an amazing turnaround.

Unlike the last 50 years or so, we were one of those franchises in the '60s that was going through coaches pretty regularly. In the late '60s, we hired a coach named Bill Austin, who had been recommended by Vince Lombardi. Everybody thought, "Well, if Lombardi recommends him, he must be the right guy."

Unfortunately, that wasn't a good hire and the late '60s was a tough stretch.

Leading up to the Super Bowl between the New York Jets and Baltimore Colts in 1969, I knew that we were talking to Chuck Noll and I knew that my dad had an eye on him. Chuck came with the recommendation of Don Shula, who was the Colts' coach and had Chuck on his staff. That certainly was a big part of the reason he got hired.

My dad got much more involved in the hiring of Chuck. He was determined to get it right that time and find somebody who was going to be able to come in and change things in a way that we had never approached them before.

Winning that first Super Bowl was fantastic. If you had lived through those 40 frustrating years prior to that, it was a taste of something that was just hard to believe. But even at that point, I don't think any of us really thought we were going to go on from there and win four Super Bowls in six years and really dominate the whole decade.

I think Chuck really was able to hold things together unlike most coaches. There are only a handful that I think of in sort of Chuck's realm—intensive guys that had great success over decades. It takes a special kind of person to lead a team for that many years, year in and year out, to have that kind of success.

TONY DUNGY: I remember, during the first team meeting that our rookie class had with Coach Noll, he said, "Welcome to the National Football League. You're now getting paid to play football, but don't make football your entire life. You've got to find what's going to fulfill you outside of football. I'm here to help you become a better player, but I'm also here to help you grow as a person."

Chuck was just special that way. He loved football, but it wasn't all-consuming to him. I played in that environment for two years and then I came back and was on his coaching staff for eight more.

I just learned so much about football and about life. He talked about champions not doing extraordinary things but doing the ordinary things better than anyone else. That resonated with me.

TOM MOORE: Chuck was the smartest person I ever met and the greatest coach going, in my mind. He used to tell the players, "I'm not here to motivate you. I'm here to coach you. If I have to motivate you, I've got to fire you."

Chuck's idea of motivation and what he preached to us as assistants was, "Motivation is teaching someone to do something that they don't know how to do. And then, when they're asked to do it and they have success, that motivates people."

He used to tell the players, "You'll never be under pressure because pressure is when someone asks you to do something and you don't have a clue how to do it. You'll never be asked to do something that you don't know how to do."

Seeing Chuck after a game, you never knew if you'd won or lost. He was always the same. After a defeat, people would ask him, "What are you going to change?"

"We're not going to change anything. We're just going to do what we do and do it better."

In the 13 years I was at Pittsburgh, I never heard Chuck Noll berate, scream, swear or yell at a player or at a coach. Ever. If he had something to say, he said it very matter-of-factly and you would get the point he was trying to get across.

I know, from a coaching standpoint and from a player's standpoint, you always knew where Chuck stood. You never walked into the facility with a knot in your stomach, wondering whether the guy was going to be up, whether he was going to be down. You always knew what he was going to be.

We had a defensive back who had a pretty good game, so he had a lot to say to the press. In the team meeting Tuesday, Chuck walked in and all he said to that defensive back was, "Do you know what Muhammad Ali's greatest asset was?"

"No, sir."

"When he shot his mouth off, he could back it up."

Chuck didn't demand it, but he commanded such an aura of respect that people could be talking and when he walked in a room, everybody would be quiet. He didn't necessarily want it that way, but that's the way it was.

I coached in one Pro Bowl with Chuck, and first day of practice, he put the players in pads. He told us, "Some of them haven't had pads on for five weeks; they've got to learn how to carry their pads."

Then he had them run gassers after practice.

Howie Long and some other guys on the team I had known said, "Hey, Tom, what the hell's with your coach?"

"He's right over there. Go talk to him."

They didn't.

ART ROONEY II: My dad, Dan Rooney, started working for the Steelers right out of college in the 1950s. In those days, working in the front office of the Steelers meant that there were three or four people you're working with and that was about it. It was a case of my dad kind of growing up in the business, alongside the business growing and the league growing as well. When Pete Rozelle became the commissioner in 1960, that was a turning point for the league, and my dad and my grandfather certainly were part of that.

My grandfather really set the tone for the Steelers being a family-run kind of organization and my dad certainly followed in that culture and thinking of the organization as a people-first organization and valuing the people in the organization, treating people right. My dad carried on and I've certainly tried to carry on as well. It's a little more of a challenge today, when we have a couple hundred people that work here instead of what we had even in the '70s, when we moved into our offices at Three Rivers Stadium.

Before we actually moved into Three Rivers, the franchise had been a little nomadic because we played at Forbes Field, which was the Pirates' stadium, and then we played at Pitt Stadium. In the '60s, we went back and forth a little bit, playing some games at Pitt Stadium and some games at Forbes Field. It didn't feel like we had a real home, and we trained at a public park facility in South Park. I don't know what the facilities were like at other teams in the league in those days, but I'm sure ours was near the bottom in terms of the quality of the setup.

JOE GREENE: My first year in Pittsburgh, 1969, was Chuck Noll's first year as the head coach. I was drafted as the fourth player overall for a team that hadn't ever won any divisional championship. The previous two years, they had won, collectively, six ballgames. Two of those wins came in 1968.

At that time, it was a 14-game season. We won our first ballgame in '69, then proceeded to lose 13 in a row.

ART ROONEY II: Moving into Three Rivers in 1970 came at the right time and it really felt like a big step up for the organization. It was great that that coincided with the team becoming successful.

Even then, there were still only a handful of people that kind of ran the organization. We probably grew, in terms of numbers, slower than most teams in the league. That was just because we wanted to keep it as a small organization, a family feel, and a culture where everybody could work together and try to get along.

JOE GREENE: The transformation was slow. We didn't have very good players and it seemed like we were doing the same thing over and over. The next year wasn't much better. But Chuck kept giving us the following benchmarks for each game: Score 17 points or more, hold the opponent to a maximum of two touchdowns, have what he called "quality" three-and-outs on defense (where you make the other team punt), and minimize your turnovers and mistakes like illegal-procedure penalties, pre-snap penalties, all of those things.

In losing so many ballgames, we never realized how many of those benchmarks we weren't reaching. But when we did win a ballgame, and we would reach some of them, the team, collectively, started to believe.

For me, the buy-in didn't come probably until the middle of my third year. Before that, I kept wondering why we didn't change what we were doing if we were not winning?

But Chuck stuck with it.

Tuesdays were big for our football team the first, second, third, and fourth years because we had new faces always coming in for tryouts. Then you'd see them on the practice field and in the meeting rooms. Chuck was changing over the roster as much as he could, because we didn't have a very good team, personnel-wise.

TERRY BRADSHAW: In 1970, I was drafted number one overall by the Steelers. Coming out of a small school, Louisiana Tech, and without the media coverage we have today, nobody knew anything about me. And I didn't know anything about anybody. I did maybe one interview before the college season started, with the local paper, the *Shreveport Times*, and then I would play football.

My senior year, we only played nine games. In a bunch of them, I didn't play past the half or the third quarter because we were so far ahead. There was talk that I'd be a tight end in the NFL. There was talk I'd be a running back. I didn't give any of that a lot of thought.

I was invited to play in the North-South Shrine college All-Star game in Miami. I was just blown away because I had seen these things on television. Louisiana Tech had never been on TV. I went down there and ended up tearing my hamstring running the 40-yard dash.

Bill Peterson, the coach at Florida State at the time, was our coach on the South squad. He had me and his own guy from Florida State as his quarterbacks. I didn't think much of the other quarterback. I didn't think much of Peterson, either, because he wasn't going to let me play much, injury or not. In practice, there was no question I should be playing a lot more.

I had gotten invited to play in the Senior Bowl in Mobile, Alabama, but I had already made my mind up: "Screw these people! I'm not going to go to the Senior Bowl. I'm going to go home and go fishing." I figured I was going to be a third- or fourth-rounder anyway. I mean, hopefully.

But my dad said that I had to go down to Mobile and at least tell Don Shula, who was coaching the South team, that I was skipping the game. I arrived at the hotel in Mobile, left my bags at the front desk, and went up to Coach Shula's room. I knocked on the door and when he opened it up, all his coaches and their wives were in there drinking beer.

"Terry, come in here!" Coach Shula said.

I was thinking, "Shit! He knows my name." Right there, I was already impressed. He introduced me to all of his coaches. I was just in awe.

"Coach, can I talk to you?"

"Sure."

He put his arm around me, and we walked away from the crowd.

"Look, I just came from the North-South game and I didn't even get a chance to play down there. And I'm not going to waste my time coming here and just sitting my ass on the bench. If you're not going to give me the chance to win the starting job, I'm going home."

"You're my starting quarterback."

"What do you mean?"

"You're going to play as long as you want to play. You don't have to worry about that."

I thanked him, went down and got my bags and checked in.

I saw all these other players from Alabama, Texas A&M, Notre Dame. My thinking was, "I'm not at that level, I'm not those other guys. That's why I went to a small school."

I just had this vision that those guys were so much better. The difference was, while I may have been the superstar quarterback at Tech, they were superstars at pretty much every position.

But in practice I said, "I'm better than all these guys." Dennis Shaw, from San Diego State and the Bills' second-round pick that year, and I were co-MVPs.

After the Senior Bowl, I went back home. Early in the morning the day of the draft, probably 5:00 AM, I was pulling my boat out and hooking it up to my truck. As I was drinking coffee in the kitchen, my dad came in and said, "Where you going?"

"I'm going fishing."

"You can't go fishing."

"Why not? The sand bass are up on the sand bars. You know how much I like to catch those things."

"Son, you're going to get drafted today."

"Well, let me know who drafts me, Dad."

"You got a call from the Chicago Bears. They lost a coin flip with the Pittsburgh Steelers for the first pick, and Chicago was trying to make a trade for the first pick so they could draft you number one. Now, the Steelers are going to draft you number one."

"Dad, you buy that? Come on."

"I got the call. You're not going anywhere."

I was pissed. My dad made me park my boat, go inside, clean up, put on slacks and a tie and a shirt and wait for the draft.

When the Steelers made me the first pick, that was shocking, to say the least. I didn't know what was going on. As a young, immature kid, I wasn't anywhere near ready for this. I came out of a university that babied me, that loved on me. They put their arm around me. They knew I needed support. They knew to always build me up and encourage me, and then I'd perform.

I had no agent. I never had an agent my entire 14 years in the NFL. My father would be kind of the person that would be in control of that. I was recruited by agents, but for some reason, maybe I just didn't trust them or think they could do the best for me.

The negotiations for my first contract were pretty fast. I had an attorney who knew nothing about the NFL. None of us had a clue. The Steelers knew we didn't know anything. In 1970, I signed a five-year contract for $25,000,

$30,000, $35,000, $40,000, $45,000. I got a $100,000 bonus and I spread it over 10 years, payable January 2.

From my bonus, I bought my mother a house full of furniture.

ART ROONEY II: When Terry came in, his arm was amazing. We had obviously never seen somebody with that kind of arm around the Steelers. People talk about whether certain guys could play today. I mean, Terry had the kind of talent that he could play in the league today. He could throw a football through a wall.

But he was raw, and Chuck really did mold him into a winner. It wasn't easy for either one of them at times, but they managed to figure out how to work together, even though their personalities, their approaches to life, probably couldn't have been more different.

TOM MOORE: I used to ride with Chuck going to golf outings and we were talking one time and he said something that that kind of rang a bell with me.

"Tom, one thing you don't ever want to do if you're ever head coach is get into financial competition with your players."

Chuck did no speaking engagements, no endorsements. He gave it all to the players.

"The players may not hold it against you," Chuck said. "But all of a sudden, some wife says, 'Honey, how come he's making that commercial and you're not? You're the guy that's playing.'"

Chuck's basic philosophy was, "Assistants are meant to be seen and not heard. There's one voice." He didn't need any media darlings that were trying to get publicity.

JOE GREENE: The origin of "Mean" Joe happened during the course of my first ballgame at North Texas State, which was referred to as the Mean Green. We were playing against Texas Western, which is now called the University of Texas El Paso. We were playing pretty good defense against those guys and in the stadium, the fans started chanting: "Go Mean Green! Go Mean Green!"

That was picked up by the wife of the sports information director, and she passed it along to her husband. He didn't think much of it at first, but he used it anyway and it kind of caught on.

When I got drafted, the media in Pittsburgh had mistakenly thought that Mean Green was referring to me. I tried to explain that I spelled my name with an "e" at the end and they were not referring to me. I think it fell on deaf ears.

The fourth ballgame of my career, we were playing the Giants at Yankee Stadium. We weren't very good and our defense was facing Francis Tarkenton. Francis was being himself, running around and talking at you. I was chasing him and he would say, "You missed! You missed!"

Finally, I hit him and I said, "What about that?"

"Yeah, what about that?"

We were five yards out of bounds. I had a yellow flag hitting me in the back. Francis started laughing.

In New York, all anyone talked about with me after that was: "That's why they call him 'Mean' Joe. He's a dirty player." I didn't like that at all, but after that, I started going along with the flow because I knew it was just futile to try and change anyone's mind.

There were times that I would go into opposing stadiums—in particular, I remember Denver and Cleveland—and I would see this poster of a very grotesque-looking guy with fangs. Underneath, it said, "Mean Joe."

I thought, "My goodness."

In '79, I made the Coca-Cola commercial where I'm limping up the tunnel after a game, with a look of pain and anger, and a boy hands me a Coke and I down it and then I smile as I toss him my jersey. After that, little old ladies would approach me smiling and saying, "You're not so mean."

"You're right."

When I started playing football, I wanted to win and I would play hard. I wasn't the strongest guy, I wasn't the fastest guy. But I was bigger than most and I played with an aggressive manner most of the time, trying to win. I got into some fights, got kicked out of ballgames.

My second year, 1970, we were playing in Philadelphia in the last game of the season. It was also the game that Frenchy Fuqua set the rushing record for the Steelers with 218 yards. We were down by a field goal and they were inside our two-yard line, somewhere around there, and they were going to score to go up 30–20.

We had maybe two minutes to play and I picked up the football, threw it in the stands, and I just walked off the field because, I assumed, I was going to get thrown out anyway. But I don't think I did, and I didn't get fined by the league.

Chuck didn't say anything to me about it after the game. Dan Rooney didn't say anything to me about it, either, at that time.

But 13 years later, when I was going to tell Dan that I was going to retire, he said, "Joe, you remember that game we played at Philadelphia in your second year?"

I said to myself, "Oh, my goodness. After all these years, now he's going to bring this up?"

"Well, Joe, I felt that same way you did."

I realized why they tolerated a lot of that nonsense I was doing, getting thrown out of ballgames and acting up, because even though I guess I was being selfish, it wasn't something that was planned. My bad actions were just from the desire to win, nothing else, and they gave me credit for that.

When people ask for an autograph, I have yet to sign my name "Mean Joe." I'm not saying I won't, but I've never done it to this point.

MEL BLOUNT: If you asked anybody in that organization back then, "Who was the building block? Who was the key? Who was the leader?" Everybody would tell you Joe Greene.

Joe Greene was not only a great nose tackle, but he was really a man among men. The way he carried himself, his demeanor, he was the guy that everybody hooked their wagon to. If Joe said, "We're going to go out here in practice and move onto X, Y, and Z," that was what we did.

As far as the reputation of being "Mean" Joe Greene, he earned it. And he was. He didn't like it, but there were stories we all witnessed.

We were playing in Denver and this guy kept holding Joe and Joe told an official, "This guy's holding me." Nothing was done about it, so a couple of plays later, Joe just wound up and hit this guy in the gut. The guy went to his knees as if somebody shot him.

Joe said, "The guy was holding me. The officials didn't do anything."

"Oh, so you're not mean anymore."

But Joe was the kind of guy every team needs up front. You need somebody that's going to kick some behind and isn't going to apologize about it. That was the kind of guy he was.

TERRY BRADSHAW: I was very fortunate that I came into the NFL when I did, where the thinking was it was going to take time to develop. If I came out today, I would probably be an undrafted free agent and I'd probably not make it because your time frame to excel and establish yourself as a quarterback is very short.

When I got to Pittsburgh, the Steelers had Kent Nix, who was the starter the year before I got there. He split time with Terry Hanratty, a second-round draft pick from Notre Dame in 1969.

I didn't know anything about how to play quarterback in the NFL. I had to learn coverages, I had to learn all this language. In college, I'd say, "I-Right Opposite" and "769." When I got to the pros, that went out the window. Plays were called, formations were called, blocking assignments were called, and adjustments were made versus coverages.

I was like, "Whoa! Where'd this come from? This is really complicated. Why have they got to make this so complicated?"

Back then, we played six preseason games. We opened up against the Miami Dolphins in Jacksonville my rookie year. I played so-so. The following week, they cut Kent Nix. I played well in all the rest of the preseason games. Then, I was announced as the starter for the opening of the season against the Houston Oilers at brand new Three Rivers Stadium.

I played poorly in that one. I blamed myself, but I also know that I didn't have the best people around me. It kind of hurts me to say that, because I don't mean to be disrespectful to anybody. But being the first pick of the draft means you went to the worst football team. We just weren't talented.

I struggled mightily as a rookie. I threw 24 interceptions to six touchdowns. I was in the lineup, out of the lineup.

I didn't have a relationship with Chuck my rookie year. I didn't know him or anything about him, so I had nothing to judge him on.

I just knew pro football was nothing like college. I didn't like the seriousness of it at all. I'd never had media say bad things about me. All of a sudden,

I was getting criticized, being called a "busted draft pick." Boy, that really hurt. I was just miserable.

BILL POLIAN: Bill Nunn was born and raised in Pittsburgh. His father, Bill Sr., was the legendary editor of the *Pittsburgh Courier*, a newspaper serving the Steel City's Black population.

Bill was an outstanding high school basketball player. He planned to play at Duquesne, with Chuck Cooper (who would go on to become the first Black player for the Boston Celtics), but his father insisted he attend West Virginia State in order to experience life at one of the historically Black colleges and universities (HBCUs). After his college hoops career came to an end, Bill returned to the *Courier*, eventually heading up the sports department. In the '50s, Bill began scouting and picking a Black College All-American team, which gained nation-wide exposure. It helped HBCU players, such as the Rams' Tank Younger, gain spots on NFL rosters.

While Bill was providing valuable talent evaluation that other NFL teams were using to good effect, the Steelers were ignoring this important resource in their own backyard. Bill was not shy about criticizing the Steelers' lack of interest in "small college players." This critique caught the eye of Dan Rooney, who invited Nunn to his office for a meeting. Bill was skeptical at first, but Rooney, respecting his work, asked him to join the Steelers' scouting staff. Bill did and the results were spectacular.

Many Hall of Famers and other great players were brought to the Steelers and mentored by Bill Nunn during his long and illustrious career. He was elected to the Pro Football Hall of Fame in 2021.

TOM MOORE: In 1950, when Bill Nunn began putting together a Black All-American team, he got to know the players and coaches from historically Black colleges and universities. In 1967, Bill went to work as a scout for the Steelers. Eventually, he became their assistant personnel director.

Everybody knew Joe Greene, but maybe not Dwight White, L.C. Greenwood, and Ernie Holmes. Bill was the guy that brought those guys to the Steelers and that kind of turned the tide.

ART ROONEY II: It just wasn't a racial thing. I can remember, back in the '60s, even though I was young, that there was a feeling that the best players were at the big schools. We really didn't look at the players at the HBCUs.

It was great that Bill came along and became available to us at the right time. I think my dad, in particular, was willing to try going in a different direction from the way we had been doing things, in terms of going after the players from the bigger schools.

Chuck was open to finding good players wherever they were. He had no bias in terms of big school versus small school, whereas I think some of our coaches prior to that didn't think that way.

Some of those players came in and became great players, some of them didn't. But Bill had opened a door that hadn't been opened before and obviously it led to a lot of success.

JOE GREENE: L.C. Greenwood and I came in together. Ernie Holmes and Dwight White came in in '71.

With their arrival, the nickname "the Steel Curtain" came about.

MEL BLOUNT: I would tell anybody that playing behind those guys probably made me one of the luckiest defensive backs that has played in this league. I mean, my goodness. If you couldn't have success playing behind L.C. and Joe and Ernie and Dwight White and Andy Russell, you couldn't have success.

Joe and that Steel Curtain made it easier for us in the secondary and the linebackers because they were just so dominant. We had run support and we did what we were supposed to do, but there weren't a lot of times where the back would get to the secondary or outside of the defense where it caused me to have to make a tackle or make a big play.

It really became so competitive to see who was going to get to the ball. I think that was a good thing to have a defense where everybody was trying to make the play instead of waiting for somebody else to do it. That was the kind of mindset we all had.

TERRY BRADSHAW: My second year, 1971, I didn't even think I'd be the starter going into training camp, but I was. In 1973, they brought in Babe

Parilli to be my quarterback coach. I just remember I played so much better, so much more relaxed because I had Babe Parilli. Babe was just like Mickey Slaughter, my quarterback coach in college. I was in a losing situation, but my confidence wasn't shaken. Babe always picked me up because I was always so hard on myself.

Then, after one year, they got rid of Babe Parilli. To this day, I have no clue why Chuck did that. Maybe Chuck thought I was too protected. Maybe Chuck thought he needed to rough me up. Maybe he thought he had to make me tougher.

One year, Chuck told me he wanted me to prepare like Johnny Unitas. I said, "I don't know how Johnny Unitas prepares." Another year, Chuck wanted me to be like Bob Griese. I said, "Shit! I don't know how to be like him."

Chuck Noll was my offensive coordinator and quarterback coach. When you look back on it, he was not a good offensive coordinator. He damn sure wasn't a good quarterback coach.

But he was my head coach and I had to listen to all this shit. I don't want to be super critical, but I am going to be honest.

BILL POLIAN: Tom Moore played quarterback at the University of Iowa. After serving in the Korean War, he embarked upon a coaching career. He had many collegiate stops along the way, most notably the University of Minnesota, where he recruited and coached a highly touted Michigan high school quarterback named Tony Dungy. They would remain exceptionally close and make football history in the years to come.

Tom joined Chuck Noll's Steelers staff in '77 as a receiver coach. He was eventually named offensive coordinator, staying with the franchise for 13 seasons. He was part of two Super Bowl teams. Among his pupils were Hall of Famers Stallworth and Swann. Tom went on to success as offensive coordinator of the Minnesota Vikings and Detroit Lions. After a stint with New Orleans, he joined the Colts under Jim Mora and later with his longtime compatriot Dungy and Dungy's successor, Jim Caldwell.

With the Colts, Tom was again part of two Super Bowl teams and coordinated every down of Peyton Manning's career in Indianapolis. He helped

Manning to a 141–67 record in that time. He created and grew the no-huddle offense that Peyton made famous.

In 2019, Tom became an offensive consultant with the Tampa Bay Bucs. In 2020, he was part of another Super Bowl–championship team, this one with Tom Brady.

TOM MOORE: I joined the Steelers from the University of Minnesota in 1977 to replace Lionel Taylor as the receiver coach. At the time, Chuck was into hiring college coaches because he wanted guys to teach. He wasn't interested in philosophy and all that stuff. The only assistant coach we had that didn't have any Pittsburgh Steeler experience was our offensive line coach, Rollie Dotsch, who had been with the Packers, Patriots, and Lions.

My interview with Chuck Noll was about 10 hours. We started at 8:00 in the morning, took an hour lunch break, and it ended about 6:00 or 6:30.

The first part of the interview was Chuck creating these scenarios where he would be a rookie receiver who had just gotten drafted and he wanted me to teach him how to run routes.

"You tell the kid to run a hook route, but how do you want him to run it?" Chuck said. "What if you get off coverage? What if you get man coverage? Inside technique? Outside technique? What if you get press coverage? What if you get Two Man, where they play underneath you and put a guy over the top of you?"

We went through every single route in the playbook, with him seeing how I was going to teach it and showing me how he wanted it taught. That was the epitome of Chuck. He could coach any position on the team better than the guy that was coaching it.

That's how smart he was.

Chuck's whole philosophy was that you've got to play fast. To play fast you have to know what to do and you have to know how to do it. That's all techniques and fundamentals. Chuck said that if you know what to do and you've got the proper techniques and fundamentals, then eventually you can break the other guy's will if your techniques are better than his.

For 13 years at training camp, the morning of the first day of practice, we spent 55 minutes teaching every player how to block and tackle by the numbers. I was even teaching Terry Bradshaw how to tackle.

Terry looked at me said, "Tom, why are you teaching me how to tackle? What's the story?"

It just so happened that Chuck was walking by.

"I'll tell you why he's teaching you how to tackle, Terry. Because you may throw an interception and I'd really like for you to make the tackle and not hurt yourself, okay?"

TERRY BRADSHAW: Before the '72 draft, Chuck Noll called me and said, "We're going to draft a running back and we are going to mold our offense after the Miami Dolphins, with Larry Csonka and Jim Kiick, and just use you like they use Bob Griese—just keep the sticks moving."

"Okay, fine."

JOE GREENE: When we drafted Franco Harris in 1972, there was a lot of debate in the organization about which Penn State running back we were going to draft, Franco or Lydell Mitchell, who ended up going to the Baltimore Colts.

ART ROONEY II: There are stories about some of the tension between my uncle Art Rooney and Chuck, and the most famous story was over the drafting of Franco in '72. There was tension there, and yet they were accomplishing things and drafting great players, so it was probably a good kind of tension and good that there were disagreements. Usually, it was my father that tried to help resolve disagreements to make sure that we got to the right decision.

Certainly, if you look at those drafts between '69 and, say, '74, it was a pretty good series of drafts and a pretty good team was built there. There were a lot of pieces to the puzzle that were coming together at the right time and in the right way.

JOE GREENE: The one thing that Franco really brought us was some stability in our offense, because we didn't have to just throw the ball all the time. It was coming together, and Franco was the one that helped bring it together.

When we got Franco, we went from winning six ballgames in '71 to 11 the following year, and we got into the playoffs for the first time in the history of the organization. And when we did, it was Franco's Immaculate Reception on that 60-yard touchdown to beat the Raiders for our first playoff win.

I don't know if, at that time, I gave the Immaculate Reception the importance that I give it now. I think it was the springboard to future success. Prior to the Immaculate Reception game, the media coverage that we got was, from my perspective, very, very local. The local sportswriters and TV people were the ones that we would see in the locker room after the game.

After the Immaculate Reception game, there were more reporters in the locker room than players. And it never stopped after that. It probably was a turning point when we became the team of NBC, which was broadcasting the AFC games at the time.

ART ROONEY II: I was in college at the time, but I can still remember, after the Immaculate Reception, my dad saying, "You need to go down and help out in the ticket office this week because we're selling more tickets than anybody can handle down there."

Prior to that, the only games we would sell out would be the Browns because half of Cleveland would come to Pittsburgh to buy tickets. After that Immaculate Reception game, we've sold out every game since.

TERRY BRADSHAW: So, we drafted Franco Harris and put in the Dolphins' offense. We put in the toss traps, the quick toss, the off-tackle traps, the weakside traps, the sucker plays. We weren't that good on the offensive line and we slowly drafted people into that position.

Back then, we weren't as big on the offensive line and we pulled the guards a lot, we pulled our tackles, we tried to do a lot of screening and stuff like that. You needed athletic linemen to do that and that was what we drafted. When you're doing tosses and fakes and misleading stuff, you're not a team that can drive people off the ball.

JOE GREENE: Gerry Mullins was a tight end, from USC, we drafted in '71. He was converted to a guard. I think I made him a star one day in practice when he blocked me pretty good and I got upset with him and grabbed him by his collar and pulled him back to the line and said, "Okay, let's go again."

He beat me again.

We called him "Moon" Mullins. He was about 250 pounds and he could run. He was a 4.7 guy.

Larry Brown went from being drafted in the fifth round in '71, as a tight end from Kansas, to becoming one of the best offensive tackles in the league, even though he never made the Pro Bowl. But he did catch a touchdown pass to help us win the Super Bowl.

Probably the heaviest guy on the line would have been Jon Kolb, at 255. Imagine offensive linemen being that small? But these guys all could run. That was something that Chuck believed in.

TERRY BRADSHAW: The Miami offense was not a hard offense to learn. The numbering system for the passing game was really simple: 40, 50, 60, 70, 80, 90. I used that offense from '72 until the day I retired, although we did implement some West Coast stuff where we would go flood right, single back, tight end, three-wide, and we'd go open, two-wide, four-wide.

When we started winning, it was because of the defense and the running game. Franco Harris and Rocky rushed for a thousand yards each in 1976, four years after Miami's Larry Csonka and Mercury Morris became the first duo in the league to achieve that.

Our offense was, "Boom! Boom! Boom!" with run plays and then play-action.

TOM MOORE: Chuck was never big on trades. If he traded, he wanted picks. He didn't want players. He didn't want someone else's problems.

We didn't have many players who had ever been on any team other than Pittsburgh because Chuck didn't want to get involved with someone saying, "Well, we did it this way at Kansas City… we did it this way at the Jets." He just wanted it to be, "This is what we do at Pittsburgh."

By 1981, Chuck had won four Super Bowls. Not long after that, Mr. Art Rooney and I were in the kitchen at our offices. He said, "You know, Tom, Chuck did his greatest job coaching his first year and he was 1–13."

"Why would you say that, Mr. Rooney?"

"Well, Tom, when we brought him in here, of course, we weren't very good. But we interviewed him, and Chuck had a plan and he knew exactly where he was going with it. He knew exactly what kind of players he wanted and what he wanted to do. They only won that first game, against Detroit, but he stuck with his plan. He never changed, and he never lost the team. After the season, I went to Dan and I said, 'We've got ourselves a coach.'"

Chuck's philosophy was, "Don't major in the minors. Just major in the majors. You don't have time for the minors."

ART ROONEY II: Hiring Chuck Noll was a key turning point. When Chuck came in, I was young. I was a ball boy at training camp for Chuck's first year. But even from that kind of position in the organization, I had an immediate feeling of, "Something's different here." There was a more serious purpose, a more serious goal about the way we were going about things. Chuck just brought a whole different paradigm to how the Steelers approached being a successful football team.

Obviously, he worked well with my father. They had a great working relationship and my Uncle Art was building a strong personnel department with people like Bill Nunn and Dick Haley.

TERRY BRADSHAW: Chuck Noll cared about his defense way more than he cared about his offense. He had been a messenger guard for Paul Brown in Cleveland, but he loved defense. Not so much offense. To him, we were just necessary, I think.

A lot of people don't know this, but one time he grabbed me going through the tunnel to play Cleveland and said, "If you don't play well in the first quarter, I'm going to bench your ass."

We hadn't even started the game and that was what I had to go out and play with. I was like, "God! You've got to be shitting me."

Chuck put in a play for a Monday night game that he liked, but I didn't like the play. That night, I was going over all the plays on the board, I was going through all the changes, everything as the quarterback. I went into Chuck's office and said, "Coach, I just don't like that play. I'm taking it out of the game plan."

He was livid. I mean, livid.

Another time, we were playing Cincinnati. We had the ball four inches from our goal line. Cincinnati was pretty good, but we were driving all the way down the field and got to like their one-foot line. I was in the huddle.

I always got on one knee and looked up at the players. As any psychiatrist will tell you, when you do that, you're in a submissive position, so you're not better than they are. They look down on you; you look up at them.

When we got to the line, our center, Mike Webster, said, "Let's call a timeout, let's call a timeout." It was first-and-six inches, so I turned around and called a timeout.

I went over to the sideline and Chuck put his hands on me. I'm thinking, "Why are you putting your hands on me?" He knew I hated when he put his hands on me, but for him that was control. When you have your hands on somebody, you've got control.

He said, "Look, we've got a play here."

I was listening, but I was thinking, "Are you shitting me? I just went 99 yards with this team, I've got nobody helping me and now we're on the six-inch line and they've got a play?"

It was laughable.

I took his hands and I pushed them off. The coaches were still talking about a play and I said, "Look, I've got a play, Chuck. I'm on the six-inch line. Don't worry, we're going to score."

I started to jog back out without the play they were talking about. The words coming out of his mouth indicated strongly that it would be a wise decision on my part if I returned to get it.

I said, "Screw you!"

I remember going back on the field. The players were looking at me and I said, "I told Chuck y'all got a play y'all want to run." They were all like, "What?" They were all nervous. It was the funniest thing you've ever seen.

We scored on the next play and Chuck was absolutely fine. He understood the situation. Chuck was a smart guy. It's just that his social skills weren't the best. I don't think he was comfortable around people and he made you uncomfortable around him.

Now in meetings, when we were looking at tape and we were doing football, that was a different story. But in a social sense, he just made you uncomfortable. You just didn't want to be around him, honestly.

Chuck wasn't one to pass out compliments. I don't recall the man ever shaking my hand, but that was okay. I didn't care. Eventually, it doesn't matter. Eventually, you do mature in the situation and you do get comfortable. You know you've got a smart coach who did a great job of signing these players and the rest of it didn't matter.

I think primarily they were waiting on me to develop into the quarterback they wanted me to be. It took me five or six years to get there.

Comfortable. Loved it. Leading the football team.

BILL POLIAN: Following the advice of Tom Moore, his collegiate position coach, Tony Dungy signed with the Steelers as an undrafted free agent. In doing so, he spurned an offer from Marv Levy and the CFL Montreal Alouettes, for whom I was a fledgling scout at the time.

Tony played two years for the Steelers, '77 and '78, as a safety and backup quarterback. He was part of the '78 Super Bowl–winning team. He played one more season with Bill Walsh's San Francisco 49ers. Upon completing his playing career, he joined Coach Noll's Steelers as one of the youngest coaches in NFL history.

Tony served as defensive coordinator in Pittsburgh, defensive backs coach in Kansas City, and defensive coordinator again in Minnesota. He became the Buccaneers' head coach in 1996 and resuscitated a moribund franchise. He was let go after the 2001 season, following four playoff appearances. Luckily for us, he joined the Colts as our head coach, leading us to a Super Bowl championship and a record of 85–27 in seven seasons. He is the winningest coach in Colts history.

Tony was inducted into the Pro Football Hall of Fame in 2016. His mantras of "do what we do" and "do the ordinary in an extraordinary way," which are so familiar to his Colts players, came directly from Chuck Noll.

TONY DUNGY: I was 25 years old and I had gotten cut by the 49ers, so I wasn't sure what I was going to do, where I was going to be in life. Coach Noll called me and he said, "You've got a great mind, you're a good communicator, you love football. I think you'd be an excellent coach."

I hadn't really thought about coaching, but the idea of working with players and continuing to develop in the game and grow intrigued me. I asked him what the job of a coach entailed. He told me something that would stay with me for the next 28 years: "Your job as a coach is very simple. Just help your players be the best they can be."

That was Chuck in a nutshell. So simple. So clean. So straightforward.

I had never heard a coach talk like that. But as he said that, it really made me understand why I loved playing for him. He didn't want to make everybody know that he was the boss. He didn't feel like he had to have all the rules in place. He didn't feel like he had to be the leader or anyone special.

He just felt like, "If I pick the right guys and I help them be the best they can be, then we're going to be successful."

That stuck with me from the grad assistant that I was at the University of Minnesota in 1980, that first year after I finished playing. It stuck with me all the way through my time as a defensive backfield coach with the Steelers and as a defensive coordinator with the Steelers and later with the Vikings, and as a head coach with the Buccaneers and Colts. I always kept in mind my job was to help my players be the best that they could be.

It reminded me so much of my mom and dad, who were teachers in the little automotive town in Central Michigan where I grew up. They always felt like that was their job, to help their students be the best they could be.

Many times, when I was coaching, my words to my team would be, "My dad used to say…" or "My mom used to say…" and everybody who played for me probably felt like they knew my mom and dad, because I referred to them so much.

Of the many things my dad used to say, one that stuck with me the most was this: "My job is to help every student earn an A and you can't do that by just having one way of doing things because you're not going to reach everyone." You've got to find out what makes people tick and help every single player that you have to be the best they can be.

TOM MOORE: A couple of weeks before we were going to coach the Senior Bowl in '82, Dick Hoak, our running back coach, and I were sitting in the office working. Chuck walked in and said, "What are you guys doing?"

I said, "We're getting the playbook ready for the Senior Bowl."

"Did you guys watch any film?"

We hadn't. Chuck told us to take the first week to watch film of the Senior Bowl players, decide what they could do, and then put together our playbook.

Our quarterback was John Fourcade. The quarterback for the other team was Jim McMahon. We saw that Fourcade couldn't throw the drop-back, so in the Senior Bowl, all we threw were play-actions, bootlegs, and nakeds. Our team won the game and Fourcade was the MVP.

We had this offensive lineman from Memphis at the Senior Bowl. Chuck looked at the guy and then said to our offensive line coach, Rollie Dotsch, "Rollie, have you tried 'Pressure G Technique' with this guy on the trap play?"

"No."

So, there was Chuck at halftime, teaching this guy who never got drafted, the "Pressure G Technique" to run the trap. Chuck loved it when free agents and low-round draft picks made it big.

That game taught me a lesson: Find out what your players can do and do that.

JOE GREENE: The '74 draft was probably the best. Our first pick there was Lynn Swann, the second pick was Jack Lambert. We didn't have a three, but the next pick, in the fourth round, was John Stallworth. Then we got Mike Webster in the fifth round.

All Hall of Famers.

As we started to get more players, and better players, we saw less and less strangers on Tuesday. That's when we started to meet those benchmarks on a regular basis.

TERRY BRADSHAW: In 1974, I lost my starting job to Joe Gilliam, who we drafted from Tennessee State in 1972. Joe was one of my best friends. We had so much fun together. I just loved him. Joe and Terry Hanratty were great friends of mine, they were great competitors.

Joe becoming the starter was a major, major story. He was the first African American quarterback to start a season opener after the 1970 AFL-NFL merger. I was this young country kid—naïve, immature. We lockered next to each other and all this media was coming in to do stories on Joe.

So, now my ego's taking a crush, just being honest here. When you come in, the first pick, you're hailed as the "savior." Now you're washed up, you're no good.

Going back to my junior year in college, I had never been replaced. I had always been the man. Now, I wasn't the man at all. Then Joe got benched after the sixth game of the '74 season and I started seven of the last eight games. Terry Hanratty started one, and we were both in and out of the lineup.

ART ROONEY II: It was not unusual for Chuck to play whoever was playing well. Whoever gave us the best chance of winning was going to be our starter. Chuck started Joe in that season and it turned out that Joe didn't have the kind of success that he would have liked, so Chuck made the change back to Terry Bradshaw fairly early in the season. That turned out to be the right thing to do.

But Chuck was going to give everybody the opportunity to compete for the starting job and he was going to play whoever earned the job. I think there was an understanding that nobody was going to be given anything. Obviously, Terry had a different view of things.

TERRY BRADSHAW: You can only imagine, when you have three starting quarterbacks in one year, the whole thing is screwed up. We had this amazing defense, but this whole thing with the quarterbacks was just bizarre.

I had had enough, so I asked to be traded. They didn't like me, I didn't like them. My career was going absolutely nowhere. I had never been so miserable, frustrated, and lost as a human being. I wanted out of there. I needed to go somewhere where I was wanted.

I had talent. I could throw the football and I could make things happen and I could do plays that other players couldn't do. I just needed to be where someone appreciated me, and I just didn't believe that that was Pittsburgh. Not with Chuck Noll anyway.

ART ROONEY II: Obviously, the relationship between Terry and Chuck was a difficult relationship. For two guys who had as much success together as they did, it's too bad that it didn't turn out to be a better relationship. But, hey, between the two of them, they made it work as best as they could, to the extent that we had a tremendous amount of success, even though on a personal level they were like oil and water.

TERRY BRADSHAW: My two best friends who were coaches were Dick Hoak, who taught me the running game, and Tom Moore. I'd go to Tom to ask, "Hey, what do you think against that coverage, this coverage, that coverage, this coverage, this play, that play?"

All my issues were between me and my head coach and me and an offense I couldn't understand, I didn't like. I mean, nobody wants to just run, run, run, run, run. That was the way we were going to win my entire career.

In 1974, we drafted John Stallworth, out of Alabama A&M, and Lynn Swann, out of USC. Then we got Bennie Cunningham, a tight end out of Clemson. We had Jim Smith, out of Michigan, and Calvin Sweeney, out of Southern Cal. We had Rocky Bleier coming back from an injury he suffered in the Vietnam War.

Of course, I wasn't traded and I did get the starting job when we played the Vikings in the Super Bowl. We beat the Vikings, so that guaranteed me at least the opening starting job for the following year.

As I matured, I understood that it really wasn't me. That's why I say today, don't bench these young quarterbacks. Put people around them that can perform. If they were drafted in the first round and they played well in college and probably in high school, the ability is there. You've just got to surround them with a good support group and encourage them.

I just think all quarterbacks are alike. They're sensitive. I'm super sensitive about myself and I had a hard time with that.

MEL BLOUNT: Chuck understood people. He would always allow us to be who we were, as long as it wasn't in violation of policies that he had in place. For the most part, we never had any trouble with guys missing practice, staying out late, getting in trouble, because I think everybody knew that that wasn't what we were about.

When guys come into a winning organization like the Steelers had, they want to be a part of it. They don't want to do anything that's going to cause them to get kicked off the team or not make the team because they know what's expected. I think a lot of that came from Chuck's leadership.

I remember when Donnie Shell was a rookie and I had four years in the league, he had gotten a little unsatisfied. I had never seen a guy play special teams like Donnie Shell, but he wasn't getting a chance to play on defense. I pulled Donnie aside and said, "Let's go out to dinner."

I talked with him about the importance of what he was doing on special teams. I told him, if he wasn't making those plays and playing special teams the way he was, we weren't going to win. I told him to just be patient. His time was going to come. I saw how valuable Donnie was to the organization and I didn't want him to disrupt the chemistry that we had.

TOM MOORE: On Saturday night before a home game, Chuck told the assistant coaches to take our wives out to dinner. He said, "You guys work enough all week. Take your wives out and have a good time." He and the trainers stayed with the team.

When you left the office, your personal life was your personal life. In the 13 years I was at Pittsburgh, Chuck called my house one time and that was to let us know when the 1982 strike was over. He didn't intrude on people's lives.

It was not necessarily Chuck and the coaches against the world, but those were the people he felt comfortable with. Now, there were only six assistants, but we had one party a year at his house and he did all the cooking. He grilled and he made sure that all the coaches' and their wives' drinks were full.

After dinner and dessert, we'd all sit in the living room and he'd play the ukulele and do a bunch of sing-along songs. He'd have been willing to do that all night, but finally, at about 12:30, his wife, Marianne, would say, "Fellas, it's time to leave."

Thursday night during the season, Chuck would go home and cook dinner. Then he'd come in Friday and tell us about the homemade lasagna that he'd made and the sauce and all that stuff.

Chuck was a gourmet cook, he was a connoisseur of wines, he flew his own airplane. When Chuck couldn't fly anymore, he got a 49-foot Grand Banks boat and he took that all over. One summer, my wife and I spent a week with him on Chesapeake Bay.

One time during that week, I started to mention something about the Steelers. Chuck stopped me.

"Tom, we're on vacation."

When Chuck worked, he worked. When football season was over, he went the other way. He could do that. I can't do that.

MEL BLOUNT: Chuck didn't say a whole lot, but people listened to the things he said because of his demeanor in practice and before games and after games and in the meeting room.

I remember a reporter asking him, "How do you win all these games?" Chuck said, "You win with good people." He didn't say good athletes. He said good people.

I think there's a lot to that because when you have good people, there's an atmosphere that's created where everybody feels important, even the guys who played special teams.

When it came to any sort of racial divide, we never had a problem because the guys respected one another and there wasn't going to be any tolerance for a guy who had those kinds of feelings. The chemistry, the quality of athletes, the quality of people, all of those things were so key to what happened in that journey with the Steelers.

Guys could come from so many different parts of the country, small colleges, and be able to focus on one thing and that was winning. You have to give a lot of that credit to the leadership of the Rooney family and also to Chuck Noll and his staff.

TOM MOORE: The locker room immediately after a game—and this was Mr. Rooney's edict—was only for players and coaches. That was it. Even he didn't come in the room.

Win or lose, Mr. Rooney wanted that to be just for the players and coaches. After a period of time, other people could come in.

I've seen a couple of places where, after a game, half the town's in the locker room. A coach needs that time to talk to his players, say what he really thinks, and to get a message across to them. He doesn't need other people hearing it, like the team doctor, who then tells his wife what Chuck said after a game.

BILL POLIAN: Since Chuck Noll's arrival in 1969, the Steelers have had three head coaches, making the franchise a paragon of consistency in all of sport.

Noll won four Super Bowls in 23 years at the helm. Bill Cowher had a .619 win percentage in 15 seasons, reaching two Super Bowls and winning one. He was inducted into the Pro Football Hall of Fame in 2020. Mike Tomlin had a .640 winning percentage through the 2020 season, with two Super Bowls and one Lombardi Trophy.

ART ROONEY II: Certainly, since Chuck and with Bill and Mike, it has still been a situation where we've tried to make sure the players understood the coach was in charge and had our support, whether it was my dad or myself. I think it's important for the players to understand the place isn't being run by a committee. There's one guy in charge when it comes to what's happening on the football field for the players.

The other aspect of it is we've understood that every season is not going to go exactly the way you hope. I remember a stretch where Bill had two or three years in a row where we didn't make the playoffs and it was the usual thing you get these days where everybody's hollering, "Time to change coaches." I think my dad and I just looked at it like, "We think Bill can still coach. There's no reason to make a change here."

We're in a business where there are some cycles to it and there are some things that are built into the way the league runs. If you have some success, now you start drafting at the bottom of the rounds and that does have an impact over time. You have to factor that into evaluating your coach, I think.

That's not always easy. Some years it is tough, but you have to kind of weather the storm. You have to help the coach weather the storm, really.

The phrase, "Staying the course" is a good one. I think it also just comes down to believing in the person that you've hired and as long as you still believe in that person. You can't give up on somebody just because a few things don't go your way in a season. There are going to be ups and downs.

Fortunately, some of our downs haven't been as down as they could have been. But we always have the same approach and the same goal, and I think our coaches have appreciated that.

BILL POLIAN: Since the days of the Steel Curtain, defense has been the Steelers' DNA. Every one of their head coaches—Chuck Noll, Bill Cowher, and Mike Tomlin—were defensive coordinators before being promoted to the big chair. This is contrary to the most accepted practice in the NFL. The results speak for themselves.

ART ROONEY II: It wasn't an accident that Chuck Noll, Bill Cowher, and Mike Tomlin were defensive coaches. I think there's been a belief that the defense sets the tone for our franchise. Obviously, that's gotten tougher over the years as they keep changing the rules, but it's still something that I think you can rely on. If you have a good defense, you're going to be in most of the games and give yourself a chance to win.

JOE GREENE: The 4-3 was the defense that we were playing when I got to Pittsburgh. We had a defense where we would slant either the left tackle or the right tackle towards the center. It would be a "Rip" or a "Liz" call. A "Rip" call would be the right tackle going to the center and a "Liz" call would be the left tackle going towards the center. Each time a tackle would move towards the center, the middle linebacker would move over in front of the guard that the tackle left for him.

I had problems consistently with my slant to the center if they were coming my way, because when they would come in my direction, I would get scooped by the center. As I was moving in his direction, he took a drop step and he got over the top of me and then the guard was off on the middle linebacker.

That happened too frequently.

BILL POLIAN: The "Stunt 4-3," which was made famous by the Steel Curtain, was largely the creation of defensive line coach George Perles. Clubs (most notably the Raiders) were double-teaming Joe Greene with a guard and center, thereby allowing one of the tandem to get out on middle linebacker Jack Lambert and facilitating the inside run game.

Perles moved Greene to the outside shoulder of the center (known as the cocked nose tackle) and upon the snap, stunted him into or away from the center, occupying the double-teamers and freeing the incredibly fast Lambert for an unblocked run to the ball-carrier. This technique is still in vogue today.

JOE GREENE: By lining up on the shoulder of the center, I was in a better position to keep the center from over-blocking me. If I could maintain that leverage in that gap—which we called the A-gap, between the guard and the center—I could prevent them from running in the A-gap. And if I stayed in the A-gap, I could keep the guard from coming off on the middle linebacker.

The strength of the defense was supposed to be our ability to keep the guard and center on the cocked nose tackle. Oftentimes, we were able to do that when they doubled me with the guard and the center. When they wanted to run inside, they would send a fullback on the middle linebacker.

Jack Lambert was so quick that he was meeting the fullback in the backfield, which negated the ability to run the ball inside. Ernie Holmes did a great job as a tackle because you couldn't block Ernie one-on-one.

The ends would do what we call a two-gap. They weren't playing one-gap outside shoulder. They were head-up and that was to keep the offensive tackle from blocking down inside. So, the middle linebacker was covered on his alignment side to keep the guard and the tackle off of him. The only guy who was free to get to the 'backer was the fullback, if you had one. That defense didn't show up until the first round of the playoffs against the Bills in '74.

You have to have a commitment to it and believe and know what you're trying to get done. In our first venture into the playoffs in '72, the Dolphins ran the football pretty good on us. And then, in '73, the Raiders ran the football pretty good on us. We were doing well with our defense up until we got to the playoffs.

From that time on, we started to work on the stunt 4-3 in practice only. We never put it into any ballgame, but we had the commitment to spend a 10-minute section of our workout on one specific thing. It was coordinated with George Perles, with the defensive line, and Dick Hoak, with the running backs, because the individual practice periods coincided.

We had four defensive linemen and they could borrow offensive linemen who weren't busy working elsewhere and they would run any play that they wanted to against the stunt 4-3. We saw where the strengths were and where the weaknesses were in the defense.

When we used it for the first time, in that playoff game against the Bills, we held O.J. Simpson to 49 yards rushing. Then we were getting ready to play the Oakland Raiders in the AFC Championship Game out in Alameda County Coliseum.

After the Raiders beat the Dolphins, stopping them from going to three Super Bowls in a row in an outstanding game, John Madden said that the best teams in football had just played.

The next day, Chuck Noll got in front of the team and said, "Out in Oakland, they think that the best two teams in football played yesterday and the Super Bowl was played yesterday. Well, I want to tell you the Super Bowl will be played in two weeks and the best team in pro football is sitting right here in this room."

That was not the way Chuck normally talked. That was a pivotal point in how I positioned myself mentally, emotionally, to deal with the Raiders, who took no prisoners. I was sitting in that chair, behind a desk that was for elementary school and junior high kids, and when Chuck did that, I felt that I had elevated out of the seat with my feet not touching the ground. I was floating the entire week and it was probably the best practice week I ever was a part of.

MEL BLOUNT: It was like Chuck had injected some rocket fuel into every player. I think that was one of the things that changed the direction of that team.

JOE GREENE: We played the Raiders in the rain. We were using the stunt 4-3 against the Raiders, who had just worn us out the year before in the playoffs and the regular season. They had won in Pittsburgh, 33–14, and ran 55 times for 232 yards.

In that 1974 conference championship game at Oakland, we won 24–13. The Raiders ran the football 21 times for 29 yards.

That particular stretch put the defense on par with what our offense had been doing and it gave us the strength and the impetus to beat the dreaded Raiders.

MEL BLOUNT: In that championship game against the Raiders, I really had a bad game. The defense that the coaches put us in had me playing inside on Cliff Branch and he kept running these deep corner routes. He had nine catches for 186 yards and a touchdown.

That game was, in my opinion, a turning point for me in my career because I got pulled out of that game and they put Jimmy Allen in. Afterward, a reporter asked me, "What did you think about Bud Carson pulling you out of that game?"

"Well, I thought it was a mistake."

That was like putting fuel on a fire because the media had all that to work with leading up to the Super Bowl.

JOE GREENE: We had the talent in '72, when we lost to the Dolphins in the conference championship game and they went undefeated. But the gut check wasn't quite there yet. There was no doubt we were going to win the Super Bowl against Minnesota, which we did.

The Vikings carried the ball 21 times for 17 yards. The ends did a great job of keeping Fran Tarkenton in the pocket, not letting him get outside. L.C. Greenwood was 6'6" and Dwight White was 6'5" and they'd get their arms up, their hands up, and Tarkenton couldn't throw the ball over them. L.C. got one or two deflections and did a great job on the right side. Dwight did a great job on the other side. He got Tarkenton down in the end zone for a safety.

MEL BLOUNT: Glen Edwards, one of our safeties, made a big-time hit on the intended receiver, John Gilliam, on a pass. The ball popped up. I came from the opposite side of the field because I was the kind of player who would always run to the ball wherever it was thrown, and I made the interception. It was a big turnover for us because Tarkenton and his group were driving.

I will never forget, after that game, I was down in Georgia, where I was born and raised. You would think a guy who had just won the Super Bowl would be one of the happiest guys in the world. But I was just the opposite. I was miserable because all the talk was that the Steelers were going to get rid of Mel Blount.

I've always had horses. Growing up, we had mules and horses in the fields because my parents were dirt farmers in Georgia. I was on the back of this horse riding across the field and I was in tears. I said, "God, if you give me the opportunity to prove that I'm a great player, I'm going to go out and show the world who I am and what I can do."

In 1975, the Steelers used their first pick in the draft on Dave Brown, a defensive back from Michigan. He was with us for one year until there was an expansion draft. Teams had to put up players for that draft and Dave was picked up by the Seattle Seahawks. He went on to have a great career with them.

But in 1975, I led the league with 11 interceptions, we went on to win another Super Bowl, and I was named NFL Defensive Player of the Year.

BILL POLIAN: The Cover Two was brought to the Steelers by defensive coordinator Bud Carson, who had employed it at Georgia Tech. Unlike standard NFL defenses of the time, its base was not man-to-man but rather zone. Cornerbacks pressed wide receivers on the line of scrimmage and jammed them, preventing a clean release. The corners then dropped into zones in the outside flat area, reading the quarterback's eyes and flowing to the ball. Two deep safeties, aligned on the hashmarks, were also reading the quarterback's eyes and receivers' routes. Upon the throw, they "rallied to the ball," causing violent collisions and interceptions at the catch point.

With all 11 defenders facing the quarterback, they pursued the ball with all-out effort, emphasizing punishing collisions and turnovers. Jack Lambert's speed and length allowed him to drop against the pass 20–25 yards deep in the middle of the field. This provided an extra middle defender, which allowed the split safeties to cover deep outside zones, thereby double-teaming outside receivers. This was unique at the time.

Dungy brought this concept to Tampa, where it became dominant and known as "Tampa Two." Tony brought it to the Colts, and it stabilized our defense and helped carry us to victory in Super Bowl XLI, thus proving that in football at least, "There is nothing new under the sun."

TONY DUNGY: I just laugh when people talk about Tampa Two, because I got to Tampa in 1996 but I had first learned the Cover Two in 1977 as a rookie defensive back in Pittsburgh. But it had gotten there in 1972 when Bud Carson was hired as defensive coordinator.

Bud came from Georgia Tech and bought this college style of defense, where the corners rolled up on both sides of the field to take away the outside. It was really put in to handle option football. You got your corners involved in tackling because that was the only way to stop the triple option.

Before Bud brought the Cover Two to Pittsburgh, professional quarterbacks had never seen it. All of a sudden, when they faced the Steelers, they didn't know what to do when the corners didn't back up and didn't play man-to-man. It just really threw them off.

Coach Noll took it to a different level by saying, "We're going to get players specifically designed for this coverage. Our corners don't have to be small, fast, quick, man-to-man guys."

When I was on the Steelers' coaching staff and getting ready for my first scouting trip, Coach Noll told me, "Don't take a stopwatch, don't take a tape measure. Take your eyes. If guys can run and hit, they can play for us."

We had a lot of undersized defensive linemen who were really good, because we didn't force them to play two gaps. They didn't have to take on an offensive blocker, beat him either way, and come off and make the tackle.

We slid our guys where they only played one gap so they could fire off the line of scrimmage, penetrate, and use their quickness. They could line up in one gap and stunt to another gap, so the offense couldn't just tee off on them.

The Steelers drafted Mel Blount, who was 6'4" and about 220 pounds, and he played the right corner. They drafted J.T. Thomas, who was a safety at Florida State and was about 6'2" and about 208–210 pounds, and he played the left corner.

Then they got some fast, active linebackers to kind of patrol the middle and go sideline to sideline. Jack Ham, a 220-pound outside linebacker, was a tremendous athlete. Jack Lambert, a 6'4", 205-pound middle linebacker, was drafted out of Kent State. So, you had these big, monstrous corners, you had these quick linebackers that people weren't used to dealing with, and then you had two ball-hawking safeties in the back.

They wreaked havoc, but if you don't have those four-down interior people that could make things happen close to the ball, then the system kind of falls apart.

MEL BLOUNT: When I came out of college, I was a man-to-man cover guy. I knew nothing about zone defenses. I had a lot of problems just recognizing formations. The first defensive backs coach I had in Pittsburgh was Charlie Sumner and he would take me after practice and after meetings and we would go over formations, we would go over coverages.

A lot of things that you see coaches put in are from what they see players do on the field. The Cover Two was really a coverage that came about because of a mistake. I remember vividly, in practice, when I should have been playing man, that I would jam and then come off because I was confused. I would just cover a guy because he was open.

I think that was the origin of the Cover Two, along with them looking at every position and being able to build something off of what they saw players doing in practice. Everybody knows about John Stallworth and Lynn Swann, but before them, we had guys like Frank Lewis and Ron Shanklin. When you get good athletes on the field, even against coverages that are designed to stop something, guys will find ways to beat it.

The coaches had a lot of film to look at and a lot of things to be creative with. Not only was Cover Two one of our leading coverages, but we also played Two Man, where we were basically playing underneath the receivers and the safeties were over the top. We led with that a lot, especially if the coaches felt the linebackers could cover. We even played a Cover Three, where I was allowed to play man-to-man on the weak side.

BILL POLIAN: As you will hear from the players, the rules in the '70s were very different than they are today. Helmet-to-helmet collisions were the norm. DBs were allowed to "chuck and jam" with impunity prior to the pass. Defensive line play was essentially "no holds barred." With the advent of Cover Two, all 11 players flew to the ball with the idea of causing massive collisions with ball-carriers and receivers and/or QBs. That would cause fumbles or knock people out of the game.

The biggest proponents of this "physical" style of play were the Steelers, Raiders, and later the '85 Bears. These teams prided themselves on "taking no prisoners" and this led to a ferociously physical rivalry between the '70s Raiders and Steelers. Fans in both cities embraced this style. This physical approach to defense is the Steelers' calling card to this day.

JOE GREENE: Being a hard-hat city, steel mills and the whole thing, we were not a finesse team. We probably took offense at anyone calling us a finesse football team.

When you two-gap, the way we did, you're not avoiding a block; you're making contact. Once you get close to those guys that way, you have to be able to get rid of them and then chase the ball. And when you get to the ball-carrier, you want to make good contact.

Chuck never believed in leaving your feet to make a tackle. He said, "You can't go with your legs. You don't fly there to make a tackle. You run through to make a tackle."

That philosophy probably brought more of a physical approach to playing football without saying, "We're trying to be physical." I think it was just the techniques that Coach talked about.

For instance, when it came to making contact as a defender, Chuck used to use terms like, "Same foot, same shoulder." Now, what does that mean? If you're going to make contact with anyone, your near leg is the one that's going to be planted and you're driving that near leg into that person, because if it's the opposite leg, it doesn't give you the power of having your hips underneath you.

It's like you're leaning on him, instead of driving. There's more force in a drive than there is in a lean. It's the same thing when you make a tackle. You don't always accomplish it, but that's what you're trying to do.

Chuck was big on techniques and fundamentals. He'd say, "If you were not having success at what we were asking you to do, go back to the basics. Ask yourself if you're doing the fundamentals properly."

That was his way.

One of the things that we were consistent with, with all of our practices, was the picture from the scout team. If I was being shown a picture by the offense, I would tell them, "I want a Rembrandt. No borderline." We wanted the best picture you could give with a minimal amount of contact. Contact was something you were going to have, let's not run away from it.

But let's not overdo it.

MEL BLOUNT: One of the things that I think we were probably doing way before any other team was that we made lifting weights throughout our training camp mandatory. I don't think Bradshaw had to lift weights, but any other position, you had to get strong.

I can't ever remember going to practice without shoulder pads. Chuck always said, "You've got to put on the equipment you're going to play with."

And that was shoulder pads and helmets. We were physical in practice and I still think, to this day, if you want to play this game, that's how you have to practice.

I hear that a lot of guys go to practice in shorts and T-shirts, but you can't just turn it on and turn it off. You have to play the way you practice. That was the way we were.

TOM MOORE: The two Super Bowls we won when I was with the Steelers, against the Cowboys and the Rams, I guarantee you, we won because of Chuck Noll. When we beat Dallas in the Super Bowl, 35–31, they would come up with what people called the double-gap blitz that you saw Mike Zimmer run at all the time.

You'd bring the safety and the linebacker into the A-gap. When Dallas did that, we had two audibles. One of them was "93," which was a tackle trap. Your center blocks back, one of your guards blocks back, your other guard goes for one of the linebackers, and you bring your tackle and trap the guy in the gap.

Dallas came up in it and Bradshaw audibled to "93" and Franco Harris went about 34 yards for a touchdown. The other thing we had in that game was something we called "90 Go." The center would block to the left, Franco would step up and just hit the linebacker in the other A-gap, and then release right straight downfield because there was no middle safety; it was zero coverage. Bradshaw hit him for a touchdown. Those were the two touchdowns that won the game for us.

That was Chuck Noll.

MEL BLOUNT: Just looking back at those first two Super Bowls, I can honestly say, to a man, that everybody felt that we would continue to win Super Bowls. In 1976, after we won the second Super Bowl, against Dallas, we started out winning one game and losing four.

But then we won our next nine games in a row. Our defense just dominated. We had five shutouts in those wins. We beat the Colts 40–14 in the divisional round of the playoffs. We were on our way to winning another championship, in my opinion, but Franco and Rocky got hurt against Baltimore.

To show you how Chuck Noll was ahead of his time, he came up with this two-tight-end offense, which we really didn't know a lot about at the time and our offense was trying to figure it out. But now, it's something that you see all the time.

We didn't have a running game and the Raiders won that championship, but we knew the kind of dominance we had over the league. I'll never forgot how we would be in the meeting rooms or on the practice field, and everybody was talking about the Cowboys being "America's Team." That was from their marketing and promotions. They did a good job of promoting themselves. But it really put a bad taste in our mouths.

We were like, "Well, how are they 'America's Team' and we're the champions?"

TOM MOORE: We played the Rams in the Super Bowl after the '79 season. That was the one game where I really saw Chuck uptight because there were three guys on the Rams staff that had previously been in Pittsburgh. They had Lionel Taylor, they had Bud Carson, and they had Dan Radakovich.

We kept two backs in the backfield for protection purposes, because Chuck was always big on protection. We took our tight end, Bennie Cunningham, out and put in a third wide receiver on third down. We knew Bud would then go to prevent defense, which he did.

We had a strong right formation, where you had two wideouts to the right side and one to the left side. We put Lynn Swann to the left side and we knew Bud would double Swann by playing a guy underneath and a guy over the top. We put Jim Smith as a flanker to the right side and we knew Bud would single him. Then, we put John Stallworth in the slot, and we knew Bud would double him by going in and out.

Anytime you get in-and-out coverage, you run an in post route because as soon as that guy comes in, the inside defender jumps the in, and the outside defender is supposed to lap over in case it's a pump. Those were the two big passes that Terry hit Stallworth to help us win that Super Bowl. Every defense has a weakness in it and when you see it, bam! Go to it and get your touchdown.

I'll never forget Lynn Swann coming in after Chuck hired me and saying, "Okay, I know you were a college coach and I'm going to help you if I can. Here's the deal, Tom: A player can make a lot of money in pro football and I want to make a lot of money. I want to play as long as I can. So, John Stallworth and I know how to catch the football. Teach us what we don't know."

"Okay, what don't you know?"

"We don't have a clue how to adjust routes, how to read coverage, how to get open."

So that was what I taught them. In training camp, we used to spend half of our time working on beating double coverage.

From that point on, I've always told assistant coaches, "When you go into your first meeting in OTAs, the first thing you have to do is take all your players and find out from them what they don't know, what they need work on, because they're not going to tell you unless you ask them. And if you ask them, that'll loosen them up and they'll feel free to tell you."

TERRY BRADSHAW: Chuck Noll, throughout my career, accomplished what he wanted to accomplish. He took a naïve, country, shy, bashful, extremely immature kid and he made me a tough-minded, emotionally strong quarterback. I think he saw what I lacked. He knew I could throw it. He knew I could run. He knew I was strong, and he knew I was fast.

He saw in me that, for us to accomplish greatness, we would experience hard times and he wanted me to be tough enough to handle those hard times and be conditioned for that. I see that now. I absolutely now appreciate our relationship from the standpoint I would never have gone into the Hall of Fame, I would never have won Super Bowls, if he hadn't conditioned me to be tough mentally and emotionally. I applaud him for that.

All the other shit, I wish we could have done without. I didn't need that.

How do you say bad things about your head coach who's in the Hall of Fame? I didn't go when he was inducted, I didn't go to his funeral. There was no relationship there. I was closer to Bum Phillips. Easily closer.

But Chuck Noll was someone that probably knew you can't be friends with your players. You're going to cut them and ask them to retire at some point. It's not going to go well. He kept his distance.

MEL BLOUNT: People don't realize how good Terry was. Someone asked me this question: "Of all the quarterbacks, who would you take if you had to go out there right now?" I said, "Terry Bradshaw."

I said that because the rules Terry played under were so different than the rules that these guys are playing under now. Terry's arm was so incredible. He had an arm—and this is no lie—that you could hear the ball whistling through the air. I saw Terry actually split the skin between guys' fingers as they caught the ball.

And I was out there trying to knock these balls down.

JOE GREENE: Terry would catch heck from Dwight White all the time in practice. The quarterbacks were supposed to be off-limits. You couldn't touch them. Dwight liked to go up there and bump him. He wouldn't hurt him; he'd just bump him.

Terry would get angry. He said, "You know you're not supposed to touch the quarterback." Dwight kept doing it and Terry was getting angrier.

TERRY BRADSHAW: Dwight just couldn't help himself. He had a clean shot at me and he wiped me out. I was so pissed. I got up, took the ball, and I drilled him with it.

I said, "Let me tell you something, Dwight. You may lose with me, but your ass ain't ever gonna win without me."

I don't know where that came from. I guess it was just some of my brilliance right there. And that became a rallying cry. George Perles, our defensive coordinator, would say it almost every day.

MEL BLOUNT: The media wanted to paint Terry as just a Southern, country hick, tobacco-chewing guy. But you could see just how much he wanted it. That offense was so potent, between the running game with Franco and Rocky and the air attack with Swann and Stallworth and Cunningham, and even Rocky catching passes out of the backfield.

It was something to see. We practiced against it every day and when we went into games, it was easy because we had practiced all week against the best.

Especially 1979. What they did was just incredible. If you looked at Super Bowl XIV, Terry and that offense just demolished the Rams.

JOE GREENE: Terry Bradshaw was a leader by what he did and there were a couple of other games when he did it from a vocal standpoint. There was a time when we really needed it and that was Super Bowl XIV. Things were going very bad for us. We were trailing the Rams at halftime and he made a speech that I thought changed it around.

He said, "Guys, we're not playing the way that we can play. We need to get out there on the same page and go out and kick some butt and win this game. We've come too far to lose this one at this point in time. So, let's go get 'em."

He came back and he threw a couple of touchdown passes.

TERRY BRADSHAW: After the fourth Super Bowl, I was able to say to myself, "It's time to go." I definitely appreciated what we accomplished. How could you not?

You hear about dynasties. Listen, we read that stuff. The greatest thing about our football team—and I give Chuck credit for this—he never let us get complacent. And we never got complacent. We wanted desperately to win.

I loved the '85 Bears, but they messed up a great thing by writing 10,000 books and having all kinds of restaurant openings. That team could have won another Super Bowl, but they didn't because they lost their focus, they lost their desire, and everybody was wanting credit. That wasn't our case at all.

At that point, I found more enjoyment in playing. I felt the Steelers needed me more. And the team was not as good defensively. The offensive rules had changed to where we were throwing the football more. I was enjoying that. It was kind of like, "Okay, this is fun."

Then I got hurt.

We were having a morning practice and the field was wet. For some reason, Chuck wanted to throw takeoffs for 50 yards or whatever. I remember, when I threw this one pass, my foot slipped and it put my elbow at an angle. I felt this sting on my right elbow. It felt like a bee sting.

I played with it, kept complaining about my elbow. I went all year like that. I'd get it shot up and we played, and it just got worse and worse. The doctor looked at it. After that, the report came out that I had tennis elbow. It was microscopically repaired; it was easy to fix.

I went to quarterback camp and picked a football up and just tossed it 10 yards and I felt that muscle slide. When I did that, I ended up just absolutely messing my elbow up. I tried electro stimulus, I tried everything in the world. Really, what I should have done was not played at all that year and I would have been fine.

I got this machine that numbed the pain. I went to practice and thought, "I'm doing really good." They announced me as the starter against the Jets, who we needed to beat to make the playoffs.

We were doing good, I was doing good. We were inside the 20 and I rolled right and I was sprinting. I looked back and I saw Gregg Garrity raise his arm on a pass route. I snapped it off across the field in a dead stride. When I did, that right elbow went, "Powww!" And I went, "Oh, shit!"

Garrity caught the pass for a touchdown. Everybody was jumping up and down and I went to the sideline. I was standing real still. Tony Parisi, our equipment manager, came over and said, "Great throw! Great throw!"

I said, "Boy, Tony, I did something to my elbow."

"What are you talking about?

"I heard it snap."

"Are you shittin' me?"

"No, man. This thing is killing me."

I actually was embarrassed that I was hurt. All of this hoopla about me coming back and starting, and now I'm hurt, right off the bat. I wasn't saying a word to anybody. I was just standing there with my elbow just screaming in pain.

I said, "Tony, I just pray to God that they don't fumble or throw a pick. I can't play, I can't stand this pain."

Sure enough, the Jets fumbled, we got the ball back. I hadn't said anything to anybody except Tony Parisi. I had my right arm hanging straight down and I wasn't moving it.

As I ran out on the field, all I was thinking was, "Run, run, run, run, run, run. We'll go in at halftime and then I'll let them all know." Then, we had a third-and-long and I thought, "Oh, shit!"

I ended up throwing a pass and we got a first down. I don't even know how I got it out of my hand. It was a wide flare. It wasn't a flat or a deep-in. It was a wide flare. We got a first down. Run, run, run, run.

Now, it was third-and-goal. I called a pick—an illegal play—and Calvin Sweeney was the intended receiver. When I dropped back, my elbow was hurting so much, I could hardly hold the ball in my hand. I threw to Calvin, who was wide open. The ball went end over end, and as it headed down to the ground, Calvin caught it for a touchdown. That was it for me in that game.

After we lost to the Raiders in the playoffs, I flew out to California to see Dr. Frank Jobe. He put my elbow in a device and moved it and he said, "You've torn the ulnar collateral ligament. There are two things to do: You can lift weights, build the muscles up around the elbow, and see if you can deal with the pain. Or we can perform the Tommy John surgery."

I opted out of surgery. That was the biggest mistake I made after the first big mistake, which was throwing the ball after surgery and that messed my shoulder up. That set rehab back a year. But I couldn't go to games and stand on the sideline. Number one, it always felt like a distraction. I'm the kind of person that I don't want anybody to have my job. I just don't. That was the thing that I was so good at, playing quarterback and throwing the football. I just couldn't stand for somebody else having my job, even though I cared about that player as a person.

If I had been encouraged by the Rooneys or the Steelers or Chuck Noll to go and get the surgery, if they had said, "We want you back whenever you're ready," I'd have gotten the surgery. But I didn't get that impression at all.

I came back for the quarterback camp the next spring and had not thrown a pass. I had lifted weights, had done everything asked of me weight-lifting-wise.

When I got in practice, I was scared to throw. I threw one pass in warmups. We always warmed up with wide flares to the backs. After I threw it, I went, "Oh, shit! Oh, my God, that hurts."

I stood there and then I just turned around and jogged back inside. I took off my helmet, pads, whatever we had on. I put my clothes on and went into the training room to see Tony Parisi. I shook his hand and hugged him and said, "I love you, man, but I'm through."

I called a friend of mine who had a plane and asked him if he would pick me up. He said he would. I tried to figure out what I could take home with me; settled on a helmet. I packed my bags and went in the training room. Chuck came in and said, "Are you okay?"

"It's over, Coach. I can't play anymore."

He shook my hand and I said, "Thank you. It's been awesome."

That was it. That was how it ended, right there. I never had a press conference, never told anybody I was retired. I just retired and signed with CBS.

Kind of the way I roll.

CHAPTER 3

The West Coast Offense I & II: From Walsh to Holmgren

BILL POLIAN: Bill Walsh became the head coach of the San Francisco 49ers in 1979 at the relatively late age of 48. He had just finished a good tenure at nearby Stanford University in his first stint as a head man.

Before taking over the Cardinal, Bill had a long run as a quarterback coach and an offensive coordinator in the NFL with the San Diego Chargers, Oakland Raiders, and most notably, the Cincinnati Bengals under legendary Hall of Famer Paul Brown.

Bill's 49ers teams revolutionized the NFL with a unique system of offensive football soon dubbed the "West Coast" offense by the media. Led by Hall of Famers Joe Montana, Steve Young, and Jerry Rice, San Francisco won three Super Bowls under Bill and two others under his successor and defensive coordinator, George Seifert.

The West Coast offense and the 49ers organization are Bill Walsh's creation, just as the original Cleveland Browns and the Cincinnati Bengals were Paul Brown's. That is no accident. Bill spent many years as Paul Brown's quarterbacks coach and de facto offensive coordinator in Cincinnati.

As a fellow football junkie, I asked Bill how the West Coast offense came to be. In his sardonic and self-deprecating way, he told me, "Our quarterback in Cincinnati was Greg Cook. [He was] 6'4", rocket arm, great intelligence, and presence—prototypical in every way. We had Isaac Curtis—tall, very fast, a flier who could go deep and catch the ball reliably. We had a vertical passing game, coupled with a trap-draw and power-run game, which was Paul Brown's and dated back to Marion Motley and Jim Brown."

Then Cook hurt his shoulder seriously and was replaced by Virgil Carter. Bill said that Carter did not have the arm to execute the vertical passing game. As a result, he had to change the entire offense. The Bengals had to go to a short, possession passing game emphasizing run after catch. Because Carter was mobile and could run, Bill began to use bootlegs off the run game. Play-action set up the vertical game.

The new iteration of the Bengals offense was successful and began to evolve. Bill said, "That's the *great* West Coast offense. It was born out of necessity."

Necessity may be the mother of invention, but the creation of a system of football and an organization that won five Super Bowls and revolutionized the game was pure Bill Walsh.

Besides George Seifert, other former Walsh assistant coaches—notably Mike Holmgren, Mike Shanahan, and Brian Billick—also went on to become head coaches. That trio led their teams to Super Bowl victories as well, while spreading the gospel of the West Coast offense through every level of the football world.

In this chapter, you will hear from Walsh (from archived radio interviews he did years ago), Holmgren, Billick, Hall of Fame quarterback Steve Young, and Hall of Fame defensive end Charles Haley.

You also will get insights from Holmgren and Hall of Fame GM Ron Wolf on how a version of the West Coast offense—which we're calling West Coast II—helped revitalize the Green Bay Packers after Holmgren became their head coach.

MIKE HOLMGREN: I had been at BYU for four years when Paul Hackett left the 49ers. He had been their quarterbacks coach and went on to become the passing game coordinator for the Dallas Cowboys. A friend of mine said, "Why don't you go for that job? You grew up in San Francisco."

I said, "They're not going to hire me."

I did get an interview with Bill Walsh and I thought it went well. He was a pretty impressive guy. I was nervous. As I suspected, I was a long shot, but at least Bill was honest with me about that.

He said, "You did a good job, but I have someone in mind. If that doesn't work out, then I'll give you a call." That usually means, "Thanks, it's been nice, but it's not going to happen." I went back to BYU.

One day I was out jogging, which I used to do before my fake hips, and after I came back, the BYU football secretary said, "Hey, a Mr. Coach Walsh just phoned. He wanted to talk to you."

"Really?"

"I told him you were out jogging, and you didn't have time to talk with him."

"What?"

Fortunately, Bill phoned me back and offered me the job. For a San Francisco kid, going to the 49ers and getting to work for Coach Walsh was kind of a dream come true.

I was coming from a place that didn't run very much at all. In fact, we would spend our whole practice at BYU passing the ball. When Bill implemented the West Coast offense, the rest of the league saw it as a change in philosophy from the mindset that most of the NFL had, which was, *Stomp, crush, kill… we've got to run and play tough defense.* It's a copycat league in certain respects, and I believe the success of the 49ers started the evolution of that West Coast offensive scheme throughout the league.

I think we did it out of necessity as much as anything else. We substituted a lot of the running plays with passing plays—our six-yard gainers, our five-yard passes, things to keep the ball moving. For me, actually, I was just going from all pass to more pass.

It wasn't a big transition for me.

BILL WALSH (from an interview with Ron Barr on *Sports Byline USA*): No one had ever labeled what we did. It was just our offense with the 49ers. And of course, I'd brought that system from Stanford and prior to that, the Chargers, and prior to that, the Bengals. It was just a system of football.

People gave it a label as though it's some purest form of the game. In reality, it's a compilation of what a lot of other people have done and a lot of original things we did. But it's a system in which you know the skills that have to be taught to each position to participate in the offense.

In other words, the tight end has certain skills and you have a way to teach him. You've found the best way to drill them and develop and enhance them. You go down through every position that way, so that when the player arrives, you know just where to start and how to develop their skills and how they can be part of it.

I assume some of it was the plays we ran. I can still see those as I change the channels with my clicker, watching the different games. Some of it's that, but more importantly, it's the attention to detail and it's the isolation of the skills that have to be taught and finding a way to teach them.

BRIAN BILLICK: I think, at its core, from Al Davis certainly and Sid Gillman, a lot of the mentality of the West Coast passing game was vertical. When you look at Bill's structure of routes, there's a vertical element in every play. It's not the primary route, but the basic "22 Z In" has that post on the back side.

Bill was always adamant that you're reading safety to linebacker. You don't care about the cornerback. If the safety does not have the curl and goes to flat, I'm going to take curl. If he hangs for the curl, I'm going to see what the linebacker does. If they give us zero coverage, or go four across, anything that might give you that post, then you had the license to go to the post.

Bill would be very precise in the way he would install the game plan. That was vintage Bill Walsh. It's the John Wooden first practice—"Here's how you put your sneakers on. Here's how you tie them." Bill would install "22 Z In," which was in the game plan every week, as if the players had never heard of it before, with attention to detail.

Bill would say, "Here's what we anticipate. And here's when we'll get the post against these guys."

He was just so detailed in his preparation and the way he installed the offense that it was much more comprehensive and easier for the quarterback. Having lived it in the old systems, it was tough on quarterbacks, because if you went deep and it didn't work, you were going to hear, "Why didn't you go to the flat?" And if you went to the flat, it was, "Dammit! The post was there. Why didn't you go there?" Whereas this was, "We'll go where the read takes us."

It was at a time when things were changing defensively. I remember when I first got the job in Baltimore, Ted Marchibroda, who had been the Ravens' coach, was kind enough to have lunch with me. Ted said, "In the old days, it was easy. On first down, you've got Cover Three. Second down, you've got Cover Two. Now, it's just so multiple."

Bill was going to provide an answer on every route combination based on what the quarterback was seeing. If that meant hitting the flare or the flat or the pivot 10 straight times, because that's what the defense is giving you, then we'll hit it 10 straight times.

Bill was very concise about the boxes he put in the game plan. He was one of the first to say, "Okay, here's our explosive box. Here's our Jerry Rice box." Meaning, if we didn't naturally get Jerry into the game, he was going to that box.

Bill just had it in his mind to get Jerry involved. He would also say, "If you don't naturally have a vertical happen within eight or nine plays, I'm going to call a specific vertical."

Now, it often happened on its own, which was great. But you had that clock in your mind the whole time.

STEVE YOUNG: It was a binary system. Against man coverage, it was one series of routes. Zone, another series of routes. Bill told Jerry Rice, "When you come off the line, you need to take a mental snapshot and understand whether you're being manned up or whether it's zone, and you've got to make this decision very quickly."

It was complicated. It was hard. I remember Jerry throwing his helmet in frustration. Nobody wants to be unable to do what looks, on paper, simple: "Figure out if it's zone or man. If it's zone, do X. If it's man, do Y." You say, "Yeah, I can do that." Then you go out on the field and people would just grind to a halt.

Some were able to understand it intuitively. For Brent Jones, our tight end, spatial awareness was just how he thought about the world. Brent wasn't going to outrun anybody, Brent wasn't going to out-physical anybody. But Brent was always open because he intuitively understood these complexities. He flourished.

But particularly for Jerry, it was a couple of times of running into zone and getting thrown the ball and getting leveled. He was like, "Okay, I'm going to figure this out." Once Jerry and John Taylor, who was an amazing talent, got it down, then we had three guys who could uniquely get into defenses. You get those guys going and you couldn't really stop it.

There were times when Bill would say, "You guys are fools if he can't just run up and down this field." I think he was right. No one could stop it. Or at least that's certainly the way it felt at times.

CHARLES HALEY: The West Coast offense was finesse, cut-blocking people, getting pass-rushers' hands down. That was Bobb McKittrick's thing as the offensive line coach: "Cut 'em, cut 'em, cut 'em." If somebody's diving at your legs, your hands are going to go down to protect your legs. You cut them a few times, guys stop coming off the ball.

It was about getting the ball out of the quarterback's hand quickly. They tried to put their best guys, like Jerry Rice, on a linebacker or a safety, catching a five-yard cross and taking it for 80. That was the West Coast offense: get their best player against the weakest player and get the ball out fast.

One of the other big things was, to be a back for the 49ers, you had to catch the ball. The outs, the screens. That was big in that system. And the running back could catch the ball and go for 20 because [the defense was] worried about Jerry Rice and the tight ends.

I played against the 49ers twice when I was with the Cowboys. In order to beat that West Coast offense, you had to get them in long down-and-distance. Third down's got to be 10–15 yards in order to really be able to go get them because they would hold the ball a little bit longer. By formation, I could kind of figure out the runs or passes, when they were going to try to bring the wide receiver or tight end down to try to hit me. That became easier because I practiced against all of it.

But when you practice against it, they don't cut you, so you don't get to see the hands go down. That was why Joe could throw the ball to Jerry Rice over the middle for five yards and not get the ball batted down. But the thing that hurts that is a quick guy. If you've got somebody getting off the ball quick, that can defeat that system.

TONY DUNGY: Playing for two Hall of Fame guys—Chuck Noll, when I was a safety for the Pittsburgh Steelers from 1977 to 1978, and Bill Walsh, when I was with the 49ers in 1979—couldn't have been better training ground for me in becoming a coach. Coach Walsh was similar to Coach Noll in a lot of ways, but he was different in that he loved matchups and he loved accentuating the positives of his players and kind of hiding the negative. He had this different style of offense built around the short passing game.

What I loved about him was he had a belief in his system. He did not waver. His first year with the 49ers was the year that I played for him. We were 2–14 and every week he would come in and say, "Hey, the system is going to work. We're getting better. I believe in it. And we're not going to change."

That had an impact on me because many years later, my first year as head coach of the Bucs, it was the same way. We started out 0–5, and then we went to 1–8. But I remember that first year and I said, "You know what? We're not going to waver; we're not going to change. We are going to build this just the way Coach Walsh did."

MIKE HOLMGREN: Bill had his philosophy, but then he had to adapt. All of a sudden, things happen—you lose a player, you gain a player—and they all have their different strengths and weaknesses. Some head coaches aren't good at adapting and some are very good at it. Bill was very, very good at adapting. We did the best things, I think, for the personnel we had. That's what you're paid to do.

Virgil Carter was quite different than Greg Cook, so after Greg got hurt you had to do something. And Virgil showed that you can move the ball and have an effective offensive football team if the quarterback is willing to buy in. Because he doesn't have to have the rocket arm. He doesn't have to be 6'4". You don't have to have those things, but your offense will help him reach his potential.

I think there are certain offenses in football that require more of a power thrower, someone who can push it down the field and is bigger and stronger. I think, in the West Coast offense, you can be that type of player, like Brett Favre was in that offense when we were in Green Bay.

You also can be someone who isn't the most imposing guy physically, like the quarterback we had when I got to San Francisco—Joe Montana.

BRIAN BILLICK: Before the 1979 draft, Denny Green and Sam Wyche had gone down to work out James Owens, a running back from UCLA. They needed a quarterback to throw to him. Well, Joe Montana was living in L.A. before the draft, so they just got Montana to come out and throw, because they wanted to look at Owens as a wide receiver.

They came back and told Bill, "You've got to look at Montana. He looks like the kind of guy you would like, Bill." Bill said, "Yeah, yeah."

We didn't have a first-round pick that year. We made James Owens our top pick of the second round, and he had a pretty forgettable career.

Then, we selected Joe Montana, from Notre Dame, in the third round. I was in the room when we took Joe, and it wasn't like, "Alright! We've got this great quarterback!" It was, "Okay, who are we going to take in the fourth round?" It was just move on to the next guy.

Obviously, the rest is history, so to speak.

But if we had not hit on a Joe Montana, wiping out on our first pick the way we did, and had the first two years that we had, I don't know if Bill would have lasted. Obviously, in Joe, we knew we had something, and it took off.

MIKE HOLMGREN: If I had to describe Joe, first of all, technically he did things about as well as you can do them as a quarterback. The physical part of it. The steps. The balance. The throwing of the ball. People used to say, "Well, he doesn't have a rifle arm." But he was plenty, plenty strong in the arm department.

After that, you had the mental part of it and the learning of the system, which was a progression system. In a split second, the quarterback has to look at the coverage and reads one, two, three, four, and five. Now, if there's a different coverage, does it change? No. It's still one, two, three, four, five. It still has to be done in a split second, and Joe was just gifted that way. He always did the right thing.

If he had protection, he couldn't miss. He was a very accurate passer. I want to throw this in, too: his teammates loved him. They'd play hard for him. You can't discount that.

CHARLES HALEY: Joe was a prankster. He'd get to practice early and take Cramergesic, a sports ointment that got hot, and put it in our jockstraps. You'd be out there practicing and the next thing you know, your balls got to burning. Everybody would be jumping around like, "What the hell's going on?" And Joe would be over there laughing.

In training camp, he would take the seat off your bike, leaving just that metal pole, so then you would have to ride all the way up to the meal hall or the practice field standing up. He'd put bikes up in trees. Joe was just a funny man. I'd never had a quarterback or friend like that before.

BRIAN BILLICK: After we drafted Joe, we flew him to San Francisco, along with our other draft picks. His flight didn't get in until 1:00 AM. As the slapdick that I was at the time, I had to go pick him up at the airport.

I was thinking I was just picking up a guy, but I will tell you—and I'm being sincere about this—the first time I met him, I looked in his eyes and there was something different about this guy. He had Björn Borg eyes—cool, calm, unflustered, unblinking.

This was a rookie who was perfect for Bill because when Bill jumped his ass about, "I want that pass a foot and a half off the lead pad of the receiver," he had the calm to say, "Got it."

Now Steve Young would have said, "Well, Bill, it was a foot and a quarter. Is that not good enough? Does it really have to be a foot and a half?"

Steve, who's a brilliant guy, would challenge Bill at every turn. He'd say, "Whoa! Three weeks ago, you said so-and-so. Now, you're saying something else." That drove Bill nuts. But Steve would burr up and want it explained again, whereas Joe would go, "Okay, I've got it."

That was the perfect match; Bill's manic obsession and a guy who was going to be so palatable and manageable to craft his game.

MIKE HOLMGREN: I remember my first three weeks on the job, Bill gave me a box of 100 videotapes of his offensive installations that he had recorded. He said, "I think this might be the best way to learn the offense." (As an aside, when I left the 49ers and Mike Shanahan came in as coach, the team gave him a box of my installations. That was how that was done.)

Studying those tapes was all I did for three weeks, because we had a mini-camp coming up and I had to be able to speak the language and understand it a little bit. I was like a quarterback still playing or a new draft choice in the room, studying and trying to learn the offense.

STEVE YOUNG: The first day I'm in San Francisco, there was a guy with a big camera on his shoulder filming Bill in a team meeting. Then he followed Bill whenever he went. He was filming him on the practice field and in the locker room. Every time Bill was speaking to the team, he was being filmed. I was thinking, "Who does he think he is? Lincoln? Does he already have a museum? What is this?"

But what he was doing was creating a tool kit—a video-based, audio-based, paper-based physical tool kit. Essentially, it was everything that he knew from installations, meetings, speeches, how he thought about nutrition and hydration and mental health and marriage counseling. He was thinking about all of these things that were going to allow his team to be better integrated.

The first meeting I went to, when the guy was filming, Bill said, "We're going to integrate this football team." I immediately think he's talking about race because when I think integration, I'm thinking it's about Black and white guys working together as a team. Bill knew that was what all of us were thinking, too.

Then he explained that we were going to integrate on all levels, that we were going to get past all the things that are separators—whether it's race, language, religion, socioeconomic background, where you went to college, the conference you came from, the position you played.

"All the quarterbacks hang out together, all the defensive backs hang out together, and the problem is, without even realizing it, you can play with a guy for 10 years and you'll know his name because you see it on the back of his jersey but you really don't know anything about him," Bill said. "So, in the locker room, in the lunchroom, on the plane, on the bus, I am going to force you to not sit and be with the people you're comfortable with. I am going to force you to integrate."

During two-a-days in training camp, do you think I wanted to talk with someone I didn't know? I wanted to hang out with a couple of quarterbacks and be done with it. But in the lunchroom, he'd make you take your tray and go over and eat with somebody else.

Why?

"Because," Bill said, "we're going to be at Lambeau Field, we're going to be in the last four minutes, we're going to be down by four, we've got to score, it's going to be freezing rain, the coldest you've ever been in your life as the wind's blowing. And I need you to look each other in the eye in the huddle and I don't want you to just see a bunch of guys that are paid to be 49ers. I want you to have an element of, at least, respect for and even love for those guys in the huddle."

This was my first meeting. I had never heard anyone speak like that in a football context, ever.

Bill built this tool kit at the height of his career, the apex of his fame. He was two or three generations ahead of everybody from an offensive perspective and from how he looked at a partnership with players. During the strike of 1987, players and ownership/management couldn't have been any further apart. It was Bill who really saw players as his partners. He fundamentally believed that he would be more successful if he developed a more transparent partnership with his players.

Bill got Eddie DeBartolo on board because Eddie was built that way. He said, "Family! Yeah, family. You're going to tell me I can be better partners with my players? I love that." His team won Super Bowls, he flew them to Hawaii to celebrate. And, of course, there was a tremendous amount of jealousy among the other owners. People just didn't want that. They thought that it was not good for the league.

When it came to the tool kit, Bill wanted all of his assistant coaches to have a leg up when they went for bigger jobs. He said, "I want them to have everything that I have." Then, when they were on their way out the door, what did he say to them? "I'll see you in the championship game." Because he knew, with this stuff he was giving them, if they used it effectively, they were going to be great.

You had the Green Bay Packers, with Mike Holmgren, in the late '90s. You had the Denver Broncos, with Mike Shanahan, who learned the Walsh system when he was the 49ers' offensive coordinator, also in the late '90s.

It provided a template to come back and get us. Who's the nutball, at the height of his power, who would do that? A guy who has a sense of legacy, a guy who has a sense for what's the best thing he can do for football. It was unnatural. But Bill gave his secrets away in a very transparent way and he knew that it would come back to bite him and to bite us.

Look around the league. If you're really honest with yourself, there are two coaching trees that have basically been grown over the last 40 years. There's the Bill Parcells tree and there's the Bill Walsh tree. I'm not going to disrespect anything about Bill Parcells; I love him and he's great. But the Bill Walsh tree has flourished like nothing else.

Bill was the first Silicon Valley CEO before there were Silicon Valley CEOs. He was worried about marriage counseling. He was worried about mental health. He was worried about nutrition. He was always the one saying, "We're not going to go out there and sweat to death and not give you water. That doesn't make any sense." He knew that before nutritionists even started talking about it.

Bill also stood up in front of the whole team and said, "I stipulate I believe that you can tackle. I'm not going to try to teach you to tackle. I believe that you can. What we're going to focus on is timing."

The result was an offense that, for the first time in history, was built around timing. He connected it with the quarterback, and that was why people couldn't defend it.

I knew Bill's foibles as well. I'm not confused about who Bill was. I saw the worst of Bill. I also recognize that Bill collected a lot of great thinking around him. It wasn't like it was all original thought, but like anyone, when someone brings it together and actually puts it into practice, that's why he's the pioneer even when we know there are many fathers of that pioneering spirit. There were Paul Brown and Sid Gillman and Al Davis. But in my mind, it was Bill who kind of put it forward. I appreciate Eddie DeBartolo allowing him to do that and then getting completely on board.

MIKE HOLMGREN: We weren't in a big fancy building or anything. Bill had an office on the other side of the hallway. Sherm Lewis, Bobb McKittrick, Denny Green, and I were all in one room across the hall.

Bill and Bobb McKittrick had been together a long time. Bobb was very set in his ways, like most offensive line coaches I've ever met in my life. Before each coaches' meeting, the staff would prepare whatever we had to prepare while Bill was in his office. Then Bill would come in, look at what we put together, and he'd usually say, "No, I want this... I don't want that." Bobb would be the one guy in the room who would push back a little bit and they'd get banging around a little. I'd go, "Oh, boy!" It prepared me for my future because line coaches are that way.

Bill would come in periodically and say to me, "How's it going? Anything you need?"

I wanted to impress him, so I would always say, "No, no, I'm good."

One day, he came in and said, "Listen, Joe Montana is coming by. Why don't you guys get together for a Coke or a cup of coffee or something? Get to know one another a little bit."

I said, "Great." Then, I got really nervous. *What in the world am I going to do? How can I coach Joe Montana? He's already been the MVP of Super Bowls.*

Joe came in, we started walking down the hallway, and as I began to speak, Joe said, "No, Mike, stop for a second. Up front, here's what I want: I want you to coach me hard. If I make a mistake, correct it. If you see something to make me better, say it."

Right away, he took the pressure off me, at least the pressure I created for myself.

BRIAN BILLICK: To be able to sit back and watch Bill piece that program together was fascinating. At first, I wasn't going to take the job, because I was trying to get into coaching. But the minute you met with Bill, you discovered he was pretty persuasive. Because we were so small organizationally, I got every shit job that came down the pike. I became everybody's assistant, which at the time was a pain in the ass, but it was great tutelage for me.

I started out as the assistant public relations director. My degree is in communication, but Bill wanted to hire a guy who could interact with the players and set up those programs that are now replete through the NFL, in terms of helping the players both while they were playing and post-career. That was how I became the first player programs guy in the NFL.

For Bill, it was all about having that singular vision. It was, "We're all going to sing from the same hymnal." He was very detailed and definitive about the duties of everybody and how they would interact, from the communications director to the chief financial officer to travel to this, that.

The way Bill structured it, there were three of us handling PR, player programs, suite sales, publications, and community relations. Today, that's 70 people. But it was because of how small we were that I got to see Bill piece these things together and it was amazing to watch. Just as on the football side, he had a very clear and defined structure of what the organization was to be, what everybody was going to do, and how they were going to interact with one another.

I think a lot of how Bill did things came from Paul Brown, for whom he was an assistant coach with the Cincinnati Bengals from 1968 to 1975. Paul was kind of that single source, so Bill knew what that autonomous total authority model was. I know he also attributed some of it to being around Al Davis for the one season that he spent coaching running backs with the Raiders. Those were his models, both from an organizational standpoint and ultimately from a football standpoint as well.

BILL WALSH (from an interview with Ron Barr on *Sports Byline USA*): The Raider system originated with Sid Gillman and [was] then refined by Al Davis. It was the most complete system in football, to be honest with you. If I've had any talent in that area, it's because I had a chance to work for the Raider organization and learn a system of football. And then, more importantly, the chance to work with the Cincinnati Bengals with Paul Brown and have some autonomy and have some confidence from Paul in what we were doing.

Because of the kind of talent we had early on with the Bengals, we necessarily went to a ball-control style. Consequently, you look more for execution, and shorter-type passes, and setting up the long pass with a play pass, things of that nature, so that by the time I actually had an opportunity to be a head coach, I knew an entire system of football. And a lot of it was related to the skills and in the execution of the game.

We still use certain kinds of plays in pass protection that Sid basically developed in the early '60s. As far as Paul was concerned, he was a great organizer with more grasp of the game and knowledge of the game and wisdom that he could bring forth that could really refine a person's skills.

MIKE HOLMGREN: Practice took some getting used to, though, because Bill was such a perfectionist. As an example, when we began our practices in training camp, we would start with drills that would have the quarterbacks doing things that they had done a thousand times. But they had to do it another thousand times. Five-step, three-step. Where's your hip? Where's your plant foot? How are you holding the football? It's like you're in first grade, teaching someone to read.

A lot of people would say, "Well, you've got Joe Montana. He's done this, he knows what the steps are." No, no. You did it because there would be times in practice where we wouldn't do it, the play would be disrupted somehow, and when that happened, Bill wouldn't yell at them. He'd yell at me.

I can remember one time we were running a post pattern to Jerry Rice against air. It was a 20-yard throw down the field. Joe dropped back, threw the ball, Jerry caught it, and I said, "Nice throw!" Bill could hear me because he was maybe 20, 30 yards away, and he said, "Miiike! Miiike! No! No!"

I said, "What?"

"I want the ball thrown six inches in front of the numbers. That's where I want the ball thrown and caught. Six inches in front of the numbers. You understand?"

"Yes, Coach."

I'd turn around and I'd be grumbling out of the corner of my mouth. We had completed a beautiful throw down the field. Six inches in front of the numbers? I'd get so frustrated, but Bill strove for perfection in everything.

We all know you can't ever be perfect. No one can be perfect. But if you're not striving for perfection, you're not going to come close. That was his theory. That was how he pounded on us and why the quarterback play was the way it was.

STEVE YOUNG: I think why we thrived with Bill was because we equally enjoyed the data and the nuance and the little details. There are a lot of players who wouldn't have enjoyed that and it wouldn't have resonated and it would have been very frustrating.

We also knew how to take in what Bill was saying. Like, who cares if the pass was a foot and a quarter and not a foot and a half in front of the receiver's lead shoulder? Or not six inches in front of the numbers? We could ingest it in a way that was productive.

The idea was putting the ball in position for what was essentially yards after catch. I can throw it for a nice three-yard gain, but what if a guy can run for 50? Bill knew that the more sensitive the timing was, the more open the ability to run would be, which was especially true against zone. With man, you beat the guy, you're going to be on your way. But we mostly saw zone because everybody was saying, "I don't know what's going on with this West Coast offense, so let's just play zone."

Bill was always thinking, "How can I make more space in zone?" It was about being more specific and getting people on the run in zone. Even though the read says sit down in zone, you essentially let the quarterback lead you and believe that where the quarterback's throwing the ball is the place to start running. What Bill was saying was, "If the quarterback throws it to the wrong side, or even directly, the receiver doesn't know where to go. I want you to tell the receiver where to go by where you throw it." That was a heck of a challenge and a fun one. That was advanced learning. I loved it. I think Joe did too.

It also depended on who was at practice. If it was some general from the Joint Chiefs that he invited to watch, he had more things to say during those practices. We'd always go, "Sure, you're trying to make yourself look like you're the king."

You had to have context with Bill.

BRIAN BILLICK: The team wasn't very good the first two years, but Bill would come in every Monday after, typically, a loss and go, "Okay, Brian, when was the last time a quarterback threw for 300 yards in consecutive games and lost? What's the record for that?" Because we had Steve DeBerg and we were putting yards up, but we weren't winning games.

Now, I'm doing this without the internet, so I'm calling the Elias Sports Bureau, trying to come up with a number. Finally, I come up with it. It was four straight games, and it was Joe Blow from wherever. So Bill got into the press conference and, though no one would really ask it, somehow he would move the conversation and say, "You know, you'll need to check this, because I'm not really sure, but I think the last time a quarterback threw for consecutive 300-yard games and lost was in '73."

Like it was just on the tip of his tongue and he just kind of pulled it out. The writers knew what he was doing.

BILL WALSH (**from an interview with Ron Barr on** *Sports Byline USA*): I just think being very thorough is so important and planning out what your approach is going to be and then, after you're through, sort of reflecting on what happened. Most people try to expect to store everything in their mind that they're anticipating doing, and then going ahead and doing it. And those people that are most thorough and more detailed, try to sort of document things in their own mind, whether with a computer or longhand or however you do it, and just try to do a better job of, point by point, deciding a course of action.

In football, we have game plans, we have practice plans, and we have an approach to dealing with the video study of previous games and upcoming games. And, of course, there's the personnel end of it, being so thorough in the scouting and having an inventory on each athlete.

So, the detail of what you do and the thoroughness is so important. Those that expect to live by the seat of their pants or some ordained thought that will come to them or just their gift for being able to talk themselves through things are the ones that never quite make it.

STEVE YOUNG: I remember Bill saying to me, "The timing's got to be right. Steve, everything you're doing is too fast. You're running through your reads great, you're seeing it. But you're getting to the fourth guy and, all of a sudden, Tom Rathman's getting the ball every time when Jerry Rice is just about to come open. You've got to stay on time."

Because I was pretty fast, physically, I took it as a challenge. Can I drop back faster than Joe? Can I throw it harder than Joe? I eventually matured out of that, but early on, that's how I thought about it.

Bill said, "You don't understand. You're hurting yourself. You're competing in the wrong places."

I really appreciated seeing that the full measure of who I could be as a player needed to come out in a much less grip-it-and-rip-it way. This is a more subtle game than you realize, and I loved diving into those subtle pieces, the more esoteric part of football. That's where Joe lived. Why was he so great? Because he lived in that place where it was about sense of timing and trust and waiting for you to make a mistake or be out of position and take advantage of it because he was so alert for what the defense was doing.

I would always make my reads based on a safety. I was focused on the offense. I was focused on my receiver coming open and where the tight end was and protection, whereas the next level is to have it all in you as reflexive recall and now be able to literally focus on a safety and to stare them down.

My favorite thing whenever I played the Cowboys was that I just stared down Darren Woodson. I remember, after games, he would be like, "Why do you keep looking at me?"

I said, "Darren, because when you look back at me, I know you're not blitzing. But when you try to look away, and you try to not make eye contact with me, I know that you're going to blitz."

"You bastard! Blah-blah-blah."

No one had ever thought about those kinds of things before, but if you own all the data, and you have the reflexive ability to kind of keep people in motion and know protection and know where everybody is and have a sense of timing, you could now really settle in to what exactly is happening with those 11 guys on the other side of the line.

MIKE HOLMGREN: At first, the way Steve Young would go through his progression would be, "One, two, run," because he could run. I mean, he was really a good runner. Then, we would have these sit-downs, these come-to-Jesus meetings, which I had with both quarterbacks.

With Steve, I said, "You've got to work the whole thing." He fought me on it because he liked to run, and he was good at it.

STEVE YOUNG: Fundamentally, early on, I couldn't wait. First of all, I didn't have the expertise. Second, I didn't have the time to hope that it all worked out. I knew that I could go make it work out. So, if I got a shot to be on the field, we had to move down and at least kick a field goal. That was how I looked at it.

But Bill was the one who told me, over and over, "Steve, people don't know where you are when you're running around. People need to know where you're going to be. The worst thing that can happen in our offense is for you to end up with the ball."

"But I just ran for a first down… I just scored."

"Yeah, but you don't understand. In the big picture, Steve, if you end up with a ball, what happens, even if it's successful, everyone around you is thinking, 'Why isn't what we're doing collectively working?'"

MIKE HOLMGREN: Steve was a great player and I loved him; he babysat my kids. But I contend he did not become a Hall of Fame player until he acknowledged the fact that, "Okay, I don't have to run. I can just dump it right over there and that guy can get seven yards or break a tackle and get 12 yards."

When Steve figured that out, plus the wear and tear that running took on his body, the sky was the limit. After that, he became the quarterback he always should have been. I don't think the transition for him was particularly easy, but he eventually adapted and, of course, the rest is history.

STEVE YOUNG: By the time I started playing more regularly in '91, I had a sense of what that was supposed to look like and how to do it. It was super fun, because then, when I ran the ball, it was really backbreaking for defenses. They actually had defended the whole thing, which is hard to do. When you'd go in on Monday and go through the film, Mike Shanahan, the offensive coordinator then, would say, "You went through the whole thing, they covered it, but then you crushed it."

That was the best compliment I could get—that I had gone through the whole thing and would still have something left that I could still do to create havoc on defense. You see, to me, that was where the real power came for me. I felt incredible power in getting the full measure of this offense that was ahead of its time.

Yes, there were times when it could be stopped, but even then, I had another answer. That was a fun place to be in the mid-90s.

MIKE HOLMGREN: Before we signed Steve, Bill talked with me about him, because he knew I had coached him at BYU. The Tampa Bay Buccaneers made him available, so we traded for him.

STEVE YOUNG: My senior year at BYU, Ted Tollner was leaving and we had to get a new offensive coordinator. At that point, we were a pretty cool place to be for offensive coordinators. LaVell Edwards told me two or three times, "Look, I don't want to do this without you. I want you to kind of talk to these guys as well."

I thought that was a cool thing for him to do. I never thought that I'd be able to talk to a future coach and have a voice in the room. Which tells you [something] about LaVell, too. He saw this as a partnership. That says a lot about his success, because we weren't nearly as talented as UCLA and Texas A&M and a lot of people that we beat through the years. It was really built off of his underpinning of partnership.

One day LaVell said, "There's this young coach coming in. Vic Rowen [who coached football and basketball at San Francisco State and was LaVell's buddy] says this young coach, who had been his offensive coordinator at San Francisco State, is really one of the best he's ever seen. His name is Mike Holmgren. He's going to come in and I want you to talk to him."

It felt like Mike was only three or four years older than me, even though it was more. But he just talked to me in a way that I loved. I went back to LaVell and I said, "Oh, my gosh, I love this Mike Holmgren." He said, "I'm happy to hear that because I think I'm headed in that direction."

We ended up hiring Mike Holmgren, and we ended up hitting it off. Mike was somebody who appreciated the complexity of offense and what BYU was doing. And we were doing things that no one else in college was doing. Mike was somebody who, I think, appreciated details and he knew that I did, so we had a great friendship.

Our coach-player relationship was respectful, but we challenged each other. He challenged me in ways that I appreciated. He had a temper and he wanted to be in control. Everybody has control issues, right? But he had a lot of them. I kind of intuitively knew that and I remember times when we'd be on the field and he'd be pissed at me and he'd call a timeout and yell, "Get over here!" I wouldn't look at him, but I knew his veins would be coming out and his neck would grow and his head would get two sizes bigger. I'd say to my teammates, "Has his head exploded yet?" And they'd be like, "Almost, almost. Hold on."

That was the kind of relationship we had, and it was a good one.

MIKE HOLMGREN: Signing Steve was a great move by the 49ers, because we had these two thoroughbreds at quarterback.

Bill would want Steve to get in the game, so he'd substitute, something he hadn't done before when Joe was playing with a backup.

It created a little tension.

STEVE YOUNG: Bill had recruited me, essentially, from Tampa Bay, which was not a hard recruit. Tampa was a classic terrible organization. Hugh Culverhouse, the team owner, was a cattle man. People confused him. The human quotient confused him. It really led to a lot of craziness and so forth. I was thinking, "I'd rather go to law school than keep playing football in these conditions."

I told Bill, "Look, I really love the 49ers, but I know that I can't come and watch. If I'm just coming in to back up Joe Montana, I don't want to do that. As much as I would love to be a 49er, I don't want to do that."

Bill said, "Don't worry about it, Steve. Joe just had his second back surgery. That's why I'm calling you. Because I think that, despite the struggles you've had, I believe that you can do great things. And I'm looking for someone to come and take Joe's place. Now, is it today? I don't believe so. But after his second back surgery, I'm not asking you to be a long-term backup for Joe Montana."

"Okay, great, because that's a super great opportunity. I'm sorry to hear that about Joe, but I'm energized to kind of give it a shot."

I remember the first practice after the first meeting with Bill when he said all that cool stuff. I was trying to make sure I was the first one out there warming up. I had never met Joe Montana in my life. Obviously, at that point, he was a superstar. The king. When I saw him come out the door of our facility and jog onto the practice field, I thought to myself, "He doesn't look very hurt. He looks like things are going pretty well."

Then, I watched him throw. *Choo, choo, choo, choo, choo.* Perfect.

After practice, I went up to Coach Walsh and said, "Joe looks like everything's fine."

Bill just shrugged and the expression on his face said, "What can I tell you?"

By the end of the day, I'm flaming pissed. I'm like, *What have I gotten myself into?*

Over the next seven years, I would find out. It was the craziest ride that could ever be. And Bill, I think, liked it.

The first year, 1987, I played parts of nine games, including the playoffs. Out of that was a loss in the playoffs when Bill took Joe out. Bill was like, "Joe, you're out. Steve, you're in." Joe was looking at me like, "Who the hell's this guy? What are we doing?"

But I think Bill believed, intuitively, that, first of all, Joe and I were not toxic personalities. Joe and I never had a cross word. We never argued one time in the seven years.

Was it awkward? Terribly awkward. Always? Almost every day. But Bill said to me in 1996, "Steve, if you look back from 1987 to 1992, who benefitted from you and Joe being together?"

I said, grudgingly, "If I had to be honest, I did." I had to say it grudgingly because I remembered, in 1989, I couldn't handle it anymore. That was when I started going to law school. I graduated from law school because I got sick of standing there.

Bill said, "Yeah, that's part of it. Do you think Joe benefitted?"

"Well, he won two more Super Bowls, one more Super Bowl MVP, and two league MVPs. I'd say that he'd probably think it was a positive for him."

"What about the 49ers?"

"Well, now that you say that, I'd say they're probably the greatest beneficiaries."

"Now you get it."

I thought, *That dang Bill Walsh. He just pisses me off to the end.*

But I think he was probably right. Who pulls that off? Joe was always upset about it; I was always upset about it. I can't remember how many times before a game Bill would call Joe and me together and say, "Hey, Joe, Steve's going to take some plays today." Joe would say, "Fine," and leave.

I remember once, early on when we were playing the Saints in the Superdome, Joe was driving the team down and then Bill said, "Steve, go run the bootleg." I went jogging in; Joe jogged off. I didn't bring the motion across the formation on the bootleg and Rickey Jackson literally bent my facemask. I was jogging off, Joe said, "Nice. That was great."

But Bill never wavered. He kept doing that and it was against what anyone thought was conventional wisdom. But he had an ability to see further and bigger. He was right.

I quickly realized that if I was going to be successful in San Francisco, I had to be the best backup that ever lived. Bill didn't say that, but I understood that this was Joe Montana. This was not nobody.

I followed Jim McMahon in college with his 78 NCAA records, by the way, so it wasn't like I wasn't used to this dilemma.

MIKE HOLMGREN: I love them both, but it was the most challenging coaching situation that I had found myself in because you have two stallions, two thoroughbreds that can really play the position. I had coached Steve in college, but when he first came to the 49ers, he was getting a smaller share the reps in practice, which is the case with the second guy. He wasn't used to that. He didn't like it very much.

Both accused me of favoring the other guy in meetings. Joe would come into my office and say, "Mike, I know you coached Steve in college, but..."

I'd stop him and say, "Joe, this is your football team." Then he'd leave and Steve would come in a half-hour later and go, "You're not coaching me. Remember when you used to coach me? You're not coaching me."

STEVE YOUNG: Mike struggled to try to convince Joe that Mike was even-handed. Joe looked at Mike with one eye closed, like, "I'm not sure about you." Mike had to earn that trust.

I don't know that it helped or hurt, but it wasn't easy that we had been together before. Mike worked hard to make sure that Joe believed he wasn't playing favorites with me. I said to him many times, "I think you're working too hard to engender trust with Joe. You're overdoing it. Enough, already. This is ridiculous."

But I don't blame him; Joe's the greatest. And I told Mike that. I said, "I would do that, too, if it was me."

Of course, I'd say, "Mike, you've got to give me some practice time." I was always complaining and moaning about it.

We'd always go in on Wednesday morning and they'd give us the play-books and Bill would do the installation of the game plan. He would have all these questions. I remember, during one of the first weeks of my rookie year, Bill said, "Okay, what are going to do here?" Joe would answer it right away. We had the playbook for all of four minutes, I was trying to go through it as fast as I could, and I didn't know how he was doing this.

Everything was a competition and I was up for it. There was not a place that I didn't want to compete. But Joe kept coming up with the answers to all the questions before I even had a chance to study the playbook. Finally, I went to Holmgren and I said, "What is it about Joe? I just got this book and he already has all the answers."

Mike said, "Well, because he gets it faxed to him on Tuesday night."

"Well, fax it to me, too!"

One day, I heard Joe say he had the game plan memorized by Wednesday morning. That was when I realized that part of playing great football was owning the data.

I got big grease boards at home and I could write down every play, every formation, every blitz, everything. If I wrote it down with my hand, I could memorize it. I could recall it photographically. But if it was typed on a piece of paper, I couldn't do it. That was one of the benefits of going to law school. I'd be in a test and I could change the pages of my own writing in my head, but if it was in a textbook, it was a big gray area.

My attitude was, "I'm going to memorize it, but I'm going to memorize it beyond what Joe's memorizing so that I could be more ready. Because in case he goes down, I'm on it."

Every week, I would prepare to start, even though I knew I wasn't going to start. But I think I earned Joe's respect because of my work ethic and my ability to be ready to play and also help him on the sidelines. Every time he had a question about what just happened on the field or something, I was intent on having an answer.

So, I hated my job as a backup, but I always said, "If you want another job, be great at the job you have." That was how I thought about it.

MIKE HOLMGREN: In 1988, Bill was bouncing the guys back and forth, playing them both, and we really were struggling offensively. We weren't clicking like we should have been. We had lost to the Raiders 9–3 to go to 6–5. We were better than our record.

That led to what I call "The Last Supper."

It was a Monday night, when you're normally in your shorts, eating off paper plates, grabbing a pizza, whatever. All of a sudden, the entire coaching staff was having a dinner in team owner Eddie DeBartolo's office, which was beautiful. Crystal, tablecloths, candles, waiters.

We were saying, "What is going on?" We were all kinds of nervous. Finally, Bill came and said, "Listen, it's not working. I think we're a little jammed up here. I'm going to go around the room and I want to know what's going on. What do you think?"

Guys were going, "Well, the left guard didn't make his block on this play." Or, "The receiver dropped the ball here." I'm thinking to myself, *No, it's a quarterback thing that's goofing everybody up here.* Bill McPherson, who was my mentor and one of the great guys in this business, was sitting next to me. He knows I can't shut up, so he's hitting me under the table, whispering, "Don't... say... anything."

Of course, I said something.

"Coach, I think the problem is you," I said. You could have heard a pin drop.

I don't know why I said it. I had young kids and I needed the job, but that didn't stop me. I said to Bill, "They listen to me, but they hear you. The quarterbacks are off-balance and the offensive team's off-balance. Choose one. Pick one."

He slammed the table and stormed out. The other coaches started throwing rolls and saying, "You dumb so-and-so!" I said, "Hey, it's not a guard who isn't pulling. It's not a dropped pass. This is the problem. And he asked us. Didn't he ask us?" They said, "Yeah, but you're still a dumb..." They were so mad at me.

Now, we were all wondering what we were supposed to do next. We were sitting around the table in our shorts with the candles still lit. Finally, Bill's secretary came in and said to me, "Coach wants you to stay here. He'll be back in just a second."

Bill came back in and you could tell he was kind of upset. He sat down and he said, "Mike was right." At that point, I felt like throwing the rolls back at the other guys. I said, "Oh, phew."

Bill said, "I haven't done this correctly. We're going to go with Joe. And that's how we're going to do it with the rest of the year."

Then he added, "But, Mike, if it doesn't work, you know what happens to you."

We played in Washington on a Monday night that week. They were good. We beat them 37–21. Joe threw for 218 yards and two touchdowns. On Tuesday morning, Bill came into my office and shut the door. He gave me the game ball and said, "Thanks."

It was one of the greatest things I've ever gotten. I've still got it on the mantel at my cabin in California. It's the only football thing my wife, Kathy, let me keep in there. It says something about Bill, that he would trust me, a young guy.

It was hard, because you had two really good football players, but it had been Joe's team. It still was Joe's team. But here you had this other guy who was going to be a Hall of Fame player as well.

BRIAN BILLICK: Bill's practice structure was so detailed, and it was organic. Of course, I lived it with Denny Green for 10 years when Denny was head coach in Minnesota, and I was the offensive coordinator. It was the basis of what I did in Baltimore. It generally consisted of how many plays you carry in each category, how you practice them, and the variations.

It was very specific. In Minnesota, we added another element to it in terms of the computer, because Bill never really did that, and it mechanized it a little bit more. But I remember when I sat with Bill once and said, "Basically, in that system, you're going to get about 150 snaps during the week, about a two-to-one ratio, not counting walk-through." This was basic, real snaps. He said, "No. There's no way we only had 150 snaps during the course of a week."

"We did, Bill."

"No, you're wrong."

We had it on our computer, so I knew exactly what the numbers were. We'd meet in his office, up the road from Stanford. He had a little broom closet with just tons of material, which for me was like I was reading the Dead Sea Scrolls.

"Okay, let's pull out a week's practice plan," I said.

So, we went through the practices and the scripting a couple of times. Finally, he said, "Damn, you're right."

That tells me that he understood the teaching sequence, how much time you had, what you could actually get practiced. And he had that formulated, at least in his mind, without really knowing that, yeah, it's two-to-one. It's 150.

Bill knew that you were in one true third-and-1 in the open field once a game on average, so why would you carry nine plays into that box? You can't get it all practiced. He would say, "Well, we'll get the first-down run, we'll have a play-action off of it, and we'll have a vertical."

It made it great for the players because they knew what the game plan was. The coaches knew what was being called. And Bill was just so mechanized in the way practice integrated with the game plan and the way it laid out.

It all began with Paul Brown and the opening 15 plays. He told the story many times. He was sitting down for breakfast with Paul on Sunday morning before a game, and Paul would say, "Okay, what are your openers? What's your first down? Second down? Earned first down? Third-and-short? Third-and-long? Third-and-medium? First red zone?"

Bill knew to show up Sunday morning and say, "Okay, here's what the plan is." And it occurred to him, "Well, why don't I give this to the players Saturday night? Why not give them the blueprint?" And then it was, "Well, if I'm going to do that Saturday, why don't we have that run-through on our openers on our walk-through on Friday morning?"

So, Bill would work back from that. From the integration of plays, to practice structure, to the teaching curve, and what could get taught, to me, was pure genius. It's literally what everybody is doing now.

Bill's attention to detail and ability to communicate that with the coaches and the scouts was brilliant in the synergy he had throughout the entire organization. He was so specific as to the talents needed at each position. As I got into coaching, we would have every play for the entire training camp, and all the individual drills, scripted before we went on vacation. That was classic Bill Walsh.

Coaches who were new to the staff would ask me, "How the hell do I know what I need to be practicing in Week 2?" I'd say, "Well, how the hell do you not know? If you're a teacher and you tell your principal, 'I don't know what I'm going to teach in November,' you're fired. How can you not know?"

Bobb McKittrick was the one guy who could tell Bill he was full of shit. Everyone else was scared to death of Bill. But Bill pushed Bobb on personnel questions like, "What are the components that your offensive linemen need? What are the skills? What do they need to do?"

Bobb came up with 27 traits between the center, guard, and tackle of what they needed to do—the first step, the hand punch, the ability to scoop, whatever. Then Bill said, "Okay, show me the drills that develop each of these traits." Bobb would do that and then the other coaches had to follow in kind.

It proved very helpful because from a scouting standpoint, it was schooling the scouts on "I need this at the slot, this at the X, and this at the Z. I need this at the right guard compared to the left guard, the right tackle versus the left tackle." So, when the scouts are looking at somebody who maybe is not rated as highly as someone else at the position, they could determine, "You know what? This guy could be a steal for us. This guy's rated as a third-rounder, but he's got those individual traits that Coach McKittrick told me he wanted."

Bill was adamant about two-back formation. He was saying, "I'm not going to give you, the defensive coordinator, a hint as to what I'm doing because I'm changing personnel by down and distance." Hence, all the great fullbacks.

He would say, "You can try to figure out what I'm doing by field position, by down and distance, but I'll be damned if I'm going to tell you what I'm doing by personnel." Where now it's 12 personnel, it's 22, it's 21. You try to do it enough to keep the bluff, but you do create tendencies by personnel, by down and distance.

Bill would do a little 12 personnel. In nickel, he would maybe do a little three-wide, but, boy, he was going to stay in that base personnel because he was looking for specific traits at the fullback—a guy who could block and catch in the flat, and a running back who obviously had to be able to catch the ball out of the backfield.

He was very much a mentor. As you can imagine, after a while, you could see where that would strain the relationship, because Bill was going to coach and teach Joe in Year Nine the same way he did it in Year One, that attention to detail. "Let me tell you about 22 Z In." And I could just imagine Joe, by Year Eight, is going, "Alright, Bill, I know where the hell to go on 22 Z In. Why am I sitting here taking notes and listening to this?"

That was probably part and parcel with Bill kind of going, "That's why there's a shelf life here because at some point, I'm going to wear him out."

The first time I really saw that specific attention to detail was on a little flare route. Joe made the read and hit the receiver right in the chest. We were all thinking, *Hey, this is great. That's a good throw.*

Bill goes off. "Joe! I want the ball thrown in his lead glove," he said. "I want it a foot and a half in front of his shoulder pads. If we're going to get the six yards we need on a flare, the ball needs to be here."

But it was that kind of manic attention to detail in terms of the nickel and dime offense that we had that was the key to that being a six-yard gain, not a three-yard gain, and where you hit the player with a very catchable ball, allowing him to go on the run.

Phil Simms told a story of when Bill went to work him out at Morehead State. The whole time, Bill kept going, "Throw it softer, throw it softer." Phil finally said, "Coach, I can throw it underhand if you want. I mean, what do you want?"

But it was the whole idea of, "I want that placement, I want a catchable ball. You don't have to overpower to where it knocks the receiver off-balance or he can't run with it." Joe was the perfect guy for that, and he had the perfect demeanor for Bill. He'd just say, "Yeah, that's cool. You got it, Coach."

For someone who was so mechanical in terms of putting the game plan together, though, Bill would always change shit up at the end of the week. On Saturday morning, which should be a time when you do your ultimate cap-it-off and reiterating of what you have planned for Sunday's game, Bill would say, "Alright, we're going to put in three new routes."

Compared to a Joe Gibbs, whose approach was what you put in Wednesday—base, nickel, red zone— was it and then you fine-tuned it, Bill was much more mercurial. He was going to tweak because he'd see something Friday night on film and say, "Oh, God, if we run that come-back on them and we add this, that will take advantage of that."

The players would joke about it, but they were used to it and were cool with it.

MIKE HOLMGREN: Bill was kind to me, but he yelled at me a lot. That was how he did it. He would yell at the coaches, but he was really directing that at the players so they would go, "Oh, I did something that got my position coach in trouble."

I remember coming home and venting to Kathy, telling her, "I am not going to do it that way." You know what happened? I wound up doing exactly the same stuff later on when I became a little wiser.

What I learned was, when you coach a group of players, those relationships are really close. As an example, Joe and I used to have a bet on the Notre Dame-USC game. Whoever lost had to take the other couple out to dinner. It was right at the time when USC was getting beat, so I had to pay up.

I mentioned in a meeting I had lost the bet. Bill called me in later and said, "You're his coach, and maybe at some point you're going to have to recommend to me that we cut him or he's getting too old or something. So you have to be careful that you're not developing a personal relationship where you can't make a decent decision."

He knew, though, that you develop a relationship with the players that you coach. You can't help it, because you're with them all the time. If I yelled at Steve Mariucci about Brett Favre, Brett didn't like that. He didn't like Steve taking that hit. So, he'd change his behavior and do it right. Players responded to that.

BRIAN BILLICK: Bill was so demanding and so detailed, but he never wanted to criticize a player. So, if the running back wasn't pass-protecting right, he'd walk over to the running back drill and go up to Billy Matthews, who was our running backs coach, and say, "Billy, can you help these players? I mean, they're not punching with the right hand. Do you have a drill for that? These players want to be good, Billy. Is there some way you can help them, Billy, to be better? Because we desperately need them to be able, in pass pro, to set with that outside hand."

The coaches knew what he was doing. That doesn't mean they liked it or wouldn't say to themselves, "Goddammit! If he comes over and embarrasses me in front of the players one more time..."

Bill did the same thing with me, and I was just a young slappy. He'd ream my ass, either because I needed it or he wanted to make an example to somebody else. During the draft, my job was to make sure we had coffee and doughnuts. And I failed miserably. This was back when the draft started at 9:00 AM in the east. We were at our facility at 4:00 AM, and coming from BYU, it never occurred to me that anybody wanted coffee at 4:00 AM.

Of course, Bill, sarcastically, would say, "Oh, don't worry about it, Brian. I'll go find us some coffee. Don't worry about it. You've got other things to do here."

Two days later or a day later, he'd show up in my office and say, "Oh, I've got these certificates for dinner over at Raphael's. Why don't you and your wife, Kim, go?" He could be charming and disarming, but he could be brutally direct and typically would do it in a way that got the message to others as well.

Bill always used to say to everybody in the organization, "Whatever task I give you, take to its logical conclusion." And if that logical conclusion is to say, "Coach, honestly, I don't think that's a good idea; I think we need to do it this way," he'd say, "Okay, great. Do it."

But if not, you'd better follow up. You'd better cross the t's and dot the i's and you'd better make sure you have all the answers and anticipate whatever questions he might have about whatever issue on which he was going to task you. He, of course, was huge on tapping into whatever resource you needed.

He would task people together, as a check and balance as much as anything else. Back in the day, NFL teams would send a PR person to the city of the opposing team to advance road games. They would be armed with sets of newspaper and video clips to hand out to the media, they'd do radio shows all week, whatever. I used to do all the advances. Bill also would tell me to make sure I communicated with our travel guy, Keith Simon, who would be working remotely from San Francisco. He'd say, "I'm going to hold you responsible for these things in terms of travel when we get there."

Clearly, having been around Paul Brown and with their relationship being strained at the end because Bill didn't feel Paul had given him much help in becoming a head coach, Bill was tireless in trying to help other coaches land those jobs. I can't tell you how many times he came down to my office and said, "So-and-so's trying to get a head-coaching job at such-and-such college. Get me all the information you can on the president and the athletic director." He was going to do his homework and make the connection to help whoever he could, based on the fact he didn't feel like Paul had supported him that way.

Bill was a Renaissance man. He very much thought of himself as someone who enjoyed wine, who enjoyed talking military history with you as much as he would football. He had that cerebral, Stanford aura, even though he went to San Jose State. But he loved that persona, which emanated from being at Stanford as a coach and being thought of on that level.

MIKE HOLMGREN: Bill was a gifted speaker. His Saturday night team meetings and his talks before the game at the stadium were inspiring. It's hard to hold the players' attention, yet they listened to him, even the guys who had been there a long time.

Even if Bill was talking about "22 Z In," which had been a staple for the 49ers forever and ever and ever, and we were in camp or in the installation in Week 14, he presented it in such a way that guys still listened. They still took notes. They still thought it was important.

What I learned from Bill was that you have to make it a little bit personal. I started doing that. For instance, when going over what we were going to do in the red zone, I'd say, "On this play, Jerry Rice, you're going to score a touchdown. And it's going to happen because you're going to do this, this, and this." Then I'd tell the other guys, "Here's how you're going to help him score."

Bill would walk around during practice, but he'd stay mainly with the offensive guys.

STEVE YOUNG: I remember Bill telling Ronnie Lott, "I know everyone's talking about this West Coast offense and all this stuff. But Ronnie, you'd better put this defense in a situation to be the best in the league." He held Ronnie accountable and Ronnie, in turn, held everyone else on defense accountable. Ronnie would say, "We're going to lead the league in defense and we're not going to get the credit. But we don't care." It became a mantra; it became a rallying cry.

When we beat Denver in the Super Bowl 55–10, the headline was not about the defense holding John Elway to 10 points. I can promise you that. But Ronnie would pound that the next year, telling the rest of the defense, "We held John Elway to 10 points! And you know we're not going to get the credit for that." But Ronnie embraced it because Bill embraced it.

Bill understood that the offense would get the credit and Bill would get the credit, but he made a space for those that weren't going to get the credit by letting them know, "I get it. I'm still with you. Trust me on this." Ronnie loved that underdog thing and the defense thrived that way. And we had the No. 1 defense for a number of years. Ironically, we also had the No. 1 rushing game for a number of years. That's because it all kind of flowed out of the way Bill thought about empowering everybody.

CHARLES HALEY: George Seifert, when he was my defensive coordinator, my God. After every game, we went in and he sat down and went over everybody's position on every play. Every play.

But first, it took him five minutes to sit there and clean his glasses. He'd be looking up and down at his glasses for five minutes. After that, he'd start going over everybody's job description.

At first, I used to get annoyed with it. Then, I said, "Man, you know what? I might as well learn something because the more you know, the more you could take advantage of."

From the first day he did that, I tried to understand and know everybody's position so that when people got out there and they got nervous, I was able to help them with their job, what they were supposed to do out there.

We weren't a physical team, not on offense nor on defense. Especially not on defense. We had like 20 base defenses, 20 red zone, 10 goal line, 15 blitzes.

We didn't just line up and hit you in the mouth.

STEVE YOUNG: Most head coaches are either offensive-minded or defensive-minded because that's their history; it's the way they think of the world. I really find most coaches don't do a good job of seeing over the fence to the other side. I feel very strongly about that because that's what my experience has been through the years, even today, watching coaches—especially defensive coaches—struggling to understand the other side of the fence.

But Bill, in my mind, was really holistic about it.

He encouraged the defense. When we'd go one-on-ones in training camp, and the defense would get the best, Bill would yell, "That's what I'm talking about! This is the best offense in the league. If you guys can beat us, you can beat anybody."

CHARLES HALEY: Bill McPherson, our defensive line coach, was a different type of guy. He would always tell us, "This is how things work: you've got God, you've got my family, the 49ers. And then the rest of you are way down here, waaaay down here."

I'm going like, "Damn! Hey, he's letting us know that if you don't do your job, you're going to be on the bus." He told me about that a few times, but I loved him because I like people being real.

He would get on my ass. He always asked me for a little bit more and I'd get mad about that. But at the end of the day, that's what brings out the best in you.

I tell my kids, when they played, and I tell players, "Real men ask their position coach, 'What do I need to do better?' Cowards are afraid to do that because they don't want to hear the truth. Most of them are afraid of the answer."

I live by that.

BRIAN BILLICK: I've said this many times: coaching is teaching, it's leading. It's all interchangeable. You could take whatever leadership book, whatever teaching book, and juxtapose the word "coach" into wherever in that text it says "leader" or "teacher," and it would make complete sense.

Bill is the best teacher I've ever seen. I remember, in another Wooden-esque moment, he would start every training camp with the coaches—and Denny was the same way—by saying, "Your No. 1 job is to get our players to the opener healthy and fresh. Now, we've got a lot of other things to do and you're going to be helped, but we need to have them there."

That came from a Cal physiologist that Bill brought in to track the players through training camp and in the season. He wanted to know at what points during the season his players were the most fatigued. And the guy came back and said, "It's easy. It's before the opening game, because you're kicking the shit out of them in training camp. That is when they're physically the most vulnerable."

Bill found the solution in the way we all now practice, where there are no padded practices back-to-back, only three practices and a special-teams walk-through. The way that the collective bargaining agreement is now, with limits on off-season practices and contact during training camp and the regular season, you go back and look at the way Bill was practicing in the late '70s, early '80s, that was exactly it. It was all about keeping the players healthy and fresh, teaching them in a way that keeps them fresh.

At a time when Joe Gibbs and Dick Vermeil were sleeping in their offices, Bill was always telling his coaches, "I want you out of here at night." He was adamant. He would tell them, "I want you as animated and energetic and at your best when you're with the players. You can't stay up all night thinking you're outworking people, which no one ever really does because everybody works hard, and then sleep your way or drool your way through presentations or coaching with the players."

It was all about what makes the player better, whether it's the teaching sequence for him to process or what we're asking him to do physically. Now, we have heart monitors on them, we've got Next Gen Stats, and so we're looking at all this data to find out when they're most vulnerable.

But Bill was very intuitive about it and Denny was that way, and I took that into Baltimore. The players respond to it, but this was the trade-off that Bill made sure they understood.

"If I'm going to take care of you, a walk-through is a practice," he said. "If you think a walk-through is that we're taking that session off, this isn't going work. If I'm going to keep you fresh and not overwork you, then you've got to give me every single minute in walk-throughs, in meetings. That way, I'll get you out of practice quicker, I'll get you out of the meeting quicker, I'll get you off your feet quicker. But you got to give me that time."

It was all about what the players could process and do to function at their best.

MIKE HOLMGREN: Dick Vermeil used to talk into a little tape recorder during practice and then listen to what he said afterwards. Bill didn't do that. When Bill saw something, he might not correct it on the spot but instead he'd write it down on one of the three-by-five cards he carried with him.

At night, Bill would walk into our meeting in training camp, pull these cards out, call the name of one of the coaches, and hand him a card with the correction he wanted. He'd go around to each position, handing out the cards, and leave. After that, we'd prepare the next day's practice plan.

It turned out that Fred von Appen, our special teams coach, was keeping track of every card to see which coach got corrected the most in training camp. He'd say, "This is not good. Holmgren, you have 27 cards."

When the offense was going in practice, Bill was talking. He was very animated, very involved in what the offense was doing. He'd get mad because he'd want it done right.

He talked about the importance of striving for perfection, but it was very much what he believed.

STEVE YOUNG: I, to this day, refer to experiences and lessons from Bill in my marriage, in my business relationships—how he looked at the world, how he thought about other humans. They do transcend.

The way to really lead today is by creating empathy for another and actually seeing them, literally walking in their shoes, and Bill was great at that. We're talking about this as a society in 2021. *This is what we need to do. Corporate America is taking this in.* Bill was doing it before everybody. And it was in football. When I tell the stories about him, people say, "Oh, is that a business leader you're talking about?" Or, "That must be a self-help guru that you're talking about."

I say, "No, he was my coach."

"He was your football coach? That's impossible."

We'd go to Washington to play the Redskins and the night before the game, one of the Joint Chiefs of Staff would come to the hotel to speak to the team. Bill would always have a suit on, which wasn't him. But you could see that he enjoyed engaging all over the place. He was not myopically focused on football. He really did enjoy conversations around politics and the military.

Bill loved boxing. He used boxing metaphors daily, talking about Muhammad Ali and Joe Frazier. He would say, "You guys are fools if you think that anyone can beat Muhammad Ali, because in the end, speed and flexibility and timing never get beat." He'd say, "Look at his body. He couldn't bench press 250. How was he the greatest of all time? Ken Norton could bench press 400, but he lost two out of three to Ali." He used those examples for why you need speed and timing.

It was bigger than football. Everything he said had an impact more than sitting there on the field.

CHARLES HALEY: Bill would bring in boxers, different Olympic athletes who won the gold medal or silver, and veteran guys would ask them questions. You got to dig into the meat and potatoes of what it takes to be successful. I was mesmerized.

The thing that I really loved was, the night before a game, Bill would get up for his speech and be like a boxer. He'd be boxing and say, "Guys going against Muhammad Ali. First round, they'd win the round. Second round, they'd win the round. Third round, Muhammad Ali would win the round. Fourth round, he knocked them out. The moral of the story is that we may not win the first quarter or the second quarter, but we're going to knock them out in the fourth quarter and we're going to win."

That was a lot for me to digest, but in my heart, I always felt like at the end that we had a chance to win because of that.

BILL WALSH (from an interview with Ron Barr on *Sports Byline USA*): It's really the job of the coach, I guess you'd say, to establish an atmosphere in which leadership can really thrive and where people begin to depend heavily on each other and demand of each other and that your teachings, in a sense, are being taught by your players and your coaches. You're not like a shepherd gathering the sheep around him, and then giving them orders, they run off and do them and then come back for more orders. They begin to learn to thrive and operate almost independently, through the teachings that you've brought to them over a period of time.

We tried to make total use of their personal, individual athletic abilities. We didn't take a man into areas where he really couldn't function well. In Joe Montana's case, we took full advantage of his mobility and the same with Steve Young.

When I worked with Dan Fouts, it was more Dan staying in the pocket. With Kenny Anderson, it was more like Joe because he could run. So, each athlete has their own unique qualities and qualifications and abilities, and you try to build on those.

Unless it's all been done on the practice field, don't expect to be able to do it spontaneously or to outthink yourself during a game. It always has to be developed on the practice field.

A good example would be Joe Montana spending hours with me on the practice field in the last year or two of his career, working on retaining and maintaining his skills. So even a guy in his mid- and late-thirties should be looking to improve his game.

STEVE YOUNG: My first son was born in 2000, so I had just retired. Eight or nine years later, my kids kept coming home from elementary school, saying, "I heard that you and Joe Montana punched each other in the face, and you bloodied his nose." The stories were just outlandish.

It hit me that I'd better tell the story, at least my story, to my own kids or else they were going to hear it from other people. And it wasn't going to be right. That started me on a five-year odyssey to write a book that I didn't intend for mass distribution. I intended to hand it to my kids, a written history of my life, but it ended up being published in 2017. It was called *QB: My Life Behind the Spiral.*

In October of '91, when I was trying to take over, trying to do what I told them I couldn't wait to do in '87 and trying to make up for lost time, I had dug myself a really deep hole. We had just lost to the Raiders 12–6. We never got beat by a stupid score like that. Afterward, Charles Haley was so upset, he had what he would later describe as a "mental breakdown," trying to fight teammates and putting his hand through a glass window and cutting up his hand and his arm. Ronnie Lott, who was with the Raiders after having been with us, had to come into our locker room to calm Charles down because "Steve Young can't be Joe!"

We had a bye and I decided to get on a plane and go back to Salt Lake City to see my brother and just get a day away. I was in the depths of hell. What got me out of it was an experience with Steve Covey, a well-known authority on leadership, and the author of a famous book, *The 7 Habits of Highly Effective People.* We met through a happenstance, on the way back from Salt Lake, where Steve lived. I ended up sitting down next to him on the plane and we talked the whole trip.

Our conversation changed my life in a way that left me with a clear focus on what I wanted to accomplish through the rest of my career and life. It empowered me to see my relationship with Joe in a completely different light. Before then, I was constantly in comparison with him. How did he throw it and how did I throw it?

But that experience with Steve Covey ended it. I always regret that "take the monkey off my back" thing I did in the locker room after winning my first Super Bowl after the '94 season, when we beat San Diego, because I took the monkey off my back in '91. By being empowered to think about that relationship in a different way that didn't have a burden, the burden left me. I left behind a bunch of crap that I had been carrying around.

I went on to become league MVP in '92 and '94, and was second to Emmitt Smith in '93, and in a lot of ways that was because I came to understand how to leave behind this burden that wasn't a burden. I'll always be grateful to Steve Covey, who passed away in 2012. How he saw the world just allowed my brain to change. I smile every time I think about it because if I would have continued down the path I was on, I don't know how that would have gone. That would have been a rough road.

It also was about developing a sense of trust with my teammates. I remember having open conversations with them, saying, "Look, I'm not Joe. You don't have to whisper. If I suck, you can say it. It's okay. But equally, if I'm doing well, let's not belabor it." Jerry Rice had the biggest struggle because he was always asked about comparisons between Joe and me. *Well, do I say something nice about Joe? If I do, I have to say something nice about Steve.* It was always a conflict.

After about three years of that with Jerry, I said, "Okay, I've had it." I did a little research and put together the number of throws I made to Jerry and the number of touchdowns, and the number of throws Joe made to Jerry and the number of touchdowns. I said, "Jerry, I'm not asking you to like me more, but if you look at touchdowns and receptions, you're doing good." He said, "Oh, you're right. I am doing good."

Sometimes it's just a matter of giving people the data.

BILL WALSH (from an interview with Ron Barr on *Sports Byline USA*): No. 1, I think players do have to feel you care and you are concerned about them, that they're not dehumanized and they're not objects. They're human beings. I think if they have that feeling, then they can absorb some of the tough decisions you have to make and that might impact them also. They know that you do, honestly, have a sensitivity and respond to them.

In the meantime, you have a job to do, they have a job to do. I've always taken the position that it's too simplistic to say sports is a business. Athletics are athletics, whether they're Little League or the highest level of professional sports. You thrive on playing them and you depend heavily on your teammates. They expect a lot of you.

You learn to communicate well and live with the stress of it, and you thrive on it and enjoy it. So, consequently, I think when our players had that kind of feeling about the atmosphere, it was easier to make our tough decisions.

Often, the player really is the last one to understand that maybe it's time to step away, because you look the same. In fact, you can look better. You certainly know more. You have much more experience and know-how, and you have a better feel for the game.

The problem with a player in the later stages of his career is that he cannot practice as often because of minor injuries that begin to continually crop up. And then he begins to miss playing time. So, it's quite possible a man, or a woman, can play well for a given game. But over a 16-game span, they're unable to really stay with it because of the minor injuries that begin to develop. They don't sometimes understand that because they can recall the great game they played. But I have to remind them, "But you missed the next two games."

It's appreciating the fact that you need the recycling or the turnover of athletes or coaches or whatever, just to keep everything in motion. There is a period of time when the player is past his or her peak, in which they may be able to play elsewhere, but you feel that you can adequately replace them, that you go ahead and do that and have the confidence that the replacement will, at the start, play about as well as the veteran. But soon thereafter, he will be performing better. And that's a tough one.

It's very personal and yet it's impersonal because the personal part is you grow to love and care and have a great relationship with the athletes, but it's impersonal from the standpoint of doing the business. And to continue to thrive and succeed, you have to make these changes.

I think it's better to be a little premature about working with a man toward stepping away from the game than waiting too long, because that's when the serious injuries can occur.

BRIAN BILLICK: Bill was very emotional, as a lot of great minds are. He had a lot of ups and downs. Those first two years, when we weren't very good, took a toll on Bill.

Back when the NFC West had Atlanta and New Orleans, we were making at least those two long trips each season. One year, we had Miami and both New Yorks, so we were going cross-country back and forth a ton.

And we'd go out and get our ass kicked.

After those games, I remember vividly Bill sitting there in the front of the plane. He would have a wine or two and literally just stare out the window for five or six hours. You could tell it was, "What am I doing wrong? What can I do to change it?"

He was always adamant that 10 years was the most you could do at one place. He would regret that in hindsight, but he stayed true to that.

There were a couple of times he thought about quitting sooner, which was an emotional response. He was so emotionally depleted at the end of the season. Part of Bill, who is a deep thinker, was thinking, "I can't do this anymore. I'm killing myself."

And then he would kind of come out of it.

BILL POLIAN: Al Davis had told Bill Walsh and others that 10 years in one place is enough. Bill had been with the Niners since 1979. Prior to Super Bowl XXIII, in 1989, speculation in the media was rampant that Bill would retire following that game.

I can say, from firsthand knowledge, that the workload on participants in Super Bowls is immense. When that is coupled with the knowledge that the upcoming game is your last, it is little wonder that Bill Walsh had a very difficult time controlling his emotions in post–Super Bowl interviews.

Mike Holmgren takes you inside the 49ers' preparation in that final season and Super Bowl, which was, in the height of irony, against the Cincinnati Bengals, where the West Coast offense was born.

MIKE HOLMGREN: I don't know when Bill made the decision that it was going to be his last season but we, as a staff, didn't know. What I did know was that the program changed just a little bit. Normally, we'd go in there and have the late meetings on Monday and Tuesday night to put the game plan together and then present it to Bill on Wednesday. I'd take it into his office and he'd scratch things off, add plays, do all sorts of stuff.

After Denny Green left to become head coach at Stanford and Bill had me coach the tight ends and receivers as well as the quarterbacks, I'd go in Bill's office with the game plan. He'd just look at it and go, "That's good." And I thought to myself, *Well, that's different.* That wasn't how it usually worked.

The second thing was he would always do the script for the first 15 plays of the game, as I did forever and ever. Then one day he came in and said, "Mike, why don't you put together the first 15?"

I said, "Okay." But I was thinking, *Boy, this is really freaking me out a little bit.*

We were getting ready for our playoff game against Minnesota at Candlestick Park. Bill called me in for a meeting at the stadium. I've got a picture of us on folding chairs and I'm just staring at him as he's talking to me. He was telling me, "Okay, why don't you call the game from upstairs? And if I don't like the play, I'll change it."

So, I swallowed hard and said, "Okay." That was not how things had been done, but I did it and got us through both of our playoff games, a 34–9 victory against the Vikings and a 28–3 win at Chicago for the NFC championship.

As we were getting ready to face Cincinnati in the Super Bowl, Bill's schedule was different, too. He had a lot of his friends there, including some guys with whom he had coached through the years. They'd go out for dinner at night and he had never done that. So, we were left to put the game plan together and Bill would just go, "Sounds good." That was how we prepared for the Super Bowl.

I called a couple plays in the beginning, then Bill kind of called some. After the game, he announced he was retiring during an interview with Brent Musburger. That was it. We didn't know. In a book Bill later wrote, he said that he realized then that I could do those things.

STEVE YOUNG: I think Bill regretted his decision to retire immediately. Eddie DeBartolo and Bill had an emotional relationship, and it was taxing. But we all do things in the moment that we think are the right thing to do. Bill told me, "I wish that I had not retired. I should have just taken some time, taken a sabbatical. Do something no one else has ever done before: take a year off."

Classic Bill, he could have pulled it off.

That has nothing to do with George or anything else. It was just the way Bill responded at the time, and I saw every bit of it. It was surprising, and I think it was too bad he didn't get back in as a coach. He was kind of sitting around the facility and advising for another five, six, seven years. His hands were in it still, but he wasn't the coach. Certainly, it changed when he retired in '88.

But the things he put in place were so entrenched. He had already given out the "tool kit" to all the players, the assistant coaches. I don't think he had planned it that way, but he had already given out all the secrets and people could go take it forward as best they could.

We all did.

BILL POLIAN: In 1991, the legendary Green Bay Packers had bottomed out. Their record in the previous five seasons was 29–49 and they had registered only two winning seasons in the previous 19. The greatness of the Vince Lombardi Packers was a distant memory. "Titletown" had become the home of also-rans, not champions.

The Packers' board of directors hired Ron Wolf as general manager with full control of football operations. Wolf had been Al Davis' top personnel man, helping to build the championship Raiders. He took over the expansion Tampa Bay Buccaneers and laid the foundation for a contender. After two years with the New York Jets, Green Bay called upon Wolf to restore the Packers greatness.

Wolf's first move was to hire Mike Holmgren, offensive coordinator of the Bill Walsh–led 49ers, as head coach. The West Coast offense was headed to the "Frozen Tundra" of Green Bay.

Wolf made two very daring moves at the outset. He traded for Brett Favre and signed Reggie White after a free-agent bidding war with Cleveland. Both men became Hall of Famers. Favre, under Holmgren's tutelage, was NFL MVP for three consecutive seasons ('95, '96, '97) and White became an All-Pro and was NFL Defensive Player of the Year in '98. In addition, wide receiver Sterling Sharpe led the league in receiving in '92, running back Dorsey Levens had a 1,400-yard rushing season in '97, and Desmond Howard led the NFL in punt-return yardage in '96. Ron Wolf's astute personnel moves made the Pack contenders in short order.

Holmgren's career in Green Bay was spectacular. From '92 through '98, Holmgren's Packers posted an 84–42 won-loss record, a win percentage of 66. They set a franchise record by reaching the playoffs six consecutive times. The Pack became Super Bowl champions in '96, beating Bill Parcells' New England Patriots, and reached the ultimate game again in '97, losing to John Elway's Denver Broncos.

Holmgren "coached what he knew"—Bill Walsh's West Coast offense. However, his quarterback, Brett Favre, was as far in style from the precise Joe Montana as he could possibly be. With a lot of gnashing of teeth and creative work, Holmgren adjusted the offense to Favre's improvisational bent and succeeded spectacularly.

Andy Reid, Holmgren's assistant in Green Bay, learned that lesson well. He is applying it today with the incredibly talented Patrick Mahomes in Kansas City.

Holmgren assembled a marvelous coaching staff in Green Bay. Reid, Steve Mariucci, Jon Gruden, Dick Jauron, Ray Rhodes, and Marty Mornhinweg, along with backup quarterback Doug Pederson, went on to become head coaches. Reid, Gruden, and Pederson won Super Bowls.

After the '98 season, Holmgren left the Packers to become president and head coach of the Seattle Seahawks, whom he led to the Super Bowl. He will likely join his partner, Ron Wolf, in the Pro Football Hall of Fame soon.

The rebirth of the Packers under Wolf and Holmgren is the epitome of the blueprint of success in the NFL. Holmgren is a rare head coach with organizational and communication skills, knowledge of a system of football that can win, and the charisma to connect with and make the players "believers." Wolf was the consummate "football man" as GM. He put a system of player selection in place and made choices that fit the coach's system. He also found a way, by varied means, to add difference-makers, particularly at quarterback and on defense.

As my mentor, Coach Marv Levy, said, "What it takes to win is simple, but it isn't easy." Ron Wolf, Mike Holmgren, and their Packers are living proof of that.

MIKE HOLMGREN: In 1992, I had the privilege of interviewing with five teams. I talked to Green Bay first, with Ron Wolf, and we hit it off right away. I just thought, *I'm gonna get my shot here.*

The Packers had gone 4–12 the year before, but I didn't think about how bad Green Bay or any of the other teams were. I just was tickled pink to get the interviews.

Ron told me he talked to Bill Parcells, who was his friend, about the job. But he said, in reference to my becoming the Packers' coach, "This could work." I left Green Bay feeling like he would offer me the job, but I told Ron that I committed to the interviews with the other teams and would go through with them. Bless his heart, he said, "I'll wait."

I went through the interview process with Pittsburgh, Indianapolis, Minnesota, and the Rams. I took the job in Green Bay and I said, "Okay, this gives me a chance to do something that was kind of in my DNA, to repair something, to have the challenge of rebuilding something."

Two years earlier, I had interviewed with the Jets and the Cardinals, and even though I wound up staying in San Francisco, I started putting together a list of who I would want on a coaching staff. I wanted a balance of veteran experience and young guys. After I was hired in Green Bay, the first of the young guys I called was Andy Reid. He had been a graduate assistant for me at BYU, and he accepted my offer to be the assistant offensive line and tight ends coach.

Two other young coaches I hired were Jon Gruden to be an offensive assistant and quality control coach and Steve Mariucci to coach the quarterbacks. Sherm Lewis and Ray Rhodes, who were my colleagues in San Francisco, came in as my offensive and defensive coordinators.

I was fortunate enough to be with Ron Wolf. He was my boss, he got final say on the roster, and I was happy with that. But he let me coach and he would always talk to me about moves. He listened to what I had to say.

I hadn't been there very long when Ron asked me to go with him to our draft room. He said, "Let's look at this quarterback thing here." There were four names on our depth chart. I was familiar with the starter, Don Majkowski, but not too familiar with the other guys. Ron said, "Look where they were drafted." We had Don Majkowski, a 10th-round pick in '87; Mike Tomczak, an undrafted free agent in 1985, and Blair Kiel, an 11th-round choice in 1984.

He said, "That doesn't work."

RON WOLF: When I was personnel director with the Jets, we thought we were going to be able to draft Brett Favre. Dick Steinberg, who was our general manager, had worked out the terms of a deal with the Cardinals that would have moved us from the 34th overall pick in the second round to 32nd, one spot in front of the Falcons. We were sitting there, and we were happier than a pig in slop.

Then, George Boone, the Cardinals' director of player personnel, called and said he wasn't going to make the deal with us anymore because the player he wanted, defensive end Mike Jones, was there. The Falcons took Brett and we took a quarterback named Browning Nagle with the next pick.

The first game I went to as executive vice president and general manager of the Green Bay Packers was against the Atlanta Falcons in Fulton County Stadium. It just so happened that Ken Herock, who had been our personnel director in Oakland, was more or less the general manager of the Falcons, although he didn't have the title.

I was sitting up in the press box, getting ready to down a hot dog, and he said to me, "If you want to see Brett Favre throw, you've got to go down to the field now because once the team comes out, they won't let him participate."

I knew right away that I had the chance to get the player who I thought in 1991 was the best player in the draft. The Falcons had made him a second-round pick and now he was a backup they were looking to trade. I tried to get down to the field, but I never got down there.

But I knew I'd have an opportunity to get this guy.

MIKE HOLMGREN: We had two first-round draft picks: No. 5 and No. 17. I thought, *This is good. We can get a couple of really good players for the future.*

One day, Ron asked me to come into his office. He said, "I'm thinking about making a trade for Brett Favre with one of our No. 1s."

Right away, I went, "Ooh, boy!"

During my last year with the 49ers, I had conducted Brett's pre-draft workout at Southern Miss, and I was trying to think about how Brett would fit into the system I wanted to run, which involved very precise passing. I just kept going back to when I ran Brett through his paces in Hattiesburg. He'd throw a swing pass. *Wham!* He'd throw a curl. *Wham!* Every ball was a rocket.

I got a chance to talk with him afterward and asked, "What do you got going the rest of the day?"

"Ah, I'm going to go drink some beer. Catch some catfish."

That was Brett.

RON WOLF: I happened to be at Brett's pro day at Hattiesburg. You could see all the stuff he had. He had an arm, he had an amazing ability to step around the rush. He also had an amazing ability to win games, which is, to me, the key at that position.

Dick Steinberg had a book about what to look for in quarterbacks, and Brett checked every box. But the No. 1 statistic, the only statistic that matters, is wins and losses. That's why they keep score.

MIKE HOLMGREN: After Ron and I spoke about trading for Brett, Ron said, "Well, think about it." Now, he had already made up his mind that we were going to make the trade, but he was kind enough to let me be a part of it.

I got out my old scouting reports on Brett from when I was in San Francisco. Under positives, I wrote that he had "excellent physical skills."

Under negatives, I said, "Not sure he can discipline himself to do the stuff we do. But really good athlete."

We made the trade and that summer, something happened in a bar and he got in trouble. We hadn't even had one play, but he had done something down in Mississippi. I remember phoning him from my cabin in Santa Cruz, California, saying, "Hey, you can't…"

"Okay, fine."

RON WOLF: Of course, we were blistered in the Wisconsin media because they had never forgotten about the John Hadl deal in 1974. That was when the Packers gave up five picks, including first- and second-rounders in 1975 and 1976 to get Hadl, who was the quarterback for the Rams, and it ended up being a disaster. You should have seen some of the letters I got.

But you get a player like Brett Favre once in a lifetime. In 38 years, this was the best player I ever got. That changed the franchise.

BILL POLIAN: When I was general manager of the Bills, I went to see Brett play at Georgia. It was early in the season and hot as hell. He'd had the car accident the previous summer, so he weighed maybe 175–180 pounds. Southern Miss was down, I think, by 17 going into the fourth quarter. And he just went *boom, boom, boom, boom, boom* down the field running, throwing.

Finally, Southern Miss was going for a two-point conversion to win the game and he hit the receiver on a perfect comeback in the end zone… and the guy dropped the ball. Otherwise, they would have beaten Georgia "between the hedges."

I came back and our owner, Mr. Ralph Wilson, asked me before the next day's Bills game, "Who did you see?"

"I saw the best quarterback in the country."

"Who's that?"

"Brett Favre."

"I never heard of the guy."

"You will."

When the draft came up, we had the 26th pick of the first round, which we used on an excellent safety named Henry Jones. But as we talked in preparation, I said, "Should we take Favre or not take Favre with the 26th pick?"

Marv said, "I'd rather not take him there because he's just going to wither on the vine. We've got Jim Kelly and Brett Favre's not going to supplant Jim with Jim's contract."

The Falcons took Favre in the second round, 33rd overall. We ended up taking defensive end Phil Hansen, who contributed greatly to our team, 21 picks later. In retrospect, we probably should have figured out a way to get Favre for his trade value alone.

MIKE HOLMGREN: Brett Favre was young and still learning. I thought we could move the ball, but instead of just flat-out doing it because we were better than the other guys, I had to fiddle with it a little bit. I had to be a little bit tricky.

If you're honest about where your own weaknesses are and you're going against a defense whose strength is your weakness, you've got to deal with it. We used different motions, different formations. I put our top receiver, Sterling Sharpe, all over the place, which was a little different, but he was our go-to guy.

If you're playing a team that uses a lot of bump-and-run and they're gonna crowd you, you use bunch formation. You bump people off, you get people open. Maybe you can't go deep, so you throw short on first downs. That was the chess game for me that I loved. That was why, as a head coach, I stayed very involved with the offense.

I was a good student. I think I learned a lot of discipline about the West Coast offense and about quarterback play from Bill Walsh—the precision involved. I tried to implement that because I'd seen it work at a professional level. As a teacher, you better teach things you understand.

I pretty much stuck with what I learned from the 49ers. With Coach Walsh, we ran a crossing game that you see a lot in today's game. The rule for receivers was you don't run into coverage. A crossing game versus man-to-man is where the guy keeps running all the way across the field. If you call the same play and if, as the receiver's running, there's a defender there, he stops. So, it's two concepts built into the same play. A quarterback has to know that.

If the receiver's looking at the quarterback, he's telling him, "I'm running away from the quarterback." If he's looking at the coverage, that means he's stopping in a certain spot. He's saying, "As soon as I cross this linebacker and before I get to the next one, I'm in the hole." Exactly where that hole is is his call, but hopefully it's in the middle.

If, say, the receiver reads man, but as the quarterback looks at him, he sees the corner come off, he doesn't throw it. Then he goes someplace else. You have something built into that pattern that if that happens, there should be something vulnerable over the top of that corner.

That's why quarterbacks make a lot of money. They've got to see that. The great ones see it and learn it.

Going into the '92 season, Don Majkowski was the starting quarterback, but Brett was the heir apparent. You're telling the world, "He's gonna be our quarterback." We didn't know when. He certainly wasn't ready to play immediately.

At the time, Brett had to learn about what he needed to do as far as studying, his preparation and how he did things. He didn't approach the game that way. He just saw the game as something that was fun to him.

We lost the first game in overtime to the Vikings and Don Majkowski played the whole game. The second game, we went down to Tampa and Majkowski threw an interception on the first play of the game.

At halftime, I said, "Favre, you've got the second half."

Don got mad. I said, "Listen, you can't start the game that way."

Brett played the second half and was not a lot better. I'd call a play, he would run something, and then I'd say, "I didn't call that. What's he doing?" It was different, but he wasn't ready to play.

Majkowski started the third game, against Cincinnati, and got hurt. The Bengals were beating us, Favre went into the game, and I was standing on the sidelines thinking, *I'm going to be the shortest-tenured coach this league has ever had. I'm going to be one-and-done. We're never going to win a game.*

But Favre brought us back with two miracle throws at the end of the game and we won. The next week, he played, and we beat Pittsburgh. Little by little, he started to learn and started to do stuff.

I had to wrap my head around the fact Brett Favre was never going to be as precise as Joe Montana. That was an adjustment for me. He was learning how to read defenses and do all that kind of stuff. And then he'd get wild—force the ball, go down to one knee and throw it underhanded. He'd do all sorts of stuff that he did in college, and it would backfire on us. It wasn't working. So, we had to kind of calm him down.

But all of a sudden, he hit a stretch where we won six in a row, finished 9–7, and almost made the playoffs. You just saw how talented he was, but he was like my wild child. He was like the son I never had.

The next year, we were making those incremental steps, but we thought we could be better. Then we lost a game in Minnesota, which was kind of our bugaboo, to fall to 1–2. It was always tough to win for us in the old dome in Minnesota.

Crazy things would happen. And Brett had one of those games where he did a couple of things, threw an interception, and the coaches weren't happy. They had worked so hard and we lost a game we thought we should have won.

In our staff meetings, the coaches were free to say what they wanted to say. When we met the Monday morning after the game, someone brought up switching to Mark Brunell. I didn't really disagree. I was upset too. I said, "Okay, we'll go around the room." We went around the room and it was pretty split on who the quarterback should be, in the opinion of the coaching staff.

Steve Mariucci, who was the quarterbacks coach, wanted to stick with Favre and work with him. I said, "Okay, I'll decide tonight."

I thought about it Monday night. I came back Tuesday and decided I was going to stick with Brett come hell or high water. I saw so much good in him, so much potential in this league. In my own ego, I thought, "I can take any quarterback and fix him."

I called Brett and told him, "Either we go to the top of the mountain together or we're going to be in the dumpster together. But we're gonna be together."

We wound up going 9–7 again and this time we made the playoffs as a wild card. We were losing in the final minutes at Detroit. I called a square-out and Brett had the guy wide open. All of a sudden, he was moving out of the pocket. I just went, "Awww!" That was when he threw a 40-yard bomb to Sterling Sharpe for the winning touchdown.

By all the rules he learned, he wasn't supposed to do that. He was supposed to throw to the split end and get a first down. He didn't do that.

He did all the five-step and three-step drops, and a lot of times it would be just textbook. But then he'd improvise.

The third season with Brett, we were playing Atlanta in Milwaukee County Stadium in our next-to-last game of the regular season. We were behind 17–14 and at the Falcons' 9-yard line with about eight seconds left. I told him, "You can't take a sack. You gotta get two shots at the end zone."

"Okay."

He dropped back to pass. Then he started to run. I was yelling, "Noooo!" He scored, barely crossing the goal line, and we won the game.

Brett came over to me and I said, "I'm really happy, but what did I tell you to do? You didn't listen to what I said."

"Mike, I knew I could make it."

I shook my head and said, "Alright."

We ended up 9–7 for the third year in a row and made the playoffs for a second straight year. We beat Detroit and then lost to the Cowboys.

Although we didn't go all the way that year or the next year, when we lost to Dallas in the 1995 NFC Championship Game, we did beat the 49ers at San Francisco in the divisional round. After that game I said, "Okay, we're ready to beat anybody."

After the season, I had a meeting with Brett. I said, "Hey, we've got to eliminate this, eliminate that."

"Mike, that's how I play."

"You want to go to the Super Bowl or do you want to be 9–5, 9–7?"

"I want to go to the Super Bowl."

"Well, then we've got to do this. Work with me."

RON WOLF: What Mike was able to do was take the players we had and take advantage of what Favre could do. We had a receiver, Sterling Sharpe, who was just remarkable. I'm sure every defensive coordinator who watched the Packers' film said, "If we take away Sharpe, we'll beat these guys." Well, they never took him away. He was the only thing we had that first year, yet still led the league in receptions.

We just needed someone with that ability to get him the ball and we needed someone like Favre to be able to do that—someone who could throw that thing, zing it in there.

MIKE HOLMGREN: Eventually, Brett got it and it was beautiful, it was fun. But it was tough love in the beginning.

I taught him the system that I knew, knowing that every once in a while, he was going to do his thing. As a coach, you don't want to take away some of that explosive, natural stuff that some of these guys have, like Patrick Mahomes. You don't want to say, "Don't run around, don't do all that stuff."

You've got to eventually trust them to make good decisions. But I told him, "You have to know when it's time to throw it away, when to live for another. Don't throw it underhand. Don't throw it from your knee."

That's a balance. That's a learned process.

CHAPTER 4

Joe Gibbs, the "Hogs," and the One-Back Offense Capture the Heart of the Nation's Capital

"Football will measure you physically and it's going to challenge you mentally because you're going to be tired and you're going to be hit."

—Joe Gibbs

BILL POLIAN: Fresh from winning two Super Bowls and an undefeated season as personnel director of the Miami Dolphins, Bobby Beathard became the general manager of the Washington Redskins in 1978. He hired Joe Gibbs as head coach and "the golden era" of Redskins football began.

George Allen and his over-the-hill gang of grizzled veterans had reached one Super Bowl but had run out of gas. They left behind a cadre of key players, such as kicker Mark Moseley, running back John Riggins, quarterback Joe Theismann, defensive tackle Dave Butz, and safety Mark Murphy.

The Beathard-Gibbs tandem went to the Super Bowl three times, winning twice. When Beathard stepped down following the '88 season, he was succeeded by his longtime assistant, Charley Casserly. The Redskins kept rolling, winning Super Bowl XXVI under quarterback Mark Rypien. Joe Gibbs won two other Super Bowls—XXII with Doug Williams at quarterback and XVII with Theismann under center. In addition to the powerful, colorful "Hogs" offensive line, Washington possessed a dominant defense coordinated by Richie Petitbon and led by Butz, Hall of Famer Darrell Green, and defensive end Dexter Manley.

Joe Gibbs had a varied and successful career as an offensive coordinator at the college and NFL levels before taking the helm of the Redskins in 1981. His principle mentor was Don Coryell, for whom he played and coached at San Diego State and with the Chargers and Cardinals. Gibbs' record with the Redskins was 124–60–0 in the regular season and 16–5 in the playoffs during his first stint with the team from 1981 to 1992; he later coached them again from 2004 to 2007. During his tenure, the Redskins battled for supremacy in the NFC and NFL with the San Francisco 49ers and New York Giants. Gibbs' teams appeared in four Super Bowls, winning three, each with a different starting quarterback.

He developed the one-back/two–tight end offense, which is standard today. The Redskins' signature was a power running game, which featured "Counter Trey," a misdirection power play, which brought blaster John Riggins around the corner, led by a tandem of huge pulling "Hogs."

Joe Theismann was a 6'0", 192-pound All-American from Notre Dame who signed with the CFL Toronto Argonauts after being selected in the fourth round of the '71 NFL draft by Miami. George Allen brought Joe to Washington in '74. He became a regular in '78 and put together a 77–47 record with the 'Skins.

Joe was a Pro Bowler in '82 and '83 and first-team All-NFL in '82, in a Super Bowl–winning year. His size and athletic style are commonplace today, but were unique in his time. His career was tragically ended by a gruesome leg injury on *Monday Night Football*. Joe was a charismatic, tough, never-say-die, inspirational leader.

Doug Williams was a huge man with a huge arm and incredible running ability. A 6'4", 224-pound All-American at Grambling, he was drafted in the first round by the Tampa Bay Buccaneers in 1978 after having been scouted by then-Bucs offensive coordinator Joe Gibbs. After five up-and-down seasons, with a bad Bucs organization and team, he signed with the USFL Oklahoma Outlaws, who merged with the Arizona Wranglers the next season and became the Arizona Outlaws. After the USFL folded, Doug returned to Washington under Joe Gibbs, first as a backup and eventually starting, winning, and being named MVP of Super Bowl XXII. Doug was the first Black quarterback to earn each of these accolades.

Charley Casserly grew up in River Edge, New Jersey, a suburb of New York City. After Springfield College, he joined the George Allen Washington Redskins as an unpaid intern in 1977. He soon advanced to a full-time scouting position and was named assistant GM by Bobby Beathard in 1982. Casserly was promoted to GM when Beathard resigned in 1989 and helped sustain Washington's success, drafting, among others, Brian Mitchell and Hall of Fame cornerback Champ Bailey.

In this chapter, you will hear from Gibbs, a Hall of Famer, as well as from Theismann, Williams, and Casserly.

JOE GIBBS: After the Chargers had lost the 1980 AFC Championship Game against the Raiders, I got a phone call from Bobby Beathard. He said, "Hey, do you want to interview for the Redskins job?"

It was one of the real thrills of my life.

We had great offensive personnel with the Chargers. We had drafted two future Hall of Fame pass-catchers, tight end Kellen Winslow and wide receiver Charlie Joiner, and we had another extremely talented wide receiver in John Jefferson. And we had Dan Fouts, another future Hall of Famer, at quarterback.

I always like to say Dan Fouts got me the Redskins job. You talk about a mentally tough guy. In the preseason of 1979, my first year coaching quarterbacks in San Diego, Dan hurt his back. We went to Seattle to open the season. When we went out for warmups, I was worried because he was even having a tough time throwing the football. But he wound up throwing for 224 yards, and we won big.

On Monday, when I'd go in the locker room, I'd see Dan and he'd have ice packs on the back of his legs, all up and down his arm, and on his back. Many times, Dan couldn't even get to the practice field Monday or Tuesday. He might dress up in sweats, come out, and walk through some stuff. Wednesday, he might take a few plays in practice. Thursday, he was a little better. Friday, he would do everything. Sunday, he would play his rear off. Dan was one of the fiercest competitors I've been around.

We had been a typical two-back-type offense, but when we drafted Winslow, we had a gifted tight end and a great receiver all in one. If you put him at the standard tight end position, he was going to get hammered by the outside "Sam" linebacker and then from the inside linebacker while trying to get a release off the line of scrimmage. That took away your passing threat.

Our head coach, Don Coryell, said, "The defense is taking away one of our great pass threats. We need to help him get off the line of scrimmage."

So, we took Kellen off the line of scrimmage, took a back out, made Kellen the H-back, and moved him all along the line of scrimmage. You could flank him out. You could put him in motion. That was what started our version of the one-back. I'm sure it was done a long time before; we didn't create that, believe me. But we used it effectively.

Don Coryell had a huge influence on me. He probably was the most intense person I've ever seen. He was so focused on football. When I was a volunteer assistant for him at San Diego State, after having played for him there, I would open the door to our office, and sometimes he would be sitting in the dark. He would just have a scrunched-up look on his face, thinking about football.

As Don got ready for each game, he would always wind up finding some way of hating the other team. He'd come up with whatever he could. I remember, when we were going to play a team that couldn't have beaten us in 100 years, Don was struggling to find a way to hate them. The night of the game, we came out of the locker room and their ball boy had put their footballs at our end of the field. It was just an honest mistake, but Coryell went ape. He came back into the locker room screaming, "They have no respect for us! They put their balls on our end of the field!"

That was his whole pregame speech.

There are a million stories about Don. He lived in Helix, on this little mountain outside of San Diego, and he used to take the trash cans down and drop them off in the morning. He would put Mindy, his daughter, in the car with him, and she'd ride down the hill to drop off the trash cans. Then, he would go to work and Mindy would walk back to the house. I think three times he went all the way to work with the trash cans and Mindy in the backseat.

Don also was probably the most honest person that I've been around. Most of us will kind of bend things to get it going our way. Don was not like that at all.

After I had made up my mind to go into coaching, I became a volunteer assistant at San Diego State. One day, Don said that I needed to start coaching on the defensive side of the ball under John Madden. I did all the grunt work, running all the game plans off the copy machine and cutting up all the game film.

On Wednesdays, John taught extension classes at Fullerton Junior College, so I would drive him back and forth in a state car. I was the chauffeur. Madden would sit in the backseat, reading a paper and eating peanuts, for the whole ride.

I was probably the most fortunate person in the coaching world to get to work with John, because he was very bright. I learned a lot from him. His defensive scheme was unusual in those days. It was a "forcer" defense, where he overloaded the strong side of an offensive set.

Back then, we had an alumni game in the spring, with the current team going against the alumni. I had just graduated, so I was on the alumni squad, and Don told me to be the player/coach. I asked him if he wanted us to try and win the game or set it up so that the current team would have a good performance.

Speaking in that characteristic, lovable lisp, Don said, "Shoot, fella, try and win." I had all my buddies who graduated with me on the team, so I wasn't going to let them down.

Three days before the game, Madden came to me and asked for the plays we were going to run.

"Coach, I'm not giving you the plays. Don told me to try to win the game."

"I want all the plays on my desk tomorrow... or you're done."

I didn't give him the plays.

I played middle linebacker. I had a little bit of an advantage from the fact that I understood the current team's offense. That helped me in scheming the alumni defense, and the game wound up being pretty close.

Afterward, before I even got to the locker room, Madden walked up to me and said, "You're done!" And that was the end of the conversation.

The next morning, I walked into Coryell's office and told him Madden had fired me.

"Well, shoot, fella, I think you need to move over here on offense with me."

Don had a full-time opening to coach the offensive line. That began my official entry into coaching offense.

From San Diego State, I went to Florida State to work for Bill Peterson, who was all about hard work. Then, I was at USC with John McKay, who was very bright and demanding. After that, I went to Arkansas with Frank Broyles, who was one of the world's great salesmen. He could just win you over.

I was probably one of the luckiest guys in the world to work under four great coaches. All of them were very successful, all of them won championships. Yet, they were four different personalities with four different ways of looking at things. Each had his own way of motivating and getting through to a team.

What I learned was that you could be successful by being yourself, and that's the most important thing in dealing with teams. When you work with the collective mind of 45 football players, they're going to figure you out. If you're trying to be somebody you're not, they'll know.

I had a chance to get back with Don Coryell in St. Louis in 1973. I was working in Arkansas, and Don asked me to coach with him in pro ball with the Cardinals. I roomed with him for three months. I would go to bed at like 10:00 PM or whatever. I would get up to go to the bathroom at like 2:00 AM and I would hear this *clink, clink, clink.* It would be a drink glass with ice in it. I'd look around the corner and it'd be Don sitting in there, alone.

He would look at me and he would say something like, "We need to experiment with Mel Gray playing running back." Mel was an All-Pro receiver, and that probably wasn't going to be an easy sell. But that's my point. Moving personnel around was the kind of stuff Don would be thinking about at 2:00 AM.

Don was not afraid to try anything. I was much more structured. When I was coaching the offensive line at San Diego State, I wanted everything to be set a certain way, but Don was flexible and creative. As an example, he would come up with swing screens that incorporated downfield routes. The receiver could run 12-yard breaking routes, the line would block screen, and the quarterback would have the option to throw the screen or the downfield route.

I remember he came to me in the middle of the year and said, "Hey, Joe, I think we ought to change our snap count."

"What? Coach, we can't change the snap count in the middle of the season."

I managed to talk him out of that. But this guy was not afraid to try anything and because of that, all of us who coached under him wound up being open to creative ideas.

Our first two years at San Diego State, he would pound the ball from the I-formation. He brought it with him from USC, where he was an assistant with Coach McKay. I played tight end and caught three passes one year (we didn't throw the ball; we ran it). Then, we got Haven Moses and Gary Garrison as our receivers and Don Horn at quarterback. All of a sudden, we started moving toward throwing it, and Don went all the way with that and became "Air Coryell."

When I was calling plays in St. Louis, Don was the only head coach who would ever come on the headset after we had played a quarter or two and say, "Hey, let's start getting after their ass!" What he meant was, "Quit running it! Start throwing this thing!"

I'd say, "Yeah, Coach, I've got you, I've got you."

After getting the call from Bobby Beathard in January 1981, I drove to L.A. that night and took a flight the next day to New York, where I interviewed with Bobby and Mr. Jack Kent Cooke for the Redskins' head coaching job. I remember thinking that I didn't know if I was going to be hired on the spot or if it was just an interview.

Somewhere in there, Mr. Cooke changed his tone and said, "Now, what we're going to do with you…"

I thought, *Oh my gosh! He's gonna give me this job.*

I had a yellow pad and I had listed nine assistant coaches I wanted to try and hire. I said, "Mr. Cooke, this is probably the most important thing we're gonna do, is try and hire these coaches. Almost all of them have good jobs, and I'm not sure we can get any of them."

I'll always remember this: he put that finger out, like he did, and said, "We'll get every single one of them." I think we actually got eight of them, which was great for me.

As I look back on those years of coaching the Redskins, the best thing I did was surround myself with great assistant coaches. That was so important, because my way of coaching—and I do it with our NASCAR business too— is you have the assistant coaches, and whatever comes up, any problem you've got, you sit there and go over it with them. You argue back and forth; everybody takes different a side. In the end, you have to make the decision, but you have to give everybody a chance to give their opinion. You gain wisdom from the collective mind of the coaches.

CHARLEY CASSERLY: Bobby had recommended that they keep Richie Petitbon on the staff and promote him from secondary coach to defensive coordinator. Joe didn't really know Richie, but he trusted Bobby.

I remember Dick Vermeil, when he was coaching the Philadelphia Eagles, made a comment that I got secondhand: "Hey, they've got a heck of a coaching staff down there. This could be trouble."

Joe always would say, "You win with people, and the single most important thing you do is hire good people." How many coaches come in and hire a bunch of friends? Now, Joe knew a lot of these guys, but they were good coaches.

JOE GIBBS: Bobby Beathard was responsible for getting the talent. He was instinctive. He would look at some player for 10 plays and go, "We've got to have this guy."

CHARLEY CASSERLY: Bobby was an instinct guy. If he got a gut, he was going with it. He had a lot of great ones, and he had some where we traded picks and the guys couldn't play. He wouldn't hesitate to trade a pick for a player at all. He felt the player was a known commodity as opposed to somebody we didn't know.

Coaches were very involved with scouting. Bobby got that from Don Shula when Bobby was director of player personnel for the Dolphins. Our coaches went on the road, and our scouts went on the road with the coaches.

The scouts formed a relationship with them. They not only got to know what they wanted, but they could also come back and translate it for everybody.

The scouts had a strong say, but Bobby did go with the coaches at the time. If they had a conviction, he'd go with it.

JOE GIBBS: The coaches worked with Bobby and his scouts and our job was to evaluate our team. But if it came down to a final decision in the draft, it was going to be Bobby's. Bobby decided what talent came to us.

Now, when it came to the makeup of the team, that was my responsibility. Mr. Cooke let Bobby and me know, "If there are any disagreements between the two of you, then you guys come to me and I'll settle it."

The bottom line was, Bobby and I made sure there was never a disagreement, because we didn't want Mr. Cooke to get after our rear.

CHARLEY CASSERLY: At Joe's initial press conference, Joe said (and I'd never heard any coach say this), "You only get one chance; you'd better be ready." It kind of set the tone for everything he did.

When we were doing the "Top Ten Coaches" segment for NFL Network, Dick Vermeil said, "I spent a week in Washington when Joe was there. Now I knew why we couldn't beat him. I never saw anybody prepare like him."

JOE GIBBS: Mr. Cooke was quite a character, but he understood winning. I felt like he was a great owner because no matter what happened—and he had very strong opinions—at the end of the meetings, he would say, "That's what I think, but you have got to be the one that makes the decision." He told me he wasn't going to ruin me like he ruined his first baseball coach when he owned the Toronto Maple Leafs minor league team.

JOE THEISMANN: In '79, we just missed out on making the playoffs after losing our final game of the season to the Cowboys. And 1980 was just a flat-out disaster, which was what led to Joe Gibbs being hired.

John Riggins had decided to retire right after that Cowboys loss. He just felt there was nothing more he could do.

JOE GIBBS: When I first got the job, one of the things everybody told me was, "You've got to get John Riggins back here." I flew out to his hometown of Centralia, Kansas. I got my rental car, drove to the first gas station, and asked the guy there, "Do you know where John Riggins lives?" Everybody in Centralia knew where John Riggins lived. He was a bigger-than-life guy, an All-American at Kansas.

I went down this dirt road and pulled up to his house. I knocked on the door. Right away, I knew I had a chance to get John back, because his wife informed me *she* would like to come back. I've found there are only two ways to get a football player to do something: you can fine him or get his wife on board.

"I'm Coach Gibbs with the Redskins and I need to talk to John. This is really important." I gave her the name and number of my hotel and said, "Please get me an appointment with John."

Later that night, the message light on my phone was on—I had an appointment with John Riggins the next morning for breakfast.

The next morning, I was thinking of my game plan to convince him to return. I was rehearsing my sales pitch as I drove out to John's house. This was a huge deal. I had my best stuff.

As soon as I pulled up, John was walking across the courtyard. He had a camouflage outfit on; he had been hunting that morning and he had a beer can in each hand. I thought, *Well, I can tell he's really impressed with me. Nobody's gonna show up for their appointment with their coach with two beer cans.* When I brought that scene up about a year later, John informed me that one of those beers was going to be for me.

As we ate breakfast and I started a casual conversation, I wasn't getting anything from John. He just sat there. So, I started my football sales pitch.

"John, new coach, new offense. I'm gonna give you the ball every down and never ask you to block."

I was going as hard as I could trying to sell the guy. He let me go on for 10 minutes, and then the first meaningful thing he said to me was, "You need to get me back there. I'll make you famous."

I thought, *Oh, my gosh! Nobody would say that to his coach. This guy has to be an egomaniac, and I'm gonna get stuck coaching him for 10 years.*

I finished my sales pitch and went back to D.C. I didn't know what had just happened or what he was thinking. I thought that maybe we needed to trade him.

Two days went by and I got a phone call. It was John.

"Joe, I've made up my mind. I'm coming back."

"Oh, my gosh! This is fantastic, this is great."

"There's only one thing I want to put in my contract."

"What's that?"

"A no-trade clause."

Somebody upstairs was looking after me, because this was one of the best deals anyone has ever made. And as I look back on that whole situation and getting John to return to play for the Redskins, many times I think about his statement: "You need to get me back there. I'll make you famous."

CHARLEY CASSERLY: Riggo comes back and he makes the famous statement: "I'm bored, I'm broke, and I'm back." That was John.

JOE GIBBS: I remember being on such a high when I got that job in Washington. Then we started off my career in coaching 0–5. I used to tell everybody I was looking for a different way home at night. I still remember my boys, J.D. and Coy, saying they can remember people yelling, "Hey, Lombardi! How ya doing?"

When I came in, Joe Theismann was our quarterback and we were depending on him to be our starter. After the fifth loss, I was at my house and I heard a knock on the door. It was Theismann.

We sat down in the living room and he said, "Look, I want this more than anything in my life. You tell me what to do and I'll do anything you want."

Joe was doing some TV shows and had some other things going on. He said he'd get rid of those. That did impress me, and that meeting was a turning point in our relationship. Joe and I talked this through man-to-man, which was always the way I felt these situations should be handled.

When I started the year off, I always liked telling our team, "Look, you're not going to read about me criticizing you in the paper. We're family. If we've got anything critical to say to somebody, it's going to be behind closed doors."

One thing I would always say was, "We're either all going up together or we're all going down together."

JOE THEISMANN: I had heard Joe was going to either cut me or bench me. Our fifth loss was against the San Francisco 49ers, so after that game I drove to his house and knocked on the door. I'll tell you, there haven't been too many people more surprised in life than Coach Gibbs was when he saw me standing on his front stoop.

I sat down with him in his den and said, "Look, I love this offense and I love what we're doing. But truthfully, I just don't feel like you're talking to me. You're just implementing plays, but we're not talking, we're not having a conversation."

Joe said, "I need somebody totally committed to be quarterback. You've got restaurants, you've got TV shows, endorsement contracts."

"I'll get rid of everything if you want me to. If that's what it takes me to prove to you that I can be your quarterback, I'll get rid of everything. But I would prefer you to do this: give me a chance. Just trust me, believe in me, give me a chance to be your quarterback."

We went 8–3 through the balance of the 1981 season.

JOE GIBBS: Joe Theismann was super bright, a great competitor, and athletic. He had a knack for making plays that resulted in game-winning drives.

When people ask me about Joe Theismann, here's a story I like to tell: we were playing the Giants at our place. It was a miserable night, kind of sleeting. Theismann had thrown three interceptions in the first half, and we were down by like 10 points. We were in a two-minute drive, and we called timeout. Joe came to the sideline. He was spitting blood and had his two front teeth knocked out. I thought he was probably going to tell me, "I'll sit the second half out."

Instead, he was cussing everyone, and I realized this guy was competing his butt off. In the fourth quarter, he took us on a 70-yard drive and Mark Moseley kicked a record-setting, at the time, 21st-straight field goal to beat the Giants 15–14. So when people ask me about Theismann, I don't tell them about the Super Bowl or this or that. I tell them about that game. Theismann was competitive and he wanted it.

Joe was a driven guy. I think part of the reason was because he was drafted in the third round in the NFL, went to Canada, and came back wanting to prove something. Billy Kilmer and Sonny Jurgensen were there when Joe arrived. There was always a dynamic with them, and Theismann kind of got left out.

JOE THEISMANN: In 1974, I was leaving the Canadian Football League, where I played for the Toronto Argonauts, and coming back to the United States. At that time, George Allen was interested in my services. He ultimately wound up trading a No. 1 pick to the Miami Dolphins for the rights to me. From '71 to '73, while I was in Canada, the Dolphins had an undefeated season and won a couple of world championships. I guess you could say I missed that train by just a little bit.

I joined the Washington Redskins—they are now the Washington Football Team, but I played for the Washington Redskins—in '74, and I did not establish myself as being a "friend of the family," so to speak. Billy Kilmer and Sonny Jurgensen were both established; Sonny's in the Pro Football Hall of Fame, and I've come to appreciate Billy as one of the toughest people I've ever known.

But when I came to town, I made this statement: "I didn't come here to sit. I came here to play."

Well, that didn't sit very well with a veteran football team. At that time, the Redskins were the most senior team in the National Football League. George Allen had brought a bunch of older guys over from the Rams who he had coached for five seasons before coming to the Redskins in '71, and then there were older guys already with the Redskins at the time.

I played one year with Sonny and I was just awed and amazed by the way he threw the football. And Billy was just the ultimate competitor. If Sonny's pass was a 10, Billy's was a .5. Every now and then, it spiraled, but he got it there. What amazed me was the way the players played for him. They played their rear ends off.

I guess you could say I got bored watching the other quarterbacks play. I was a punt returner at Notre Dame for seven games before I got a chance to start. In the Canadian Football League, I caught punts at the end of the half or the end of the game if they were in the end zone, and I would punt the ball back out because, in the CFL, if the ball stayed in the end zone, it was worth a point for the team that was kicking it in. So every day after practice with the Redskins, I would catch punts.

Finally, against the Giants in the middle of the '74 season, our kick returner, Herb Mul-Key, got hurt, and then Kenny Houston, a Hall of Fame safety who returned punts, also got hurt. I walked up next to George Allen on the sideline, and sort of out of his line of sight, I said, "Kenny's hurt. Do you want me to go catch the punt?"

"Go on in."

I ran by him and he turned to Paul Lanham, our special teams coach. Pointing at me, he said, "What's he doing out there?"

"You sent him in to return a punt."

"Get him off the field, will you?"

But once I crossed the white line, I never came back. I wound up returning punts for my first two years with Washington.

Fast-forward to 1985. We were playing the Bears in Chicago. Jeff Hayes, who was our punter and kickoff guy, tore his thigh muscle on the opening kickoff. I was standing on the sidelines, and Joe Gibbs said, "We don't have a punter."

I said, "I can punt."

"What?"

"I said, 'I can punt.' How hard can it be? Drop the ball, raise your foot, ball's gone." I was also thinking to myself that Danny White was doing it while quarterbacking the Cowboys. Why couldn't I do it?

We got the ball at our 13-yard line. All of a sudden, it was fourth-and-8 and we had to punt. I was on the goal line with my hands up saying, "Mom, look at me, I'm a punter in the National Football League. How great is this?"

I called for the snap and the ball hit my hands. My teammates had said to kick the ball to the right, so that was what I was going to do. I dropped the ball, raised my foot, and sent the ball spiraling through the air. It traveled all of 16 yards. I was 15 yards behind the line.

I have the second-shortest punt in the history of the National Football League, at one yard. Sean Landeta has the record at minus-seven yards, but I would argue that he never touched the ball. And it happened to be in the same exact spot at Soldier Field in which I executed my stellar punt.

I went jogging to the sideline and sat down on the bench. The Bears went in and scored. After that, I walked up to Coach Gibbs, who was looking down at his clipboard getting ready for our next offensive series, and I asked, "What do you want to run?"

"Spread Right Short Motion 60 Outside."

"Okay, fine."

I started laughing and then asked, "You want me to punt again?"

Joe used to wear these giant glasses. He pushed his glasses up, looked at me, and said, "I never want to hear the word 'punt' come out of your mouth again."

But back to when George Allen was coach. If you were a young player, as I was then, he was all about proving to him that you were worth going out on the field. He loved veteran players, and that was his commitment.

Sonny Jurgensen retired in '75 and Billy Kilmer was at the end of his career. I played a little bit at quarterback in '76 and a little bit in '77. George got fired after the '77 season and Jack Pardee took over.

In 1978, I became the starting quarterback and really had the support of the coaching staff. We started that season at 6–2 and I was on the cover of *The Sporting News* and all of these magazine covers under headlines reading, "Here Comes the New Kid in Town."

JOE GIBBS: If you go through those tough times and handle them the right way, that's actually when you grow the most and learn the most. For instance, it's the best time to study everybody around you.

During that 0–5 stretch, Mr. Cooke called me and said, "I need to meet with you." I remember sweating bullets. Mr. Cooke came in the room and he had three or four books under his arm.

We talked for a while. At one point, he said, "You know what they're calling me when I leave that stadium?"

"Yes, Mr. Cooke. They're calling me the same thing."

"Well, I've got other problems. I just got a windfall and I've got these books and I've got to figure out how I can get out of paying the taxes."

Mr. Cooke had a real feel for sports. He loved baseball; he owned a minor league team called the Toronto Maple Leafs who played in the International League.

CHARLEY CASSERLY: Jack Kent Cooke had a relationship with Branch Rickey, who had so much to do with creating the farm system in baseball. The Maple Leafs were independent, so Jack would sell players to Branch Rickey. In fact, Jack was an executive of the year in minor league baseball.

He understood the concept of player development, which was something he got from Rickey. We had a big injured-reserve list. We were never penalized, but we had a big IR and he never questioned paying those players who weren't playing. Jack also understood the importance of going on the road and scouting players as a general manager.

He went to the Los Angeles Lakers and built a championship team with them. He built up the L.A. Kings hockey team. He was very demanding.

Jack wanted a high level of accountability from his people. He also only listened to the head coach and general manager—nobody else. He did not pay attention to the media whatsoever. Friends' opinions? He ignored them, too.

Really, what you had was an ideal situation. He challenged you when you made decisions, but in the end, you won 99 percent of them.

JOE GIBBS: Mr. Cooke promoted the first Muhammad Ali–Joe Frazier fight. He built The Forum in Los Angeles. I think he really understood sports. Most of all, he wanted Washington to really feel like he was doing everything he could to give them a winner.

I always felt Mr. Cooke was at his best when we were at our worst, when it was really tough. He had these different quotes he would use from history. One of them was, "I'm going to lay down and bleed awhile, and then we'll get up and fight again."

Another thing he would always say was, "I'm going to go and try and make some money so you can throw it away."

CHARLEY CASSERLY: The way Mr. Cooke would handle a conversation about paying a player was he would sometimes start off being negative about it, but it was a test. It was a big test. But in the end, you could pass the test. You were going to have to fight like heck, because you had to prove it.

He was looking for you to have a conviction that we had to pay that player. If you had a conviction, you were going to get it done.

He had a saying: "When you need one, get two."

JOE GIBBS: Our first meeting in the morning with the team focused on special teams. I'd sit in there for an hour because one of the things with being a head coach, if you're an offensive guy as I was, then you've got to be careful that guys on special teams and defense aren't saying, "Hey, Coach is over there with the offense. That's all he cares about."

That certainly wasn't the case with me. You want everybody together as a team.

We had John Riggins and Terry Metcalf in our backfield. John had been off for a year, and I remember it was kind of slow for him at the beginning. We went through a couple of preseason games and he looked rusty.

Then, all of a sudden, it was as if he said, "This is it, I'm playing. I've got to start rolling." And he did.

John was so physical and big, he was hard to get down. He had great balance and great feet. The people in his town swore, when he was in high school and he was playing eight-man football, he would have 250 yards by halftime and they would take him out of the game. He'd just run over everybody. They also marveled about his speed for such a big guy.

But you didn't want either John Riggins or Terry Metcalf to be blocking. You wanted them carrying the ball. If you put both of them in there, with Riggins at fullback, that wasn't going to work.

During that 0–5 start, we said, "That's not smart. We've got two guys who should be toting the ball." We had drafted some tight ends who were more athletic and smaller, and we could use them as H-backs. That would allow us to keep Terry and John carrying the ball.

The second thing that caused us to change our offensive scheme was Lawrence Taylor. What we learned right away when we were playing the Giants was that you could not block him with a back. You try to block Lawrence Taylor with a back, you're going to get a sack. It was very hard to turn a tackle out on him too.

The Giants played a 3-4 front. In some cases, we would dual-read the guard. In other words, we'd have the guard key the inside linebacker and if he didn't come on a blitz, we'd have the guard pick up the outside linebacker. That caused us having Joe Theismann having two teeth knocked out and a fumble.

Eventually, we said we needed to put a tight end in that guy's face. At least you'd have a chance by making him negotiate a tight end.

JOE THEISMANN: Coach Gibbs changed our approach. When he came from San Diego, it was throw it all over the place like Dan Fouts did for the Chargers. Well, we didn't have J.J. Jefferson, we didn't have Charlie Joiner, we didn't have Kellen Winslow. But we tried to do those things.

CHARLEY CASSERLY: Joe came in with the San Diego Chargers offense, Air Coryell. We were gonna spread 'em out, throw the ball all over the field. We weren't quite built for that.

In the process of losing the first five games, we outgained everybody. But we were turning the ball over and we weren't winning.

JOE THEISMANN: After that, we went to more of a running attack and John Riggins became the centerpiece of what we were able to do. My job was to keep the chains moving, pick up first downs, and once we got down around the goal line and into the red zone, Coach Gibbs would come up with plays.

I've said this many times: Joe Gibbs could give a clinic on red-zone offense. That's how incredible he was when it came to conceptualizing what we needed to do.

Joe would look for matchups. For example, in Super Bowl XVII, we knew that the Miami Dolphins would match up man-to-man, so Joe came up with what was called an "explode package." I would get to the line of scrimmage and go, "Hut!" And we would all explode with different formations.

We had Art Monk, a Hall of Fame receiver, in the backfield. We had John Riggins up on a wing. We had Alvin Garrett and Virgil Seay on opposite sides. We had the tight end on the opposite side.

Now, you could picture what it was like coming out defensively to identify the formation. It wasn't easy.

JOE GIBBS: Besides the offensive changes, we also made some personnel changes. When you go through tough times like that, you have a chance to study your players and you can see the guys who say, "I don't care what the score is, I don't care how many games we've lost. We're gonna lay it on the line. We're gonna fight our butt off."

I can remember the first game we won was against Chicago. It was one of the ugliest games anybody's ever seen. They used the "Bear defense," and to be truthful I'd never seen that thing before.

I was up all night for five straight nights trying to figure out what to do. I think we ran the ball 49 times or something and we picked up a fumble. A few other things went our way, and somehow, we won.

I really feel that 0–5 start propelled us to two Super Bowls, for sure, because none of us wanted to go back to that. Not the coaches, not the players, none of us. We were highly, highly motivated. You love winning so much and I think it really drove us for a number of years.

BILL POLIAN: By the time Joe Gibbs became the Redskins' coach, his offensive philosophy was fully formed. He was prepared to implement Air Coryell in the nation's capital until he found he didn't have players like Dan Fouts, Charlie Joiner, and Kellen Winslow in Burgundy and Gold. Out of necessity, he transitioned to a power running game featuring John Riggins and a powerful, huge offensive line that became known as the "Hogs."

Gibbs designed the one-back offense with three things in mind. First, he wanted an H-Back, a second tight end who replaced the fullback, to cause safeties to switch responsibility when the H-Back went in motion. This often pitted a small, light free safety against a power-pulling Hog, an obvious mismatch. Second, he wanted the H-Back, a big receiver, to be matched in the passing game against a less-nimble strong safety or linebacker, another mismatch in favor of the offense. Third, and perhaps most important, he needed the second tight end to play over the Giants' All-World outside linebacker, Lawrence Taylor, in order to help stymie Taylor both in run and pass. Taylor could not be handled one-on-one.

The zone-blocking run game to either side was complemented by "Counter Trey," the Redskins' signature run play. Upon the snap, the single back faked one way and then reversed field, following a pulling Hog tackle and guard around the opposite corner. Theismann had play-action passes and bootlegs off all this run action, which made this offense both very physical and very tough to defend.

The one-back offense is a staple in the NFL now. When Joe Gibbs brought it forth, it was revolutionary.

JOE GIBBS: Our philosophy in the running game was that we were always trying, formation-wise, to get the safeties out of run support. We used multiple formations to try to get that done.

We get credit for using the counter gap, but really I stole it. There's probably nothing new in football. We happened to be watching film of a Nebraska game, evaluating players for the draft. All of a sudden, they ran this play, and I went, "Wait a minute. Run that back." That was the first time I had seen that form of a counter game.

JOE THEISMANN: Coach Gibbs slept at Redskin Park three nights a week: Monday, Tuesday, and Wednesday. I used to walk in at 7:00 AM for the 7:30 meeting and Don Breaux, our offensive coordinator, would be sound asleep on the chairs. The coaches worked into 3:00, 4:00, 5:00 in the morning.

I guess, sometimes when you're exhausted, things pop into your head. I think most of our offense came from late-night meetings when they probably had no idea what they were thinking about. They just had an open mind to write stuff down.

CHARLEY CASSERLY: Joe Gibbs' involvement in the defense wasn't much. He would go in every Tuesday morning to go over the tape with the defensive coaches and he would have some comments. But he let them pretty much run it. If things didn't go right, he stepped in.

In a 1989 loss to Philadelphia, we couldn't tackle anybody, so in the practices that followed, we had tackling drills. We had never done tackling drills up to that point, but Joe felt we needed it because we had tackled so poorly against the Eagles.

JOE THEISMANN: It was great playing for Joe because he always challenged the players. He just kept giving us more and more to see if we could handle it—more and more movement, more and more different formations, more and more play combinations. I was given the flexibility at the line of scrimmage just to get into good plays and out of bad ones.

When a playcaller calls a play like Coach Gibbs did, it's not a question of what the play is. It's the question of why it was called. Did you call this play because we're going to go for it on fourth down? Did you call this play because, if I get the look that I want, or you think we're going to get, I get the chance to take the shot? It's a much more in-depth process than meets the eye.

Joe used to do things that always made the game interesting for us. On Wednesday, when we would install our game plan, Joe would always come up with something unique, whether it was three tight ends, whether it was no backs, whether it was John on the wing, Art on the wing, and we would run a particular play. We would have a running play, a pass play, and a play-action play out of it. It made football fun.

You'd get to a point in the game where you'd say, "This is where he's going to call it." And he did. It was like, "Man, that was great. I can't wait to see what he comes up with next."

He was very creative when it came to placing personnel in different places, and he really understood what people wanted to try to do.

JOE GIBBS: Counter gap became a big part of our running game, and it was very successful versus the 3-4 front. The basic concept is you gap-block the strong side and you trap with your backside guard while bringing your backside tackle up through the hole.

When we added counter gap to our run game, it also led to a very effective play-action pass scheme. The first time we ran that play-action pass was against Seattle, and I had never seen a receiver that wide open. I mean, he was 15 yards behind the coverage.

JOE THEISMANN: The reason we ran the two-tight-end offense was back in the '80s, you used to have a designated weak safety and a designated strong safety. By going two tight ends, we forced the weak safety to become a tackler and the strong safety to become a pass-cover guy. We took what their strengths were and turned them into weaknesses.

So, with a balanced formation, you didn't know which way we were going to go, whether we were going to run 60 outside, 90 outside, 40 gut, 50 gut. Then, we could motion and change it to trips if we wanted to.

CHARLEY CASSERLY: Joe Gibbs took a lot of criticism for the offense for years. How can you run an offense without a fullback? How can you have a running game without a fullback? How come the tight end doesn't go out and catch any passes?

But Joe believed in the offense. It evolved in that first year because Air Coryell wasn't working. We had a power back, we had a third-down back. Joe's attitude was, "Hey, we're gonna line up with two tight ends, and this is how we're going to play."

It's an example of a coach evaluating his talent and changing in midstream. He believed in the running game; that was something he always did.

He said, "We can create 1,000-yard receivers in the concept of what we're doing, but I've got to have a back."

JOE GIBBS: In 1982, our second season, we beat Minnesota in a divisional-round playoff game. John Riggins ran for 185 yards and I took him out in the fourth quarter. As he started walking off the field, the fans began going crazy. He stopped, took his helmet off, and he bowed—east, north, west, and south. John had a great feel for special moments.

He wasn't one to celebrate often. When he would score a touchdown, he usually just took the ball and flipped it back to the ref. That was John.

He could sense big games, and those were the games he wanted to be in. He would rarely talk to me. He would send a message through the coaches, through Joe Bugel, our offensive line coach, or Don Breaux, one of our other offensive coaches. There'd be a big game, and John would say things like, "Tell Joe to load the wagon. I'm ready to go. Just give it to me."

There were also a couple of times where we would be getting ready to play a game when we had already locked up the playoffs, and he would send a message to me: "Tell Joe to take it easy on me today."

The offensive line loved John Riggins.

CHARLEY CASSERLY: You have to look back at George Allen, who left in '77. Joe Gibbs came in '81. Three seasons separate them, but when you look at the '82 championship team, you've got Mark Moseley, who was MVP of the league as the kicker (that kind of tells you about the offense in '82), and he was a George Allen signing; John Riggins was the MVP of the Super Bowl, and he was a George Allen signing; Joe Theismann was a George Allen trade, and he was the MVP in '83.

George Starke, the right tackle of the Hogs, was a holdover. Mark Murphy, who was the leading tackler in '82 and led the league in interceptions in '83, was a holdover. And then you had Dave Butz, who was the cornerstone of the inside of the defense. Those parts were there when we won the first championship in '82.

JOE THEISMANN: In 1982, there was a players' strike. We were out for seven weeks. I organized practices at a high school field. The interesting part of that was, for the first five weeks, we had 35 guys showing up.

We were feeling like a pretty good football team and really developed a camaraderie, more so than anything that could be done in a room at the facility. It was us committed to one another. When we came back from the strike, we wound up being just an unbelievable football team.

CHARLEY CASSERLY: The last game of the year was against St. Louis at RFK Stadium. Someone, somewhere, out of 55,000 fans, started chanting, "We want Dallas! We want Dallas!" And then more people joined in and pretty soon, the whole stadium was chanting, "We want Dallas!"

We finished 8–1 in the strike-shortened '82 season and went into the playoffs as the No. 1 seed, so we were at home to face Detroit. The play I remember most from that game was Riggo coming down the sideline. He was 250 pounds and he ran about a 4.9 40, but when he got going, that was a big 4.9.

Some Detroit defensive back came up to hit him with his shoulder and I swear, Riggo knocked that guy about five feet in the air. He ran over the guy. And in the fourth quarter, the fans started chanting again: "We want Dallas! We want Dallas!" The place was shaking.

Our next playoff game was against Minnesota. The first drive—*bang, bang, bang*—we went down and scored. This time, the fans didn't wait until the fourth quarter. The first quarter had just started and they were already chanting, "We want Dallas! We want Dallas!"

Now, we were getting ready to face the Cowboys in the NFC Championship Game. The Friday before the game, I had just gotten back from the Senior

Bowl. Redskin Park was in an industrial park and as I was driving past all these buildings on my way there, I saw these signs, written on sheets, hanging in front of them that read BEAT DALLAS! and DALLAS SUCKS!

Next to one of the buildings, people were outside in the parking lot singing "Hail to the Redskins!" It was like a high school atmosphere.

Some guy held up a sign on Constitution Avenue that read PARK IF YOU HATE THE COWBOYS. That started a massive traffic jam. Fans went over to the hotel where the Cowboys were staying and started screaming and yelling outside.

An hour before kickoff, there were 30,000 people in the stands. It was deafening.

JOE THEISMANN: They had brought in all of these aluminum seats in the stadium to give more people a chance to watch the game. They were pounding their feet against those aluminum seats. The ground beneath my feet actually shook. Every time I tell the story, I get goosebumps. It was like an out-of-body experience.

A lot of times, people will ask me, "What's the most memorable game you've ever played in?" I think most people would expect me to say Super Bowl XVII, because it was a world championship and we won.

But the game that stands out most in my mind is that NFC Championship Game. The Dallas Cowboys had been our nemesis since I joined the Redskins in '74. It was always us against the Cowboys. George Allen made it that way, Jack Pardee made it that way. Joe really hadn't gotten into all of the stuff that the other coaches did, but we knew that if we wanted to advance or be competitive in the division, the Cowboys were always going to be a roadblock for us.

Now we were playing at RFK Stadium, in front of our fans, with the right to go to the Super Bowl. I'll never forget. It was the hardest-hitting game I've ever played in in my life.

CHARLEY CASSERLY: On the opening kickoff, Otis Wonsley, who was a fullback, went down and leveled the Cowboys returner. It was kind of like one of those signature hits; we've all been around them. Everybody understood, *Hey, we came to play today.*

As we went through the game, Dexter Manley knocked out Danny White. That was huge. Gary Hogeboom came in and he got hot, but Dexter again made a big play by tapping a pass in the air that Darryl Grant intercepted and ran in for a touchdown. Riggo ran for more than 100 yards.

In the fourth quarter, it was time to take control of the game.

JOE THEISMANN: We got the ball back with five or six minutes to go. I stepped into the huddle and called the play Joe had signaled to me from the sideline: "Spread Right Sixty Outside." And Russ Grimm said, "No!"

"What do you mean, no?"

"No, I want to run Fifty Gut."

Now, here I was, middle management, and I had to make an executive decision. Do I go with the guy on the field or do I go with my boss?

So, I said, "Okay. Fifty Gut."

We gained five yards. I looked to the sideline, and Don Breaux signaled, "Sixty Outside." I stepped into the huddle and said, "Alright, Spread Right Sixty Outside."

Russ said, "No."

"No?"

"No, I want to run Fifty Gut."

I looked to the sidelines again, and then I just said, "Okay, Fifty Gut."

CHARLEY CASSERLY: Grimm wanted us to run the ball over him. He was going to block Randy White and he was going to make a point: *We're going to run it right over this sucker's face.* And we did. We only had those two run plays: "Forty Gut" and "Fifty Gut." Gut right and gut left.

JOE THEISMANN: We ran 11 consecutive "Fifty Guts." By the fourth one, I didn't even look at the sideline anymore. I knew what the answer was going to be.

I also had a lot of faith in Russ Grimm. He had played center for me one week when Jeff Bostic got hurt. Russ had the biggest rear end I've ever been behind in my life. It felt like there wasn't anybody around you. Russ is in the Hall of Fame as a guard, but he could have gotten in as a tackle, he could have gotten in as a center. He was just that good, that talented.

In that championship game, Russ was right there. He was in the trenches. He knew what was working. Players are the guys who can tell you what's going on.

We won 31–17. In the final seconds, all of the Cowboys players had gone to the locker room, but time hadn't expired and they had to get 11 Dallas players to come back for the last snap. We had knocked out both of their quarterbacks, Danny White and Gary Hogeboom, and receiver Drew Pearson, who was my high school teammate, had to take the snap.

It became the answer to a trivia question: Which two former high school teammates quarterbacked each other in an NFC championship game?

It's funny. You don't know what to be afraid of if you haven't been on an adventure yet. You don't know what pitfalls are out there, you don't know what you should or shouldn't do. You're just living for the moment.

That was the story of the 1982 Washington Redskins football team going to Super Bowl XVII to face the Dolphins.

Our linebackers and defensive backs were dressed in battle fatigues. Our two wide receivers, Alvin Garrett and Virgil Seay, went off to Disneyland with the Smurfs, which was what our receivers were called. John Riggins showed up Friday night at a party for Mr. Cooke in top hat, tails, Safari shorts, cowboy boots, and a cane.

Okay, were we really taking this seriously?

On game day, I remember walking the entire football field at the Rose Bowl. I said to myself, "I don't know if I'm going to get to see all of this field or part of this field." I walked from one end line to the other. During the introductions—and that's monumental in its nature to be introduced before the Super Bowl—when I ran onto the field and I got to the goal line, I sort of hopped over it. I said, "The last thing I wanted to do was trip over the goal line during introductions and embarrass myself completely."

The Dolphins led for much of the first half and were up 17–10 at half-time after Fulton Walker returned a kickoff 98 yards for a touchdown. But Joe had told us the night before—and this was really what Joe Gibbs was all about—"If we can stay within three to seven points of these guys, we can wear them out at the end of the game because we're bigger and stronger up front than they are."

What Coach Gibbs said pretty much happened. We managed to just run John Riggins constantly. Four yards here, five yards there. Then, he broke a big one, 43 yards, for a touchdown. All of a sudden, we were world champions.

The images I had in my mind were of Joe Namath waving his finger in the air and Terry Bradshaw holding up the ball after their Super Bowl wins. I thought I was actually going to be one of those guys, a world champion quarterback for the Washington Redskins.

CHARLEY CASSERLY: No one has ever done this before, but Jack Kent Cooke, our owner, and Joe Robbie, the owner of the Dolphins, agreed to have a joint party after the game and the loser would pay for it.

About five Dolphins showed up, and Robbie had to pay for the party. Cooke said to him, sarcastically, "I told you this would work, didn't I?"

JOE THEISMANN: Unfortunately, 11 of us had to miss the parade in Washington because we flew to Hawaii for the Pro Bowl. It was a miserable, rainy day, yet half a million people showed up in Washington to celebrate.

We were watching it on TV from Honolulu. It was the bittersweet aspect of the game. You're honored by playing in the Pro Bowl, but you can't be at the parade.

JOE GIBBS: At old Redskin Park, we had an equipment shed out behind the practice field. John and his buddies would hang out in that shed after practice. Their group became known as the "Five o'Clock Club." They'd have some beers and, honestly, I really didn't even know about it.

John Madden came to our practice before one of our nationally televised games and Riggins invited him out to the "Five o'Clock Club." The next day, during the game, John started telling the story about the "Five o'Clock Club," saying, "These guys go have some beers before they go home."

Once that was all over TV, I said to myself, "This is not good."

It was one of the few times I ever went looking for John during the week. I went downstairs to the locker room and I walked right up to him.

"Hey, John, you've got to help me with something. Madden talked about the Five o'Clock Club during the game and now everybody's talking about it. That's not good for a lot of reasons."

John looked right at me and said, "Don't worry about this. I've got it. I'll take care of it."

I thought to myself, *Hey, that was easy.*

I went back to my office. John's solution? He moved the Five o'Clock Club down the street to some other place that I didn't know about.

JOE THEISMANN: We used to have volleyball games every Saturday morning, offense versus defense or special teams. We played volleyball over the goalpost before our special teams practices on Saturday. It was really all about building camaraderie.

In the five seasons I played for him, I saw Joe Gibbs walk through our locker room maybe five times. He believed that the locker room belonged to the players.

Joe Gibbs, to his credit, let us be ourselves. We ran our football team. We respected him, but he never raised his voice. The only time I ever saw him get really upset was when he took his knuckle and rammed it through the glass of an overhead projector. Somebody had done something and he found out about it.

JOE GIBBS: I think people felt, because I was kind of a milquetoast guy—even though I didn't picture myself that way—that I didn't enjoy all the fun stuff. But, really, I did enjoy it and thought it was very important for the chemistry of the football team to have guys with personalities and who were characters.

JOE THEISMANN: Jeff Bostic was my center. To me, the most underrated position in football is the center position. They're the traffic cops. They're the ones who direct the slide of the line. They're the ones who have to get you the ball and then reach to do a cut-off block. They have the toughest challenge up front, equal to what I believe the quarterback has to do under center. And Jeff was terrific.

CHARLEY CASSERLY: When I went and scouted Joe Jacoby at Louisville in the fall of 1980, we had him rated as a free-agent offensive tackle, which probably everybody did. I was watching the tape and he played David

Galloway, a defensive lineman, from Florida, and did well. Galloway ended up being a second-round pick of the St. Louis Cardinals. He played Greg Meisner from Pittsburgh, and Joe shut him out. Meisner was a third-round pick of the Los Angeles Rams.

I told Joe Jacoby we were going to come back in the spring and work him out again and that I wanted to see him in better shape. We went through the draft meetings and no one really liked him except Joe Bugel and me. Joe Jacoby wasn't drafted; we brought him in, signed him, and took him to see Joe Gibbs.

Coach Gibbs took one look at this 6'7", 295-pound guy and said, "Hey, this is a great place to come. We drafted five offensive linemen. God, we need defensive tackles like you."

We told Coach Gibbs, "No, he's an offensive tackle." Coach Gibbs then asked if we could get out of the contract, and we said, "No, we can't get out of the contract."

Our first-round pick in '81, Mark May, an offensive tackle from Pitt, was holding out, so we put Joe Jacoby at left tackle and he looked like a natural there. He was a big guy, he had long arms, and he could stay on his feet. He ended up staying at left tackle and we put May at right tackle.

In the third round, we took Russ Grimm, a center from Pitt who we moved to guard. Bobby believed in this guy. He thought he could be a great player and he was.

In the fifth round, we took Dexter Manley, a defensive end from Oklahoma State. Dexter was a hell of a pass-rusher. He loved football and worked his ass off in practice.

One of my favorite stories about Dexter was when we were playing the Dallas Cowboys for the first time in his rookie year. They must have run a trap like 10 times in a row. He never read the frickin' thing. In year two, the first time they ran that trap, he shoved it right back in their faces.

JOE THEISMANN: As an offense, we were lost in '81; we didn't have an identity. We had an identity that Joe had brought with him, but it didn't suit our personnel.

We were still looking for ourselves in '82—our kicker, Mark Moseley, was the MVP of the NFL that year—and we found ourselves in '83. That was when we led the NFL in scoring with 541 points and that really became the foundation of everything Joe did after I left in '85. We were unstoppable.

It was a question of us being the attackers. We were always going to push the envelope in and out of the huddle. Get to the line of scrimmage and make them defend us, make them identify personnel, make them identify movement. Our goal was, because of the movement and placement of personnel, to basically have them play a base defense where it would be easy for me to read, it would be easy for our offensive linemen to read where they were lined up, and it helped with the efficiency of what we wanted to do on the offensive side of the ball.

We went at them fast; we went at them at a pace. We asked certain players on the defensive side of the ball to do things that they weren't comfortable with. If they went four across the board, trying not to play the strong safety too close or not to play the free safety too far back, then we'd run play action. We could run a post route up top on one of those safeties or we could run a tight end right down the middle against either one of the safeties.

It was an offense that built on itself, and each week it would be a little bit different. We could give you the same look, but it was going to be a different play.

Even though everybody talked about our offense and Joe Gibbs in 1983, our giveaway-takeaway ratio was plus-43. That was better than any other team in any era. In fact, I don't think there's anybody that could get half of that. So, yeah, we had a great offense that scored a lot of points, but what we managed to do was have a defense that got us the ball in position to do it.

Then, all of a sudden, we could just turn our running game loose. It was somewhat of a simple formula: play great defense, take the lead, make them start to put the ball in the air, make them one-dimensional.

JOE GIBBS: It seems like when everybody talks about me, they normally talk about offense, and I feel bad. I've always believed defense leads you and that special teams are the heart of your team.

Our defense led us to Super Bowls. Richie Petitbon, our defensive coordinator; LaVern Torgeson, our defensive line coach; Larry Peccatiello, our linebackers coach; and Emmitt Thomas, our defensive backs coach, just did a fantastic job. Wayne Sevier, my friend from the college years, did an unbelievable job coaching our special teams.

CHARLEY CASSERLY: In the '83 draft, we made Darrell Green the last pick of the first round. Miami had picked Dan Marino one spot earlier. After picking Darrell, Bobby Beathard said, "That saved me from all those Dan Marino questions." Both guys are in the Hall of Fame.

Darrell's talent at Texas A&M–Kingsville wasn't a secret, but he was only 5'8" and 169 pounds. I used to say he could go to Tysons Corner, the big mall near our practice facility in Virginia, and people wouldn't know who the hell he was.

He was lightning fast. He tied with Carl Lewis for fastest 100 meters in the world. He could have gone to the Olympics, but he was a football player first.

In our draft meetings, there was never any question in my mind that this was the guy Bobby wanted. There were people in the building who were kind of questioning it, but Bobby never questioned it.

After minicamp, some of the coaches weren't sure about Darrell. He wasn't a technician. I don't know if he ever was a technician. But he had the speed with great instincts and reflexes, and he could jump.

The opening game of his rookie year we were playing Dallas. Tony Dorsett took off on a run and it looked like he was going the distance. But here comes this guy out of nowhere and Dorsett looks like he's in slow motion. Darrell tackled him.

JOE THEISMANN: We went 14–2, beat San Francisco in the NFC Championship Game, and went back to the Super Bowl, facing the Los Angeles Raiders in Super Bowl XVIII in Tampa. We had beaten the Raiders in the regular season 37–35 at our place. The problem was that they didn't have Mike Haynes at cornerback. Marcus Allen didn't play in that game, either.

When we got to Tampa, it just didn't feel right. The year before, we didn't know what to expect in the Super Bowl. Now, we knew what to expect. We had a great practice on Thursday. Friday, I got a little stale. Saturday, I got a little staler. Sunday, I played a terrible football game.

We were down 14–3 and on our 12-yard line with 12 seconds to go in the half. We called timeout. I walked to the sideline and asked Coach Gibbs what he wanted to run. He said he wanted to run "Rocket Screen."

"Coach, I don't like putting the ball in the air backed up this far. It doesn't make sense."

"It worked against them last time."

I was thinking, *You don't think they know that?*

I started jogging on the field. I got five yards away and I turned around. Joe pointed his finger at me and said, "Run it!"

I thought, *Okay, fine. I'm the quarterback, you're the coach.*

It looked like the Raiders were in zone. They had taken out Matt Millen and put in Jack Squirek, specifically to cover our running back, Joe Washington, coming out of the backfield. I took the snap, I dropped back, I looked to my right to look the safety off. I turned to throw the ball to Joe. All of a sudden, I saw Jack start breaking for Joe, but the ball had already left my hand.

Remember the movie with Bruce Dern, *Black Sunday*, where he's up in the air in a dirigible and he's got a high-powered rifle and the ball gets shot out of the air? That was what I was hoping for. I was hoping that the ball would just go *poom*, and just fall harmlessly to the ground and we would go into the locker room down 14–3. I wasn't that fortunate. Squirek intercepted and returned it five yards for a touchdown to give the Raiders a 21–3 halftime lead. We lost 38–9.

About six years after that, I was with Joe Gibbs at a function for his Youth for Tomorrow charity. I said, "Coach, I've been eating this thing for a long time and it's bothered me."

"What's the problem?"

"You know that call you made in Super Bowl XVIII, Rocket Screen? Of all the time that we were together, that was one of the worst calls you made."

"You know what, Joe? I agree with you. But I've got to tell you something: that pass you threw was one of the worst I've seen too."

JOE GIBBS: Doug Williams, another of the great quarterbacks I was blessed to coach, is a great story. When I was in Tampa, as an assistant under John McKay in 1978, we had the 17th pick in the first round. Coach McKay came to me and said, "Hey, there's a quarterback at Grambling I want you to go see. Try and find out everything you can about this kid, Doug Williams."

I was there for three days and got to know Doug really well. I sat in the back of some of the classes he was teaching as a student teacher in Monroe, Louisiana. We'd go to McDonald's and get burgers, and then we would get in front of the blackboard and talk football.

DOUG WILLIAMS: In 1978, Coach Gibbs was the only coach who came down to visit me at Grambling. I was doing student teaching in Monroe, and Coach spent two days with me. He sat in the back of the class. He didn't say anything. He just watched.

When school was out, we spent two or three hours talking about life in general, then football. We did that for a couple of days. He took me to lunch at McDonald's. That was big.

JOE GIBBS: Now, don't get me wrong. Coach McKay deserves the credit for selecting Doug. He was the one who told me to go see Doug. That was his draft choice.

When I came back, I did say, "Listen, Coach, this guy's really football bright and he can throw it. This guy's legit."

DOUG WILLIAMS: My rookie year at Tampa, I got to training camp late because of the contract negotiation, so I missed a week of practice. When I got there, Coach Gibbs would take me home with him, and I had dinner at his house every night during training camp. We sat at the table going over the offensive scheme and everything. And he did this with a wife and two sons at home.

The quarterbacks coach was Bill Nelsen, bless his soul. His voice was real loud, even when he was just talking. One day, something went wrong—I missed something—and Bill just started screaming at me.

Joe, who was coaching the running backs at that time and would be there for only one year before becoming offensive coordinator of the Chargers, sprinted from one end of the field all the way to the other and he told Bill, "Don't holler at him! He just got here, and he's got to learn like everybody else. Do not holler at him!"

It was almost one of those situations where the whole field stood still. You've got your first-round pick, your prized rookie coming in, and the coach is hollering at him and another coach is telling him, "Don't holler at him anymore." It was an interesting situation, especially for me coming from Grambling. That didn't happen.

What made it even more meaningful to me was the fact that Joe Gibbs took the time out to say, "Whatever you don't know, we're going to make sure you know it. You're going to go home with me every day after practice."

The first game of my rookie year, we played the New York Giants, and as I was scrambling to the sideline, Gary Jeter hit me late. I didn't think anything of it. I went to the huddle, then I walked to the line of scrimmage for the next play.

But when I moved my left arm to put it up under center, there was so much pain, I fell to the ground. John McKay, our coach, said, "Damn! They shot him!" It turned out that I had a separated shoulder and I missed some games.

It was tough playing in Tampa at that time, because from a racial standpoint and being one of the only Blacks in the league playing quarterback, a lot of people weren't ready for that. I remembered sitting in the locker room in Tampa when you get a box in the mail with a rotten watermelon in it with a note saying, "Throw this to the end. Maybe they can catch this."

I got all kinds of mail like that. I got to the point in Tampa where, when I got mail without a return address, I didn't even open it; I threw it in the trash can. I felt like every time I got one without an address on it, it was a derogatory type of letter.

We showed some promise early. The first win I was part of as a Buccaneer was against the Vikings in Minnesota. They had the great Hall of Famer Fran Tarkenton. After the game, I looked for him to shake his hand, but Fran was nowhere to be found.

I got my jaw broke when we played against the Rams at the L.A. Coliseum. I thought I just had a couple of teeth knocked out, and I told the dentist to just go on and pull them out. I wanted to go back in to play, and he said, "No, it's a little worse than that. Your jaw is broken in three places."

I had to fly back from L.A. to Tampa with a wrap around my head, and for seven weeks I had my jaw wired shut. I had lost 20 pounds, and I decided to play the last game of the season with rubber bands in my mouth.

I thought I was gonna be in Tampa all my life as a player. After the 1982 season, when my father was in New Orleans, getting his leg amputated, Ken Herock, our director of player personnel, called me and said, "When are you going to come back here? We're going to try to work something out." They had offered me $400,000, and I turned them down.

I flew to Tampa and Phil Krueger, who was working in the front office, said "the old man," Hugh Culverhouse, was not happy.

"What do you mean?

"By you not signing your contract, the ticket sales are going down. And this is what we figure. Rather than offer $400,000, we'll offer you $375,000 and give you an incentive package. If you finish in the top 10, we'll give you this much. If you do this, we'll give you this much."

I stopped him.

"Hey, Phil, I've been here five years. I've gotten my ass kicked. I haven't said one word about anybody's blocking. I haven't said one word about catching the ball. I don't want any gift money. It is what it is."

"Well, you're not going to make the Hall of Fame."

I went down to Coach McKay's office and told him that it wasn't going to work out.

"Dougie, why don't you just sign a one-year deal at that $400,000 and we'll go from there?"

"No, Coach, don't worry about it."

That same year my wife, Janice, passed away. At that time, I had a five-month-old daughter. Football didn't resonate as much as it did early on because I realized that I could live without football. I had just lost my wife, so I wasn't going to take any deal they were offering.

Ken Herock called me and said, 'Would you take $500,000?"

"Yeah."

Ken tried to get Mr. C. to go up to $500,000 and he wouldn't even move. I just sat out the whole 1983 season and did substitute teaching at my brother's high school in Louisiana.

In '84, I signed with the United States Football League. We played a year in Tulsa and then we moved to Arizona. After the USFL folded, only one coach called me, and that was Joe Gibbs. Joe Theismann had gotten hurt in 1985, and in '86, Coach Gibbs, who was the only guy who called me

Douglas, called me and said, "Douglas, could you come to Washington to be the backup?"

"Coach, I can be anything you want me to be because I don't have a job."

Coming from Tampa to the Washington Redskins at that time was a world of difference. In Washington, you had nostalgia and an established team, and from a fan standpoint and an organizational standpoint, it was two different worlds. The coaching staff had unity, had been there for a while, and I was fortunate to be with a bunch of veterans who had been there and been to the Super Bowl. The offensive line was intact. You had skilled people who were intact.

The first season I was in Washington, I threw one pass all year and that was toward the end of the season.

JOE GIBBS: When the USFL folded, we got Doug and receivers Gary Clark, Ricky Sanders, and Clarence Verdin, whose nickname was CNN because he was always talking trash.

We had Jay Schroeder as our starter. He was a young guy with a lot of talent. When we had young guys at quarterback, I wanted a veteran behind him. If it was the opposite, with a veteran guy starting, I liked having a young guy as a backup. That was the case when Theismann was a seasoned veteran and we had Jay Schroeder.

Our best practices during training camp in Carlisle, Pennsylvania, were Wednesday nights. I remember the Wednesday night that the USFL guys showed up to run the other team's plays. With Doug throwing and these three fresh receivers, they shredded us. Our defense was saying, "Where in the hell did these guys come from?"

In '86, Doug got some limited playing time and really looked good. The next year, word came out that we were considering trading Doug to the Raiders. Bobby Beathard and all of us talked it over and we kind of made up our mind we were going to do it.

Then, overnight, as we thought about it, we came to the conclusion that we needed Doug backing up Jay. I called Doug into my office the next morning and told him we weren't going to make that trade. I remember Doug standing there and saying, "You can't do that! I'm going to the Raiders."

"Doug, we're not doing this. We really need you here. You're gonna do something special for us."

He was so upset with me, but to show you what kind of person Doug was, after he left my office, he never—to my knowledge—said another word about it during the rest of his time with the Redskins. He went downstairs to the weight room.

Afterwards I asked the weight coach, Dan Riley, who I had great respect for, "What was he like?"

"He was fine. He worked his butt off. He didn't say anything about not being traded." Doug was a class act.

DOUG WILLIAMS: In 1987, we played the Rams in L.A. during the preseason. We flew back overnight and when I came down the stairs of our plane, Coach Gibbs and Bobby Beathard were at the bottom. They pulled me aside and said, "Hey, we traded you to the Raiders."

I was happy because now I had a chance to be a star. The Raiders had tried to trade for me when I was in Tampa, but Al Davis, the Raiders' owner, and Hugh Culverhouse, who owned the Buccaneers, didn't have a great relationship. The Buccaneers would not trade me to the Raiders.

Coach Gibbs told me to come by his office by 11:00 that morning. I went to my apartment and packed up all my clothes. I called home in Louisiana and told everybody I was going to be playing for the Raiders. When I went to Coach Gibbs' office, I was sitting in front of his desk and he looked at me and he just started laughing. He said, "I've changed my mind."

I got out of my chair and said, "Coach, you can't change your mind."

That was the first time I saw Coach get upset.

"Hey, I don't work for the Raiders," he said. "I work for the Washington Redskins."

I sat back down in my chair. Before I left Coach Gibbs' office, he told me, "I've got a good feeling that somewhere along the line, you're gonna come in here and we're gonna win this thing."

At the time, that didn't mean anything to me because I had just been shunned from an opportunity to be a star quarterback and I had a coach telling me he had a gut feeling. That didn't resonate.

I just went back to my locker and got ready for the season. I was disappointed, but there was nothing you could do about it except roll with the punches.

But the first game of the season, Jay Schroeder got hurt against the Philadelphia Eagles and I came in and led the team to victory.

CHARLEY CASSERLY: After the second game of the '87 season, the players went on strike. We signed replacement players. We signed some guys who hadn't played in a year. We picked up some guys out of Canada. We signed four guys from a halfway house. We basically were signing anybody.

None of our players crossed the picket line. Joe Gibbs told the team, "You go out together, you come back together."

We played three games with replacements. The first one was against the St. Louis Cardinals, who had 14 guys cross the picket line. We were struggling in the game. We were about ready to pull our quarterback, a guy named Ed Rubbert, and put in Tony Robinson, who was one of the guys we signed from the halfway house. This was street football.

Finally, Dan Henning, our offensive coordinator, said, "Tell Anthony Allen to run a post-corner route and let's see what happens." Allen ran the post-corner, they couldn't cover him, and he wound up catching seven passes for 255 yards and three touchdowns. We won the game.

Next, we played the Giants, who filled most of their roster with a minor league team from Connecticut. We were playing a 4:00 game. John Madden and Pat Summerall were doing the TV broadcast. There were 4,000 people in the stands at Giants Stadium. In the fourth quarter, one of the CBS cameras showed a player from the Giants asleep while sitting on the bench. Lionel Vital, our running back, ran for 128 yards and we won that game big.

The last replacement game was on a Monday night against the Cowboys. They had some starters on the team—Danny White, Randy White, Tony Dorsett, Ed "Too Tall" Jones. What we were told later was that there were annuities for them that had to be funded, but that they would only be funded if they played.

I thought we had zero chance to win the game. But Joe Gibbs gave a great speech. I wasn't there, but I verified it with him afterward. He said, "Men, this is why you're here, to prove you could play in the National Football League. So what greater stage to have than *Monday Night Football* with every other team watching you against the Dallas Cowboys, with their best players out there. These are the guys you want to play against. This is your chance to prove you can play in the league."

Those kids went out there and played their ass off. Vital ran for 136 yards, Tony Robinson threw a couple of touchdown passes, and we won 13–7.

Our first game after the strike was against the Jets at RFK. We were playing like crap and the fans started to chant, "We want the scabs! We want the scabs!"

Our players rallied and we won the game.

DOUG WILLIAMS: I came off the bench during three games after Jay Schroeder came out because he was inefficient, and we won all three games.

One of the games was the day after Christmas. We were in Minnesota and we had already clinched a spot in the playoffs. But we were trailing. Coach Gibbs put me in in the fourth quarter, and we came back and won the game. In the postgame interview—and I had no idea he was going to do this—Coach Gibbs announced that I was going to be the starting quarterback for the playoffs. It surprised me, but it was a good surprise.

We had to go to Chicago the next week.

CHARLEY CASSERLY: Our video guy was Nate Fine, who to that point had filmed every game in the history of the Redskins—from 1937 to 1987. He had cancer and he was dying, but he hadn't missed a practice or a game. Everybody loved Nate.

The night before the Bears playoff game, Joe Gibbs got up in front of the team and said, "Men, there's nothing more I want to do than hand a Super Bowl trophy to Nate Fine." There wasn't a dry eye in the place.

DOUG WILLIAMS: With the wind chill and everything, it was 13-below at Soldier Field. I had never played in weather that cold in my life. We were trailing 14–0 and we came back and ended up winning 21–17.

The following week we had to play the Vikings, who we had just played three weeks earlier. We won 17–10. I probably had the worst game I'd had in a long time as far as my stats. I was 9-for-26, but I had two TD passes. I was so disappointed in the way I played. After the game, our offensive coordinator, Dan Henning, sat at my locker and asked me what was wrong.

"I played like shit."

"What do you mean? You threw about four balls away to keep from getting sacked. You didn't throw any interceptions. You threw two TD passes. And we won."

That did help cheer me up. My thing was to never take sacks and not worry about what my completion percentage was going to be or anything like that. I had this mentality that it was better to be third-and-10 than third-and-15, third-and-17.

JOE GIBBS: Doug had one of the best arms I had ever seen. He was the only quarterback I had been around, when he would throw the ball in practice, many times the players would say, "Did you see that?" He also had touch. He was big and super strong.

The other thing about Doug was he had great vision. He would come to the sideline and tell me, "Hey, I think that we can work that free safety." Doug was also a real leader. I think a lot of the players looked up to him.

By the end of that season, Doug was our starter and got us to the Super Bowl.

All of us looked at Doug as just our quarterback. But when we got to San Diego for Super Bowl XXII against the Broncos, everybody was talking about him being the first Black quarterback to start the Super Bowl.

DOUG WILLIAMS: The two weeks before the Super Bowl, every reporter wanted to interview me. And it was all about being Black. It was nothing about football. It was all about being the first Black quarterback to start in the Super Bowl.

I had told myself that I wasn't going to get caught up in it because I thought it was going to be a distraction, not only for me but for the team as a whole. I made a concerted effort to dodge all those questions, so I just stayed out of the way of the public basically the whole week. I just went to practice and went home each day.

We flew to San Diego and all the reporters were there looking for a sound-bite. I said to myself I was only going to do the interviews I was required to do by the league.

The first day that we did interviews, I had all these reporters around me. One of them was Butch Jones, a writer from Jackson, Miss. I knew Butch because he covered Grambling. There were so many people around and everybody was trying to get a question in, and I knew where Butch was coming from when he got this question in that became something people have talked about and written about ever since: "How long have you been a Black quarterback?"

Everybody looked at him like, "What?" I didn't want to embarrass Butch, so I said, "The emphasis of me being a Black quarterback only started when I left Grambling."

I got an email from Butch before he passed away. He told me that he appreciated the way I handled the question because even though it made him look bad, I answered it in a way that put him at ease.

The morning before the game, I woke up and had a toothache. It came out of the clear blue. I went to Dr. Barry Rudolph, who was our team dentist, and he called a friend of his in La Jolla, not too far from San Diego. We went to his office and took an X-ray, and I ended up spending four hours having a root canal done.

I didn't practice at all on that Saturday. When I got back to our hotel, we were packing up to move to the hotel that we were going to stay in the night before the game. I was taking medication, but it was still painful.

We were staying at the Lawrence Welk Resort. Anthony Jones was my roommate and when we walked into our room, we heard Lawrence Welk music being piped in. If you've ever listened to Lawrence Welk music, it doesn't go good with pain. I said, "A.J., you've got to find the volume, man. I can't live with that." We were able to turn the music down.

I sat in meetings, came back to the room. I ate a bag of Hershey's Kisses every Saturday night before a game, and I still had my kisses. I ate them on the side opposite the root canal, the right side, and spent most of the night looking at the playbook and going over the game plan and the signals. I woke up the next morning and went to breakfast, and I didn't feel one iota of pain.

I got on the bus and we were driving back to San Diego to Jack Murphy Stadium for our game against Denver. For me, it was a chance to reflect on my whole life, looking back from where I came and the road that I traveled to get to that game.

I thought about how grateful I was to have played for Eddie Robinson at Grambling and all the people I played for along the way. Coach Robinson was that mentor, that guy you hung your hat on because he gave you value. It wasn't about just football with him. It wasn't the Xs and Os. Coach talked about being a good American.

Coach Rob had never ever seen me play football in high school. Back then, we had a guy named Adolph Byrd who lived in the Baton Rouge area and who recruited me. Adolph had played for Coach Robinson, who recruited through his ex-players. Coach Rob believed if one of his former players called him and said, "You need to sign this guy," Coach Rob would sign that guy because Coach Rob knew the former player knew what Coach Rob wanted in a player.

Growing up in rural Louisiana, we had a Southern Bell party line phone. Coach Rob called late one night. I was sleeping and my mom came and woke me up. She said, "Coach Robinson's on the line and you're going to Grambling."

Actually, I wanted to go to Southern University, which was about 15 minutes from my house. I wanted to go there because now my mom and dad would get a chance to see me play. Grambling was like a four-hour drive from my house, but she said, "You're going to Grambling."

My older brother had gone to Grambling. We had a lot of people from my high school who went to Grambling.

I asked my mom, "Why am I going to Grambling?"

"Because Coach Robinson said you're going to go to class and you're going to graduate." My dad would have had a big problem if I'd have argued with my mom and told her I wasn't going to Grambling.

Coach Rob redshirted me my first year. The following spring, I thought I had the best spring practice of all the quarterbacks. When the season began, I wasn't playing. We lost against Alcorn and then we barely beat Northwestern State. I thought I was gonna play that game because we were playing that bad.

I was crying because I wanted to play. My brother came to me and said, "What you crying for?"

"I should have been playing."

On Monday of the following week, I didn't go to practice. Fred Hobdy, who was the basketball coach and the athletic director at the time, and Coach Rob were buddy-buddy. They called each other "Lefty." They were very tight. I was in my dorm room watching *The Big Valley*, and Coach Hobdy came up and said, "Hell, what do you think you're doing?"

"Coach, I quit. I ain't playing anymore."

"You better get your ass out there."

When I came down, practice was half over. I thought I was going to give everybody the silent treatment. I wasn't saying anything to anybody. Not one word. But I realized that nobody was saying anything to me, either. Finally, Coach Ernie Sterling, our defensive line coach, came to me and said, "Coach Rob wants to see you."

When I went to see Coach Rob, he was getting dressed, putting on his shoes.

"Sit down, Cat," he said. Coach Rob called everyone "Cat." He asked me what was on my mind.

"Coach, I'm going to transfer over to Southern."

"Hell. You ain't going to transfer and come back and beat the hell out of me. The only reason why you ain't playing is because of me. Hell, if I put you in there, those other boys aren't ever going to play again."

Joe Comeaux was the starter. Terry Brown was the backup, and I was third team. Coach Rob believed in seniority and wanted me to wait my turn.

When I did get my first taste of playing in college against Prairie View in Dallas, I led a drive all the way down the field and threw my first touchdown pass to Sammy White. We were blowing them out and Coach Rob took me out and put in Terry. I didn't understand it, but then I realized Coach Rob didn't want me to outshine Terry.

The next week, we were playing Tennessee State. Joe Comeaux broke his wrist, and Coach Rob put Terry in. We weren't moving the football, so he took Terry out. Coach Rob said, "Where's that Williams boy at?" I was looking for my helmet. I found it, I went into the game, and we ended up winning.

In the sixth game of my freshman year, I started, and the rest was history. I played the next three and a half years at quarterback. When I left Grambling in 1977, I was the all-time passing leader in NCAA history with 8,400 yards and 93 TDs.

I thought about the journey taking me to the USFL, where I took a pretty good beating physically. All that kind of stuff resonated with me on that bus ride. Just being able to put all that stuff behind me was a great moment.

Running out of that dressing room before the game and the flyover and everything, and then standing on the sideline and looking around the stadium, knowing that my mom and about 12 other people from my family were behind me with a big sign that read ZACHARY, LOUISIANA, I felt that it was football and I had dodged the bullet of getting caught up in being Black.

I always looked at it from the standpoint that Washington did not bring me to San Diego as a Black quarterback. They brought me to San Diego as the quarterback who just happened to be Black.

The first quarter was terrible for us. We couldn't get anything going. On one play, Gary Clark, who's probably one of the toughest SOBs I've ever played with and sure-handed, dropped a third-down pass that hit him in the hands and would have given us a first down.

The next series, I went back to pass, did a split while being sacked, and hyperextended my knee. Jay Schroeder came in for two plays in the last couple of minutes of the first quarter. He got sacked on the first one and threw an incompletion on the second, and we had to punt.

JOE GIBBS: We were down 10–0 in the first quarter. The Raiders had beat us in our second Super Bowl, and I thought, "We're gonna get our butt kicked again."

DOUG WILLIAMS: While the trainers were tending to me, Coach Gibbs said, "Doug, you good to go?"

"Yeah, Coach, I can go."

He hit me on my knee and said, "Okay, we're going to get this sucker rolling."

Our first play of the second quarter was a routine play called "Charlie-10 Hitch." That was a fake to the fullback up the middle and the receiver would run a seven-yard hitch. Mark Haynes came up to press Ricky Sanders. We always said, with our receivers, whether it was Gary Clark, Ricky Sanders, or Art Monk, if it's press coverage with no safety help, we win. On the fake, everything converted to fade. Mark Haynes went up to stab Ricky with his left hand and missed. I just lobbed the ball up, Ricky took it, and 75 yards later, we scored.

On the next 18 plays in the second quarter, we scored 35 points. It seemed like we were running on all cylinders. Our offensive line was blowing the defensive line out of the box. The receivers were getting open. Everything we called, anything we checked to, was working.

JOE GIBBS: From that point on, it seemed I could shut my eyes and everything we called would have gone for 10 yards. I'd never been a part of anything like that.

DOUG WILLIAMS: We went into halftime with a 35–10 lead. My knee was hurting. I was in excruciating pain. Joe Bugel, our assistant head coach and offensive line coach, used to call me "Stud," because he knew if I was in the pocket, I wasn't going anywhere. He used to always tell his offensive line, "He's going to be in the pocket, so protect him."

Coach Bugel walked up to me at halftime and said, "Stud, it's 35–10. I think we can hold them from here. You don't have to play if you don't want to." I said, "Buges, I started this game, I'm gonna finish this game."

I went to the doctors. They took this long needle and they shot my knee up. It felt pretty good once I went back out there. We didn't throw the ball much; we ran the ball and killed the clock. We only scored another seven points. Coach Gibbs and Dan Reeves, the Broncos' coach, were friends. And Coach Gibbs is probably one of best sportsmanship guys you ever want to see. What we did wasn't about embarrassing the Broncos; it was about keeping the ball away from them.

One of the most chilling moments for me was, when they announced me as MVP, all the players came and tapped me on the helmet. It was one of those situations when you realized it was all about the team. It wasn't about one individual. And it was all happening for me because they knew what I had been through with everybody wanting to make it about the Black quarterback.

I was walking off the field with Joe Jacoby. He said, "Doug Williams, red, purple, green, it doesn't matter. You are our quarterback."

That was one of the best comments to be made from a teammate.

Going through the tunnel after the game, I saw Coach Robinson. I didn't know he was at the game. The NFL had brought him in. When I saw him, he started crying and I started crying. He said, "Hey, Cat. Today was like Joe Louis knocking out Max Schmeling. You don't understand now, but you'll understand down the road."

I went in the locker room and Joe Gibbs said, "I told you."

The hunch he had in the preseason that I was going to come in and we were going to win this thing was a dream come true.

JOE GIBBS: Our quarterback in 1991 when we went 14–2 was Mark Rypien. Mark was born in Canada. We had drafted him in the sixth round from Washington State in 1986.

Mark's football intelligence was just off the charts. If I was drawing something on the board, and I asked a question, he would answer the question before anybody else could answer. He was so in tuned to football.

We could do anything with Rypien. I think two of his years he was the least-sacked quarterback in the league. And here was a guy who was not going to run. But he was so smart, he knew every outlet, he knew every hot read. He could see pressure and get rid of the ball.

The other thing about Mark I'll always remember was he never missed anything deep. If you had something open deep, that man hit it.

CHARLEY CASSERLY: The 1991 season was magical. We opened the playoffs at home against Atlanta. We had beaten the Falcons 56–17 during the season. Jerry Glanville, with his big mouth, bragged that they were going to come and beat us in the playoffs.

It was raining the day of the game. We got off to a slow start and we eventually ended up grinding them out. We had given away seat cushions for the game. Well, guess what? The raindrops stopped falling and then it began raining seat cushions as fans started throwing them on the field to celebrate the fact we were advancing.

In Redskins history, if you say, "Seat Cushion Game," they remember it, just like the "Body Bag Game" the year before when Buddy Ryan told the media they were going to administer a beating so bad that our players would "have to be carted off in body bags." Philadelphia won that game and nine of our guys left with injuries.

We faced Detroit in the conference championship game and dominated. That put us in Super Bowl XXVI against Buffalo.

BILL POLIAN: We had just come off a 13–3 season and an extremely hard-fought AFC Championship Game against the Denver Broncos in which the first points were not scored until well into the third quarter on an interception return by our inside linebacker, Carlton Bailey.

We went into the game with some injury issues. Bruce Smith's knee was not 100 percent. Strong safety Leonard Smith was out. And early in the first quarter, inside linebacker Shane Conlan was lost for the game with a knee injury. It was not the best of matchups versus the Hogs, and that proved to be true.

Offensively, we couldn't handle the Washington pass rush and Jim Kelly was sacked five times and was eventually concussed. The Redskins defense took a calculated gamble that the officiating would be on the loose side. They were physically aggressive in defending Andre Reed, and as a result disrupted the timing of our passing game, which played a major role in Jim throwing four interceptions.

Boo to the officials and "Hail to the Redskins."

There were a number of weird occurrences before and during this game. We had designed a trap play for Thurman Thomas to run as our opening play. We thought it would be a huge gainer, possibly a touchdown. The problem was that Thurman wasn't in the game; his backup, Kenneth Davis, was. We used a different run for the opening play, and Kenneth gained only one yard. We called it on the second play, and it was ready to break open, just as we expected it would. Unfortunately, Kenneth ran to the wrong hole and Jim Kelly, with no one to hand the ball to, ran for four yards.

Thurman was not in the game because he couldn't find his helmet on the sideline. The theory is that during the national anthem, which was performed near our bench, one of Harry Connick Jr.'s musicians or support staff moved Thurman's helmet from its normal location. Weird.

Wait. It gets better. We line up for the opening kickoff. The official, Jerry Markbreit signals, "Go." The ball is kicked, we're covering, the Redskins are returning, and all of a sudden, whistles blow the play dead.

What? It was announced that CBS was still in commercial, so we had to kick off again. In hindsight, maybe we should have ended it there.

The final and most hurtful self-inflicted wound was caused by assistant coach Chuck Dickerson, who unbeknownst to most of us made fun of the Hogs during a pregame press availability. Ironically, Marv Levy always preached to the players that we should avoid giving the opposition "bulletin-board material." Dickerson must not have been listening.

As Coach Levy said after the game, we were soundly beaten by a better team.

CHARLEY CASSERLY: Jack Kent Cooke had always predicted we were going to win the Super Bowl. It was a given, as far as he was concerned. He made it clear that the accountability was to win the Super Bowl—that there was only one standard—and he held you to it.

Then, as we were riding in a cart under the tunnel, he said to me, "I can't believe we won the Super Bowl."

I almost fell out of the cart. That was his way of showing he understood how tough it was.

CHAPTER 5

From Dark Days to "Big Blue"

"A championship team understands how to play the game with the resources that they possess. They have the discipline to take care of the ball. They have the intelligence to play within the system. And they have the energy to sustain effort when their opponents won't."

—Bill Parcells

BILL POLIAN: The New York Football Giants are one of the NFL's oldest franchises, founded in 1925 by family patriarch Tim Mara.

They are still run by a third-generation Mara, team president John K. Mara. Tim Mara had two sons, John (Jack) and Wellington. They literally grew up on the sidelines of the pre–World War II NFL. The brothers eventually took over the franchise, with Jack running the business side and Wellington overseeing football.

When Jack passed away, the CEO role fell to Wellington. His acumen on all aspects of the business, coupled with his intelligence and stellar character, made him one of the NFL's most important, respected, and influential owners. John Mara admirably and ably continues his father's and grandfather's legacies both with the team and the league.

Prior to 1956, the Giants played at the Polo Grounds, summer home of the New York Baseball Giants. They were a perennial contender, appearing in eight championship games and winning three NFL titles. In '56, they moved to much larger Yankee Stadium and played a major role in making the NFL

America's No. 1 sport. They beat the Chicago Bears that year for the NFL crown and reached the championship game in '58, '59, '61, '62, and '63.

It was in 1958, however, that they lost to the Baltimore Colts in overtime in what became known as "the greatest game ever played." It was the first NFL championship game to be nationally televised and its stars, setting, and drama captured the interest of America's sporting public.

The Giants, led by Frank Gifford, Andy Robustelli, Sam Huff, and Rosey Brown, had already won the hearts of New Yorkers, including this writer and all of his friends, many of whom still own Giants season tickets to this day. Those Giants were coached by Jim Lee Howell and two assistant coaches who became NFL legends, Vince Lombardi and Tom Landry.

The Colts were led by Hall of Famers Johnny Unitas, Lenny Moore, Raymond Berry, Gino Marchetti, and Art Donovan. They were coached by Hall of Famer Weeb Ewbank, who would go on to win a Super Bowl in New York with the AFL refugee Jets.

After a Steve Myhra field goal capped a brilliant two-minute Unitas drive to send the game into overtime, Colts fullback Alan Ameche scored on a goal-line plunge to give the NFL title to the Colts. The iconic photo of Ameche crossing the goal line in the gathering darkness of Yankee Stadium remains the enduring image of the game that catapulted the NFL to the top of the sports world.

After the '63 championship game loss to the Bears, hard times fell upon the Giants. In 1976, they left New York City to move to a new stadium in the New Jersey Meadowlands. The new Giants Stadium didn't help the team's play on the field. The Giants' record from 1964 to 1979 was 80–144–4, with no playoff appearances.

Wellington Mara and his co-owner, nephew Tim Mara, were feuding. But with help from NFL commissioner Pete Rozelle, they settled on a new general manager, George Young, who had been the personnel director of Don Shula's Super Bowl–champion Miami Dolphins. George began his journey to the Hall of Fame by drafting quarterback Phil Simms and linebackers Lawrence Taylor and Carl Banks and inheriting Hall of Fame linebacker Harry Carson.

Young's original head-coaching hire was Ray Perkins. When Perkins departed for Alabama in '83, Young named a little-known "Jersey Guy," defensive coordinator Bill Parcells, head coach. The Parcells Giants became what Giants fans proudly refer to today as "Big Blue."

Playing ferocious defense and power offense, they won two Super Bowls, in the '86 season over Denver and in the '90 season over the Buffalo Bills, while I was the Bills' GM.

The saying "life is stranger than fiction" is certainly apropos in this saga.

Wellington Mara and Vince Lombardi were contemporaries at Fordham University, which is located four blocks from where I went to grade school. The Giants often practiced there. I, along with some close friends who were Giants fanatics, occasionally "missed class" to watch them.

Bill Parcells and I are contemporaries and grew up 20 minutes as the crow flies from one another—Bill in northern New Jersey, me in the Bronx. We're both baseball fanatics, he with the baseball Giants and me with the Yankees. When Parcells became head coach, he named as his defensive coordinator Bill Belichick, who as head coach of the New England Patriots became our principal rival when I was with the Indianapolis Colts.

Finally, George Young, after college, became a successful high school coach in Baltimore. In a time when NFL staffs were very small, he moonlighted as a scout and later became a full-time coach for the Unitas-Donovan-Marchetti Colts. To complete the *Ripley's Believe It or Not!* tale, Young and I served together on the NFL Competition Committee, the original iteration of which included Wellington Mara and Vince Lombardi. At different times, both George and I served as vice president of football operations under NFL Commissioner Paul Tagliabue.

In this chapter, you will hear about the Giants' return to prominence and what defined their "Big Blue" success through the voices of John Mara, Parcells, Simms, Banks, and Carson. You'll also get insights into the brilliant coaching mind of Bill Belichick, who was Parcells' defensive coordinator.

JOHN MARA: The dark period for us extended from 1964 through 1980, where we had very few winning seasons. We were never in the playoffs and really were just kind of floundering.

It was pretty brutal living through it as a youngster, when you see your father take that type of criticism. I still have this horrible image of him being hung in effigy from the third deck of Giants Stadium.

We were always trying to find Y.A. Tittle's replacement at quarterback. We had made a lot of trades in that era, gave up a lot of picks to try to find him. We found some success with Fran Tarkenton for a while, but never quite enough to get us over the hump. We made some poor trades. We gave up a lot of draft picks for Craig Morton, who was a decent player, but he certainly was not going to get us over the hump. We kept trying to engineer a quick fix and it just never quite worked. The draft was the way to have done it.

The '81 season was when it really started to change. I still remember one of the happiest experiences I ever had with my father was when we beat the Cowboys in the final game of the '81 season. It looked like we were going to the playoffs for the first time in all those years. The press box elevator was not working, so we had to walk through the stands to get to the locker room. The walk with him from the press box down to the locker room would have been unthinkable a few years prior to that.

But walking down—with people congratulating him, slapping him on the back, shaking his hand—it occurred to me: *It's unbelievable how quickly things change.* When you're losing, everybody hates you. Everybody thinks you're dishonest, immoral, and greedy. All of a sudden, you start winning some games and the entire perception changes, even about your character, which is ridiculous. But that's just always been the society we live in. Winners get a certain respect that losers never do. To me, that was such a key moment in our history. Having a winning season in '81 and going to the playoffs just changed the whole narrative about the franchise.

My father and his nephew, my cousin Tim Mara, started having some disagreements. In 1978, it really kind of boiled over. That was when Andy Robustelli, who had been a Hall of Fame defensive end for us, decided he wasn't coming back as our general manager. My father and Tim had a dispute over who was going to be the replacement and how we were going to get that replacement.

Unfortunately, it became public and it seemed like every day, for eternity, we were living through it on the front pages of the tabloids during that period of 1978 going into 1979. Pete Rozelle attempted to mediate that, and it got to the point where Tim rejected anybody my father and I suggested, and it was going nowhere.

I can remember my father talking to Joe Paterno, talking to John Madden, talking to Dan Reeves. Dan even flew up from Dallas; he was with the Cowboys at the time. My father met with him at our home. Tim would find out that my father was talking to some of these people and Tim would contact them and say my father didn't have authority to have the conversation. It was just a nasty thing.

My big regret was that I wasn't mature enough at the time to try to mediate and get the thing settled without all the public acrimony and all the press conferences and whatnot, which really was an embarrassment to the family. I was hot-headed and not mature enough to be able to deal with it. It was just one of those things.

A guy who was offered the job was Jan Van Duser, who was the personnel director for the NFL. Pete Rozelle had recommended him, Tim had interviewed him and liked him, and my father liked him. But Van Duser turned the job down. Maybe he felt he didn't want to work for two owners who weren't getting along and that it would be an impossible situation. Maybe he just didn't want to run a club.

All of a sudden, two of our former players—Hall of Famer Frank Gifford and Tom Scott—said, "What about this guy with the Miami Dolphins, George Young?" My father did some research on him and thought he might be somebody we ought to consider. But he knew, if he suggested it, my cousin would reject it right away. So, my father went to Pete Rozelle and said, "Why don't you suggest George Young to Tim." Pete did.

Tim was very close with Frank Gifford. I had given Frank a good recommendation on George. When Tim went back and checked with Frank, he was sold. That was how George ended up getting hired as GM on Valentine's Day 1979. It was one of the most important moments in the history of the franchise.

George Young came aboard in 1979 and rebuilt our whole scouting department and our whole grading system, and we started having those strong drafts that brought us back to a place where we could be a contender. His first pick in '79 was Phil Simms.

In that draft, the two highest-rated quarterbacks at the time were Jack Thompson, "the Throwin' Samoan" from Washington State, and much lesser-known Phil Simms from Morehead State. The public and the media wanted us to take Jack Thompson. I remember George telling me that he and Ray Perkins had scouted Simms, and both were struck by his ability. Perkins was really excited and enthused about him.

I also remember feeling sick to my stomach at the time, because I had never heard of Phil Simms from Morehead State. I wanted Thompson. He was the glamour guy at the time. Fortunately, they went ahead and chose Phil. That really started us back.

PHIL SIMMS: I probably had 20 private workouts at Morehead State. People would show up and sit in the stands because the word would spread: "Hey, today, the Kansas City Chiefs are going to be here." The Giants drafted me. I was expecting it, but the understatement of all time was it caught a lot of people by surprise to see a quarterback from Morehead State selected in the first round with the seventh pick.

There were six to seven teams that basically told me they were going to draft me in the first round, so I really felt confident about that. My favorite team that I worked out for was the 49ers and Bill Walsh, because everything he was telling me was almost the opposite of what everybody else told me. I think back to that and go, "Boy, I wish I would have listened and carried that workout over into my pro career." Just the rhythm and the pacing and the footwork and everything he was showing me that day. Everybody else wanted me to throw as hard as I could. They'd say, "How far can you throw it?" But after I threw about 10 passes for Bill Walsh, he said, "What are you doing? I want to see you be more graceful. Throw it softer. Make it look pretty." I'd never heard that from a coach.

It was a different era back then. It was about downfield throwing and power throwing. That was what I had kind of done my whole life up to that point, so I carried it over to the NFL. I'll never forget when we were gonna play the Atlanta Falcons, who at that time were in the same division with the 49ers, and we were watching film of Joe Montana, who was dropping back and it was just completion after completion.

I was going, *Oh, my God, they make it look so easy.*

Then I thought, *Man, could I have done this if I went to San Francisco?*

JOHN MARA: Phil set the tone for everybody else with his toughness, his desire to win, playing through all those injuries. He had the Super Bowl MVP year in '86, but people forget, in '90, he was the starter when we began the season 10–0. He got hurt against Buffalo and was down for the rest of the season and missed the postseason. But even though he wasn't the Super Bowl XXV quarterback, he got us off to that great start that allowed us to be in the postseason.

Phil was certainly the leader on offense and really one of the key leaders, along with Harry Carson and George Martin, on the team. He meant the world to us.

I remember Bill Parcells saying, "Phil will really be appreciated by fans and the media when he's gone. People will be wondering, 'When are we going to have another Phil Simms?'" I think that was largely true. I think it took a while for fans to really appreciate how good a player he was and how much he meant to us. I think the one quality for me that stood out was his toughness. I think of some of the hits he took over the years, some of the injuries he played through and just kept going.

He also had some great exchanges with Parcells on the sideline with the two of them barking back and forth. But they had so much respect for one another. They could have those type of exchanges because they both wanted the same thing in the end.

There's no way we even come close to having the success that we had in that period without Phil Simms as the quarterback.

CARL BANKS: We knew Phil could throw the football. I think he was an underrated thrower, just because of the style that we played. But when we needed a ball down the field, he could throw it and the beautiful part about it was he could throw it better than a lot of people in Giants Stadium, because he knew the weather—because we had to practice in it every day.

Aside from his talent, he understood how to throw the football almost like a golfer has to adjust to the wind. He knew what type of plays worked and how they would work. That was the science of playing quarterback in Giants Stadium and being good at it. We had players who could get down the field and he could throw it with the best of them. It just didn't look as sexy because all the pictures of him were in the weight room powerlifting with his offensive linemen all the time.

PHIL SIMMS: I did get hurt late in my second year. Injuries were a very common theme to my career. Scott Brunner came in and won some games, went to the playoffs.

As I look back and watch today's game, most of the injuries I had were my fault just because I played too aggressive. I stood in there too much, which was really the mantra of the day: "Stay in there, hang in the pocket, throw it, and take the hit." They say none of those things nowadays.

JOHN MARA: George Young just made us so much more of a professional football organization. We had fallen way behind the times and he added some staff and he added a new way of looking at players. He brought Tom Boisture in as director of player personnel. All of a sudden, our drafts went from becoming weak to being among the most respected in the league.

We got Lawrence Taylor in '81. Thankfully, New Orleans took George Rogers, a running back from South Carolina, with the No. 1 overall pick and there was Lawrence, who was so dominant as an outside linebacker at North Carolina, sitting there for us at No. 2. That transformed our whole team.

You always did worry about Lawrence off the field. That's been pretty well-documented. There were conversations we had about whether we should move him somewhere. But after discussions back and forth, it was decided that, "No, we're not going to move him. He's just too good. We can help him deal with some of his issues and get him to be a productive player and still be a productive human being as well."

I remember a line that Parcells had about Lawrence: "He's the pilot of a burning plane."

Fortunately, we were able to contain him long enough for him to continue playing with us because it was definitely a concern to me, with the drug use, which, again, is well-documented. But he always showed up to play on Sundays. He had as much pride as, if not more than, anybody. He was another guy who hated to lose.

We tried to help him. He did some rehab stints back then. My father developed a very close relationship with him, and he was able to play his whole career with us and obviously have a huge impact on the National Football League. When he came on board in '81, there really weren't any players who could rush the passer like that from that linebacker spot.

You had to know where he was at all times. He really affected the game and how offenses had to protect.

CARL BANKS: Whatever people thought of Lawrence Taylor in terms of, "Yeah, it came easy for him, he saw the game differently than everybody else," when it came to practice, he practiced at game speed. Even if he was on scout team, if Parcells needed him to give our offensive line a look, it was game speed. My first practice, I looked out and this guy was moving faster than I'd ever seen anybody move before.

I knew, in order to be a part of that group, I needed to be at my best all the time. I thought, "I'm merging now onto a freeway where, in my mind, I'm going like 50 or 60 mph and these guys are just flying." So I knew that I had to raise my game a level in order to even be on the field with those guys.

JOHN MARA: We added a lot of talent in those years, guys like defensive end Leonard Marshall, a second-round pick from LSU in 1983, and linebacker Carl Banks, the third overall pick of the '84 draft from Michigan State.

CARL BANKS: When I was at Michigan State, George Perles had Jack Ham, the Hall of Fame linebacker from the Pittsburgh Steelers, come in and spend the whole spring with me, teaching me techniques that helped me avoid getting hook-blocked. With Jack, nothing was really a lot of effort. He was more about footwork and leverage and knew exactly how to do it. My life changed after that spring.

I could look at offensive linemen and tight ends today, having not played a down of football in 30 years, and I could tell you which way they're gonna block, especially blocking tight ends. If they want to release or to get outside, they tighten down their stance to get you to get tighter, and then they try to hook you. If they want to come off to block you, they're going to give a wide stance so that they can get some room to get back inside.

Jack also taught me how to read releases in the pass game and how to disrupt tight ends' releases off the ball by their alignment.

JOHN MARA: We were built to win in that climate, with the wind blowing in that stadium. We had a tough defense and we could run the ball, which was what you had to do, and we had that steady-handed quarterback who was as tough as any of the guys.

PHIL SIMMS: The core of the whole team was this: big and strong; when in doubt, draft somebody big. It seemed like George Young just loved big players.

I don't think I realized until my career was over how amazing our defensive front was with Leonard Marshall, Jim Burt, Harry Carson, Pepper Johnson, Lawrence Taylor, Carl Banks. What a front! And we had reserves who should have started in the league, but they couldn't because players couldn't move from team to team back then like they do now.

We wanted to be the big, bad bullies. I'll always remember what Lawrence Taylor would say after I would turn the ball over at midfield, "Don't worry, we'll get it back to you right here."

JOHN MARA: George did a very good job of navigating between my father and Tim. He kept both of them informed at all times, so it worked. We trusted him to make the right decisions, which he did more often than not.

When George hired Ray Perkins, I remember the line that George had after he interviewed him. He said, "Ray will make it very uncomfortable in that locker room for them to lose."

That's a line that always stuck with me. Ray was so young at the time and he hadn't had a lot of experience, but George found him to be very focused, very football-smart, and very tough-minded. George felt we needed that toughness that we didn't have.

Ray was doing a good job for us. He got us into the playoffs in '81. He changed the culture in that locker room and helped us bring in some players who were tough both mentally and physically.

PHIL SIMMS: It was a transition. They basically tore the team apart to start over. And we lived up to it. We were awful. We won our first game of 1980; I threw five touchdowns. I think it was Week 10 before we had another good game on the offensive side.

It was really tough, but I learned a lot. I had some big moments. We beat the Dallas Cowboys, who at the time were 7–2 and we were 1–8. That was by far the highlight for me and the football team in my second year.

BILL PARCELLS: I had a long relationship with Ray Perkins back to when

we were both college coaches. Then he went to New England as an assistant. After that, he became offensive coordinator in San Diego and wound up getting the Giants job in '79. I joined his staff as a linebackers coach that year, my first coaching job in the NFL, and then I went to New England to coach the linebackers there.

Ray had been with the Giants for a couple of years when he asked me if I wanted to come with him and kind of run the defense for him. They had not had a good year in '80, so they were looking for help defensively in '81.

When I first got there, we were going to change the scheme to a 3-4 from a 4-3. That was what we were playing at New England and Ray told me when he hired me that he wanted to play that because he had been there and was familiar with it. We both knew what we were talking about, but that's always a transition of sorts.

We had, I would say, a small nucleus of good players who were carry-overs from the mid-70s to the late '70s. George Martin, a defensive end who wound up being my team captain for many years in the '80s, was a very good player. Harry Carson, a linebacker, is in the Hall of Fame. Both were easy to plug in.

We had a young defensive end named Curtis McGriff who fit in well, but other than Brad Van Pelt, who had been a veteran Giants linebacker and four-, five-time Pro Bowler, and Brian Kelley, another veteran linebacker who was part of the tradition, we really needed linemen and linebackers.

In the draft that year we got two outside linebackers, Lawrence Taylor and Byron Hunt, and that kind of gave us the nucleus of our front seven. We also were able to get a couple of nose tackles, Jim Burt and Bill Neill. We started to get some depth at both linebacker and the frontline personnel.

We didn't even have a nickel defense until about the seventh game of the season in '81. We started putting a third corner in the game and doing some things to balance the front on the pass rush.

Obviously, Taylor was a very integral and dominant player, so he was attracting a lot of attention. That let guys like Martin, who was another good pass-rusher, flourish on the other side in the passing situations.

My first year there, we were fortunate enough to get to the playoffs and play the Eagles in Philadelphia in the wild-card game. We won that. Then we played San Francisco on the West Coast in '81 and got beat. I know we didn't play too well on defense that day. That was basically the essence of the transition.

The second year was the strike year. We were still in our developmental stages and even though we had a pretty good group of veterans, it wasn't enough. The young players are immature, and the strike wasn't something the young players really knew much about and they were caught up in it. I would say that second year there certainly wasn't something we were capable of. We were not a good team and we didn't act like it.

PHIL SIMMS: One of our key draft picks was Joe Morris from Syracuse in the second round in 1982. He was 5'7" and probably the strongest guy on the team. I think he was the hardest worker too. Joe trained twice a day during the off-season.

Bill Parcells once said, "Man, I shortened his career because we used him and we used him." When in doubt, hand it to Joe. But I don't think that bothered Joe because he was a power runner at his size. He could get a foot off the ground with his shoulder pads on. It was hard to bring him down.

In 1989, we drafted Dave Meggett, who was even smaller than Joe. I heard Bill say once, "What are we gonna do with all these small guys?" After Meggett took his first or second punt in a preseason game 70 yards for a touchdown, all of a sudden Bill said, "Oh, I like this guy. You've got to get him in the offense a little more."

Every once in a while, you've got to break the profile of what you want on your team when there's a talent that can make you better, and those two did it for sure.

JOHN MARA: Ray Perkins left us at the end of the '82 season, which was a strike year, to become head coach at Alabama. George promoted Bill Parcells from defensive coordinator to be the replacement, because he thought we had something going in the right direction and he didn't want to bring in a whole new staff. And Bill was the one guy who had some head coaching experience, one season at Air Force in 1978, so we hired him in '83.

BILL PARCELLS: My first year we were 3–12–1, so I was just another coach who came in there and if things didn't get better quickly, I would be gone. Even at the end of the season, there were some questions about whether I would return. But when I did get that opportunity for the second year, I had a much different attitude and a much different resolve.

JOHN MARA: In '83, we suffered a ridiculous number of injuries throughout the year. We had a terrible year. George Young had made up his mind at the end of that year that maybe Bill Parcells wasn't the guy to lead us. George had conversations with Howard Schnellenberger, who was the hot coach who had won a national championship at the University of Miami. George came back to my father and me and said, "I don't think I can get him this year, but I think I can get him next year."

That gave Parcells one more year, which ended up being 1984, when we won a playoff game. That, to me, was such a critical point in our development because it allowed us to stay with Bill and a lot of success followed that.

Had Schnellenberger said yes after the 1983 season, who the hell knows what would have happened after that?

PHIL SIMMS: I won't say Bill was quiet that first year, because that's never the word for Bill, but he wasn't as loud as he turned out to be.

BILL PARCELLS: Looking back on it, I think I was trying to be what I thought a head coach was supposed to be instead of just being Bill Parcells, my own personality, kind of what had always served me well.

Some of the defensive players who I had coached in '81 and '82 even came to me and said, "What's the matter with you? What's going on?" That's what kind of snapped me out of it. They were calling my attention to things that I was very on top of as an assistant coach, and I was kind of—I wouldn't say letting them slide intentionally—but I wasn't as cognizant of what was really going on.

It took me that whole year to add the threat of losing my job, which I was very close to doing. I said, *You know, Parcells, you better get going here.* If they were going to get me, they were going to get me doing it my way.

JOHN MARA: I remember Bill, during that first season and prior to that, being kind of an outgoing, friendly guy. I didn't necessarily see that tough side of him. But after he went through that experience in '83 of almost getting fired, that was when I think he started to change and develop some of those attitudes and thoughts and expressions and whatnot. I think he felt like he had to develop a much tougher personality.

I think Bill always resented the fact he almost was terminated after not having really a fair chance. He was with us one year, and half the team got hurt, so he really didn't have a fair opportunity to build the team.

Bill and George Young didn't always see eye-to-eye, but they had similar football philosophies, similar ways of looking at players and grading players, and that allowed our drafts to be very strong during that period. The arguments that they had were never about the qualities that they wanted in their players.

They wanted big, physical players, especially in Giants Stadium. You had to be able to run the football. You had to have a defense that could stop the run and rush the passer. And the defensive linemen and linebackers had to have certain physical characteristics—certain height, weight, and speed. That was where I think they were closely aligned.

Obviously, there's a lot more to being a football player than just those measurables, but Bill and George had very similar views on what they had to be. As a result, we had big, physical players during that period, both on the defensive line and at linebacker.

We never had Pro Bowl receivers or anything, but we had good running backs, a good, sturdy offensive line, a tough-ass quarterback in Phil Simms, and a defense that was formidable.

BILL PARCELLS: I never really had a conflict on philosophy on personnel, on what we were looking for. When we changed to the 3-4, George and his personnel staff were obviously inquiring about what we were looking for prototypically in the defense. So I had to spend a lot of time explaining to them what fit this system.

The 3-4, as I played it, was not a gap defense; it was a lane defense. We played a two-gap scheme on the front line, which means the three down linemen had the areas inside or outside. But our philosophy against all runs was to force the ball to the perimeter. We were not trying to contain runs. We were trying to force them to the sideline and then using a secondary player to turn to play in, in most cases.

Occasionally, we'd use a linebacker to do that, but in most cases it was the secondary player because we were a zone team and lot of the time, we tried to force the ball to the perimeter. And we tried to shuffle down on the backside for the cutback lanes and the reverses and things of that nature.

The inside linebackers were on what we called a fast, slow, and direct read system. If something broke the perimeter to the corner, that would be a fast read. If something was uncertain, that would be a slow read. Then there's obviously the ball that comes directly at them that they'd have to attack a certain way.

As the offenses began to spread just a little bit more, they were obviously trying to get our linebackers out in space, where they were not threats in the pass rush. So we had to occasionally alter our scheme, particularly in long yardage, which we could do with Taylor because he could do either one.

Carl Banks was pretty good on the other side, so we had the versatility to drop them in coverage, which wasn't Taylor's best asset. But we could balance the line and get a good rush and then get the nickel defense in and still have our best players on the field, because we weren't taking out too many of our frontline players.

Most of the time, no matter where I was coaching, I would always take the personnel of the other teams in the division that we were playing, put it up in a visible area, and then compare our personnel to it. I would try to explain to our personnel people, "Here's where we may have an advantage, but here's where they have two or three advantages, in my opinion. And here's what this player does for them, and we don't have a guy who does that yet."

Most of the time, the philosophy on personnel acquisition was not a problem with George. Now, there were a few isolated instances where I probably didn't conduct myself the best when we were going to pick a guy that I really didn't want. But most of the time it worked out.

PHIL SIMMS: I'm just gonna be honest, I don't think I was the guy Bill wanted to be his quarterback at first. I think most of our other coaches definitely favored me over Scott Brunner. I'm not saying anything against Scott, but I was a better athlete; I had the better arm.

But I could just tell during that first training camp under Bill that he wanted to play Scott, because I think Bill thought I was a hothead, which I am, and he just had more trust in Scott as a quarterback. I could sense it: the body language, things that were said, things that I heard that he didn't think that I heard.

I knew my time was going to come because, as a quarterback, when you're on the field practicing every day, when you're the better thrower, sooner or later they're going to give you a shot. I got in against Philadelphia and went right down the field and scored a touchdown. The very next drive, I threw and my hand hit Carl Hairston's helmet or facemask and almost tore my thumb off. That was the end of my season that year. It also probably saved my career in New York because the team fell apart.

They were thinking about replacing Bill Parcells with Howard Schnellenberger. Fortunately, as I look back on it, Bill survived. That off-season he said to me, "Simms, this year we're going to do it my way." Then he let Scott Brunner go, so I knew it was going to be my job.

I was down in the weight room early one day during that off-season and he came down and we started talking. I think we both knew if we were going to survive, we had to do this together.

BILL PARCELLS: Phil Simms' personality was just like mine: it was fiery. We understood each other. I just had such a high regard for him. He went through the gauntlet. They were booing him in that stadium, just like they were booing me. We had kind of been through it together. He wound up being a good player for us.

Phil wasn't a celebrity quarterback. He's a celebrity now because I see him on television all the time, but he wasn't then. He was in the weight room with those offensive linemen, and it wasn't for show. He was there to work. He just won a lot of respect; the defensive players loved him, too. That's important. The defensive players have got to like and be confident in your quarterback, and they were confident in Phil because of his toughness and work ethic.

I always told Phil, "What we need in the huddle is a battlefield commander. We need a guy who is going to press the issue, who's going to get his team in the end zone, and that should be his only concern. We're not worried about passing stats; we're not worried about touchdown passes. Your job as my quarterback for our team is to get your team in the end zone. And I don't care how we get there. Run, pass."

In fact, I was preaching running the ball into the end zone. And Phil responded to that.

We had some injuries and we really didn't have any receivers left to play, so we were playing multiple tight ends with Mark Bavaro and Zeke Mowatt. We were running the ball a lot. Phil's passing stats weren't good, but we beat our three division rivals three weeks in a row—Washington, Philadelphia, and Dallas. Phil would be like 9-for-16, maybe one interception. There were a couple of drops in there. And the press was on him. They were putting the blame where it shouldn't have been. *You can't throw the ball well enough. Our pass offense isn't good enough.*

I called Phil into the office and I said, "Look, I don't know what you're thinking, but here's what I'm thinking: you just beat your three biggest division rivals. You got your team in first place. I just want you to forget about what everybody's saying. You can play on my team and get out there and be as aggressive as you can, using good judgment."

That was the turning point for Phil and me. Not that we were contenders, because we weren't. But that let him know that I was backing him, no matter what happened. He got a little more aggressive and we came back to beat the Minnesota Vikings on the road. It was a critical game for that first championship season in '86. We had a fourth-and-17, he executed it, and we kicked a field goal to win the game.

We were really off to the races after that. We won 12 games in a row, including the postseason, and it was all because Phil's confidence was up and he was able to understand and put away those ancillary issues that really had nothing to do with the outcome.

PHIL SIMMS: We were a power running team, but Bill Parcells loved big plays in the passing game. If I threw a five-yard flat route to the fullback, he'd go, "What are you doin' thrown' it to him?"

"Well, the guy was covered down the field."

"Oh, you're just worried about your completion percentage now. Throw it down the field, Simms! We need big plays!"

BILL PARCELLS: After that first season as head coach, I was a little more adamant. I was definitely much tougher on the team. That '84 camp would be illegal today. We were in pads twice a day and we were doing that for weeks on end. Even when the preseason was going on, we were practicing twice a day, but that served us well.

We got a little more battle-hardened. I happened to have the exact right kind of players, particularly the defensive players, who understood me at the most critical time. And they backed me and they supported me. I don't mean we were buddy-buddy. They were trying to help me get where they knew I wanted the team to go.

CARL BANKS: The Giants had just come off a really bad season, so for Parcells during that training camp, it was the most vulnerable I've ever seen him to this day.

Close to the end of camp, he said to us, "Look, I'm gonna make some tough decisions. They're going to fire my ass if we don't win, so we've got to do this my way. I need to know that the guys who are gonna be on this final roster are gonna be my guys. I'm going to give you everything I've got, but I need you to give me everything you've got. I need your word. I'm giving you my word."

You heard that phrase a lot: "He's a Parcells guy." That was kind of the birth of that. From that moment on, it was just a bond. It wasn't a coach-player relationship. It was, "Hold me accountable because I'm going to hold you accountable."

HARRY CARSON: When we went to training camp at Pace University in Pleasantville, New York, we had been working our asses off and we had been doing everything that Bill wanted us to do. I could see the fatigue that guys were going through and that they were kind of wondering when it was going to let up. He was driving the team really, really hard.

One of the things I brought to the table as a captain was that I was an advocate for those guys I played with. So I went to Bill and I said, "You know, the guys have done everything that you wanted them to do." He said something to the effect of, "I fear what's coming next. What are you thinking about?"

"Well, I think the old adage is true. You work hard, you get a break, and these guys have been working really, really hard. So, I think they should get a break. Can I do something to help the guys loosen up?"

"What are you proposing, Carson? I'm afraid to hear what you have in mind."

"I want your permission to have a little party in the dorms for the guys. Maybe we'll have a keg of beer."

"You do what you want to do, but I'm going to tell you this: if there's any problems, I'm going to hold your ass to the fire."

"Okay."

In the back of this magazine, they had ads where you could hire exotic dancers for parties and all this stuff. I called one of the numbers and arranged for three female dancers to show up at camp. I told the guys right up front that it was okay with the coach, and that anyone who didn't want to come to the party didn't have to come.

I'm not a beer drinker, but I was just looking at what could be done to lighten everybody up. It was July, August, and we were dealing with the heat and humidity.

We all had dinner as a team in the cafeteria, went to our meetings, and then everybody sort of assembled for some entertainment. The dancers performed. Nobody got out of line, nobody misbehaved. Everybody was respectful.

It was exactly what I wanted it to be, something to get away from the monotony of football and meetings and so forth. The next morning, everybody was up and peppy and energized. All we needed was that break and we got it.

That was one of those things that Bill trusted me, as a captain, to take care of. I don't think he would have ever thought of doing anything like that. It was me and my own little warped mentality of what would be good to energize these guys.

Bill was always willing to listen. When things weren't going well during the season and we lost four or five games in a row, I would go to him and say, "How much money do we have in the fine jar? I want to use it to take everybody out to dinner."

When you're going through adversity, you bring guys together. We used to go to a Beefsteak Charlie's or something like that. We would reserve a catering room and we would have shrimp cocktail and steak and drinks and all that stuff.

It was an opportunity for guys to sit there and not talk football, but to get to know each other on a more personal level. And when you know a guy on a different level, not just as a player with a number, but a guy who has a family, who's just sort of hanging out, it makes a difference. Bill was one of these coaches who believed and trusted in the guys that he had in leadership positions to take care of things off the field.

PHIL SIMMS: Between 1983 and 1984, he transformed into Bill Parcells, the guy that we know now. At practice, he was yelling, talking, cutting people up, putting mental pressure on you, just everything. Bill was the greatest manipulator in the history of coaching, in my eyes, because he just had a way of doing it. His personality just took over the football team.

BILL PARCELLS: We got to the playoffs in '84 and were able to win on the road against the Rams. We had to again play the 49ers, who had what I think was their best team ever. We lost in San Francisco 21–10, and that doesn't sound like it was too close, but we had the ball across midfield five times in the second half and we did not get any points. That was our fault, but the opportunities were there and our players kind of knew that after that game.

I was taught at a young age in coaching, by a Hall of Fame coach named Sid Gillman, that 100 yards of field position should be worth seven points. Everybody knows what the passing stats are, everybody knows what the rushing stats are, but very few people take the time to study the hidden yardage in the game. What's the difference in penalty yardage? Do we have more penalties that are taking yards away from us? If they have more penalties, then we're gaining yards. If our net punting is four or five yards better than theirs on six or seven punts, that's 30 or 40 yards a game. That's worth two or three points. So, if 100 yards is worth seven points, then 30 or 40 is certainly worth three or four.

I taught my team about the field-position game, how we want to play on their end. There are certain things we're not going to do when we're deep in our own territory. You can look at all the film of games that I coached. We never pitched the ball out when we were coming out on our own 5-yard line. No pitches, always handoffs. Our goal was to make two first downs so that we could put them into neutral field position. We were trying to get the ball out to at least the 30- or 35-yard line, just so we could punt it.

We were preaching no turnovers, but not because it gave the opponent a chance to score, which is the reason everybody thinks of first. We didn't want the turnover because if that happened, we didn't get to punt it. And if we didn't get to punt it, that's 40 yards we lose and that's probably two points in the game.

Most of my players, and certainly all of my ex-coaches (some of whom are still coaching in the league), can recite these things about the field position, the 100 yards, and the points derived from the difference in penalties, difference in net punting, difference in net return game. All those kinds of things add up.

That doesn't mean run the ball. That means we want to play on your end of the field, where we're threatening to score, where you're backed up trying to get out of there, where we want to play. We're trying to keep you there as long as we can.

We also wanted to have a balanced attack. I believe to rely totally on the passing game on some Sundays in the elements in the Northeast is going to be prohibitive. So I was preaching a good running game with very good play-action passing and trying to keep the third downs to a minimum.

PHIL SIMMS: Mark Bavaro joined us in 1985, a guy that nobody thought could catch the football because they didn't throw it to him at Notre Dame. And lo and behold, oh my gosh, could he catch the football. Mark had great hands.

I think we really started the seam passes. We threw more seams than anybody in the NFL by far. And we did it every different way because we had Mark Bavaro and Zeke Mowatt at tight end. We were playing the Pittsburgh Steelers in a preseason game. Mark was running the seam, I thought the linebacker had him covered and I dropped it down.

The next day, we were watching the game tape and Parcells said, "Why didn't you throw it to Mark Bavaro?" I kind of looked at him and I said, "He was covered."

"Simms, listen to me; when he's covered, he's open."

I didn't say anything because I knew what Bill meant and that he was right. After that, we started throwing it behind Mark, over the top. No matter where I threw it, he could adjust because he knew I was going to put it wherever the guy was.

We also did it with our wide receivers, who were small. We threw seams, back shoulders, 20-yard in-cuts, and 12-yard speed-outs. That was our passing offense. The rest of it was run the ball and let our defense do its thing.

BILL PARCELLS: I also wanted the cornerbacks to know that we would throw the ball deep. We were going to throw it deep a few times a game because we didn't want them sleeping very well in those hotels the night before the game. We wanted them to know that was coming.

BILL POLIAN: During the '80s and early '90s, the NFC had as many dominant teams in one conference as had existed in NFL history. The Bill Walsh 49ers ruled the Western Division. The NFC East was filled with rivals who despised each other and battled for NFL supremacy year in and year out. The Washington Redskins, New York Giants, and early Dallas Cowboys all won multiple Super Bowls, as did the 49ers.

Murderers' Row in the NFC.

CARL BANKS: Everything was about beating the Washington Redskins, which was their name at the time. They had John Riggins and a lot of other great players. They were just so difficult for the Giants. Everything that Bill Parcells and Bill Belichick did was around beating the most physical team in the division.

Physically and emotionally, the Redskins game was always the one you circled on the calendar. Coaches and players spent their off-season trying to figure out how to either keep an advantage or gain an advantage. For me, it was tight end Donnie Warren. He was the toughest SOB I've ever played against. He just never backed down. A tie was a win when you played against him because he was such an incredible blocker. You spent time looking at film and seeing what it was you could do better, what it was he did so well.

We also knew who the weak links were. There were a few of their guys who needed a kick in the butt from their teammates, and if we could get to some of those guys early, it would be to our advantage.

We would game plan against somebody's emotional distraction. An example was Andre Waters of the Eagles. Andre loved to block kicks. He'd come off the edge and knock your kicker down. I was a wing guy on the line of scrimmage. Bill Parcells said, "Can you piss him off enough that we can run a fake field goal?"

So, when we lined up, I said to Andre, "You're not going to block this kick because I'm going to cut-block your ass." Now, he was pissed off. The first field-goal attempt we had, I took his knees out. Now, he was m—fing me. I told Parcells, "If we get the chance, we'll get the fake, because I've got him where I need him."

Sure enough, we got in field-goal range another time and I started trash-talking him. I said, "Here it comes again, I'm about to take your knees out." Andre started m—fing me, the ball was snapped, he charged hard, I released outside, and I caught a touchdown on a fake field goal.

If we could find where these guys were mentally, how they tick, we knew that there was a play we could put in to take advantage of that. During pregame warmups against Washington my second year, Harry Carson came and got Pepper Johnson, Gary Reasons, and me and we literally walked through Washington's team stretches. It was like walking into a saloon in the Old West. Harry walked straight up to George Rogers and said, "George, homeboy, you're gonna fumble twice today." Then Harry turned around and walked out.

Sure enough, Rogers had two fumbles.

Sometimes we would do that stuff with our own guys to get them ready for an opponent that would do it to them. Dexter Manley, a defensive end for the Redskins, used to have his way with one of our tackles, Brad Benson, so we would jerk Brad around a bit in practice to get him wired up because that was what Dexter was going to do. We wanted to see if Brad could keep his composure or if he could turn the tables on Dexter. There were games where Brad trash-talked him or cheap-shotted him. And once Dexter lost his cool, there was a run coming right inside of him.

PHIL SIMMS: As a quarterback, the division was brutal. You had Washington, with Charles Mann and Dexter Manley, big, aggressive line-backers on the outside. Oh, and there was a guy named Darrell Green, the Hall of Fame cornerback. Bill Parcells would tell me every game we played Washington, "Simms, no matter what you do, don't you dare throw the ball at Darrell Green."

"Well, what if they double-cover the other receiver?"

"Are you hearing me? Do not throw the ball at Darrell Green!"

Of course, I did once, and he almost intercepted and ran it back for a touchdown. Thank God, he dropped it. I thought Bill was going to come out and fight me on the field, he was so mad.

I learned my lesson. I think I threw at Darrell Green three times in my career. I'm not exaggerating.

Those battles with Washington were great. Even though they won Super Bowls, we thought we had their number.

The Cowboys were coming along at that time. Of course, when they traded for Charles Haley, that was another bad day for me. I thought, *Oh, my God! Now I've got to play him twice a year.* After they got Charles, they turned it around and were eight-deep on their defensive line. That was extraordinary.

Buddy Ryan going to Philadelphia was another nightmare. I can remember like yesterday sitting in the locker room before a game at Veterans Stadium in Philadelphia. Usually I'd be going through the checks of what I wanted to do in the game. *"Okay, if they do this, now you make sure you do that."* But when we were getting ready to play Buddy's Eagles, all I was doing was rocking in my chair going, *Hang in there, it's going to be rough. You've just gotta hang in there.* It was just so physical with Reggie White and Jerome Brown and Clyde

Simmons. I don't care who you were. They beat up every quarterback. They had our number.

Thank God the St. Louis and then Arizona Cardinals were in the division at the time, because you said, *Okay, we've got two there.* But you couldn't pick out the other wins in the division a lot of times, or when we were playing the Chicago Bears and San Francisco every year.

With the 49ers, we always talk about their offense, but their defense was outstanding. They tore up quarterbacks. When we beat them 49–3 in a playoff game, I probably took one of the worst beatings I ever took in a game in my whole career. Charles Haley was a rookie then, in 1986, and he was just running me over. When I watched the game on YouTube during COVID in 2020, I went, *Oh, my gosh! I forgot how many unbelievable hits I took in a game against the 49ers.*

Their defense never really got the credit it deserved.

BILL PARCELLS: Bill Walsh was famous for the script he used for his first 15 offensive plays. In '85, we were playing the 49ers in the first playoff game at Giants Stadium. The league mandates that when one team's phones go out, the other side puts their phones down, too, until both are working. After the 49ers won the toss, their phones mysteriously went out.

Well, they have that script already orchestrated. We could kind of anticipate some of the stuff, so we were able to function on our side. But it was a little bit disconcerting for just a second. We won that game, not by a lot, but we won.

The next year, we were playing the 49ers again in the playoffs at our place. In pregame warmups, I saw Bill Walsh and we started talking and I said, "Bill, I've got tell you. If you pull the same shit that you pulled last year with these phones going out, I want you to know that I'm going to expose you."

He winked at me and said, "You know, it's just a little gamesmanship."

"Yeah, I know. It's a little gamesmanship."

I never said a word about it. I didn't roll over on him, I didn't complain in public. And that solidified our relationship forever.

BILL POLIAN: Bill Parcells believed that he had to put maximum pressure on players and coaches during the practice week. His thinking was that practice should be harder than the game, thereby making the game pressure-free.

This philosophy was espoused years before by a coach at St. Cecilia High School in northern New Jersey who went on to coach in the NFL. His name was Vince Lombardi.

BILL PARCELLS: My mother was Italian. She was highly confrontational. Nothing would slide. It was always confronted. My father was a well-educated man who taught me that you only get medals for results. Trying is what you're supposed to do.

In some convoluted way, I used to try to get that through to my players because I believe the pressure is something that individuals respond to. Some respond favorably, and others respond unfavorably.

In practice, I wanted constant pressure on execution and success, so that when the time came in the game, they would respond favorably. But it all comes basically from my mother, because I learned then that confrontation was a good thing.

I used to tell my players, "Listen, when a player has problems with the coach, most of the time it's because the coach's expectations for the player are higher than his. If I think you can do better than what you're showing, then we're gonna have a problem." Most of the real competitors will say, "Well, your expectations aren't higher than mine." And I said, "Well, why don't we get together here and start working to solve these problems because it's not going real good right now."

Some people call it badgering, but it's not badgering. That's just like nuisance nitpicking. I never was a nuisance nitpicking guy. It was always a broader spectrum.

HARRY CARSON: Bill Parcells loved being a joker. He loved being in the locker room. He loved bullshitting around with players. He didn't always act like a head coach with his players.

The whole thing with us beginning the tradition of NFL players dumping Gatorade on the head coach near the end of a win—which we did with Bill

Parcells—started with him trying to prepare Jim Burt for a 1985 game against Washington and its center, Rick Donnalley.

Bill asked Jim if he had watched the film of what Donnalley did against Detroit, Washington's previous opponent. Bill said, "Rick Donnalley kicked his ass. And you know what, Burt? If you're not ready, he's gonna have you for lunch. He's gonna kick your ass like he kicked the other guy's ass." Bill knew exactly what buttons to push with Jim Burt.

During the week, Jim would be in his stance and be working with dumbbells to help increase his speed of getting his hands up on Donnalley. Parcells was really riding him the whole week. That was his way of motivating his player to be prepared for what he was going to be facing. Burt was playing well that season. Parcells didn't want him to let his guard down, so he found his way to needle him.

At one point in the game, Jim asked me, "Is he getting to you?"

"Who?"

"The center. Is he getting to you?"

"No, you're doing a good job."

We were on our way to winning the game, and toward the end, Burt came up to me and said, "That Parcells is such a prick. We should get him or something."

"What do you mean *we* should get him?"

"Because you're a Parcells guy and if I do something with him, he will get pissed. But if you do it with me, he won't say a word."

"Okay, Jim. What do you want to do?"

"Let's get him with the Gatorade."

"Get him with the Gatorade?"

"Yeah, let's douse him with the Gatorade."

"Okay, I'll do it with you, but we've got to wait until he takes his headphones off because he might be electrocuted if we throw Gatorade on him before that."

Bill was surprised when it happened, with the cold temperature and the ice and everything, but we got him. He just laughed.

PHIL SIMMS: I was walking to practice at training camp one day. I can't remember the year; it might have been 1988. Bill was in front of me and I was kind of hustling to get to the practice field because the quarterbacks have got to be out there first. I didn't want to walk by him because I knew if I walked by him, he was gonna say something really derogatory to me or yell at me or whatever. Finally, I decided I just had to walk by him. Sure enough, just as I did, he said, "Hey, Simms."

"Coach, I've got to get to the field."

"Hey, you're with me? Come here. Listen, really proud of you. You're having a great camp. You're doing everything I want. You're leading, you're playing well. You couldn't be better. I'm just so proud of you."

I knew there was going to be a "but" in there somewhere. There always was.

Bill said, "But I just want you to know, today, I'm gonna rip your ass."

"Can't we wait to see what happens before you do that?"

"No, no. I've got to rip your ass in front of the team because the rest of these SOBs, they're not doing what I want. So, I've gotta use you."

"Okay, whatever."

We were having a great practice. I mean, the ball was not even hitting the ground. Back in those times, practice was real. It was a war. Finally, I threw an incompletion. Bill stopped practice and just yelled, "Simms!" And he just went into this tirade.

I stood there, knowing this was all orchestrated and I had to take it.

At that time at training camp, the fans were really close and they were all laughing. Everybody was laughing and Bill loved that. He would yell at a player and the rest of the team was allowed to join in and make fun of you.

"Yeah! Get him, Bill! Stick it to him, Bill!"

The other thing was you were allowed to yell back at him. I'd say, "Oh, Coach, just be quiet. I'm tired of listening to you!"

He would just smile and go, "Oh, you don't like me now? You want to hit me? Is that what you want to do? You'd love to hit me, wouldn't you?"

Eventually, all you could do was say, "Man, you're crazy," and just walk away.

Bill was great with picking on the offensive linemen. Almost every one of them was a target. I mean, he'd wear them out. He had nicknames for all of them; they were all funny. He called them the "Suburbanites."

JOHN MARA: One of the keys for us was that the offensive line was a prideful, tough-minded group—guys like Bart Oates and Brad Benson, Karl Nelson. They were nicknamed the Suburbanites early on, which was kind of an insulting nickname, at least for them, because it almost implied softness. They were anything but that.

PHIL SIMMS: Occasionally, Bill would make Lawrence the focal point of his ire. Bill would say, "You know, Taylor, I'm just gonna change your name to 'What's the matter with?'" Lawrence would say, "What are you talking about?"

"That's all the reporters keep asking me: 'What's the matter with Lawrence Taylor?'"

I hated those days, even though Lawrence wasn't supposed to hit me in practice.

HARRY CARSON: Bill did that needling with most of the players because he believed finding that button to push motivated them. He found it in me when he called Willie Jeffries, my coach at South Carolina State, and had a conversation about me. I knew nothing about it.

Coach Jeffries was like a surrogate father to me. Bill called him to find out what got me pissed off or whatever. He did his homework.

In practice, we'd be doing running drills, and Bill would say, "Carson, you can do better than that. If Willie was here, you'd be singing a different tune, blah, blah, blah." Then he'd say something to the effect of, "Alright, Don-Don."

That was when I knew he had spoken to Willie Jeffries, because nobody from the Giants knew my nickname was "Don-Don." That goes back to my hometown of Florence, South Carolina, because my middle name is Donald.

Bill told me he had spoken to Willie. Now, Bill had the dirt he wanted to get to motivate me in some way. Not that he needed to motivate me, but it was just to let me know he did his own due diligence on me and what made me tick.

Bill did due diligence on other players. When you have a coach who would go so far as to tap into a high school or college coach who coached you to find out little things about you, it shows that this guy really does care. But he's also looking for ammunition to kind of get under your skin to get the best out of you.

PHIL SIMMS: When I walked in that building every day, I was on alert. I was uptight, because the pressure was on. Every day was the most important day of our lives. I was the first one in almost every day to our locker room.

I walked in there one morning after a game and Bill was sitting in our little sitting room. He said, "Hey, come here Simms."

"Good morning, Coach."

"How many passes did you complete yesterday?"

"I don't know."

"I'll tell you how many. Not very many. I couldn't sleep all night. I'm tossing and turning because you couldn't throw the ball worth anything. And my wife says, 'Oh, Bill, what's the matter? Why are you tossing and turning?' I said, 'Because my damn quarterback can't complete a pass. That's why.'"

This was at 7:30 in the morning. I was so nervous the whole day. We went out to practice. Our wide receivers coach, Pat Hodgson, had heard about the tirade. He said, "I will tell the receivers to be ready today."

"Coach, you tell them I'm going to knock their heads off."

What Bill did that day was very common. He set the stage and put the pressure on us every day of practice, in meetings. It was rough, but I never begrudged it because I knew that was why we were winning, too.

Bill never lightened up in those seven years after his first season. He would find a reason to be mad every day.

When we beat the 49ers 49–3 in the playoffs after the '86 season, he came in the next day, stood behind the lectern, put that yellow notepad down, and just started to rip. It wasn't like, "Great win, guys!" Instead he said, "O-line, let me tell you what. It's amazing our quarterback's still here."

For 10 minutes, he just killed the offensive line.

CARL BANKS: Bill was a guy who, during the course of our careers, coached a game with gallstones. He was laying up in the training room and we were all teasing him. He was in so much pain because he couldn't pass the stone and he still went out and coached. Those were the things that were just so endearing to us as players because he would often ask us to make sacrifices that today many players would not even consider.

I played with a surgically repaired wrist the better part of the '91 season and didn't think twice about it. I played an important division game against Washington with one hand. Bill asked me if I could go and it was a yes or no answer. He wouldn't have held it against me if I said no, but I knew he felt that I could give them something. So, I said to the trainer, "If you can pad it up where I can't hurt it anymore, I'll play." I took three Tylenol and went out and played.

PHIL SIMMS: In his State of the Union Address, which came on Wednesday mornings before the week of practice, Bill wasn't a rah-rah coach before the game. He would give a 20-, 30-minute dissertation that began with: "Here's what we're going to do." He'd go through all the things that we had to do to win, and that was how we practiced. Game time, he would just look at us and say, "Alright guys, let's go! Let's do what we did in practice."

Only once do I ever remember him giving a halftime speech. It was 1986 and we were playing the 49ers in San Francisco. We were down 17–0, which was usually the case against them. He just came in and said, "When are we going to end this thing against the 49ers? When are we going to do it?"

Those words hit me. I couldn't imagine what it did to other players. We scored three touchdowns in the third quarter, our defense shut them out, and we won the game. We beat them in the playoffs, too.

Bill coached everything and everybody. I don't care who you were. He was the quarterbacks coach. He coached the punt returner.

CARL BANKS: We were assigned individual players to scout from the other team. We'd start that on Monday and by Friday, with a full download, we would go group by group, talking about what gave the players we scouted problems, what we saw from them in certain situations, what worked and didn't work against them.

PHIL SIMMS: Bill Parcells and Bill Belichick just did a great job with everything they had. Sometimes we would do some things that, out of nowhere, would be different. They were willing to take chances and change things from game to game on both sides of the ball to give us the best chance to win.

I remember—I'm not sure the year, maybe '89—we were getting ready to play against Washington and all of our wide receivers were hurt. We were going to use Lee Rouson, a running back, as a receiver. The offensive line was missing some key pieces. So, Bill put in a small game plan. It was so small that I said, "This is all we got?"

We did three-step drops, shotgun catch-and-throw, double-moves. We had just a couple little concepts for the whole game. Tom Coughlin, who was our wide receivers coach at the time, was just frantic about the game plan. He said, "How can we do this? This is just not enough. We need more plays. We can't beat this team."

We played the game and we torched them. We were throwing quick outs, we were throwing slant-goes. After the game, Tom Coughlin looked at me and, talking about Bill, he said, "He's a genius. He's a damn genius."

Against teams in the division, Bill really had a great feel for, whatever you did the first time, you had to reinvent yourself the second time.

CARL BANKS: Bill Parcells and Bill Belichick subscribe to the same philosophies when it comes to winning. They both thought or felt with deep conviction that technique and good fundamentals would always carry the day. It was a religion to them. Parcells preached it, Belichick taught it.

As a tactician and a teacher of fundamentals, Belichick broke down every movement and every single function on a particular play. If you were supposed to take on a guard with your right shoulder, that became a drill. It was footwork, it was leverage, it was shoulders. He taught everything that could possibly happen in a game as part of your fundamental package. It wasn't run fast, get in position, and strike, which is fine if people can teach it that way.

But there was always a reason why you had to do things a certain way. It was tedious. It was annoying at times. And there were a lot of times when we would ask, "Why do we have to do this?"

Then, when you got into actual drills, Bill Parcells would walk right in the middle of a drill to make sure that you were doing things the right way—like if your knees weren't bent, if your hands weren't up or something. He was literally standing in the middle of a nine-on-seven drill. He was barking out what you weren't doing right. They both deeply believed in fundamentals and they taught it. And then your athleticism, to whatever degree you had it, would take over.

HARRY CARSON: *I've thought to myself, Wow, I was really in the first row to see how Belichick and Parcells came together and worked together and how Belichick learned from Parcells, what he learned from Parcells and what he learned from the players he coached, that he continues to draw strength from the core group of guys—Taylor, Banks, Reasons, Carson—as well as those other guys who are reserve players who made their presence felt.*

I think what made the defense unique is we all understood what our jobs were and oftentimes you'd hear Bill Belichick say—even now when you see him on the sideline—"Do your job!" I knew what my job was. He didn't want me to be a Lawrence Taylor and rush the quarterback, sack the quarterback. That wasn't my job. My job was to be the inside run defender that they needed and wanted at that time.

Carl Banks understood what his job was. Gary Reasons understood what his job was. The nose tackle, the ends, they knew what their jobs were. When you know what your purpose is, you go out there and you give your all.

The way Belichick coached, if you went out there and you screwed up, he didn't sugarcoat anything. He would call you out in front of everybody. By doing that, he gave guys the incentive to not want to be called out. He also gave guys the incentive that if they were doing something right, he would reinforce and praise what they were doing. But he didn't pull any punches. The guys knew what their jobs were, and he challenged them to get better and better.

When Belichick took over as a defensive coordinator, he would draw defenses on the board. From a player's perspective, you looked at it and you said, "I don't know if this is going to work." We had our doubts as to certain things that he would want us to do, but then we'd go out on the field and start to implement them within the game plan. Then we could see that there was a very strong possibility that what he put on the board might work. So when we'd go into a game, and we'd throw something at an opposing offense and they weren't prepared for it and it worked in our favor, it made us believers.

I think you have a deeper respect for a coach who has played linebacker. Parcells played linebacker, so it's a given that he knows what he's talking about because he has been there. Belichick played lacrosse and football in college. Oftentimes, unbeknownst to him, we'd look at each other and say, "Does this guy know what he's actually asking us to do?" And then week in and week out, there were certain things that he wanted us to do and we bought into it gradually and it made us better as a defense.

If you look at some of the things that Belichick would run up in New England, like two rushers and everybody else falling back into pass coverage, all of that stuff started with the Giants back in the '80s.

BILL POLIAN: One of Bill Parcells' favorite sayings, which he put on a sign for his players to see, was, "Individuals play the game. Teams win titles."

BILL PARCELLS: I was trying to preach unity with that sign. We're not getting anywhere on a personal basis. It's only the team that counts. I'm not interested in who had the most rushing yards, who had the most passing yards, who had the most catches. And don't ask me what your role is because I'll figure that out. You don't try to figure it out. I'll figure it out.

BILL POLIAN: Another Bill Parcells saying: "There's a way to win every game. You just have to find it."

BILL PARCELLS: That's my high school basketball coach there, Mickey Corcoran. He said, "You know, fellas, there's a way to win these games if you're just smart enough to understand how we have to do it." I can't tell you how many times I've stood up in front of the professional teams that I coached and I said, "Look, we're capable of winning this game if everybody understands how we have to do it."

In certain cases, it was, "We've got to be aggressive with our offensive attack. We've got to go out there and go for their throat." Another day it might have been, "The wind's blowing 35 mph. If we don't hold the ball and we're relying on trying to throw the ball into the wind, we're gonna get beat today. So, you punt returners better get out there and work in pregame warmup with the wind, because I don't want any punts hitting the ground, either."

The best bit of coaching I ever got was in a high school basketball game. We were playing in a state tournament. There were eight seconds to go in the game, and we had the ball out on our side. And my coach, Mickey Corcoran, said to me, "I'm going to get you the ball at the foul line extended, and there are going to be about six seconds to go when you get the ball."

Everybody in the building knew that we had score to a basket, so he didn't have to tell me that. It was such a great bit of coaching because he solved all my problems for me. He told me where I was going to be on the floor and when I was going to get the ball. After that, it was my job to get the ball in the basket.

I can remember using that similar technique with Lawrence Taylor. When he first came into the league, he was a big speed rusher—speed and power, speed and power. Tackles were starting to get smart. They'd split wider, they'd start pushing him by, they started running draw plays inside him. And Lawrence didn't have an answer.

So I said, "Do you want to make this easy or hard on yourself? You're trying to run a better speed rush, and that's what they're looking for. You need to take them up the field like you're going speed, and then turn in on them hard."

"What about the draw?"

"Once you start up the field, and you see it's a draw, retrace your steps."

That solved his problems for him. Then he had that turn-in power rush, and when the draw came, he knew what to do: go back the way he came. I'll bet he made eight or 10 plays in his career on that one thing.

Solving problems for the players is what the coach is supposed to do.

BILL POLIAN: Another Parcells favorite: "I want beavers. What do beavers do other than chop down trees? Nothing. They just chop down trees. I want guys that just think football."

BILL PARCELLS: I was lucky to have some of those, too. We called the other ones "Saint Bernards." You had to hit them with a bat to get them out of the huddle. And then there were the "Louisville Sluggers." I'd say, "I've got to hit you guys with a bat to get you moving."

BILL POLIAN: And another Parcells saying that I quote all the time is, "If they don't bite as pups, they probably won't bite."

BILL PARCELLS: You hear people rationalize, "Oh, he's from a small school, he needs time." Yeah. If they don't bite at the start, usually they don't ever bite. I learned that in the boxing gyms in New Jersey. When you were a young kid in the PAL or the CYO, the first thing they did was put boxing gloves on you. *Let's see what you've got.* I wouldn't want to expose my children to some of the things I was exposed to, but still, in all, it serves you pretty well sometimes.

BILL POLIAN: As the Giants approached the '86 season, the heavy lifting of building and training a championship team had been done. George Young had put difference-makers like Phil Simms, Lawrence Taylor, Carl Banks, and Mark Bavaro in place. Bill Parcells had built solid offensive and defensive lines and a culture of power and toughness. Team leaders like Harry Carson and George Martin were in place.

Full speed ahead for "Big Blue."

PHIL SIMMS: In training camp in 1985, we were practicing against the Bears' "46" defense. I had never really studied it before then, and I said, "What is this? The linebackers are doing what? The safeties are where?"

We spent a week working on them even though they weren't on our schedule, but then, lo and behold, we played them in the playoffs after that season and they beat us 21–0. We played them tough; the score was misleading. We were down inside the 1-yard line and didn't score; we missed a field goal. We whiffed on a punt to give them a touchdown.

When we went to training camp in 1986, I thought, *Man, we can be the Super Bowl champions this year.* I don't know if a lot of people were behind us or thinking that way, but we had won a playoff game in '84, and we won another one against San Francisco in '85.

The Bears were so dominating when they won the Super Bowl, yet I knew how close we were in that playoff game against them. We fought through a tremendous amount of injuries at wide receiver that year, but we kept winning a lot of close games. There was a lot going on that gave us confidence that we could challenge them or other teams and win the Super Bowl.

JOHN MARA: Well into the '86 season we were just beating everybody. That was the first time in my life that I sat there and said, "We are the best team in the league." I had never felt that prior to that. I maybe felt that once or twice since.

Late in that regular season and into the playoffs, we were just convinced that we were the best team because we were beating teams by pretty good margins and everything was just clicking.

CARL BANKS: The '86 season was predetermined by the loss in Chicago in 1985. At that time, both of our teams thought we had pretty good defenses. We met those guys in the divisional round. We lost and things didn't go well. But what we realized was that after that game, there was still another level, because we were a really good football team, a really good defensive team.

Coming out of that game, we vowed that we would win the Super Bowl the next year. Before we got in the locker room, we knew our off-season was set. Our mindset was just to go to a whole other level in '86 and just dominate the league.

We faced the 49ers in the playoffs. They had John Frank as a tight end. I played against John in college a lot; he was an undersized guy. When I was looking at film, I wasn't looking for anything. All of a sudden, there were certain plays when John Frank's inside hand just twitched. I was running it back and I was like, *Wait a minute, he doesn't do this a lot.* I ran it back again. Then, I ran about 20 plays, and he was only doing it on an outside run to his right. I just made a note of it. Everything else was pretty steady.

In the game, they were backed up with their heels to the goal line. And there John was, in a three-point stance, and he was twitching his hand. I said to Eric Dorsey, our defensive tackle, "Step to your left on the snap." He said, "What?"

"Just step to your left on the snap."

He did. I stepped to the left, too, and it was a tackle for a loss, almost a safety. But it was that one little thing that just showed up in that whole process.

I spent so much time the week before that Super Bowl against Denver looking at film. The film study became more than just the Xs and Os. I watched it for the rhythm of the game, just to get a feel for how things would go during the course of the game for me from a defensive standpoint.

You hear players say they want to have the perfect game. For me, that was that game. If I could have had my best game as a defensive player in the biggest game of the year, I had it in that Super Bowl. There was nothing that happened in the game that I didn't anticipate. You talk about being in the zone, there was nothing Denver did offensively—run, pass, everything—I didn't have a feel for. I might have made nine tackles in the game. I was just in the zone.

When you want to find things out about a team, just put the film on and don't look for it, because some of those things start to show up. I did that the first hour of film study just watching the flow of a game, watching the flow of the offense, watching to see what jumped out before I even started to dig into what the plays were, what their tendencies were, things like that.

There are things that often show up that never appear when you're looking for them. I made a big play down on the goal line right before the half and the Broncos ended up missing a field goal. It was a play that I just felt that I could make chasing from behind the line of scrimmage, but it was something I saw in film. It was not because of a lack of blocking, but just the pace of the play. That was the way I studied before I even dug into the Xs and Os.

That game was one of the most complete games that both Phil and I had played.

BILL PARCELLS: We had played Denver in the regular season. It was a close game in New York. That game could have easily gone to them. We made a couple of very, very big plays—one defensively for a long touchdown.

But we were a lot better by the time we got to them the second time than when we played them the first time. We were going to be aggressive in our attack. The first play of the game was a play-action in-cut we completed.

Almost everything we threw was complete. Phil only had two incompletions in the whole game. We started a little shaky. They had to lead, but we made a goal-line stand in the first half, and that kind of turned the tide. We got a safety and then the third quarter was very one-sided in our favor. That was pretty much the game.

JOHN MARA: We started off the '90 season 10–0, then Phil Simms got hurt. Jeff Hostetler came in and he played fairly well. But we were playing with a backup quarterback, so I couldn't say that I went into the playoffs in '90 expecting that we were going to make any great run because we still had a backup quarterback in there.

Our first playoff game was against the Bears. We beat them fairly easy. It was a cold, windy day. We started to build some confidence as that went along, but I never had that feeling that I expected we were going to win or that nobody was as good as we were.

I had that feeling in '86. I didn't necessarily have it in '90, especially playing against Buffalo's high-powered offense at that time.

CARL BANKS: That '90 season was pretty much set up by the year prior to that. We were a better football team and Flipper Anderson of the Rams cut that short when he caught a touchdown bomb from Jim Everett in overtime. When you have a team that's together long enough, you kind of know when you're good enough. You kind of expect it to be at a certain level every single year, barring injury.

Losing to the Rams the way we did only incentivized us because we knew we were going to get back in and make a run at it again. When Phil Simms went out and we lost our running back and I had the wrist injury in '89 and I didn't come back until the latter part of the year, we went 10–0, but it was a "yeah, but" season. People would say, "They won, but… They won, but…" We rode that all the way into the playoffs.

That year, there was no extra week between the conference championship games and the Super Bowl, so if you were the road team for the conference championship game and advanced, you were heading straight to Tampa. The Monday as we were getting prepared to go to San Francisco for the NFC title game, Bill Parcells came in the meeting room with a little suitcase and said,

"I need to know if you're packing for one week or two weeks. I'm packing for two. If you're packing for one week, don't plan on taking the trip. So you need to go home and tell your wives, your girlfriends, your mother, you're gonna be going for two weeks. That's my goal."

You always had to account for the San Francisco 49ers, even though they were not even in your division. We did that when we were drafting, when we were putting in plays, when we were doing our off-season work, when we were doing our in-season work. During the course of the weeks during the season, there were always plays from San Francisco that were sprinkled in throughout practice because we knew if we were in the playoffs, we were going to have to face them.

PHIL SIMMS: The '90 season was the year the team was extremely orchestrated. We ran the ball, were persistent, ate clock up, let our defense do its thing. That was what we were, and I played into it. Statistically, I was having a really good season for most of the year.

I broke my foot in a game late that year against Buffalo. It was the last play before the half. I was walking off the field and Parcells said, "What's wrong?"

"I think I broke my foot."

"Oh, no, it's not broke. You're okay."

I walked into the locker room and they taped it up. I was warming up and I couldn't plant my foot and throw. I said, "Aw, I'll just backpedal every play."

The very first third down of the second half, Dave Meggett was open in the flat. I went to turn to throw it and it was like somebody shot me. I fell flat on my back. Somehow the ball stayed in the air forever and Meggett caught it and got a first down. And that was the end of my year.

I have no regrets about it. I was a part of that and I'm glad we won the damn game. It hurt. Of course, it hurt.

Would we have won that Super Bowl if I was the quarterback? I don't know. In the conference championship game against the 49ers, Jeff Hostetler did a few scrambles, which I would not have done, that could have been the difference in the game.

The Super Bowl game against the Bills, I don't know. Bill Parcells always kind of thought I could match up pretty well against the Bills defense. But we would probably have played almost the same exact game as we did with

Jeff Hostetler if I was the quarterback. I was in on the meetings before that game just seeing what we were going to try to do, I said, "We're going to try to grind this game to a halt."

CARL BANKS: The Bills' K-Gun offense, at the level it was going into the Super Bowl, was something we had never seen. Before we even discussed the game plan, we put the film on and the offense was moving at such a clip, the coaches' tape couldn't keep up with every play. Bill Belichick got the network-broadcast copies of every offensive play just so we could see the whole play.

That AFC Championship Game against the Raiders was a track meet. I mean, the Raiders didn't even get their feet set before there was another 15 yards gained and the Bills were in the end zone. The network copies also gave us every angle, so we were able to see every facet of the play. If you were just relying on coaches' tape, you were gonna miss a lot of different things.

The thing that really set the tone for us was not so much our game plan, but what Bill Belichick talked about with Buffalo. This is where the genius of a Bill Belichick comes into play in terms of how he never leaves a stone unturned. He always starts by explaining the why and the how. He said, "They figured out a really great way to effectively run the ball without ever handing the ball off. And they've done it to perfection. This is not a tendency, because you can only find those over two- or three-game samples. This is a trend. They've been doing this since Week 8 of the season.

"A draw is their only inside run and their outside runs are screen passes. This is their running game. We have to let Thurman Thomas rush for 100 yards."

We lost our mind in the meeting room, because we just didn't believe in giving up 100-yard rushing games. But he set the stage as to why. It wasn't a situation where they could change up, where he was saying, "Over three games we saw this." No. He said, "This is a trend. It's not a tendency. It's a trend."

Then, Belichick said, "If they're running the ball, that means they're not passing it," which was the most difficult aspect of what we had to defend. And then he talked about how it was going to be difficult to line up in the huddle, break the huddle, set your guys, and anticipate plays. So he said that we were basically going to run a no-huddle defense, unless the ball was spotted.

We were going to rush two guys, and we were going to put players at intersections of where the receivers were going to be. That was from looking at the Raiders' game and seeing that by the time their inside linebackers got set in their pass drops, the ball was caught and gone. And these guys were just getting set.

Belichick said, "We're going to line up and, based on down and distance, these are going to be our intersection points. We're going to jam, we're going to hit. Anybody crossing, we've got to punish. Punish, punish, punish. We've got to be where we're supposed to be so we can see everything in front of us."

We rushed two and, every once in a while, we rushed three. But the whole emphasis was that we had to intersect their receivers on crossing routes and not let them catch and run with the football. If they were doing shallow crosses, we needed to hit them within five yards. If they caught the ball, we needed to punish them. And it was primarily Andre Reed, because James Lofton was the outside guy most of the time.

They eventually started running Thurman a lot, and had they started that five minutes earlier, it probably would have been a different game, because he ended up getting 100 yards, but if Mark Levy would have said, "You know what? We need to run this ball and we probably could do some things."

When they did start giving him the ball, we didn't have the personnel on the field to really stop it until he got seven or eight yards down the field. But, again, because it was a trend and not a tendency, we were betting on the fact that Marv wasn't gonna change what he was doing, because it was working and had all the defenses flummoxed through the last part of the year. They were just a well-oiled machine.

What we wanted to do on the other side of the football was to take the air out of the ball. We wanted to be very efficient passing, but very, very deliberate running the football. We found a way to start running the ball with O.J. Anderson, passing only when necessary. We wanted to stay in third-and-manageable situations, and we wanted to eat the clock. We had the ball for a pretty good chunk of time during that game.

And when you look at the last drive Buffalo had, if Sean Landeta doesn't hit the punt that he hits, that field goal goes in. They're much closer.

We played the cards we were dealt, but the dealer was Sean Landeta. His punt was the one that really set the table for us to have the success that we had on that last drive because it took every ounce we had to get a stop and hold them to that area.

They were still moving the football. They weren't moving it on their terms, but they were still moving it. If you're talking about a difference of five yards, 10 yards, it's a different ballgame. Maybe, if it were closer than 47 yards, Scott Norwood's field-goal try in the final seconds goes through rather than sailing wide right.

BILL PARCELLS: I used to tell my players, "Sometimes, winning isn't a matter of playing better. It's just a matter of playing longer and who's willing to play harder longer. If you're willing to do it, most of the time you're going to come out on top. You can't play dumb football and turn the ball over. Don't crack when the pressure's on. Make them crack."

That's not a sense of arrogance. That's an approach, a mentality I wanted my players thinking about. That Buffalo team that played in Super Bowl XXV was very resilient. If we got a three- or four-point lead, we were tough to beat because we wouldn't crack.

JOHN MARA: It was a surreal experience. I was in a suite with my parents, which was unusual because my father would never sit with the rest of the family. He would always sit with me and maybe some of my brothers, but never with my mother or anybody else. But given the fact it was the Super Bowl and you had the Gulf War just starting, everything was very security-tight. So, we were all crammed into this one box.

BILL PARCELLS: That was a one-play-either-way game. We played the Bills in the preseason and in the regular season and the Bills had beaten us in the regular season in New York. That game in New York taught us that we were not ready for that hurry-up, K-Gun offense that the Bills were running. We were not properly prepared to deal with that, and we spent a lot of time deciding how we were going to approach the Super Bowl.

The Bills were averaging 31 points a game going into the Super Bowl, and our whole mantra for that was, "We've got to keep these guys off the field."

We had one very long stretch in the game at the end of the second quarter, beginning of the third quarter, where we just had the ball the whole time. And that really wasn't even enough because the Bills still had a chance to win the game.

I thought Jeff Wright, the Bills' nose tackle, made one of the greatest plays that I've ever seen on the goal line. He ran behind the center's reach block and tackled O.J. Anderson, and we wound up having to kick a field goal. Everybody else on the defense was either on the ground or being blocked out of the way, or that would have been a touchdown and it wouldn't have come down to that field goal, but it did. It was certainly, discipline-wise for our team, our finest hour.

BILL POLIAN: Jeff Hostetler, in my humble opinion, made the most consequential play of Super Bowl XXV. In the mid-second quarter, we (the Buffalo Bills) led 10–3. We had the Giants offense backed against their goal line. Bruce Smith broke through and was sacking Hostetler in the end zone. Trying to cause a fumble, Smith had Hostetler's right wrist in a vice grip. If the ball came out and the Bills recovered, which was very likely because there were defenders all around him, it would have been a touchdown and we would have been up by 14 points.

If nothing changed from that play forward, we would have won the game. At worst, a Bills TD would have changed the Giants' strategy of ball- and clock-control to a large degree. But Hostetler didn't fumble. How he held onto the ball, I'll never know, but he did. On such plays do Super Bowls turn.

BILL PARCELLS: God plays in some of these games. Everson Walls tackling Thurman Thomas in the open field? Come on. I told Everson after the game, "That's the best play you ever made in your life."

JOHN MARA: I remember being upset that Jim Kelly drove down the field so effortlessly on that final drive. We were going with the three-man pass rush and it seemed like we were being a little bit too loose back there.

All of a sudden, they were in field-goal range. I didn't know what to expect at that point. You just cross your fingers and hope for the best. I was thinking, *We had a great season no matter what happens.*

The other incredible thing about that Super Bowl was I was in the final stages of negotiating with Bob Tisch, who was about to purchase my cousin's half of the Giants. Bob had pretty much worked out his agreement with my cousin, but still had to work out a number of important details in our operating agreement.

Once that game was over and we had won and became the toast of the town, it further motivated Bob to close the deal, which we did.

BILL POLIAN: After the game, I asked Wellington Mara, "Did it ever occur to you that you've got more powerful Hail Marys than we do? Because there were a hell of a lot said on both sidelines when that ball was kicked."

JOHN MARA: That's one of the benefits of attending mass every day.

CHAPTER 6

Jerry Jones, Jimmy Johnson, and the Dallas Cowboys: What Might Have Been

"I asked John Madden one time, after we played the Giants, 'Am I screwed up or is the NFL as big as the president?' John said, 'Jerry, this is big shit we're into. Big shit.'"

—Jerry Jones

BILL POLIAN: Under Tex Schramm, Tom Landry, and Gil Brandt, the Dallas Cowboys had gone from an expansion team to an NFL power. In the early Super Bowl era, from 1967 to 1978, the Cowboys reached five Super Bowls, winning two. Schramm had christened them "America's Team" and the name, much to the discomfort of their NFL brethren, stuck.

By 1989, when Jerry Jones purchased the team from H.R. "Bum" Bright, it had fallen on hard times. The Cowboys' record in the previous three seasons was 17–30. They had reached the playoffs only once in the previous five seasons and had not been to the Super Bowl since the 1977 season.

Jerry Jones was an offensive guard and co-captain of the 1964 University of Arkansas national championship team. While still captivated by football, Jerry went into the oil and gas business after college. He eventually made a fortune in one of the most volatile and risky facets of that business, "wildcatting," which is high-risk exploratory drilling in areas that have no solid history of success or have already been tapped out. Having established the net worth to do so, Jerry audaciously put up all of his capital to fulfill the lifetime dream of owning an NFL team. Not only did he get a team, but he got one of sport's most iconic franchises, the Dallas Cowboys.

Introducing himself to the Cowboys' fanbase, Jerry made it clear he would be a "hands-on owner," not passive as his predecessors had been. He famously said he would "count every sock and jock."

Jones promptly replaced the venerated Coach Landry with his former college teammate, Jimmy Johnson. Jimmy had a stellar career as a college coach. He built Oklahoma State into a power and then took the University of Miami Hurricanes to the top of the collegiate football world with a 52–9 record from '84 to '88. The U won the national championship in 1987.

The arrival of Jerry Jones and Jimmy Johnson was met with skepticism by many in the media. What they missed was Jerry's incredible drive, business vision, and passion, along with Jimmy's tremendous ability to identify, organize, and motivate talent.

Jerry and Jimmy inherited a team on the decline, but one valuable piece was in place in 1989 number one overall draft choice, Troy Aikman. Troy began his career at the University of Oklahoma under Barry Switzer, but soon realized that the Oklahoma Wishbone was not going to develop his NFL-quality talent and transferred to UCLA. That decision proved correct, as did the Cowboys' decision to make Aikman the top pick in '89.

Aikman led the team to three Super Bowl wins. His 90 victories are the most of any NFL quarterback in the decade of the '90s. He holds 47 Dallas passing records, was named an All-Pro in 1993 and was named to six Pro Bowls.

One of Aikman's favorite targets in the passing game and the lead blocker for all-time leading rusher Emmitt Smith was fullback Daryl Johnston. From the western New York community of Youngstown, Johnston was a star at Syracuse and a second-round choice of the Cowboys. He became a starter in '91 and remained so for each of the following three Super Bowls. "Moose" made the Pro Bowl in 1993 and 1994 and played in 149 consecutive games before a neck injury sidelined him.

The defensive catalyst for the Cowboys was Charles Haley. He came from the 49ers in a trade in 1992. A 6'5", 242-pound outside linebacker/defensive end from James Madison, Haley was selected in the fourth round by San Francisco in 1986. He led the 49ers in sacks in each of his first six seasons. Psychological issues, discovered later in life, made him difficult for coaches to deal with at times.

There was, however, no denying his talent or passion. He was named NFC Defensive Player of the Year twice and All-Pro twice. Charles was named to five Pro Bowls, was a member of 10 division championship teams and was the first player ever to play on five winning Super Bowl teams. Charles finished his career with 100½ sacks and was elected to the Pro Football Hall of Fame in 2015. He is my Hall of Fame classmate and friend.

The Jerry Jones/Jimmy Johnson iteration of the Dallas Cowboys was a resounding success. In the first decade of Jerry Jones' ownership, the Cowboys won six division titles, made the playoffs seven times, and won three Super Bowls in four seasons. Jimmy Johnson won the first two and Barry Switzer the third after Jimmy and Jerry had their parting of the ways.

Jimmy went on to coach the Miami Dolphins with a modicum of success, but not what he achieved in Dallas. Jerry went on to become the most visionary business leader in all of sports with the magnificent and phenomenally successful AT&T Stadium as his crown jewel, but had not, through the 2020 season, been back to the Super Bowl.

Both Jerry and Jimmy have been enshrined in the Pro Football Hall of Fame. They joined Troy Aikman, Larry Allen, Charles Haley, Michael Irvin, Emmitt Smith, and Deion Sanders from their Super Bowl teams.

In this chapter, you will hear from Jerry, Jimmy, Troy, Charles, and Daryl Johnston. They, along with Cowboy fans everywhere, have been left to wonder what might have been.

JERRY JONES: My dad and mother were middle-class entrepreneurs in the grocery business. I grew up around a breakfast table or supper table, listening to their adventures relative to money going from one pocket to the other to keep their business alive. We lived above the store until I was in about the fifth or sixth grade.

The biggest thing that stuck with me from my parents was their ability to operate with what I call tolerance for ambiguity. They were able to function not knowing where their business was going to be the next month or what the next month even was.

Some people—great talents, great mental giants—have to know what it's going to look like at the end of the month. Once they know, then they can operate brilliantly. They need to know that the square peg is going to be in the square hole, and they could be the greatest people in their fields you've ever seen. On the other hand, you take a Mississippi riverboat gambler. He's at his absolute best when that next card will have him owning the boat or thrown in the damn river.

If I got anything from growing up being entrepreneurial, it was being able to make decisions scared shitless and realizing maybe that's when you're your best.

Around the end of my days at the University of Arkansas, I was torn between entrepreneurship, being a business guy, or being a coach. I would have loved, deep down, to have been a coach. My master's thesis was the role of marketing in modern-day football. My interviews for the thesis were with Bear Bryant, Paul Dietzel, Woody Hayes, all the great coaches of that time.

Bear Bryant was from Arkansas and I was from Arkansas, so he kind of had a little bit of an affinity for anybody that was from that part of the country. He was easy for me to talk to.

Bear Bryant said, "Jerry, you take the fake out of me, there's not much left. I'm an actor for different roles. That's a coach. A coach has to have a lot of wardrobes and wear a lot of different hats and he's got to come on in a lot of different ways to a lot of different kinds of people. I'm Bear Bryant, because they had this old bear at a fair, but it looked like everything on him was taped up or boxed up. So, I got out there and squeezed around with him a little bit and I got to be Bear Bryant. And I had to act like Bear Bryant."

He was that candid.

My dad used to get so frustrated. He had asked me, "Jerry, what do you want to do with your life?"

"I want to be a sports promoter. I watched those AFL teams and, boy, somehow I want to be involved."

When I was 22, 23 years old, I would sit in a hotel lobby in Houston, waiting on the owners of the AFL to come out for a break from their meetings and just go up and introduce myself. When I bought the Cowboys, I went up to Joe Robbie, the owner of the Dolphins, and said, "Do you remember me, Mr. Robbie?" Right after Joe Robbie got the Dolphins, me and a coach named Wilson pushed the first desk up the steps into the Miami Dolphins' office. It was a metal desk. I was at the back; Wilson was at the front. I was down there trying to figure out some way, somehow to get involved.

All during my late teens and early twenties, while selling insurance after school, my daydream was about being involved in football. I didn't feel that coaching was the place. I read an article in *Look* magazine about Art Modell when he bought the Cleveland Browns, and they were talking about him coming in and bringing his television expertise into the NFL. I saw that picture with his boys and his actress wife, and I thought, "My God, that's my dream." But as the values of those teams went from the $15 million that the DeBartolos paid for the 49ers and just evolved during my time, it just looked so far out of reach.

In my late thirties and early forties, I had very good success in the oil and gas business, beyond anything that I deserved or was smart enough to attain. Five or six years before I bought the Cowboys, the oil business fell through the floor. Dallas, Texas, looked like a bomb had gone off in it. The buildings that were completed were empty. The buildings that were half-completed were the majority of the buildings in the city. Every bank, without exception, was crippled or broke. It was the shits as far as the scene of economics.

But I was able to survive. I was forced to get liquid and come out of the collapse of the oil business with viability, with both feet on the ground. As everybody else in that industry was in courtrooms and fighting to stay alive, I was able to go on offense. The oil business's downturn was very, very beneficial because it caused me to be able to get involved at the right level financially.

All of a sudden, I had a pathway to be standing there when the opportunity to buy the Dallas Cowboys came by in 1989.

I was with my son, Stephen, on a fishing trip in Mexico. We'd had too much tequila, and I looked at a San Diego paper and it said Bum Bright was going to sell the Dallas Cowboys. As soon as I could, I got on an old garbled switchboard from Mexico, called Bum Bright and said, "You don't know me from Adam. My name is Jerry Jones. I think I'm dying, but if I survive, I'm going to come back to Dallas and buy the Cowboys."

We flew right from Mexico to Dallas, sat down with Mr. Bum Bright, and worked out the beginnings of what, over the next 30 days, culminated in my buying the Dallas Cowboys.

Right before I bought the team, I met with Dan Burke, who was the chairman of a company called Capital Cities, which owned ABC network and ESPN. He was in New York and his people said I would have about an hour with him. I wanted to hear what he thought about the future of football and television. I got there at 9:00 in the morning and I was still there at 11:00 at night. We had a couple of meals and we had some good scotch. We were having a hell of a time.

This was how Dan Burke summed it up: "Number one, your game is where all the money is. The fourth quarter, and a little bit of the first quarter, is when most of the people that we're interested in getting a message to get in front of a TV set. And advertisers will pay us a lot of money for that. No other sport is at its apex the way football is in the fourth quarter.

"Secondly, it's not intrusive to the game to make 30-second spots that run during huddles and all kinds of stoppages. Consequently, we can get more money with those spots than any other thing there is. That's big.

"Number three, and the biggest part of all of it, is that you're a soap opera between the games every day, all year round. In season, out of season, on and off the field, you've got shit going on all the time that we can put on television. You are a promoter's dream. That's why you're always going to be at the top of the heap."

JIMMY JOHNSON: While I was at the University of Miami, Jerry had me call Tex Schramm to introduce Jerry and let Tex know that Jerry was a legitimate buyer. I had sat with Tex and Tom Landry in a box at the Super Bowl just a few months prior, so I had a good relationship with Tex.

Jerry told me there was a $5 million note on the Cowboys' complex at Valley Ranch. He said, "I need to see if it's worth a damn or if I want to default on that $5 million."

After I checked it out, I told him, "It's a damn country club, but I think I can handle it."

Jerry flew down, picked me up, and we went to Little Rock, Arkansas. He said, "Listen, I want you to handle all the football. I'm going to handle all the business, I'm going to do all the finances. We'll go to back-to-back Super Bowls, and we'll make sports history."

He never even asked me to do the job. He just kind of assumed I would.

JERRY JONES: The University of Arkansas was, at that time and had been for many years, the only non-Texas team in the Southwest Conference. So you really could have been coming from about any place, relative to sports and football, to buy the Cowboys—except Arkansas. That was a little bit of a problem right there and it was duly noted.

Coach Landry was being criticized and there was already talk of a replacement going on by all the writers. But the minute I came in and actually made the change, it made him perceived as a martyr. He was honored as though he had been Abraham Lincoln, without exaggeration. It was really a PR nightmare.

The facts are, this team was so down and out, somebody coming in and committing $175–$180 million to it should have had the flag raised for him as a hero. It was the opposite, and I truly became a real symbol of everything that I wasn't. In addition to that, Tex Schramm was really on a campaign to try to convert his 30 percent interest in the Cowboys to ultimately trying to leverage it into owning the Cowboys. And I never knew it. Boy, did Tex know how to play the game. The media campaign to undermine me was unbelievable. I mean, it was some of the worst publicity that you could ever imagine.

The Leader, which was right on par with the *Dallas Morning News*, made a statement about my financial capabilities, or lack thereof. And then it ran a retraction. I was endeared to a lot of friends, both corporate and otherwise, who took the position, "But for you go I."

I actually had empathy for both Tom and Tex. Had I gotten to them earlier, I could have probably been talked into staying with Tom and Tex for a year or two. But I made my bed early and decided, when I was doing the negotiation, that I would make the change.

The biggest reason I was standing in Dallas, Texas, was Tom Landry—the respect and the feel that I had for what he brought to football. That's not getting melty. That's just what it was. I respected everything about what Tom and Tex were.

At the time I purchased the Cowboys, you couldn't borrow a penny on the team. You couldn't borrow a cent on the stadium. No lending institutions would loan it. I literally had to make almost a total equity purchase. I was leveraged to buy the Dallas Cowboys. I had to use my total assets and funds, everything, to make that purchase.

At that time, it was the largest amount that had ever been paid for anything in sports. Donald Trump was one of the people that looked at it and said, "I feel sorry for the guy that buys the Cowboys. It doesn't work." We were losing $1 million a month in cash flow with the Dallas Cowboys at the time.

Herschel Walker's contract, which was supposed to have been guaranteed with the league, hadn't been guaranteed. Tom Landry's and Tex Schramm's pensions, which were supposed to have been funded, hadn't been funded. When I bought the team, I had to fund Herschel Walker's contract for $10 million with the league. I had to fund those pensions, plus spend $140 million to buy the Dallas Cowboys.

Mr. Bright, rest his soul, was really compromised financially. I bought 15 percent of the team from the FDIC; it had been foreclosed on. There was another 50 percent headed to the courthouse within weeks that involved control, and I was going to buy that from the courts.

Shortly after that, the networks wanted to reduce the television rights by about 20–30 percent and extend that for a couple more years. That would change in 1993, when Rupert Murdoch came into the league with Fox and changed our economics. Compared to where we were, Murdoch four-timesed it. I honestly think it was the most significant thing for the NFL, financially. But when I got the Cowboys, it was not a pretty financial picture in the National Football League.

I was shook like I would have been had I been shot at. I just knew that I was going to go down as the triple idiot that had some success and, because he wanted to be in football, had blown it. It was a dark time.

JIMMY JOHNSON: Bob Ackles, who was a scouting administrator for us, called me at home one day and said, "Jimmy, Jerry just fired Chris."

"Chris? Chris who?"

Bob told me Chris answered the phone in scouting. I said, "Well, you can get somebody to answer the phone."

"No, you don't understand. He's the only guy that knows the computer system that can program the computers. We are lost without him. We've got to get Chris back. Call Jerry."

I called Jerry.

"Did you fire Chris over in scouting?"

"Chris? Chris who?"

I reminded him and he said, "Oh, yeah."

"Why did you fire him?"

"I'm cutting down all the departments and he was the lowest-paid guy in that department, so I fired him." Chris was making $15,000 a year.

"Jerry, we've got to hire him back. Give him a raise. We need him." Chris stayed with the Cowboys ever since.

JERRY JONES: You readily saw the traditional sources for revenue for an NFL team—television, tickets—were not going to get it done. You had to think about how to create new ways to create revenue for a team.

That was where sponsors came in.

For instance, the NFL had done a fabulous job of creating interest. They dominated the sports pages. Tex Schramm was a master. He would carry 50–60 media on the away trips, with the coaches and players. But getting attention on the sports pages was different than using that and marketing with it and encouraging people to pay to get to be associated with the team.

The NFL had a tremendous amount of visibility and awareness, but did not have good marketable return. You had to use that visibility to create some money to go make the teams viable. And that's what we did.

JIMMY JOHNSON: Jerry talked about a contract for me. I said, "Jerry, don't worry about a contract. Just pay me what I'm making at the University of Miami. Eventually, we'll work out the contract."

"Well, I'm going to give you a 10-year contract."

"Okay, fine."

My attorney did the contract and he put in that I had final say, total responsibility, on all football matters—coaches, trades, strength coaches, on and on and on.

We sat down with Bum Bright for two days when he finalized everything for the sale. Then Bum said to me, "You need to get your ass out of town, because I'm going to make this press conference announcement. I don't want you anywhere to be seen with me."

I flew back to Miami, Bum did the press conference, and then I flew back in for my press conference.

JERRY JONES: Jimmy Johnson was a smart, smart, smart, great coach for the Dallas Cowboys. Frank Broyles had told me that he had recruited two genius IQs on his football teams at Arkansas. "And Jones, you sure as hell weren't one of them," he said. "Barry Switzer and Jimmy Johnson were my two genius recruits. They were smart as could be."

My wife, Gene, and I would go visit Jimmy when he was coaching at Oklahoma State. We'd go up to Hot Springs, Arkansas; he and his staff would be there, playing a little golf. We'd go to one of the lakes and spend a night or two with Jimmy and his coaching staff. We did that for five years before the Cowboys.

I had a lot of confidence in Jimmy's abilities. I never even gave a second thought about anything that would get involved in getting off-base relative to loyalty or anything like that. And still don't. Our experience together was absolutely fabulous. To have gotten to experience what we did together was worth any price that I could have ever paid.

JIMMY JOHNSON: At the University of Miami, we had so many great players. I thought I was a hell of a coach, but come to find out, I had better players than everybody. That was why we won all those games. I realized that after I joined the Cowboys.

The first thing I did when I got to Dallas was put the players through some conditioning drills. We timed them in the 40 and I was just taken aback. I said, "This is the oldest, slowest team I've ever seen. There is no talent on this team."

I ended up trading the starting quarterback, Steve Pelluer, to Kansas City. Our starting wide receiver, who led the team in catches, ran a 5.0 40, so I cut him right off the bat. I started looking at this thing and I said, "Jesus, what did I get myself into? Tom Landry, one of the greatest coaches of all time, had three straight losing seasons. And they were 3–13 in the season before I got there."

I didn't know anything about drafting players, but that was my responsibility. Gil Brandt, who had been the Cowboys' longtime vice president of player personnel, helped me out a little bit on it. They did things different, though. They didn't have their coaches do a lot of evaluation. A few of them went out on the road, but I was my own recruiting coordinator at Miami and Oklahoma State, so I wanted to look at these players. With the Cowboys, all the coaches went out on the road and I looked at a lot of the players.

I got into the draft room for our first draft and John Wooten, who was on our player-personnel staff, wanted me to take Tony Mandarich, an offensive tackle from Michigan State, with the first overall pick. He said, "You'll have an all-pro tackle for 10 straight years."

"No, I've got to get a quarterback."

So, we picked Troy Aikman. The Green Bay Packers took Mandarich with the second pick.

Everybody looks back and thinks drafting Troy was a slam-dunk. It wasn't a slam dunk. Troy wasn't even All-Pac 10. Rodney Peete was the All-Pac 10 quarterback, but I had been in Troy's home as a sophomore. I knew who he was and what I wanted.

TROY AIKMAN: In the middle of that 1988 season, the two teams that were vying for the worst record in the NFL, shortly after Thanksgiving, were the Packers and the Cowboys. Lindy Infante was the head coach of the Packers at the time and he had actually flown into Los Angeles and met with me at UCLA while the season was going on. He told me that if they had the number one pick, they were definitely going to take me. I had nothing against Green Bay, but I really was somewhat of a fair-weather quarterback. I struggled in inclement weather and I just knew that I was probably not a great fit for Green Bay.

As we moved through the season, the Packers and Cowboys kept jockeying back and forth as to who had the worst record. In the final week of the season, I was in Scottsdale, Arizona, at the home of a girl I was dating at the time. The Packers were playing the Cardinals at Phoenix, and we went to the game. The Packers had to win and the Cowboys had to lose in order for the Cowboys to have the number one pick overall. No one thought Green Bay could beat the Cardinals that afternoon, but they did and the Cowboys lost to Philadelphia, so I walked out of that stadium that day at least knowing there was a chance that I'd go somewhere other than Green Bay and that maybe Dallas would take me.

We played in the Cotton Bowl in Dallas my senior year, and Gil Brandt, Tex Schramm, and Tom Landry were still in charge of the Cowboys. They were at all my practices. I struggled one particular day, and Terry Donahue, my head coach at UCLA, was really worried about it and I think he expressed that to the powers that be with the Cowboys.

I got a call at my hotel room from Gil Brandt and he said, "Hey, Troy, we don't care if you go out in this game and you throw 10 interceptions. You're going to be our guy. We're taking you with the number one pick."

We won the game and leading up to the draft, I was in Indianapolis for the NFL Scouting Combine. I was meeting with one of the scouts for the Cowboys and he started asking me where I was born, where I grew up, if I had any siblings. It was like, this guy had no idea who I was.

I said, "Wait a minute. I don't mind answering your questions, but you're talking to me as though you have no idea even who I am. I was told by Gil Brandt that I was going to be your first pick."

I'll never forget his response. He said, "Sometimes, Gil says things that he maybe shouldn't say."

Right before the draft is when, all of a sudden, Jerry Jones bought the team and fired Tom Landry. So, everything changed… except the Cowboys' decision to make me the number one pick.

JERRY JONES: The watershed thing was having the first pick in the draft, which Tom Landry had earned, and Troy Aikman being right there at the top of the draft. If you want to come into the NFL, come in and have your first pick ever be the number one pick and have a Troy Aikman sitting there at the top of the draft.

TROY AIKMAN: Jimmy Johnson was recruiting me when I was 15 years old out of Henryetta, Oklahoma. I went to his football camp when I was 16 years old. I was his number one recruit at Oklahoma State and decided to go to Oklahoma. Then he recruited me when I was transferring, and I ended up going to UCLA. It was kind of a strange time to all of a sudden have him back in my life.

I got drafted by the Cowboys and I was thrilled. It was the closest professional team to where I grew up, in Oklahoma. It was a three-hour drive to Henryetta.

I think because of the popularity of the Cowboys, people now would say, "You'd have been crazy to not want to be drafted by the Dallas Cowboys with all that comes with that as the quarterback."

But at the time that I was drafted, the Cowboys, of course, had been the worst team in football. That was why they had the number one pick. They hadn't made the playoffs in a long time.

My rookie year, we had about 30,000–35,000 people coming to games. It was not a full stadium. The whole aura, if you will, of the '70s Cowboys and what we now know of the Cowboy machine was not in existence. Nowhere, in any of that, was I excited about the Cowboys because of the star and the history of that franchise. It was just that I thought it'd be a great place to live and it was close to where I grew up.

JIMMY JOHNSON: Our next pick in '89 was 29th overall, at the top of the second round. I wanted Daryl Johnston, a fullback from Syracuse, but reading all the reports and talking to the people around, nobody was going to draft Daryl that high. I didn't know that many people in pro football, so I called Al Davis and asked him if he wanted to trade up. He said, "Let's swap twos and I'll give you my three."

"Fine."

When I got off the phone, Tex Schramm looked at me and said, "What are you doing? We don't even speak to Al Davis, much less trade with him."

"Well, I didn't want to take Daryl with the first pick in the second round and I don't want to take someone else just because he's the best player available. I don't understand this, 'Take the best player available.' If I don't want that player, if he doesn't fit into our system, I want to get out of that pick."

We did end up taking Steve Wisniewski, a guard from Penn State, at No. 29 and then traded him right away to the Raiders for their second-round pick, at No. 39, and that was where we drafted Daryl.

DARYL JOHNSTON: I was fortunate that Don Shula said, going into that draft, "I'm going to take the fullback from Syracuse in the second round." So, on draft day, I was already kind of expecting where I would go and how things would play out.

Then Louis Oliver, a safety from Florida, started dropping in the first round. I have no reason why. But as he kept dropping, the Dolphins, who had taken running back Sammie Smith with the ninth pick, traded away their second- and third-round picks to move back into the first to grab Louis at No. 25.

I had had a good workout with Washington, so I thought that would be a possible landing spot. But shortly after the Dolphins drafted Oliver, Washington traded a second-round pick and the following year's first-round pick for running back Gerald Riggs from Atlanta.

After that, I thought, "Well, we could be in for a long afternoon."

The Cowboys' trade with the Raiders to move down to take me kind of came out of the blue. Two of the Cowboy coaches, Dave Campo and Tony Wise, had come up to work out all the seniors at Syracuse. They had both been coaches there before, so I thought that was just Jimmy sending those guys up there because they had familiarity with the program and weren't specifically looking at me. I had a good workout, but never anticipated getting drafted in the second round to Dallas.

One of the highlights for me will always be having had an opportunity to talk with Gil Brandt on the phone that day. He said, "How do you feel about having a star on your helmet?"

JERRY JONES: For about 39 days after I bought the team, Tex Schramm was still with the Cowboys and our offices were in the same area. There's no question about it: my purchase of the Cowboys was hard, hard, hard for him. For all intents and purposes, Tex made all the decisions for the Dallas Cowboys.

My attorneys advised me, "Get ready. You're going to have a huge lawsuit. It'll probably come from Tex since he's been there from Day

One, organized the team, did everything but fund the team. Tex does not understand that he doesn't own the Dallas Cowboys. And you've got to understand why he doesn't understand that. If you had been in that position and called every shot, you would feel the very same way." I was advised that I might have this money tied up for what I was doing with the purchase and could be in court for years with a contentious Tex Schramm involved at that particular time.

Tex had given me a list of about 20 things that he wanted relative to leaving the Dallas Cowboys. Pete Rozelle, who was in his final days as NFL commissioner, had his back all the way. This had nothing to do with what I paid the owner. These were things that Tex wanted. Very, very onerous things, but things that I did for the most part because I wanted the Dallas Cowboys.

JIMMY JOHNSON: I made two or three more trades the rest of the way. After the draft, I went into Jerry and said, "Listen, I think we did pretty good. But to be honest with you, I was just shooting from the hip. I've got no background on this stuff, but I think there's a better way to do it as far as knowing the value of the picks.

"The league office will give us a record of all the trades that have been made over the last 10 years. I can't involve players because we don't know the value of players. But if we get a record of all the trades, pick for pick, that have been made over the last 10 years, we can do a graph that can help guide us on these trades."

I asked Mike McCoy, who was a real smart guy in the oil and gas business and was a minority owner and vice president of the Cowboys, to give me a line graph and get an arbitrary number, starting at one and going all the way through the draft, and then put everybody's trades on this graph.

I said, "That way, we can get a relative value of this by adding up the numbers and I won't be shooting from the hip. I'll have it right there in front of me. I can get somebody on the phone and say, 'Hey, we'll swap twos and I'll give you my four, because I know what the value of these picks are.'"

That helped me in the next couple of drafts, as far as making a lot of trades. We made 51 trades in five years. That was more than the entire NFL had made in those five years. To give you an example, the New York Giants had made one trade in that five-year period.

That was with me on a long snapper and it was a screwup on my part. I traded Steve DeOssie for a pick. The only reason I did that was Steve came to one of our minicamps and got in an argument with our defensive coordinator, Dave Wannstedt, so I got rid of him. I should have kept him because he was a great long snapper.

TROY AIKMAN: I remember, during the OTAs of my rookie year, the supplemental draft was coming up and Jerry Jones called to tell me the Cowboys were going to draft Timm Rosenbach, a quarterback at Washington State that I had played against. Jerry said they were only going to draft him for trade value, so I didn't think anything of it. I didn't even know what the supplemental draft was or how it worked.

The Cowboys did get the pick, but they didn't take Rosenbach. They drafted Steve Walsh, who, of course, had a history with Jimmy Johnson as his quarterback at the University of Miami. They had won a national championship together.

Now, essentially, two first-round picks as quarterbacks are competing for the starting job as rookies. So, it was a little tense.

DARYL JOHNSTON: The coaches from the University of Miami were really kind of leaning towards Steve Walsh. Listen, I love Steve and he had a great college career. He's one of those guys who's able to get more from himself and his team than you would think possible.

But you couldn't put those two guys on the field and watch them throw it and think that Steve Walsh should be ahead of Troy Aikman. You had to be crazy. Troy could throw it like nobody I'd ever seen before.

JERRY JONES: After we had bought the team, Tex Schramm and I had talked three or four times about trading Herschel Walker, and about how that could be a really good move for us. Tex talked about, when he was with the Rams, the great trade that he had made and said he actually brought in three or four quarterbacks at the same time and ended up trading two or three of them and getting a great amount of picks and players that helped build the Rams.

JIMMY JOHNSON: I used to go jogging with all my coaches. We were talking that first year and I said, "There's no way in the world we're going to be able to build up the talent good enough to win. We've got to do something to jump-start this thing. Making some trades will help, but the only thing that we've got that anybody wants is Herschel Walker. He's the only Pro Bowler we've got. What do you think about trading him?"

David Shula, our offensive coordinator, looked at me and said, "Trade him? We won't score a point if we don't have Herschel."

"Well, it doesn't make a shit a difference. We're going to get our ass beat anyway."

Ernie Accorsi, who was the GM of the Browns at the time, actually started it when he called me and said, "Jimmy, I hear you might be interested in trading Herschel."

"Yeah."

"Well, what would it take?"

Of course, I was going to shoot for the moon. I said, "What is that Guy Lombardo deal? A one… and a two… and a one… and a two… and a one… and a two."

He laughed and said, "We don't have a one next year. I've got a linebacker from Florida, Clifford Charlton. I'll throw in him and we'll give you our two next year. And then a one and a two the next year. And maybe a three or something the third year."

"Let me give it some thought."

"I'm going to have our owner, Art Modell, call you tonight."

"Okay."

I got off the phone with him and, just before practice, I went to Jerry and said, "I think I got a hell of a deal on this Herschel Walker trade."

"Herschel? You're going to trade Herschel?"

"We've got to do something. I think it's a good deal with Cleveland, but I think maybe we can better it. Herschel's from Georgia, you know Rankin Smith," who owned the Atlanta Falcons. "Why don't you call Rankin and see what he'd do? I've been talking to Mike Lynn [the GM of the Vikings] a bunch about trading Steve Walsh to him. I'll call San Francisco because they wanted Walsh as well. I'll call the people I know, and we'll go from there."

I got back in from practice, and my secretary, Barbara Goodman, said, "You've got a fax here from Mike Lynn."

I looked at his trade proposal for Herschel and it was kind of complicated. It had one first-round pick, like three years down the road, but he had five players. I could tell all five of these players were players that he could get rid of: Jesse Solomon, a linebacker who had a bad knee; David Howard, who was an old linebacker; Issiac Holt, a cornerback who was a little bit of a headcase. They had a little running back from Stanford that never even showed up. And then they had a disgruntled young defensive tackle.

But the way Mike put it was, every player was tied to a pick so, if the Cowboys kept those players, we wouldn't get any of those picks. As I looked at it, I was thinking, "Well, these players are better than anything we've got, but I don't want these players. But I might, down the road, be able to work out a deal to get the picks."

Herschel's agent, Peter Johnson, balked at us making the trade and said Herschel was going to retire unless Jerry gave him a million dollars, which Jerry did.

JERRY JONES: What a lot of people don't know is that Herschel Walker had to agree to be traded, because he could void the trade. For that time, Herschel Walker was one of the most compensated football players for endorsements and getting funds. So, we also had to pay him a lot of money, because of what he was leaving behind and that was a whole other negotiation.

But on the trading chart, because of the Herschel Walker trade, for three years in a row we had over 8,000 points in the draft. We had like four or five times the firepower of any other team in terms of draft picks because we got Minnesota's one, two, three; one, two, three; and one, two, three. And then we had the first pick of the draft in two of those three years: 1989, when we got Troy Aikman, and 1991, when we took defensive tackle Russell Maryland.

It was like going to Las Vegas with a pocketful of extra money. You can go and roll if you don't have to pay for the baby's pablum. And we were able to roll. There's no question that that firepower is where you got the big punch to punch this thing to the success that we had.

Not to take anything away from Troy Aikman. Not to take anything away from Michael Irvin. Not to take anything away from Charles Haley, who we were able to get because of those extra picks, or any of the players. Not to take anything away from Jimmy or any of the coaching.

But that firepower was really what put us in that spot.

JIMMY JOHNSON: We made the trade with the Vikings and we got gashed in the media. I've still got Randy Galloway's column in the *Dallas Morning News*: "Who are these buffoons? What are they doing trading away their only good player for a bunch of cripples and has-beens?" All these players came in, except for the little running back, so I got that pick. The defensive tackle was an asshole, so I cut him right off the bat.

Jesse Solomon came in and if he had been healthy, he would have been a really good player. David Howard was a really great person, a try-hard guy. Issiac Holt was a talented guy, but he was just here, there, and everywhere.

I told Wannstedt, "Listen, I know they're better than anything we've got, but don't start them and don't fall in love with them. If you want to put them in in the second quarter, that's fine. Put them on the kickoff team to open the game, but don't put them in until the second quarter because I don't want the fans to fall in love with them, either."

I was going to get those picks rather than having to send them back to the Vikings.

Herschel did really well in the first game for Minnesota, but then they tailed off. Mike Lynn was getting criticism for trading away all those players that became picks for us. At the end of the year, I called him and said, "As it stands now, I'm going to cut all these players."

"Oh, shit, Jimmy, I'm taking a beating up here."

"Well, I'll tell you what, those three guys that we've got left, I'll keep them and I'll kick back a pick or two. That way you get something out of it."

He hung up on me. I called Jerry Burns, the Vikings' coach, and Jerry Burns said, "I've got nothing to do with it. That's Mike's deal."

I kept trying to call Mike. He wouldn't call me back. It was getting down to the point that I had to do something, so I sent a certified letter to the league office saying, "As of a certain day, these three players are going to be released, unless the Minnesota Vikings and Mike Lynn cancel this trade and work out an arrangement with me."

Mike Lynn called and said, "Okay, what do you want to give us?"

I gave him a three and we got those three players. Now those three players never played for us. They were kind of transitional guys and when we got to be good, they weren't even around. But it helped us in the meantime.

TROY AIKMAN: I was a huge Herschel Walker fan when I was in high school and he was at Georgia. Rarely do your heroes surpass your thoughts of them and your expectations, but he was one of those that did. It was really awesome to me as a rookie.

When we traded him, I thought, "Holy cow! He's the one player that we know can play. We don't have anybody else." I also remember thinking, with all the draft picks, the trade was only going to be as good as the guys that we got with those picks.

Jimmy had a lot of strengths as a head coach, but I think his greatest strength was as a talent evaluator and being able to work deals and manipulate the roster. That trade, of course, as most people know, is what really got us going on the right track with a young, talented team a lot sooner than people would have ever imagined.

JIMMY JOHNSON: I ended up getting a one, two and a three for Steve Walsh. That was a tough deal, too, because Steve had played for me at the University of Miami, been on an undefeated team and a national championship team. It pissed Troy off, but I couldn't come right out and say, "Hey, Troy's our guy," because I wanted to build up trade value for Steve.

There was a little bit of tension that first year until I was able to trade Steve. After that, I had to make in-roads with Troy. I went over to his house and we set up a tropical fish tank and had some beers and bullshitted around.

But I couldn't do that until I got rid of Steve.

TROY AIKMAN: We weren't very talented and through that first season, we went through a lot of players. I mean, a lot of players. It seemed like every Monday or every Wednesday we came into practice, we had new faces in the huddle.

JIMMY JOHNSON: It was a revolving door. Every Tuesday, I was just looking at players, just trying them out. We would bring in guys on Tuesday and maybe we would keep one, he'd play a week or two and we'd get rid of him. Then, we'd bring in two or three more.

DARYL JOHNSTON: Jimmy was in search to find the right type of people and personalities that were going to be able to perform in that environment. That first year was tough.

JIMMY JOHNSON: I remember there was one player from the University of Tulsa that I worked out on Tuesday and signed that afternoon. He practiced Wednesday and Thursday, he was in the team picture on Friday, played in the game on Sunday, and I cut him on Monday. I was just trying out guys to see what fit. Obviously, all the players were on edge.

When I first got there, I had a talk with Randy White, a great person who was at the end of the line, and he retired. Then, I kind of encouraged Danny White to retire. Too Tall Jones was a tremendous professional, but he was over the hill.

When I first got there, they had an outdoor weight room. It was an old chain-link fence around a few weights. The first time I saw it, it was the off-season and there were no players lifting. I went to the strength coach, Bob Ward, and said, "Bob, where are all our players?"

"Well, shit, it's cold out here. Plus, in the off-season, they don't work out here. They work out in spas."

"Well, why in the hell did we hire you? What are you doing?"

The same thing happened when we went to Thousand Oaks, California, for training camp. There was this huge publicity about these trucks of weights coming out to Thousand Oaks, but every day after practice, I never saw anybody working out. The only guy that ever worked out in that little weight area was Brad Sham, our radio guy. He was always on the bicycle.

We were in one of our nightly personnel meetings and I asked Bob Ward, "Why aren't our players working out?"

"Coach, you go with these three-a-day practices, they don't have enough energy to lift weights."

"Why in the hell are we bringing out a truckload of weights if nobody's going to work out here?"

I got rid of Bob after that season and brought in Mike Woicik from Syracuse University.

DARYL JOHNSTON: There are two teams that won three Super Bowls in a four-year span. Mike Woicik was the strength coach for both: the Dallas Cowboys and the New England Patriots. I don't think it's a coincidence.

Mike was the best at what he did. He made you work in the weight room. I remember Jimmy coming up to me towards the end of the '89 season and he said, "Hey, we're thinking about bringing your old strength coach in for an interview."

I kind of chuckled a little bit and said, "Oh, these guys aren't ready to work that hard. They're not ready for Mike."

"You may have just got your friend a job."

Mike was what Jimmy was looking for, someone off the field to be demanding and challenging and pushing guys to be the best that they can be the way that he challenged his coaching staff on the practice field. That was one of the first additions that was really a big missing piece. We got bigger, stronger, faster really quick.

Number one, you were going to do squatting. If you couldn't squat, you were going to find a way to get your legs and your glutes stronger. The game is played from explosive power. Plyometrics—transitioning strength to movement, becoming explosive. Box jumps, lateral hops. He had an old Eastern Bloc style of training. He had magazines that were printed in German and Russian just to let you see the photographs of what the training elements were.

Robert Williams was more of a track guy out of Baylor playing corner. He ran a 4.34 40 and Mike was trying to get him to embrace his style of training. Robert said to him, "You're not going to be able to get me any faster."

"Give me one off-season and if you don't like what I'm doing, then I'll adjust, and we'll integrate some of the stuff that you'd like to do."

Mike did speed training with Robert. He used resistance running, where you have bands, parachutes, a number of different ways. That helps you with your stride frequency and building strength through the foot. He also used assisted running, where you're tethered to another guy and it makes you over-stride. Assisted running increases your stride length, while being very, very careful not to overstride and not pull a hamstring.

At the end of that off-season, Williams ran a 4.29. That was when the light bulb went on for him. That was how Mike did things. He got advocates in his weight room. He changed people, he showed people how they could become faster, how they could become stronger, and how that transitioned onto the playing field.

Now, all of a sudden, you've got your little army of warriors that are out there and when anybody doubts your program, you can share your story. That was huge for me because I was one of his first guys. I would say, "Listen, when I got to Syracuse, I was 6'2", 212 pounds and I ran a 4.85 40. I was the last guy offered a scholarship. When I graduated, I was 6'2", 242 pounds and ran a 4.61 40."

I had put on 30 pounds and my 40 time had dropped two-and-a-half tenths of a second. I said, "That's what this guy will do for you if you just buy in and believe in him."

One day, Emmitt Smith was in the squat rack and hurt his back. The story came out that Emmitt got hurt squatting. Jimmy came to Mike and said, "I'm thinking of pulling the squat out of this for certain guys and I just want to make sure you're okay with that."

"Once you take the squat out of this program, you're gonna have to fire me."

"Whoa! Whoa! Whoa! You believe in it that strongly?"

"Well, not only do I believe in it that strongly, but do you know how Emmitt got hurt?"

"He got hurt in the squat rack?"

"No. Emmitt had 225 pounds on his back, and somebody called his name, and he turned. You're rotating and you can't stop that weight without really bracing. So, he tweaked his back not being smart in the rack."

"Alright, don't worry about that. We're still squatting."

JIMMY JOHNSON: It was such a culture change. A couple of reporters said, "This team will be dead by the time they get to November, because they're working out four days a week."

But I didn't know any different. That was what we had been in college. We were doing the three-man monkey rolls. You should have seen Too Tall Jones trying to do a three-man monkey roll. I felt so bad for him. It was brutal.

TROY AIKMAN: I oftentimes thought that my team at UCLA, when I left, was probably a more talented team than the team I was playing for professionally.

I was 0–11 as a rookie and the one game we won in going 1–15 that year was against Washington, and Steve Walsh was the starter. There were games where I didn't play particularly well, but there were also some games where I thought I played really well, only to lose at the last minutes.

I just thought, "Man, I don't know what you have to do to win in this league."

JIMMY JOHNSON: In the preseason, we had scrimmaged San Diego and we had a goal-line stand. You would have thought we won the damn Super Bowl because we had that goal-line stand. We went 3–1 in the preseason and I was thinking, "Hey, we may be okay."

The opening game was against New Orleans. They killed us.

DARYL JOHNSTON: The Saints beat us 28–0. I think, from our tallies, we missed 26 tackles that day. That was when all of us realized, especially the rookies, the younger guys, there's a huge difference between the NFL preseason and the NFL regular season.

I remember the tone being set that first meeting that week, where Jimmy said, "Hey, you know what? You guys are men. I expected you to act that way, but you had your chance and you blew it. Now we're going to do things my way."

That was when everything ramped up. We were doing middle drill on Wednesdays, live tackling, backs to the ground. Our practices became very, very physical, very, very challenging.

That was Jimmy's first real big transition and his thumbprint on what this was going to be like moving forward, to build that toughness, that physicality. It was going to be a grind every week.

JERRY JONES: The first season, we won one football game. That went off me like water off a duck's back. I didn't even think twice about it because I had so many other matters on my mind. Just to be involved in the NFL, to walk out on the practice field, to walk out and just be around the team, hell, that was the breath of fresh air.

People would ask, "How did you get through that first year when you won one football game? How did you handle the second and third year? What about when you traded Herschel Walker?"

Well, that was against the backdrop of actually feeling like you're dancing with the devil, gone to hell and back, and you were just lucky to be doing what you were doing. That was the fun part. That was the good part of it.

JIMMY JOHNSON: As much as we struggled early on, I believed in what we were doing just because I didn't know any better. Maybe I wasn't smart enough to know that we were really bad. I was just accustomed to winning.

When we went to Oklahoma State, they weren't any good and we rebuilt that program. We lost one regular season game in four years at the University of Miami and we were playing a national schedule. My last two years, I think we played 12 teams that were in the top 20 and eight teams that were in the top 10. Every other week, it was Michigan or Penn State or Oklahoma or Florida or Florida State, on and on. We won all those games, so when we got to Dallas, we didn't know any different.

I brought in my coaching staff, I brought in my trainer, I brought in my administrative assistant to handle all the travel, I brought in my publicity director. They were people that had been with me everywhere. We all just believed because that was the only thing we had ever done.

TROY AIKMAN: If you went to practice, you'd have been amazed at how physical we practiced and the intensity of our practices. Jimmy brought a lot of the college atmosphere. He was still kind of, I would say, learning the ropes.

We were young and he felt, "Hey, this is the way you mold a football team." We were in pads every day and we hit every day. And we were young enough to absorb all that.

JIMMY JOHNSON: Not knowing anything about pro football, I spent time watching pro teams work so I wouldn't completely be an idiot about it. I spent four days with John Robinson with the Rams. I spent time with the Atlanta Falcons. I spent time with the Raiders.

For the first year, I retained one coach to help the defense, Dick Nolan. I also kept one coach to help the offense, Neill Armstrong, and I kept the special teams coach, Al Lowry.

I didn't want to fall into a trap that first year of not knowing something. I wanted to have a little bit of pro experience in all three phases. They knew it was just going to be for one year until we got our feet on the ground.

DARYL JOHNSTON: Jimmy allowed his coaches to be aggressive, which was great, and there was also some transparency. He'd come to the defensive guys and say, "Hey, we're gonna do a surprise onsides kick and if we don't get it, you guys are gonna be on a short field. I expect you to hold them to at least a field goal. We can't have a touchdown here. But we're gonna roll the dice on it, so you guys be ready to go because if this thing goes the other way, you're gonna be right back out on the field."

JIMMY JOHNSON: When we were getting ready for the second draft, Jerry said, "Jimmy, do we actually need all these scouts?"

"Well, they bring back a bunch of information."

"You've got your coaches on the road doing the scouting. I just think that maybe we don't need all these guys. I hear you guys talking about who the top players are. I got *Sports Illustrated* here. It's about the same players."

"Well, when we get into that third, fourth, fifth, sixth round, *Sports Illustrated* doesn't have that."

All the trades we made weren't all that great, but we made enough of them that it was kind of like a fishing-net approach. You get a lot of trash fish, but you get a lot of good fish, too. If you got enough picks, you're going to hit on some of them.

TROY AIKMAN: My first game of my second year, in 1990, we beat the San Diego Chargers. So, I got that monkey off my back. But as we began having success in the years ahead, I never lost track of how hard my rookie year was and how hard it was to win.

A lot of people did take winning for granted, but I never did. I always knew that it was really hard to win consistently in this league. The players are too good, the coaches are too good and the organizations, as a whole, are just too good.

JIMMY JOHNSON: Troy didn't say much the first five years. He wouldn't get all vocal. He was really kind of quiet.

CHARLES HALEY: Troy never talked. The only time I would hear him talk was when he was giving out cadence. The day before a game, I'd be over there clowning like I normally do and Troy would be laughing and end up swallowing his tobacco or snuff, whatever it was, and he'd be running to the bathroom to throw up.

TROY AIKMAN: I didn't care about passing titles, I didn't care about rushing titles, I didn't care about any of that. If somebody got it, great, but it wasn't relevant in my world.

For instance, Emmitt would be asked at the start of the year, "What's your goal this year? How many yards do you think you can rush for? Is 2,000 a reality?"

I was asked, "What's going on with Jimmy and Jerry? Are they gonna be able to get along?" or, "How come they haven't signed so-and-so yet? Are you upset about that?"

I was asked the hard questions where I had to kind of walk a tightrope. I thought there was a lot of attention on our game back when I was playing, but it's nothing like it is now and I really think an important part of the quarterback's duties is to be a good representative of the organization and be careful as to what they say.

I would tell Jerry, "I'm not involved in this negotiation. I mean, I want to have this player here, I think he's a great player. But you just have to know that publicly, I have to say these things so that those players know that I'm with them. I'm not trying to upset you. I'm not trying to influence what you're doing, but I'm a player first and I'm a teammate first."

Jerry certainly understood that.

JIMMY JOHNSON: Our second year, when Troy hurt his shoulder and we didn't make the playoffs, I pushed to try to get Troy into the Pro Bowl and he didn't make it. I remember, to this day, I walked out on that little brick wall by the practice field before we started practice when they announced who was going to go to the Pro Bowl.

I said, "Troy, I'm sorry. I apologize. You deserve to be in the Pro Bowl. I tried to get you in. It just didn't happen."

"Coach, don't worry about me going to the Pro Bowl. You just keep surrounding me with great players. I'll go to plenty of Pro Bowls."

That tells you a little bit about Troy.

TROY AIKMAN: We started 3–7 my second year, and that was the low point of my career. A lot of people would have thought maybe my rookie year would have been the low point. But when you start your first year, at least for me, the team was already bad. They were already the worst team in football. It's hard to take ownership of how bad your team is when they were already bad before you got there.

Then, when you go into Year Two, now you start really saying, "Hey, I'm a part of the problem now if we don't get this thing going." You're no longer able to deflect it.

When we started out 3–7, the locker room morale was not good. We were not playing particularly good football. We went to play the Los Angeles Rams, and they were good. Jim Everett was their quarterback. Ernie Zampese and Norv Turner were on their offensive staff. And out of nowhere, we win the game.

We ended up winning four games in a row and put ourselves in a position to make the postseason. We came up just short. But we went 7–9 that year and we started thinking, "Hey, we might be a decent team. It feels like we're kind of on the right track."

JIMMY JOHNSON: Our first year, I had David Shula as offensive coordinator. He had been with the Miami Dolphins as a quarterbacks coach and receivers coach the previous seven seasons and was using the offense they had run. I wasn't happy with it.

TROY AIKMAN: David Shula had been our offensive coordinator my first two years and we just weren't very good. My second year, there were 28 teams in the league and we were 28ᵗʰ in offense. A change was made.

JIMMY JOHNSON: Two years into it, I was going to make a change at offensive coordinator and I was going to put David Shula with the receivers. I liked what Ernie Zampese had done and I wanted to hire him away from the Los Angeles Rams. Ernie turned me down, but he recommended Norv Turner, who had been his receivers coach with the Rams. I knew Norv because I watched the Rams practice.

TROY AIKMAN: There were about four guys that we wanted, and none of them could get out of their contracts—or one thing after another as to why we couldn't get any of them. I had always liked what the Rams were doing with Ernie Zampese. The offense was similar to what I had run at UCLA.

Jimmy called me and said, "I think we can get the guy with the Rams."

"Ernie Zampese? I had heard he'd never leave L.A., never leave California."

"No, it's not Zampese. It's their wide receivers coach, Norv Turner."

I didn't know anything about him. Then, I went into a meeting room with Norv and he started drawing up some plays. I just asked him, "If you come here, is this going to be the L.A. Rams' offense?"

"One hundred percent."

That was all I needed to hear.

Norv didn't wow me as far as saying, "We're going to get along great," or anything like that. But, man, I liked his offense. I told Jimmy, "I really like this guy, I think he'd be great."

JIMMY JOHNSON: When I hired Norv, I told him, "I want Ernie Zampese's passing game, but here's our running game: We're going to have a bunch of young guys, so it's going to be power right, it's going to be power left. It's going to be toss right, it's going to be toss left. It's going to be wham right, wham left. It's going to be simple, so everybody's going to know what to do and I can insert a rookie in there and he's going to be able to handle it.

"On our passing game, which fits into what Ernie did, we're going to number all the routes. That way, if Michael Irvin's at X or Z or slot or whatever, he'll know exactly what to do." Norv and I spent a ton of time weaving it all together.

TROY AIKMAN: Norv installed the Rams' offense, but with pretty much the same personnel that we had my first two years. All of a sudden, we went from worst in the league in offense to ninth in his first year. In his second year, we were in the top five, and his third year we were top three. He was a great playcaller, he was a great innovator. It was a perfect fit.

I know he was great for me. That was why he was my presenter when I went into the Hall of Fame. As great as Jimmy was for me, my career was not what it was without Norv Turner.

So many quarterbacks, I believe, have come into this league with a lot of ability and they've just not been in the right situation or they haven't had the chance to work with the right person. I believe, had that been the case, they could have gone on and had great success. Had I stayed where I was my first two years, I probably would have left the league regarded as a bust.

Norv got us all going on the same track. I've heard Michael Irvin say that Norv was responsible for his career. I've heard Emmitt Smith say the same thing. So did our offensive linemen. He brought a sense of direction and confidence.

Nobody called a game better than Norv. We would put in a play that was only for a specific coverage and if they didn't bring that coverage, we didn't have anything. I asked, "What if they bring a blitz?"

"If they bring a blitz, just throw it away. We don't have anything. We just hope we get it."

Norv would call the play, I'd walk up to the line of scrimmage, they'd start to show the coverage exactly the way we were hoping it would be and… boom! We were hitting a big play. It's one thing to know offense. It's another thing to know when to call the plays. Norv was just so good at breaking down the defense's weaknesses.

He was only with me for three years, but he had a profound impact on me and my life and my career. He's one of my closest friends to this day.

JIMMY JOHNSON: I always prided myself that I was always the first guy in the office. I always liked to do two or three hours of work before the coaches

got there, before we had our first meeting in the morning. In fact, I would always go home like 10:00 or so, because I knew if I stayed there, they would stay there, even if it was busy work.

I'm an early riser. Even to this day, I get up at 4:30, 5:00 every morning. Well, I'd go in at 5:00 and Norv would be in there watching tape. This was in the off-season. A couple days later, he was still in there when I arrived. He had beaten me every morning.

I said, "Norv, this is going to get old here. I'm going to try to beat you into the office and you're not going to let me beat you. We've got to set some standards here."

Norv worked his ass off, as far as combining the pass and the run. We did get into a little bit of problem with the running game. After the first few practices, Norv said, "Jimmy, the only thing we didn't address on this 'Power Right' is we do have to audible. We can't just go, 'Black Power Right!' We're going to have to add some numbers to some of this stuff."

We made the adjustments.

The main thing with our passing game was that it was simple with the receiver routes being numbered. All they had to do was learn the route tree. If it was "347," one receiver ran a three route, another ran a four route, and another ran a seven route. So, if Michael Irvin was strong side, he ran a three. If he was weak side, he ran a seven.

It was very, very simple and we could change formations without anyone getting confused as far as what route they were running. Troy Aikman knew exactly where the routes were, so when he read the coverage, he was going to see which route was going to be open.

DARYL JOHNSTON: When Norv came in, we started watching Rams film in the spring. We were just watching how that personnel mirrored our personnel: What John Jefferson and Charlie Joiner and the guys outside were doing. What Kellen Winslow was doing.

You could see the pieces of the puzzle really starting to fit with what our personnel did well and how that really mirrored that scheme. I was very confident in my blocking. I've always felt good as a receiver out of the backfield. Everything that he was going to ask the H and the F in that system kind of accentuated the strengths of my game. But that was true for everybody:

Michael Irvin on the outside, Jay Novacek at tight end. The pieces that we had on our roster fit seamlessly into what Norv did.

By the time we finished OTAs, we walked into training camp extremely confident that we were going to be a very, very good offensive football team. That was when we went from 7–9 to 11–5.

Everybody will go to different games, but when we beat the Redskins at RFK, when they were 11–0 and we were 6–5, that was the epitome of what that offense became. We walked onto the field with more than seven minutes left on the clock in the fourth quarter, up 24–21, and we never left. We killed that clock for seven minutes. Washington knew what we were doing and couldn't stop it.

We thought, "This is going to be fun moving forward. And Norv is just going to be able to add to it."

He also used a little bit of anticipatory management. We'd have a Philadelphia game back in the early '90s and in the Saturday night meeting, Norv would tell Nate Newton, "I don't want you to get on the phone and tell me we need to run the ball because that's not what the game plan is. We're gonna loosen it up, we're gonna throw it a little bit more than we have in the first half. I need you to be ready to go in the second half when we get them tired from rushing the passer and all the other stuff we're going to do. I need you to be ready to go then."

As good as Norv was on Sunday afternoon calling plays, he was every bit as good Saturday night, explaining everything and how everything was gonna play out so everybody had a really good idea of how the game should go if we do our jobs.

JIMMY JOHNSON: We were running the same defense that we did at Oklahoma State and Miami. That was what Butch Davis and Dave Campo knew, because they had been doing it for 15 years. It was "Switch" and "Double Switch."

There's a lot of teams doing it now. It was out of Cover Two, but we would invert it. We'd invert weak side, we'd invert strong side and we'd even invert it on both sides. When the 49ers were really good, we inverted it on both sides, but we pressed both corners. They thought it was a hard Cover Two and they ran the slant right into those safeties.

I visited with the Steelers when we were running this when I was defensive coordinator at Pitt before I even went to Oklahoma State. Their defensive secondary coach grabbed me one night at the Black Angus Restaurant, and said, "You cannot run that coverage."

"Well, I guess we can't, but we're just kicking everybody's ass with it."

My first year at Dallas, Bill Parcells told me a story about when the Giants played us and his quarterback, Phil Simms, said, "They're running that college coverage." Parcells told him, "Hey, you'd better study that college coverage because these bastards know what they're doing."

Now, everybody runs a portion of it. Bill Belichick said he tried to do a little bit, but you've got to almost do it full-scale for it to be effective. Back then, everybody was running one-free, man coverage, three-deep. They didn't do a whole lot of inverted two. Now, a lot of teams do it.

BILL POLIAN: With "Switch" and "Double Switch," Jimmy's reference is to a coverage concept, originally developed at the college level, to deal with option offenses. The four defensive backs line up in what is called a Cover Two look. The corners are aligned over the wide receivers at a six- to seven-yard depth. The safeties are aligned just outside the hashmarks at a 10- to 12-yard depth.

In his pre-snap look, the quarterback sees what looks like a zone defense designed to stop deep throws. A basic offensive audible versus this coverage would be to throw a slant to one of the wide receivers. On the snap, one or both safeties "invert," meaning that they drive toward the line of scrimmage with their aiming point seven yards of depth on the outside shoulder of the offensive tackle. That landmark is exactly where the slant audible would be thrown. The result is a blown-up receiver, an incompletion, or an interception.

This coverage works equally well versus the run. As Jimmy states, you can run it with press cornerbacks, giving the quarterback a totally different look and creating different post-snap reads.

JIMMY JOHNSON: Our third year, '91, we won our first playoff game against Chicago. Then, we went to Detroit and Detroit just threw the ball all over the field and beat us.

After the game, my first words in the locker room were, "We've made progress, but we've got to improve our pass defense and our pass rush. We do that, then we can take some steps forward."

Luckily, John McVay, who was vice president and director of football operations for San Francisco, called during the off-season. I had made trades with him for running back Terrence Flagler and defensive end Danny Stubbs, so he knew I was willing to listen to a deal he would propose. He said, "Jimmy, would you be interested in Charles Haley?"

I was looking for a pass-rusher, and Charles was a Pro Bowler so I told him we'd be interested. Then John said, "He can't get along with the coaches here."

I had my assistant coaches, Dave Campo and Butch Davis, call the 49ers' assistants. I had some of the players call their players. They all said, "Charles is passionate. He's a great player. He's smart, but he just can't get along with guys telling him what to do."

I just thought to myself, "If he's smart and he's passionate and a great player, I can reason with him. If he's dumb, I can't handle it. I can't reason with a dumb guy."

CHARLES HALEY: George Seifert—our coach in San Francisco—and I had a little altercation, a difference of opinion and philosophy or whatever you want to say. It got a little heated. I was sent home.

Some of the veteran guys were telling me I needed to come back and apologize to George. I came back the next day, but I can't say I'm sorry for the truth. I didn't apologize. He just told me to go home and within an hour I was sent to the Cowboys.

JIMMY JOHNSON: We ended up making the trade in 1992 and then, in that year's draft, I took Kevin Smith and Darren Woodson. That improved our pass defense and our pass rush. We went from 15th to leading the league in total defense.

CHARLES HALEY: You know how it is when you wish shit like that to happen, and then when it happens, you get mad about it? I said, "Damn! What did I do? What did I do?"

I had to get on a plane that day to fly to Dallas. As I was walking off the plane with one of my suitcases, I couldn't even see because there were so many cameras and lights there. And then Jerry Jones stuck his damn hand out and said, "I'm Jerry Jones, the owner of the Dallas Cowboys."

I'm looking at him going, "Yeah, right. No owner ever came out to say hi to Charles Haley. What the hell's going on?"

I guess Jerry wanted to look crazy right in the eyes. And I was looking at him like he was crazy. He grabbed my suitcase. I couldn't believe this was Jerry Jones, the owner of the Cowboys, carrying my suitcase.

I was feeling dejected, whatever. By the time I got to my hotel room, I felt like I had a brother. He told me, "Whatever happened when you were at the 49ers, that's at the 49ers. If you want to live with one foot in the past and one foot forward, you ain't gonna be worth a damn. But if you need somebody to push you forward, I'll be that guy. And if you ever need a hand, I'll help you out." He always said he had my back, and that meant something to me because I never had anybody, other than Bill Walsh, say that.

Before the last preseason game after I got to the Cowboys, nobody wanted to talk to me. They were all in a corner, shaking and shivering, wondering, "What the hell have they done?"

The other guys on the D-line looked over and they were sizing me up, going, "Look at this guy, he's only 235 pounds." What they did wrong was they didn't look in my damn eyes because they would have seen what hell looked like.

The next day, I walked in and there were 25 guys in the tub. Half of them were looking at me and the other half were talking about me. And they were too damn dumb to know that I was standing there listening. Now, I guess about 95 percent of what they said was true, but the other 5 percent pissed me off.

I got in one of the one-man Jacuzzi tubs and the guys started coming by telling me they didn't mean anything by what they said. I told them what my mama said: "Boy, respect is not given; it's earned." And I told them, "I'm going to earn it today."

I went out there and practiced, even though I had gotten a scope on my knee five days before the trade. During the stretch, I went all the way back to the goalposts because my whole theory in life is first, I have to visualize; I have to see myself being successful. Then, I have to verbalize; I have to tell myself what I'm gonna do. And then, I've gotta go do it.

I whupped their ass. I put every defensive lineman on their back. I went over there and kicked every offensive lineman's ass. Then, I went in. I said, "My day's work is done."

They still never felt what hell felt like because I never released it all. I had to stay in control because I didn't want to hurt anybody.

JIMMY JOHNSON: I had two incidents with Charles and we straightened both of them out. The first one was after we won a game at Minnesota when we already had the playoffs sewed up. We went into the locker room and I had a rule that once I closed the door, nobody got in. Charles wasn't there. Then, here came Charles, late.

Sure enough, he went to the back of the room as I was talking to team. I said, "Charles, get your ass up here." He looked at me. I said, "Get your ass up here. I ain't gonna tell you again."

He came up. He got right in my face and said, "Is this close enough?"

"Yeah, that's close enough."

The second time also was in the locker room. As I was reaming the team out, Charles was in the back of the room. I said, "Charles, get your ass up here!"

Afterward, he came in and said, "Coach, just don't embarrass me in front of the other players. I love playing for you, I'll do anything you ask, but don't embarrass me in front of the players."

Charles was a trip, but after those incidents, our relationship was fantastic. We'd laugh and cut up. He just said don't embarrass him in front of the other players, and everything would be fine. And it was.

CHARLES HALEY: Jimmy was a no-nonsense type of head coach. He was, "It's my way or the highway." He'd say, "Repetition is the motherhood of learning. We're gonna do some damn learning today."

He'd have guys out there for hours. He'd go, "Start it over! Start it over!" It'd be five minutes before practice was over and he'd go back to stretching and do the whole damn thing over again. That was crazy, but he had full control of the situation, 100 percent.

Guys respected that. They wanted that discipline and they got that discipline.

TROY AIKMAN: Jerry Jones and Jimmy Johnson have always said we probably wouldn't have made the Super Bowl without Charles Haley. I believe that.

He brought a credibility to our defense and a pass rush that we just simply didn't have, that a team had to game plan for. He was just a ferocious competitor. He kind of put us over the top and then we were off and running at that point.

DARYL JOHNSTON: The one thing we were missing was the guy from the edge. Then, Jimmy went out and got that fixed with Charles Haley.

So now, as good as we felt after the '91 season, going into '92 with Charles coming in and seeing what he could do and knowing about him, that was kind of when we knew we were going to be unique.

Charles was one of the greatest teammates you'll ever have. He was so misunderstood. He's been great with my kids, he's been great with my family. He's one of the more giving people you'll ever meet.

He's very open with his struggle with his bipolar condition. I think that's what some of the behavioral issues are a part of. And at that time, we didn't embrace mental health as much as we do today.

CHARLES HALEY: When I would go into my depression, I wouldn't talk for about two or three weeks. When I got there, I became a leader and guys looked up to me. They looked for that leadership and I wasn't there to help them because I couldn't understand what I was going through.

My problem was I never talked out stuff when it happened. I would always let it fester. Then, when it came out, everyone was going, "What the hell? What happened?"

Before Jimmy went in the Hall of Fame, I got a chance to sit down with him and hug his neck and tell him that I was sorry, especially after I went through my diagnosis and I got treatment for it and medicine. I told him how much I regretted a lot of the stuff I did. I explained to him we had the same mission. He humiliated them; I did the same thing as a player. And our goal was to win.

Winning is everything. If it ain't, why keep score?

DARYL JOHNSTON: The first day Charles came to the facility, he was the first person I met that morning. I was sitting in the hot tub. He was the greatest guy you could ever meet.

I used to see him stay out late after practice with Mark Tuinei and show him, from a defensive edge rusher, the things he needed to know as an offensive tackle. He shares his craft with other people, especially on the opposite side of the ball. For us on the offense, the most important thing to know is how a linebacker thinks.

CHARLES HALEY: I ain't never seen that much damn talent amassed anywhere. Ever. They could run like deer. They could run, jump, do it all, man. It was amazing.

Guys would get hurt and they couldn't get their job back because the guy behind them was an "A" player, just like they were. I had never seen anything like that before.

TROY AIKMAN: In the '92 season, we knew we were a good team. We really didn't know how good we were. We played the 49ers in the NFC Championship Game. They were a veteran team and played a lot of playoff games and won a lot of Super Bowls. Steve Young was in his first year as a starter and we were underdogs going in, but we won the game.

I remember being in the locker room and it was euphoric. Everyone was excited and no one expected it to happen and everyone's saying, "Man, we're going to the Super Bowl!"

As a quarterback—and I think it's probably the same way as a GM and as a coach—it hit me before I had even taken my pads off and got in the shower: "Wow! As great as this moment is, it really doesn't mean anything right now if we don't take care of business in a couple of weeks."

We were going to play the Bills, who were more of a veteran team than we were. I thought, "Man, this team, they know what it's all about. They've been there. They've had some devastating losses the last two years. What are the odds that they could lose three in a row?"

There was a lot of pressure, but it was an interesting time. Winning was still new and expectations weren't where they ultimately got. There was a young innocence to a young team that was just enjoying the moment and just playing football and not really thinking about whatever the consequences were, whether you win or lose. It was a really magical time and my favorite year of my career.

JIMMY JOHNSON: We didn't cut anybody any slack. Before every season, I told them, "Listen, guys, I'm going to be very consistent with all of you. All this fair and equal bullshit, we all know, in this room, things are not fair and equal. I'm going to treat every single one of you differently. How I treat you is, the harder you work, the more you meet the guidelines and the rules and regulations and do the things that we ask you to do, I'm going to cut you some slack, especially if you're a good player. But—and don't forget this—if you're a marginal player and you don't meet the rules and regulations and the guidelines, and you don't do the things we ask you to do, your ass is out of here."

There was no sitting on helmets. You were not to be a minute late for meetings or practice.

I traded for John Roper, a backup linebacker who was actually a decent player for Chicago. But he was late for a meeting, he was late for this, late for that. We were in the film room, getting ready to play the 49ers, and I was looking at him and he was sleeping. I think he was making like $600,000 a year, and he was sleeping.

At first, I thought, "I'm going to cut him a break."

Then, I kind of thought about it, and sometimes when something's on your mind, it just starts festering. I turned back and he was still sleeping. I said, "John, get your ass up here. You're not getting enough sleep at home. We're putting you on waivers."

When we were leaving for a game in Detroit, I left Michael Irvin at home because he was two minutes late for the plane. Troy said, "Coach, there's Michael right there on the tarmac."

"Bullshit! Close that door! He'll get his own way there."

We took off, even though he was on the tarmac. If the door's closed, I leave you. I don't give a shit who you are. I left Troy after a 49er game in San Francisco as we were going to the bus. He said he was doing media interviews. I said, "You should have cut them short." That was the way I operated.

But I had to. We had so many young players and I could get away with it because they were young. If we had a whole bunch of veterans, they might have balked. But we didn't.

A week after beating Washington for our first win of that first season, we traveled to Phoenix. We were 1–8 with a rookie quarterback, Troy Aikman, and a rookie running back, Paul Palmer. We had all these young players and we were leading, 20–17, late in the fourth quarter.

Here we were, I thought, about to win our second game in a row. Then Tom Tupa, the Cardinals' quarterback, threw a 72-yard touchdown pass right over Everson Walls' head and they beat us by four points. Oh, I was sick.

Now, pro players kind of mingle around after games. I saw Everson with the receiver that had caught the pass and they were laughing it up. I said, "Everson! What the hell is going on? He just caught the pass that beat us."

"Coach, we're 1–8, we're not going to playoffs."

It was almost as if they were accustomed to losing, even a great player like Everson. When I got the team in the locker room, I let it all out. I said, "You get in the habit of losing and you accept it. And we aren't going to accept it."

In 1992, we were playing Washington in the 14th game of the season. We had already clinched a playoff spot. We flopped around and ended up losing. We got on the plane and the flight attendants started to roll out the trays for dinner. I said, "Uh-uh. Sit back down. They're not eating. They don't deserve to eat."

So we didn't serve them a meal.

TROY AIKMAN: We almost bonded in spite of Jimmy. I mean, Jimmy was tough. He was tough. He demanded a lot. Jimmy knew that not everybody was a self-starter and not everyone took losing the way he wanted them to take it.

After we lost that game in Washington in '92, Jimmy was sitting up there in first class watching the television broadcast of the game, as he always did on the flight. He got into the Heinekens and he got madder and madder as that game went along. And, man, he came to the back of the plane and he was ripping into everybody that wasn't in their seat, that was talking. He wanted it just deathly silent for the flight. There were some veteran players that didn't appreciate it and he didn't care. He threatened to get rid of them the next day.

There was nobody who made it more miserable when we lost than Jimmy. Our facility was just not a fun place to go into on Monday morning after a loss. But when we won, it was a party and he made it fun. He might have been mad after the game, but if we won the game on Sunday, on Monday it was a great environment. And everybody couldn't wait.

I think Jimmy's sheer personality is what brought the team together.

JIMMY JOHNSON: Dave Wannstedt came up to me next morning after that Washington game and said, "Jimmy, you didn't even serve them a meal. Don't you think you were being too hard on them?"

"Dave, they accepted we were in the playoffs and they lost a ballgame. And they played like shit. I don't care if they hate me. When we lose, I want them to hurt. I want them to be sick to their stomach. I wanted to make a point."

When we won, it was party time on the plane. They could do whatever the hell they wanted to do, and I was going to be right there with them. But when they lost, I wanted them to feel it. We had to change the culture. That was the only way I knew how to change the culture.

We scrimmaged throughout the year. Every Wednesday, we had what we called our middle drill. The middle drill was two tackles, two guards, a center, a fullback, and a running back going against the interior defensive line and linebackers. You could not run outside the tackles. If they could make a yard or two yards, that was pretty good. They had to break two tackles to get past the line of scrimmage. I mean, it was a toughness drill. It was for the defense, but it was also for our offensive line.

It was full-speed tackling, take them to the ground. Now, I held Emmitt Smith out of a lot of it. But the rest of them, it was full go. Kenny Norton had held out the first week or two of training camp one year. Finally, he signed his contract and came in. Kenny was really vocal, and everybody loved him. We were in the middle drill and he said, "Okay, bring 'em on! Bring 'em on!"

We had this fullback that we'd signed just for training camp for middle drill. I told the guard to block down and that fullback hit him right in the chin and knocked him colder than a cucumber. We scrimmaged throughout the year. And when I say scrimmage, it wasn't butt and square up. It was take them to the ground.

I think it helped our tackling. I've always said because we were so physical in practices—and I know they can't do it now—the body adjusted to it and we had fewer injuries on Sunday. I've talked to some strength and conditioning coaches, and a lot of them feel that it takes the body a while to get accustomed to being hit and how to fall and how to protect yourself and all this stuff.

We were playing Chicago in the last game of the '92 season. We had the playoffs already set. This was before the first Super Bowl and I was resting Emmitt Smith. Curvin Richards, who was starting in his place, fumbled. So I brought him to the sidelines and said, "You hold on to the damn ball. I don't give a shit how many yards you get, but you hold on to the damn ball." He fumbled again. So we got in the locker room and I said, "Hey, get your ass out of here. You're on waivers."

Joel Bussert, the NFL's senior vice president of player personnel and football operations, called me and said, "Jimmy, you know you're going to have to pay him that playoff money."

"I don't give a shit. I don't want him on the team. I told him to hold on to the damn ball and he didn't hold on to the ball."

CHARLES HALEY: Jimmy found a way to get the best out of guys. As I tell people, the difference between the 49ers and the Cowboys was, at the 49ers, you had 80 percent of the guys motivated to play every week and at the Cowboys, you had 90 percent unmotivated because guys relied on talent and not skill. When you rely on talent, you get your ass whupped. When you learn a skill, you whup ass. It took a while to get guys to understand that.

Jimmy was so hard, man. Guys would jump offside and Jimmy would say, "You jump offside again, I'm gonna cut you!" So, they'd back five yards off the line of scrimmage. How do you get after the passer doing that? I would jump offside just for the hell of it because I wanted guys to know, "Man, we can't play like that. That's not how we're going to win."

Me and Jimmy would have a conversation about that. He got on my ass. We got on each other's ass sometimes, but I needed it.

The two of us would be taking a piss and Jimmy would say, "Yeah, I'll flush your career down the toilet like this piss." It took everything I had to bite that tongue of mine.

JIMMY JOHNSON: Michael Irvin was obviously a great competitor and would work fearlessly. In practice, he ran every single route as fast as he could run it. One of the things Norv Turner preached was timing. Once we got out of stretch and warmups, everything was full speed so that, if we had a seven-step drop, the timing was such that Troy knew exactly the spot the receiver was going to be.

Michael was very precise. Obviously, Troy was a great, great player, but he needed everything to be precise. He wasn't a guy that would go out on the sandlot and just make things happen. Everything had to be exactly like they practiced.

Michael was vocal and all of that stuff. People say Michael was a great leader, and he was a great leader, but we had a bunch of them that were great leaders. It's always been hard for me to single out any one or two. They all were pretty good. On championship teams, you've got a bunch of them.

DARYL JOHNSTON: When Darren Woodson came in as a rookie, he saw all the guys he'd been watching on television. He said, "The lightbulb went on for me. I used to watch you guys on Sunday. You guys would go out and play well, you played hard. It was awesome to watch you guys do it. And then I come here and see that all the key guys on the team are the hardest workers in the off-season."

Michael was the hardest worker on our team. Just an unbelievable worker. Troy Aikman, unbelievable worker. Emmitt Smith. Guys took him under their wing and he finally got it.

JIMMY JOHNSON: Before we drafted Emmitt Smith, I wanted to draft a defensive player. I tried to trade up. In Plan B, we had signed a running back who I thought was going to be decent, so I didn't think I really needed a running back. We were going through the draft and we were getting toward our pick at 14.

I was looking at the board and I said, "Shit, I'm not going to be able to get a defensive player and if we wait until our pick at 21, the best player that stands out is Rodney Hampton, who ended up going to the Giants at 24. If we're going to have to take a running back, I've got Emmitt Smith as the number four player on the board. I'd rather trade up and get Emmitt instead of being stuck with Rodney Hampton."

I had my little draft-value trade chart and I started calling around, seeing if we could move up. We had tried to move up even before then, because I knew I was going to have to take a running back and if I was going to take one, I was going to take the best one. I ended up trading a third-round pick to swap ones with Pittsburgh, which was at 17. We picked Emmitt and the Steelers ended up taking Eric Green, a tight end from Liberty.

Right after I picked Emmitt, Ken Herock of the Falcons called and said, "Hey, you want to trade Emmitt Smith?"

"No, no. I've got who I want."

I was not bothered about the questions about Emmitt's speed. Our running backs coach in Dallas was Joe Brodsky, who was also my running backs coach at the University of Miami. I sent Joe out on the road to look at all the running backs in the 1990 draft. He came back and said the number one running back on his list was Anthony Thompson, from Indiana. He had led the nation in rushing.

I said, "Joe, you've fallen in love with this guy."

"He's just a great person. He's durable, he's tough. He can catch the football. He's got good size."

"Joe, all I know is what I see on film. He's playing Northwestern—and back then Northwestern was horrible—and he's playing some of these Big 10 teams that can't play defense a lick and his longest run for his whole career is 38 yards. Now, Emmitt's smaller, not as fast, and maybe not as good. But shit, I study him on film and he's going 80 against Alabama, he's going 60 against Tennessee. He's not as big and fast, but all I know is he's making all these long runs against great defenses."

I told our scouts and coaches: We all know if they can play or not play, but here's the five things that I'm looking for after we identify that they're a good player. Number one, intelligence. Hit me in the head with a hammer the next time I take a dumb guy. You make more mistakes, you've got more off-the-field problems with dumb guys. And they never get better. Those smart guys get better and better and better. Number two, I want a gym rat. I want somebody that's passionate about the game, that loves the game, loves to compete.

If he's shooting pool, he's a competitor. If it's his off day, he's in there shooting hoops with his buddies.

The third thing is quickness for his position. Quickness with Russell Maryland, at defensive tackle, might be those first two or three steps. It doesn't necessarily mean 40-yard dash. The fourth thing I want is a playmaker. And a playmaker doesn't necessarily touch the ball. A playmaker might be that offensive guard who makes the key block. We were trying to make a decision between Kevin Smith and Troy Vincent. Kevin Smith led the Southwest Conference in punt returns and had umpteen interceptions. Troy Vincent was a great player, but he didn't touch the ball. With Russell Maryland, you'd see a little hand reach out of a pile and he'd make the tackle on key plays. And then the fifth thing was character. You can't win this game with bums. I don't want bums.

But we didn't know if Emmitt could catch the ball. And Emmitt will tell you different, but he was about a 4.6 40 guy.

But he did have great balance. He was amazing. You never got a hit on him. You look at him run in slow motion and it was just a little dip, a little dodge, this, that, and he just never took a full hit.

I would use one word with Emmitt and that's pride. He is an extremely proud person. He was a great player in junior high, high school, and college. He was a great player from Day One. He didn't just, all of a sudden, become great in Dallas. I tried to recruit him at Miami, and he wouldn't give us a sniff because we were throwing the ball too much. He wanted to run the ball.

I could cuss at Michael Irvin all day. And every time I'd cuss him, he just worked that much harder. He would just get mad, grit his teeth, and work. If I hollered at Emmitt, he'd go into a shell because that was Emmitt.

When Emmitt held out those first couple of games, we had Derrick Lassic as our running back. The defense was just turning him for a flip. When Emmitt signed, it was the third week of training camp, and we ran that middle drill and Emmitt made one little dip and, boom, there he goes.

Norv looked at me and said, "We're back."

TROY AIKMAN: Michael Irvin was drafted the year before me as the number one pick, and the Cowboys went 3–13 his rookie year in 1988. I came in in

'89 and we were 1–15. Emmitt Smith came in in 1990 and we went 7–9. So, all three of us, in our first year, had losing records and we didn't make the playoffs and we hadn't done anything.

People around the league today, especially in Dallas, when they have a quarterback, a running back, and a receiver that are good, say, "Ah, this is the new Triplets." Well, it kind of doesn't tell the whole story about us and what the Triplets meant, at least to me.

Michael, Emmitt, and I were three guys that came in, essentially, at the same time and enjoyed all of our successes at the same time. None of us had ever won without the others. And then we grew together. I believe that was why we never had the egos as to who was getting the credit. Ever.

Of course, we ran the ball a lot. But we could throw it when we had to throw it. If teams loaded up at the line of scrimmage and we had to throw it, then, heck, that was what we would do and Michael would get his yards. Then, if they started covering him and playing Two Deep, we started running the ball some more and Emmitt would get his yards.

I think we all always appreciated that when we started out, we weren't really good. And when we got good, the egos didn't destroy us—at least, with the players. Unfortunately, it did in the front office between the owner and the head coach. But with the players, I think all of us realized, without the collective group, none of us was really all that great and we needed each other.

Now, we had some big personalities. I didn't feel that it was my job to manage them. All I demanded from my teammates was that when we hit the practice field that everybody give it everything they had, and they knew their assignment. As the leader of the team that was what I felt my job was. Beyond that, I really did not care what they did when we were not together.

DARYL JOHNSTON: Troy's contribution comes in as, number one, the undisputed leader of the offense. The offense had several huge personalities, but everybody knew, first and foremost, it was Troy Aikman's offense.

The other thing is he was driven by the desire to win. Statistics didn't matter to him. I've done a thing a number of times on TV where I go back and grab a six-year segment of Roger Staubach and a six-year segment of Troy Aikman. So, it's from the '70s and it's from the '90s and it just shows how the game can be played well and consistently. A consistent day for Troy was 18 out of 24 for 195–205 yards, one touchdown, no interceptions. That was how we were functioning.

For Troy to come into the NFL as the number one overall pick in the draft and not want to throw up numbers and be able to be compared to all the greats in the game was amazing. He was a Hall of Famer based on the fact he was a three-time Super Bowl champion, and the first quarterback to lead his team to three Super Bowls in four years.

Emmitt Smith can't become the NFL's all-time leading rusher if he's got a quarterback that's statistically driven. It's just not going to happen. But if you had a team that said, "We are not going to let Dallas run the football on us," Troy would destroy them.

That was our rub. We were challenging people, saying, "You want to load up the box? Go ahead. How are you going to cover Michael Irvin and Jay Novacek at the same time?"

If that happened, you had Alvin Harper on the outside taking the top off of everything. With Kelvin Martin and Kevin Williams working underneath, our team was functioning back in the early '90s like the teams do today. As soon as you start to load up the box, we're going to hit you down the field. But if you didn't load up the box, we honestly felt like you couldn't stop us.

JIMMY JOHNSON: We signed a dozen guys or so in Plan B. We signed a couple of tight ends from Phoenix. One of them was Jay Novacek.

I wanted a receiving tight end; I didn't want a blocker. Jay was such an athlete. He would just wall people off. He'd get bounced around trying to block somebody, but he was really good for our offense in that he could run routes and he was athletic enough. Of course, nowadays, they split the tight ends out and do everything with them, but back then they didn't.

DARYL JOHNSTON: Back then, the communication device in the helmet wasn't all that great, with the quarterback putting his hands over his ears because he was struggling to hear the call. Troy would step out of the huddle to try and get the play call as it came in from Norv.

Our huddle would be utter chaos. The offensive line would be arguing with Michael because Michael wanted to throw the ball and Nate Newton wanted to run the ball. I mean, it was a comedy. You'd just shake your head and be like, "If people could only hear what's going on in this huddle right now."

As soon as Troy stepped back into the huddle, you could hear a pin drop. It was his huddle. That's something that's earned, and he had that right away. Troy's one of those guys where the leadership exudes naturally. I wanted him to think that I was a good football player. I wanted him to think that our team wouldn't be as good without me in the lineup. That was my motivation. I wanted him to respect me as a football player, and he could do that to people. And that's a gift.

One of the other motivations was you didn't want those eyes burning a hole in you. If you made a mistake on the football field, it was two eyes right through you. You didn't want to disappoint him. You didn't want to be the reason the play didn't work because you had to sit in that film room with him. You've seen those film clips of him on game day where he'd be going up and down our sideline fired up. I loved it.

I've always said, if your quarterback doesn't have a little bit of prick in him, then he's not your guy.

TROY AIKMAN: Over the years, the thing that meant the most to me was when former teammates of mine have said, "Hey, none of this would have been possible if it weren't for you, if you hadn't been the guy who really held people accountable and made sure that we were doing what we needed to do."

I had great friendships, but I never felt like my job as the quarterback was to make friends, although I had a lot of them. I think all of my teammates were friends, but my job was to win. I thought I was paid a check by Jerry Jones to win football games; I thought all of us were.

CHARLES HALEY: On defense, I set the tone. I don't want to toot my horn or anything, man, but I pointed guys out that sucked, that got their ass whupped on Sunday. I just felt it was about leadership, it was about winning. These guys wanted to talk to me about winning Super Bowls and I wanted to talk to them about the fact a lot of them would go out or miss curfew or something like that.

I said, "I didn't like that in college and I damn sure don't like it as a pro, where you're gonna cost me the game because you're not disciplined."

As a defensive line, we would walk down the tunnel together and I would tell them, "We're gonna be mobile, agile, and violent." And they had to pick out which one we were gonna be this week. Some weeks, they said, "Let's just be violent."

"Okay, because I'll take that glove off."

I always wore one glove, on my right hand, because of Michael Jackson, because he was a thriller. If I took that glove off, I'm bringing some violence to the game, baby, some real shit.

TROY AIKMAN: When Norv was getting ready to leave the Cowboys to become head coach at Washington, I asked him, "Who is there for us to hire?"

"There's only one guy: Ernie Zampese."

"Yeah, but he won't leave California."

"He'll leave California for this job."

We got Ernie, who brought the same offense we were running with Norv, who had learned it from Ernie in the first place. It was awesome. It was a great four years. I spent so much time talking with Ernie about the years with Dan Fouts and Charlie Joiner and Kellen Winslow, and the things that they did and how the game had changed. And Fouts was just a Rolodex of information. I was blessed.

For seven of my 12 years, I had some really iconic offensive coordinators.

JIMMY JOHNSON: Tony Wise, our offensive line coach, was with me at Pitt, Oklahoma State, and Miami. He was the worst recruiter I had ever seen in my life. The main thing was that he was always honest. He would recruit somebody, and they'd say, "Coach, you think I can play as a freshman?"

"Are you crazy? You'll be lucky if you play as a junior."

Obviously, we never got that player.

But Tony was a great offensive line coach. Everybody talks about that offensive line being one of the best ever. Well, one reason was Emmitt, but the other reason was Tony Wise. At left tackle, we had Mark Tuinei, a free-agent defensive tackle that we moved to offensive tackle. He was a great player.

We had a guy that was a castoff from the USFL, Nate Newton, that everybody said was too fat, at left guard. Our center, Mark Stepnoski, was a 245-pound offensive guard at Pitt that we drafted in the third round. He had never played center in his life, and I asked Tony, "Can you convert him to center?" And Tony converted him. Mark was a hell of a player for us and ended up making the Pro Bowl.

We had two right guards, John Gesek, who we traded for from the Raiders, and Kevin Gogan, who was an eighth-round pick who tried to play tackle and struggled because he didn't have quick enough feet. At right tackle, we had a third-round pick from Central Ohio, Eric Williams. But that was, supposedly, one of the best offensive lines ever. Two third-round picks, an eighth-round pick, and two free agents.

TROY AIKMAN: They were ready to run Nate Newton out of town when I got to Dallas in 1989. A lot of people thought we couldn't win with those guys.

DARYL JOHNSTON: After Tony Wise left for the Chicago Bears in 1993, Hudson Houck took over as offensive line coach. The guys loved Tony because Tony was a heavy-hand, come-off-the-ball style coach. Hudson wasn't teaching a true bucket step, but it was kind of a gather step. Tony was off-the-ball and pad-level and just knock those guys off the line of scrimmage. And that was perfect for all their personalities.

Hudson was very similar to Jimmy. He came in and guys fought him on his technique a little bit at the beginning and he stayed true to it. He stayed with what he believed in. And the linemen really came to respect Hudson, not only for his knowledge as a coach but his belief in his system because it was very different.

How many guys get to go from Tony Wise to Hudson Houck?

And our guys were mean. I've always hated when someone says about an offensive lineman, "That guy's got a defensive mentality. He's very physical." Really? How would you like to go against our offensive line? You don't think they're physical? You don't think they're mean? They were a nasty group of guys.

TROY AIKMAN: When you have an offense that's successful, the offense tends to always overshadow the defense. But we knew how good our defense was. History certainly shows that, but I think when people look back on those teams, the defense doesn't get the recognition that they deserve.

In '92 and '94, we had the number one defense in the league in yards allowed and top five in points allowed in '92, '93, and '94. It was a well-coached group, really talented. It didn't seem like there was ever animosity about the offense maybe overshadowing them. We were all really close.

BILL POLIAN: The first Super Bowl for Jimmy Johnson's Cowboys, Super Bowl XXVII, was the third for the Bills. It looked like we had made a big difference-making play early on when Steve Tasker blocked a punt that went out of bounds inside the Dallas 20 and we drove for a touchdown.

JIMMY JOHNSON: It was good coaching on the Bills' part. We lost our starting left tackle on our punt team, Robert Jones. We had to put another guy in there at tackle and the Bills went right over that spot and blocked the punt.

BILL POLIAN: We thought that we would have an advantage because the Cowboys had not seen a lot of our no-huddle. They were, however, really well prepared.

JIMMY JOHNSON: Because the Bills had that no-huddle and were just wearing people out with it, defenses couldn't get ready for them. The week of practice prior to the game, we didn't have enough players to run two scout teams, so we took our starting players and we had two units going machine gun, rapid fire at our defense. *Bang, bang, bang, bang.* I'm talking about Emmitt Smith, Troy Aikman, all of them were part of the scout team getting ready for the no-huddle stuff.

We felt like we were going to be ready for the no-huddle. We did it to where the defensive guys were gasping for air. As soon as one play was over with, the offense was on the line of scrimmage ready to run another one. That got us ready for the no-huddle.

Every Monday of game week, I always tried to talk to the team about how we were going to win the game. I would always identify certain players. I'd say, "They're going to have to run an eight-man front." I pointed to Michael and said, "Michael, that's going to put you one-on-one against so-and-so and so-and-so. Can you kick his ass? Tell me right now! Can you kick his ass?"

"Coach, I'll do it."

"Okay, get ready for it."

On the Wednesday before we left for Pasadena, I was trying to think, "What am I going to say about Buffalo getting ready for the Super Bowl?"

I walked in the meeting room and said, "Guys, let me tell you something: every one of you knows we're playing a hell of a football team. They've got some great players. And they've been to a couple of Super Bowls. Everybody's saying, 'Dallas is the underdog, youngest team in the league. There's no way they're going to handle all the pressure.'

"Every one of you in this room, you know if the game is out here on this practice field, you'll kick their ass. With nobody watching, you'll kick their ass because you're a better football team than they are. If I had a two-by-four and I put it right here on the floor, and said, 'Troy, walk from one end to the other,' he'd walk one end to the other. If I said, 'Michael, get up here and walk from one end to the other... Nate, you're a big fat ass, get up and walk from one end to the other.'

"But if we put this two-by-four out there, at 10 feet," and I started demonstrating, "you'd be saying to yourself, 'Don't fall, don't fall, don't fall.' And what do you do? You're falling. Everybody's saying, 'Bruce Smith, Darryl Talley, Andre Reed, Jim Kelly, Thurman Thomas. All these great players, this great team.'

"I don't care who they are. I don't care how many millions of people are watching. The thought you should have on your mind every play you're out there is that you're on this practice field, with nobody watching and you're going to kick their ass because you're a better team than they are. You don't turn the ball over."

The other thing was, because the Bills had just killed everybody all year long with the no-huddle stuff, they turned the ball over some. Of course, we hadn't had many turnovers. The night before the game, I told the team, "Guys, listen, here's what we're going to do. We're going to start out a little conservative right off the bat. But we're going to get some turnovers. And once we get the turnovers, we're going to open it up because we don't turn the ball over."

BILL POLIAN: I've always said that game turned on two plays. One was fate, an interception that bounced off Pete Metzelaars after he slipped and fell. The other was the great play by Ken Norton on a goal-line stand, followed by another interception.

JIMMY JOHNSON: Ken Norton hit the backup running back, Kenny Davis, square up, for no gain. It was a hell of a play.

BILL POLIAN: George Toma was the groundskeeper. He had been the groundskeeper when Marv and I were in Kansas City. The day before the game, we worked out at the Rose Bowl, and George came over to Marv and I and he said, "Hey, there's a high-water table here. You get into the second quarter, because this game starts late in the day, it's going to start to get slick. So, remind your guys to change their cleats."

We were driving in second quarter, going toward the mountain end of the Rose Bowl. Jim Kelly had a turn route to Pete Metzelaars over the middle, about a 12-yard route. He threw the ball to the inside, where it was supposed to be thrown, and Pete slipped.

The ball bounced off his shoulder and was intercepted and returned for a touchdown. The rout was on. The two plays came almost back-to-back, the great hit by Norton, which denied a touchdown, and then another turnover.

JIMMY JOHNSON: The day before the game, George Toma walked with me. I had a chart of the field and some of the turf was replaced and some of it wasn't. I charted the whole field about where it was slick and where it was not slick, from the old turf and the new, because he didn't replace the entire field.

The next morning, before pregame meal, I got our coaching staff together and I had a big chalkboard with a drawing of the whole field on it. I said to Butch Davis, "If you're in this area, I don't want you blitzing, playing man. Put it on your chart."

I said to Joe Avezzano, our special teams coach, "On this end of the field, I don't want any sideline returns. I want everything up the middle because if you try to make a cut on that sideline, you're going to slip."

I told Norv Turner, "Don't run a toss to Emmitt if you're over in this corner. Put it on your call sheet, where not to run it or where to run it."

We went through the entire game plan before pregame meal, and we put an asterisk on where and where not to do certain things for the whole game.

TROY AIKMAN: After we had won the Super Bowl in '92, immediately you're asked, "Hey, do you think you can repeat?" I remember we lost to the Bills in Week 2 of the '93 season. Now, we were 0–2. I was doing an interview and a reporter said, "No team had ever started the season 0–2 and made it to the Super Bowl. Does that concern you?"

"Well, that doesn't concern me, but if you told me that no team that started the year 0–2 had ever gone on to be 1–2, that'd be a real concern because right now the Super Bowl is the furthest thing from my mind. We're just trying to win a football game."

JIMMY JOHNSON: Getting ready for the second Super Bowl against the Bills, I came back from practice, went to the hotel and turned on ESPN. The ESPN guys were talking and running footage of the Bills stretching and stuff before their practice. Then I saw Jim Kelly taking the ball and pitching it to Thurman Thomas with a shuffle pass. He did it two or three times.

I called Butch Davis and said, "Butch, check the computer printouts. Have the Bills run the shuffle pass?"

"They haven't run it all year long."

Then I remembered that in preseason, we played the Miami Dolphins, and the Dolphins had run it against us and gashed us two or three times.

"Shit!" I said. "They're going to run the shuffle pass."

So, we practiced against it all week long. Sure enough, three of the biggest plays in the ballgame came against the shuffle pass. One, was when we knocked the ball loose, got the fumble and ran it in right before the half. Another was an incompletion. The third was a no gainer.

That's why coaches are paranoid about cameras out there on the practice field.

BILL POLIAN: I had left the Bills in '93 to become vice president for football operations of the NFL. Most people thought the second Bills-Cowboys Super Bowl, which came after the '93 season, would be another Cowboy rout. That was not the case. The Bills played hard and well and were ahead at halftime.

DARYL JOHNSTON: Jimmy's best coaching moment, to me, was the second Super Bowl down in Atlanta. The Bills had just stoned us in the first half. They were slanting their tackles, wrapping the 'backers—where the linebacker moves behind the slanting defensive lineman up into the line of scrimmage to attack the play and confuse the blocking assignments of the offensive linemen—and crashing their ends inside. The spot-on movement was challenging for our guys, who were big guys coming off the ball. If you were quick and you had movement, it could give us some problems.

At halftime, when we were down 13–6, and we were coming in, Jimmy was outside the locker room door. He said, "Listen, we know what they're doing, we know how they're stopping the run game. We've got a play that we were running about four or five weeks ago that we think is going to force them out of what they're doing. And then we can get back to what we want to do. You guys go in, get off your feet, the coaches are gonna go talk, we'll bring it back out, we'll go over it, we'll make sure nobody has any questions about it. And then we'll roll it out in the second half."

Our opening drive of the second half was that play—just an outside power run, left and right, left and right—all the way down the field. As Cornelius Bennett was crashing, there were times where I would bypass Cornelius and I could go to the corner, I could go down to the safety, just because I knew he was coming in so hard that that play was going to be out and around him. We kept waiting and waiting and waiting for the defensive line to kind of slow down the stunts and movement, and it never did. So, we just stayed with that play the whole second half.

We were washing everything down. Sometimes, there was no kick-out at the end of the line. Sometimes, the end of the line crossed the face of the tight end, so he got washed. And we were coming around, so I could check the inside linebacker's scrape. I could leave that for the guard or take that for myself.

From a calming standpoint, just having Jimmy there at the door telling us, "We know what they're doing and we're gonna force them out of it," was huge. It was just like, "Thank God, because this is just frustrating out there."

BILL POLIAN: On the first drive of the third quarter, Thurman Thomas, who never fumbled, lost the ball and James Washington returned it for a touchdown to put Dallas ahead. Another turnover at the start of the fourth quarter sealed the Bills' fate.

JIMMY JOHNSON: Jerry Jones and I used to communicate almost daily until about the third or fourth year. That was the downfall of Jerry and I: We stopped communicating.

People talk about Jerry meddling. He never meddled. There was never really a difference of opinion. Jerry just wanted to be informed. Jerry is running his businesses and he has people doing things.

The season before we won our first Super Bowl, we got in a big argument about Tony Casillas during training camp at St. Edward's down in Austin. Ken Herock called, and I was talking to him about trading for Tony. We ended up getting a three that could go to a two.

I ran into Jerry and I said, "Jerry, I made a nice trade. We traded for Tony Casillas, a defensive lineman from Atlanta.

"Oh, yeah, okay, good, good."

I went back to my room. No more than 30 minutes later, I turned the TV on and I was sitting with Rhonda—my girlfriend then, my wife now—and Jerry was on camera, saying, "Well, I just traded for a defensive lineman." He wasn't sure who Tony Casillas was.

Rhonda said, "Jerry didn't mention your name."

"Aww, shit."

Jerry wanted me to redo my contract and he wanted me to take out the personnel responsibilities and all that stuff. I said, "I'm never taking that out. Add years to it, whatever, but that's my responsibility and I'm not going to do it any other way. Just like the Tony Casillas thing, Jerry. I don't want all the accolades or credit or anything else. But you could have said, 'We,' or 'Jimmy and I,' or this and that."

"Jimmy, when we got into this thing, I know what we said about football and business and stuff. But I can make $5 million dollars and nobody really gives a shit. You can trade for a backup offensive guard and everybody goes, 'Ooh, boy!' I want to be part of that."

"I understand, but sometimes, Jerry, I can't come down there and talk to you and say, 'Hey, I may have a deal.' Sometimes, you've got to pull the trigger and you've got to do what you've got to do."

That was when we started kind of going in opposite directions.

JERRY JONES: Jimmy was an integral part as far as the coaching. Jimmy wanted to be a bigger part as far as a lot of the other stuff. And that was good. I was fine with that.

But I got here trading. I got here making deals every day. Jimmy had never traded for a goldfish when he got here.

We got in the business of wheeling and dealing. I came from the world of wheeling and dealing. That's how I got the Cowboys.

JIMMY JOHNSON: I could be so mad at him. Norv used to say, "Jimmy's going to be pissed off. He's going to go in there and talk to Jerry. And Jerry's going to tell him how great he is and Jimmy's going to come back and he's going to be fine."

If you're with him, you've got to love the guy. He never, ever stops working.

I'll say all this about Jerry: He is passionate about that team and he will work around the clock. He never stops thinking about what they can do, how they can improve.

TROY AIKMAN: Jimmy and I had gotten really close, which was interesting because there was a period early in my career where he and I didn't speak. There was no real moment as to why. It was just total frustration on both of our parts. It was a real struggle.

We had a history together, but the relationship never got going the way that it should have because of him drafting Steve Walsh in the supplemental draft. I'm all for competition, but Jimmy felt like he needed to pull back because he already had a relationship with Steve.

Jimmy wanted to win. It wasn't like it was a foregone conclusion that I was the starter. It was competition. But Jimmy then removed himself from really having much of a relationship with me.

We were losing, so that's never good. I didn't like the things that they were doing. They probably didn't like things that I was doing.

And then, in 1992, we started to break the ice a little bit and worked through some things. At the end, we were really close, probably as close as any head coach and quarterback has ever been. The last couple of years together were some of the most fun that I've ever had with a head coach. And he asked me to present him in Canton.

I was sensing there was some stuff going on with Jimmy and Jerry. I never imagined that second Super Bowl, in '93, would be the last time Jimmy coached us. I knew it was not going to last much longer, but I think Jimmy really wanted to try for three Super Bowl wins in a row. I think that was important to Jimmy.

But when Jerry made his comments at the owners' meetings that any of 500 coaches could have won the Super Bowls, I think Jimmy, being a smart guy, realized that was the crack in the door that he needed in order to get out and maybe keep some money and get paid some money. So, he took advantage of that. It was unusual, but I got it. I understood it, so I wasn't upset with Jerry. He paid for the team and all that.

But I think a lot of players were upset about it. I know Michael Irvin was. I talked to those guys, because right away Jerry said, "If this doesn't work out with Jimmy, I am going to hire Switzer."

The announcement was made that Jerry was hiring Switzer. I played for Barry for two years at OU. He was a tough guy back then at Oklahoma. He demanded a lot. I told the team, "I think this is gonna be a great fit, I think we'll be fine." And then I found out, after Barry got there—and this is not a criticism of him—but he was at a different time in his life and he wasn't the same coach I played for at Oklahoma.

I've always felt, if you have great coaching in college, you can win a fair amount of football games. If you have great players and not-so-great coaching, you can still win a fair amount of football games. But in the NFL, you've got to have it all. You've got to have great players and you've got to have great coaching, and you've got to have a great front office.

There's just so much that goes into being successful and if you start letting things go and you don't pay attention to the details, it catches up to you. The margin between winning and losing is so small, that can be the difference in winning and losing a game.

That, really, is what began to happen with us. We didn't practice with the same intensity. The accountability wasn't the same. We didn't draft as well. We didn't handle our roster as well. Little by little, we just weren't as good a football team.

JIMMY JOHNSON: After I left and Barry came in, Troy just all of a sudden felt like he needed to be the bad guy. He was on the other players' case time after time after time. He will tell you to this day that he completely changed because he had to. He had to be the guy demanding that they do stuff.

To give you an idea, I always called the timeouts. Anytime, regardless what was happening. Troy would look over to me and I'd call the timeout.

In Barry's first season, something happened in a game and Troy was looking toward the sideline. Barry was over there sitting on the bench talking to somebody. Troy was going, "What the hell?"

"You're looking to me? I don't call timeouts. The quarterback calls timeouts."

TROY AIKMAN: In '94, Jimmy's first year away, we were not as good as we were in '93, but we made it to the NFC Championship game and then lost to San Francisco. In '95, we weren't as good as we were in '94, but we were good enough, and we won the Super Bowl.

In '96, we still made the postseason and won a playoff game. But we just were not as good each year. We were losing our edge. And then by '97, the wheels had totally come off. It just doesn't take long if you're not minding the business, and that was what happened to us.

It was really unfortunate.

CHARLES HALEY: Barry was a players' coach. So, you go from Jimmy to Barry, and players were still waiting for somebody to stay on them like Jimmy did and keep that foot in their ass. Barry treated them like men, and that was when shit just went crazy. Guys did everything under the sun and we didn't hit our goal.

But Barry was trying to make them men. When you do everything for somebody, you're not helping them grow.

TROY AIKMAN: With Jimmy Johnson, I just got to focus on playing football and being a great teammate. When Jimmy left, I had to absorb a much bigger role, and a role no player should have to absorb.

People ask me a lot, "How many Super Bowls do you think you might have won had Jimmy stayed?" I don't know. I think we would have won a few more. But the biggest thing I believe is we would have been competitive for a lot longer. Jimmy would have drafted well. He would have run the organization in a way that made players accountable, and I think that we would have been at least in a position every year in the postseason with an opportunity. And that's all you can ask for.

DARYL JOHNSTON: Jerry Jones was just very hands-on. As a broadcaster, getting out and seeing other organizations and how they're run, you see ownership and this was a different environment. Jerry loves the game of football. He loves being around the game of football. We could tell that he wanted to be more involved with the day-to-day functioning of the team. But through that run, the parameters were put in place. If only they could have figured it out. This is one of the ones that makes you shake your head.

Early on, I don't know if Jimmy ever expected us to do what we did, but I do believe he expected us to be good. He did say, "When we get this thing turned around, there's going to be enough credit for everybody to go around."

I'll always remember that, because the demise of the team was because the two guys at the top couldn't get to the point where there was enough credit to go around. They couldn't share the credit.

That was something that, for me, was really disappointing because Jimmy was spot on. Everybody was able to share in all the success that we had as players. But the fact that Jerry and Jimmy could never get on that same page at that time to really kind of push that over the top and just get to a place where there was shared credit was unfortunate.

Jimmy was great at bringing guys in. Jerry was great at the deals and getting people extended. And then the way Jerry revolutionized the business side of football. The amount of money these franchises are worth today? That's all Jerry. I mean, he made training camp profitable.

People can say what they want about us moving from Thousand Oaks, California, to Austin, Texas. Do you want to reengage the Texas fan base? Well, sure that makes sense. Do you want to train in the Texas heat because you're gonna play in the Texas heat? Yeah, okay. You can lump that one in, too.

But let's not be foolish. There's not a lot of Cowboy fans that are going to travel all the way out to California. If you can get them to your practice facility and start selling merchandise and selling sponsorships and take the team out to a golfing event, you do it. He took the money pit of training camp and monetized it.

I've always believed that a football team functions as your second family. The whole Jones family—Jerry, Jean, Charlotte, Stephen, and Jerry Jr.—they didn't just talk about that. They did things to generate that. Still to this day, if you're a part of the Cowboy franchise, you are family. That, to me, is the great thing they've done.

JERRY JONES: With tremendous, unbelievable, good fortune, we ended up winning two Super Bowls—and we ended up having to change coaches. The main reason that that happened was my lack of tolerance. It was on me to accept Jimmy becoming full of himself, for him becoming emboldened with his and our success. I know that was natural.

But my ass had danced so close to the devil and had gone through a traumatic experience, I lost any tolerance for bullshit. So, when we had a confrontation, or when we had to talk about it, I couldn't handle it. At that particular time, it was an emotional lack of understanding, the disloyalty that I perceived was there. I got beat up in my own mind so badly that I had no tolerance for my teammate.

It was so ridiculous that the day after we had made the change, I got Barry Switzer to come in. Barry drove to Dallas from Norman, Oklahoma, and came in and said, "Where's Jimmy?"

"Jimmy's gone."

"Oh, get out of here. Get him up here."

"What do you want him up here for?"

"I want to take you two knotheads, you little assholes, sit you on that couch and ask you both how you could screw this up? How do you screw up winning two Super Bowls?"

"Well, he's gone, you're here, and we're here to talk about you being the coach of the Cowboys."

Paul Tagliabue came to me after we had won the third Super Bowl with Barry as coach and said, "I'm going to have a committee of owners, and would you lead the committee? We're going to talk about how to hire coaches."

"Paul, I need to be out in the audience. I don't need to be on the panel. I have run out of college teammates. I don't know how to hire a damn coach now."

CHAPTER 7

Marv Levy, the No-Huddle, and a "Simple, but Not Easy" Path to Winning

BILL POLIAN: The contribution Marv Levy made to his Buffalo Bills goes far beyond implementing the revolutionary no-huddle offense and leading them to four Super Bowls. They were the result of his unique coaching talents, which I was fortunate to witness up close, as were our quarterbacks: Hall of Famer Jim Kelly and Frank Reich, who became head coach of the Indianapolis Colts in 2018. They join Marv and I in providing a behind-the-scenes look at that remarkable Super Bowl run.

When the Bills let go of Hank Bullough after our 2–7 start to the 1986 season, I walked down to the office of our team owner, Ralph Wilson, and recommended that he hire Marv. Ralph knew that, a few years earlier, Marv had been let go as coach of the Kansas City Chiefs. He called Lamar Hunt, the owner of the Chiefs, and Lamar said, "Ralph, we made a big mistake in letting Marv go."

We didn't make the same mistake and brought Marv aboard six days before our 10th game, against the Pittsburgh Steelers. I knew that before he walked into the building, of course. When he was the head coach of the Montreal Alouettes of the Canadian Football League, I was a part-time scout for them, assigned to NFL and college teams on the East Coast.

My first extended conversation with Marv didn't occur until near the end of the season when he called me in to compliment my work and offered me a chance to stay on the scouting staff, which I was thrilled to accept. I got to know Marv better when he became head coach of the Chiefs and I joined their scouting staff as a pro scout advancing upcoming opponents. I had seen him motivate and delegate authority to his assistant coaches like no head coach I had ever seen before.

While in Kansas City, I witnessed a great example of his elevated motivational skills before a scrimmage at Arrowhead Stadium against the Houston Oilers after the first two weeks of training camp. Our camp practices were on grass and Arrowhead was artificial turf, so at the end of the practice the day before the scrimmage, Marv called everybody together and said, "You know, there are a lot of new players here, especially you rookies, and I want to remind you to bring your turf shoes." I was waiting for him to add, "If you don't do that, we'll fine you or we won't look kindly on it," which is what most coaches would have said.

Marv didn't. He said, "You've worked hard these last two weeks and I'm really happy with the effort you've put out. I know you want to do your best tomorrow and we want you to do your best. We want your effort to be rewarded, so please make sure you pack your turf shoes."

I was astounded. I'd never heard a coach approach such a situation from that point of view. Typically, it would have been more disciplinary. *"If you don't bring your shoes and you play poorly, you're not going to make the team!"* But Marv struck the right balance between giving his players an order and then telling them why it was good for them. He used positive reinforcement to the fullest.

When it came to his assistant coaches, Marv not only believed in delegating authority but was comfortable enough in his own skin to allow them to run their areas of the team as they saw fit. I remember when we were with the Chiefs, getting ready to cut the squad to 53, we had a long snapper who really didn't have a regular position. Because of Marv's emphasis on special teams, we were one of the first teams to have a designated long snapper who wouldn't have made an NFL roster at any other position.

During the meeting, someone said, "Okay, we're going to keep this long snapper. What group does he work with when the kicking team isn't practicing?"

The player had been a college linebacker, so Marv said, "Well, let him work with the linebackers."

Rod Rust, our defensive coordinator, who also coached the linebackers, said, "I don't want him."

"Oh, don't worry about it," Marv said. "He won't get in the way. He's been a linebacker before."

Rod wouldn't budge.

"I don't want him," he said. "I don't want him in the meeting room."

Finally, Marv said, "Okay, we'll figure out a way to handle it."

The solution was that the player would service the offense by snapping the ball as the scout-team center. Ultimately, he spent a lot more time working with the holder and the kicker and punter.

Most of the time, at least in my experience, if the head coach said, "We're going to do this this way," the assistant would grumble and maybe even smile and do it. Rod wasn't being insubordinate. He was just making his point.

Being a great delegator, Marv allowed everybody, coaches as well as players, to be themselves. That was diametrically opposed to the way Hank Bullough was doing things.

Our players recognized that quality the first time Marv met with them. After introducing him and giving his biography in front of the team, I turned it over to Marv. His speech wasn't very long.

When Marv finished, he simply said, "Okay, let's go beat the Steelers." The players stood up and applauded.

They had met him for all of 15 minutes and were giving him a standing ovation. I'll remember that to my dying day.

MARV LEVY: I said, "I've got good news for you. What it takes to win is simple, but it isn't easy. If you run, throw, block, tackle, catch, kick better than your opponent, you're going to win.

"We're not going to turn the football over and give people gifts. We're not going to lead the league in penalties. We're not going to be dumb and we're not going to be dirty. Play hard, play clean, play to win. But win or lose, dig right back in. And honor the game.

"I have only three rules. One: Be on time. Two: Every time you're here, give everything you have. Three: Be a good citizen, both in the community and within the team."

JIM KELLY: When I got to Buffalo in 1986, after two seasons in the United States Football League, there was so much negativity in the locker room about our head coach at the time, Hank Bullough, that it almost was affecting the way we played because nobody really wanted to win that much. I mean, they had the desire to win, of course, but they were more interested in doing what they could to get a new head coach in there.

I know that doesn't paint a good picture of Hank, but that was just the vibe. It was tough, especially after back-to-back 2–14 seasons in 1984 and 1985, with Kay Stephenson, the coach through the first four games of '85 before Hank took over.

I remember when we were playing at Tampa Bay, on November 2, 1986, and we were one touchdown away from winning the game. And I remember Fred Smerlas, our veteran nose tackle, coming up to me before I took the field with like two minutes to go in the game.

"Hey, Kel, if you score, I will break your arm."

"What?"

"If you score and we win this game, Hank Bullough is still going to be here. Don't score!"

That was my first year in the NFL and Fred was the leader of the team. As much as I respected Fred and didn't want him to break my arm, I could never avoid trying to win a game on purpose. I led us right down the field. On our last play, I threw a pass to running back Robb Riddick, who was open in the end zone. Rob had already caught seven passes for 50 yards that day. But he wouldn't get an eighth one. The ball went right through his hands, one of which was covered with a cast because it was broken.

We wound up losing, Hank was fired, and Marv became the new coach. I still wonder if Fred would have really broken my arm if I completed that pass.

BILL POLIAN: I've often said that I've never met anyone who's as good a teacher as Marv Levy. And he did it through aphorisms and sayings and poems, things that are certainly off the beaten path as far as football is concerned.

One of Marv's most memorable sayings was, "Where would you rather be than right here, right now?"

MARV LEVY: In 1958, when I was head coach at the University of New Mexico and the youngest major college head coach in the country at the time, we were getting ready for our opening day game. With the Sandia Mountains in the background, the sun was shining, the band was playing, cheerleaders dancing up and down in front of us, and as the players gathered around for the final words of encouragement, I looked around and I couldn't think of anything else but the feeling in my heart and looks on their faces.

The next thing I said was, "Where else would you rather be than right here, right now?" That's what I would say before the kickoff of every game that I coached through the next 40-some years.

BILL POLIAN: My next all-time favorite Marv-ism was, "If it's too tough for them, it's just right for us."

MARV LEVY: The 1990 AFC Championship Game against the then-Los Angeles Raiders was on a bitter, bitter cold day. Just before the kickoff, I said something that I used as a trademark through the rest of my coaching career: "Fellas, when it's too tough for them, it's just right for us." We went out and won the game, 51–3, to advance to our first of four consecutive Super Bowls.

BILL POLIAN: History lessons were a huge part of Marv's coaching. In '86, the Bills had a road losing streak of 22 straight and we were going to Kansas City to play the Chiefs.

Marv said to me, "You might want to come to my meeting Saturday night at the hotel."

I said, "Sure." Anytime I could hear him speak to the team, I jumped at it.

MARV LEVY: I said, "Fellas, I don't know how much you guys know about World War II history, but you know that Adolf Hitler was the despicable dictator of Germany. At one time, he was, by far, the most powerful military force in the world. He had overcome Poland. He had defeated France.

"Now, England was on the brink of being defeated. World history was on the verge of changing. And then, inexplicably, Hitler turned east. His troops marched through Russia, mile after mile after mile. He was close to the city of Stalingrad and it began to snow something awful. Now, the Germans were a long way from home and unable to deal with the brutal weather. Things went wrong, the tide of the war changed, and Hitler was overwhelmed."

I paused. Then, I said, "You know why Hitler lost the war? He couldn't win on the road. If you want to be a champion, you've got to win on the road."

There was some laughter, along with a few confused looks and blank stares, I'm sure. But the point was made and I think it resonated with the players, because we did go on to win the game, 17–14.

I probably used more quotes from writers and poets than other coaches did. I was an English literature major and English history major in college. I was moved by some of the great writers of all times, whether it was Charles Dickens or many others.

My mother, an immigrant who came from Russia at the age of four and only had gone as far as first grade in elementary school, had read the complete works of so many great poets and she had quite an influence on me. She gave me a book of poetry when I went into the service, and I started to read it on the train going to basic training. I was 18 years old at that time.

There was one poem I read then that rushed through my mind after the loss of that first Super Bowl, decades later. It was from a 16th century Scottish warrior.

"Fight on, my men, Sir Andrew said. A little I'm hurt, but not yet slain. I'll just lie down and bleed a while. And then I'll rise and fight again."

"That's what we're going to do," I told the players. "We lost the Super Bowl, but we're going to rise and fight again."

I coached the way I thought would be best, because I realized player morale is important and how you inspire response and hard work from players was important. It might differ a little bit from player to player. Every now and then, one of them, particularly Thurman Thomas, would roll their eyes like, "Oh, my God, here it comes."

BILL POLIAN: On numerous occasions when Marv would use multisyllabic words, he'd let it kind of hang up in the air. Then, he'd turn to Thurman Thomas and say, "Look it up, Thurman, and give the rest of us the definition." The room would howl with laughter.

In all seriousness, Marv had high regard for the intelligence of the players. And they knew it.

FRANK REICH: I just don't think there ever will be anybody quite like Marv Levy. There are a lot of great coaches, there are a lot of great techniques, but he was so selfless and so focused on what would make the team and the individual better. And he just knew how to connect.

By using all of that history stuff, he was able to communicate in a way that was authentically him. It was never about pontificating or flaunting how smart he was, with all the degrees and the honors that he had. The stories were always about how to help us as a team, how to connect to us as a team on the mission that we were on.

It was like he knew how to touch everybody in that locker room in a unique way, on top of a quick wit and a great sense of humor. It was never about him or about how smart he was. It was always about the other person.

There's so much that I think about and do as a coach that is because of having Marv as a head coach for the years that I did. In 2019, we had a captain of the week with the Colts and I would pick a word to assign to each captain. I would do a study on the word and write up the notes, going into the etymology and roots of the word that I would give the captain to read. I got all of that from Marv.

He knew that NFL football players are smart, that the adage of "dumb jock" was far from the truth. By talking to us, one intellectual to another, that raised the perception of the whole team.

BILL POLIAN: Regardless of the ways Marv delivered the message, what counted was that it was always received. In early '87, we were out on the practice field. In those days, you had a lot of guys on injured reserve, so the guys who were on defense, for example, would not have to serve as the scout team for the offense. There were rookies and injured guys who did that.

During this particular practice, some of our starters on defense—Darryl Talley, Shane Conlan, Nate Odomes, and Scott Radecic—were kneeling next to each other on the sideline. A play took place and a couple of the young guys on the defensive scout team began to rough up somebody on offense. It started to turn into a little scrap that broke up quickly.

I was standing behind Scott and Nate, and they immediately yelled out, "Hey! Don't be dumb and don't be dirty!"

As we were walking off the field, I told Marv about the incident and said, "You're getting through. They're responding."

MARV LEVY: Everybody should coach according to their own personality. Mine was influenced by many coaches. Bud Wilkinson at Oklahoma and Bear Bryant at Alabama were two that I just idolized in my early coaching years. They had vastly different personalities. Wilkinson was very intellectual in his approach, while Bryant was very authoritarian and demanding.

Bud put on coaching clinics throughout the country and I went to all of them. About the fifth one, I was sitting in the front row. Bud looked down and said, "Are you here again?"

He invited me to his spring practices over the years, and that allowed me to become more familiar with his system. His offense was about 20 percent the size of any I ever knew before, which stuck with me. He would get great repetitions from his players, but he wasn't overly stressing the need for contact in practice. That stuck with me, too.

Over time, I learned the guy knew history in and out. He knew literature. He knew poetry. He also could sing every college football song in the country.

JIM KELLY: The first thing I think about with Marv is how he allowed us to be ourselves. We did have a lot of egos on our team, without a doubt. We had players that were very, very good, Hall of Famers. But without somebody behind us, allowing us to be ourselves but in a way that made us want to listen to him, I don't think any of us would have gotten to where we did.

I'm sure that he knew a lot of things that we did, like going to The Big Tree, our favorite bar right up the road from the stadium, on Fridays after practice. Even though I was part of that, I knew I could not party like a rock 'n' roll star on Friday night and be ready to call my own plays on Sunday.

But to be allowed to be ourselves and do the things that we did in the past, I think that says a lot about the individual and the coach that Marv was. Not only in the way he treated us at practice and as football players, but also as human beings.

MARV LEVY: First of all, I wanted the players to have fun. I wanted them to be themselves, as long as it wasn't something that was truly bad for other people, for the game, for their reputations, things of that nature.

You had to be on time. We did not take roll when players boarded the plane for road trips, because barring any mechanical or weather issue, it was going to leave as scheduled. Our players would get there an hour and a half early to be sure they had enough time in case they had car trouble or got in a traffic jam or something like that.

We didn't go overboard and try to be disciplinarians. Every now and then, there was a guy we had to fine. You'd have to talk with someone. You'd have to counsel them. And they'd listen. One such player, in my early days, was Bruce Smith. At the time, he was an overweight guy who just didn't pay attention. He wanted things his way, would show up late for practice. In short, he wasn't displaying the kind of characteristics we were seeking, even though we knew he was immensely talented.

Finally, I called him into my office one day and told him he had to follow a certain off-season program and get on the path to turning himself around. I said, in no uncertain terms, "Bruce, if you don't do it, you're not going to play with the Buffalo Bills."

When I got done talking with him, he was angry. He stomped out of the office. Later, he came back in and said, "Coach, you know when I listen to you the most?"

"When's that, Bruce?"

"When you lower your voice."

One of the big things that helped Bruce Smith wasn't just what he heard from his coach, something for which I've taken a lot of credit. Equally, if not more, important was, when he went back to Virginia Tech to finish his degree, there was a woman named Carmen who was a counselor that talked to the players and gave them guidance. Bruce listened, he followed it.

Not only that, he fell in love with her, they got married, and I tell you, she was a better coach for him than I was. Boy, she really got him on track again. He turned out to be a wonderful citizen, good businessman, wonderful father.

There have been times—five, six, seven, 20 years later—where I've had players who were so taken by some of the type of discipline that we may have exacted on them, they'd thank me for it.

I remember Andre Reed one time saying, "You know, Marv, we used to fool you the night before every game. You would come around to take bed check, but those were dummies in the bed. We were really out at the bar scene."

"Andre, let me tell you something," I said. "Even when you guys weren't out at the bar scene, there were dummies in those beds."

JIM KELLY: If we ever stepped over the line, there was no doubt that even though there wasn't a lot of screaming, the tone of voice that Marv would have in the meeting room would put you in your place.

It was more about him being disappointed than angry. If you were a minute late for a meeting, your heart was beating hard, because you never wanted to let Marv down. You always wanted to play and live by his rules because you knew his rules worked.

BILL POLIAN: Marv believed everyone in the building contributed to winning. Trainers, doctors, scouts, equipment/video staff, marketing, ticketing—all needed to be invested and share in the quest to win.

As our team and organization matured, we finally got to the point where we were physically "one" on game day. Jim Kelly had a spacious house in Orchard Park, near the stadium, and invited everyone in the organization—players, coaches, etc.—and their relatives to his house after every home game.

MARV LEVY: It's the total organization that wins. It's coach, players, general manager, personnel director, scouts, team owner, the people who work in the front office, the people who work at night and sweep up the place.

Is football a team game? You bet. Is success a team effort? Every bit as much.

Nothing symbolized that more than Ralph Wilson taking everybody in the organization to all four Super Bowls. He covered plane fares, hotels, everything. There was just a great feeling that everyone shared, a recognition that each employee played a part in the success of the team, which was absolutely true.

BILL POLIAN: In many ways, the roster we put together reflected Marv. In 1987, we were in a meeting prior to his first draft as the Bills' coach. We were far along in the process and we were setting the board.

We had the third overall pick. We were hoping we could get Cornelius Bennett, an amazingly talented linebacker from Alabama who would join us later that year in a trade, but we figured he wouldn't get past Indianapolis at No. 2—and he didn't. So, we traded down to the eighth spot.

Norm Pollom, our personnel director, was really talking up Reggie Rogers, a defensive end from the University of Washington.

"I'm not sold on him," Marv said. "And, neither, frankly, is Bill." Both of us had concerns about his off-the-field conduct.

"You know, Reggie Rogers has a chance to be a Pro Bowl player for a long time," Norm said.

Marv shot back in a manner that was way out of character for him. "Dammit! I want Super Bowl players," he said. "I don't want Pro Bowl players."

It reinforced to everyone in the room, which included the entire scouting staff, that there was much more to evaluating players than that—that there had to be other things, the biggest of which was character. That was something with which he stayed throughout and with which I stayed through the rest of my career.

As it turned out, Rogers was selected seventh overall by Detroit and never did make it to the Pro Bowl. The player we chose with the next pick, linebacker Shane Conlan, was a three-time Pro Bowl selection and helped the Bills reach four Super Bowls.

MARV LEVY: The reason our team was so resilient, the reason they were able to fight their way back like they did, the reason they are such memorable guys and so many of them are in the Hall of Fame, is because way back when

I was hired and sat in that office with Bill Polian and with Ralph Wilson, I presented a profile for our players and they jumped on it.

I said, "We're only going to bring aboard guys who have character. Their personalities may differ. Some may be outgoing, some may be quiet and laid back. But do they show up for work on time? Do they not blame their teammates? Did they go back to work after disappointments? Were they good citizens? Did they care about the fans?"

Our players fit that mold. By staying true to that criteria, we were able to put together the kind of team that would do what no other club in NFL history has been able to in reaching four Super Bowls in a row.

Along the way, we also made history by making the no-huddle our primary offense rather than limiting it to conventional two-minute situations at the end of the game or the half.

BILL POLIAN: The Bills' version of the no-huddle was effectively born during our 1989 divisional-round playoff game at Cleveland. Our kicker, Scott Norwood, was hurt and he could hardly kick off. We didn't have anybody to take his place, so every time we scored, the Browns would return Scott's short kicks to midfield and they'd score practically every time.

It turned into a ping-pong match of big pass plays and scoring by both teams, led by two former University of Miami greats: Jim Kelly and Bernie Kosar.

MARV LEVY: We went into the fourth quarter of that Cleveland playoff game down by 10 points. We knew we couldn't have a long, time-consuming march down the field and make a difference. So, we decided we'd better go to our two-minute drill. And lo and behold, Jim steered us down the field. Touchdown.

We finally played some tough defense and got the ball back with not much time to go. Trailing 34–30 in the final minute, Jim was leading us on one of the greatest two-minute drives I've ever seen. It looked as if we were going to pull off a win when Jim threw to Ronnie Harmon in the left side of the end zone. But Ronnie wanted to be sure his feet were in bounds, he glanced down, and he let what would have been the winning touchdown to go through his hands.

With nine seconds left, Jim tried to drill another pass into the end zone, this time over the middle to Thurman Thomas. It was intercepted. All that was left to do was remove my headset.

Walking off the field with Ted Marchibroda, my offensive coordinator, on one side and Tom Bresnahan, my offensive line coach, on the other side, I don't know who said it—Ted, Tom, or me—but we all kind of went, "What if we made that our offense next year? We've got the exact right quarterback to do it, for one thing, and we've got a lot of the other right tools at receiver and running back."

JIM KELLY: Marv allowed Ted and Jim Shofner and the other coaches to take complete control of the offense. It takes a guy with the type of personality like Marv's to do that.

When we started to run that no-huddle full-time, I just thrived in it. For me, the no-huddle, quick pace is pretty much how I've lived my life ever since I was a little kid. My mom's favorite saying was, "Son, you need to slow down." But I never was like that. I always liked to do things fast. That's just the way I was growing up and I never have stopped that.

Even when I speak, I have a note in front of me that says, "Slow down!" That means, when I start talking on something I totally believe in and my heart is in it, like the no-huddle offense, I start getting a little bit too excited and I need to slow down.

BILL POLIAN: The no-huddle really changed everything we did because it made us practice so much faster. Everything went boom, boom, boom, boom, boom. We never huddled.

I always contended it helped our defense because they had to be on their toes much more often than a defense would.

JIM KELLY: There were no quarterbacks calling their own plays back in the day and for a head coach to allow that to happen, he had to have a lot of confidence in his quarterback. Yes, I was very blessed to have a great offensive coordinator in Ted Marchibroda, a good quarterbacks coach in Jim Shofner, and also a backup like Frank Reich there with me.

But to have a head coach that allowed me to do that says a lot about the individual, because if I screwed up, it wasn't just on me. It was on Marv, too. Our success depended on how I played. If we did not play well, I'm sure that no-huddle offense would not have thrived, and I probably would not be in the Pro Football Hall of Fame.

But Marv did have to have a little say in the offense. He was the one who called all of our short-yardage and goal-line plays. I remember many times, when we would go down the field and all of a sudden, we would get inside the five-yard line and Marv would be yelling, "Tough! Tough! Tough!" That means he was sending in the big guys.

Of course, sometimes I'd hurry to get everybody up on the line of scrimmage and pretend like I didn't see them coming onto the field because I didn't want them on the field. I'd yell, "I have a play! We got 'em right where we want 'em! Let's go! Let's go! Let's go!"

Marv would be like, "Shit, I had a good play." Every once in a while, I did let the big guys come in just to pad his ego.

BILL POLIAN: Marv Levy, Jim Kelly, and the no-huddle was a match made in football heaven. Jim's "go-go" personality and confident and competitive zeal, coupled with the great offensive players we had, were the perfect mix of talent and system.

We had to add very few pieces. One was Hall of Fame receiver James Lofton, who we acquired as a free agent during the 1989 season after he was released by the Los Angeles Raiders. James was at the end of a career that began as a first-round draft pick of the Green Bay Packers. But he was an accomplished deep receiver who could run every route on the weak side. That made him an ideal complement to Don Beebe on the other side, Hall of Famer Andre Reed in the slot, and tight ends Pete Metzelaars and Keith McKeller. James also became an immediate leader.

JIM KELLY: I was smart enough to realize and Marv was, too, that I had Hall of Fame receivers Andre Reed and James Lofton. I had another Hall of Famer, Thurman Thomas, in my backfield. And I had a great center, Kent Hull, in front of me.

I knew my speed was in James and Don Beebe on the outside. I knew hardly anybody could cover Andre inside, one-on-one, and I loved it.

I also believed in the cliché, "Take what they give you," so I loved throwing to our tight end, Pete Metzelaars. A lot of times, teams would take away deep passes, so if you have to throw it to the running back time and time again, do it until they start bringing those safeties and linebackers up close. Then, you could start dropping passes behind them. If that was helping lead us down the field to score touchdowns and score some field goals, we would do that.

I knew what plays I liked. You're pretty much defeated if you get a play from the sidelines that you don't like. If you don't have confidence in it, you're probably not going to complete it. Frank and I would go in meetings on Wednesday and say, "Hey, here's the plays that we really like by watching film." And we would go over them with Ted, and he'd keep the ones we liked and throw out the ones we didn't like.

If Chuck Dickerson, an assistant coach who signaled in plays from the sidelines along with Frank, would signal in a play I didn't like, I would flip him off. I'd be walking back to huddle and I'd give him the middle finger. It was my way of saying, "I ain't calling that play—that's horrible." Then I would call my own play.

There were certain plays that I'd run all the time, say, on third-and-3 to third-and-5. But there also were times, when it was the same down and distance, I would run the same play, but from a different formation, just to confuse the opponent a little bit.

MARV LEVY: Another very important person in that no-huddle offense operation that rarely has gotten the credit he deserves was our center, Kent Hull. He had to line up and as soon as Jim called the play, Kent would have to make a code call to the players about a certain blocking scheme. He'd have to remember the starting count, then he'd have to block 260 pounds of dynamite across from him.

Kent was fantastic. He was one of the most underrated players and one of the most high-character, delightful guys it has been my privilege to coach. Unfortunately, he died at an early age of cancer.

BILL POLIAN: The Cincinnati Bengals were already running a version of the no-huddle offense, called "Sugar Huddle," which we had faced in the 1988 AFC Championship Game.

Sam Wyche, the Bengals' late coach, had devised the scheme in order to confuse and delay defensive substitution. The Bengals' offense would linger at the line of scrimmage, or on the sideline, with 12 or 13 people in their "huddle." They would stand there, letting the play clock run down and, with under 10 seconds left, they would run the extra people off the field. Then they would quick snap and try to catch the opponent with too many or too few men on the field.

Unlike the Bills' no-huddle, the "Sugar Huddle" was not designed to snap the ball on an up-tempo basis. It was designed to prevent the defense from matching up with Cincinnati's personnel group. It was, in essence, the opposite of what we would do. Our approach presented completely different problems for defenses because we rarely substituted.

JIM KELLY: Even though Boomer Esiason and the Bengals really went with no-huddle before we did, there was nobody that ran the no-huddle like us. We were running it at a pace of about 15 seconds per play. Not 15 seconds on the clock, but 15 seconds in real time.

I remember Howie Long, the Raiders' Hall of Fame defensive end, yelling at me in the AFC Championship Game to "slow this shit down!"

Kent Hull said, "Hell on that! Speed it up!"

Without being able to substitute, those defensive linemen were getting so tired, they could not rush the passer. And that, to me, was a big plus because now I was able to step up in the pocket and be able to hit my second and third read, and not have to worry if the first one wasn't open. So, for the offensive linemen, it was, "Go! Go! Go!"

We didn't care what personnel the defense was trying to bring in. If they were trying to run somebody on the field, there was a better chance they would confuse themselves than having us catch them with too many players on the field or not enough.

Our attitude was, "Do you want nickel? Do you want dime? Do you want regular? No matter which way you go, we're going to do what we do."

We didn't win a Super Bowl with it, but that was a system that I loved.

FRANK REICH: I certainly give credit to Sam Wyche and Boomer, their version of a no-huddle, but it was a lot different than our version. I've listened to Boomer talk about their version. It was very wordy. It involved a lot of communication.

At some level, the "Sugar Huddle" was a version of the no-huddle that was an important part of the progression of the game. But I do feel what we did in our version of the no-huddle was revolutionary in that it had people thinking, "Can you really play a whole game running a play every 20 seconds? Can you play a whole season like that?"

Nobody thought that could be done. And we did it for five years.

JIM KELLY: I know some people say that I didn't run a lot of plays. Well, when you have James Lofton and you have Andre Reed and you have a mismatch against whoever is trying to cover them, then you should run the same play over and over. And there would be times when I'd call the same play, but I'd put it in a different formation, so that made it almost like a different play.

Besides, why would you want to have 75 to 100 plays? Why do you have to have 15 words to call each play? All you're doing is confusing your own players, who pretty much would have to be under your system for years to really have it all sink in.

Ours play calls were very simple. You'd have, "Eight! Cubs! Ninety-Three Double Switch! Noah!"

"Eight" was the formation. That meant the tight end was on the right. If I said, "Nine," the tight end would be on the left. Even numbers to the right, odd to the left.

"Cubs" was a weak-side pass protection. "Bears" meant strong side, bears being strong. If you said, "Flood," that meant we were going to flood one of the zones with receivers.

"Ninety-One Double Switch" was a pass play. This was Andre Reed's favorite play. The tight end would go up 10 yards and run a square-in. Andre, who would line up outside the tight end, would take two or three steps and cut hard across the middle (known today as the shallow cross). The outside guys would go up about five yards.

The switch was flopping the formation to one side or the other. Depending on where Andre lined up, he would be covered by either a nickel back or a safety. Either way, it was a mismatch in Andre's favor because he could stutter-step and run away from whoever was covering him man-to-man. Against zone, he could sit down between defenders, and be wide open as an outlet.

BILL POLIAN: If "Ninety-One Double Switch" sounds familiar, think about Wes Welker and Julian Edelman running the routes they ran with Tom Brady in New England. That proves, once again, there is nothing new under the sun.

JIM KELLY: "Noah" was the snap count. The snap count could also be "Louisville" or "Zita." Our plays didn't have all the words and numbers that the West Coast offense had. We weren't saying, "Flip Right Double X Jet 36 Counter Naked Waggle at 7 X Quarter."

There are so many things that some of these teams still say when calling a play. I remember watching a video of Jon Gruden having one of his quarterbacks on the Raiders call a play. The guy had to do it at least three times, because it was like 12–14 words long and he had trouble remembering it.

Defenses never really caught on to all that we were doing, because they were so damn tired trying to get back to the huddle that they didn't listen to what I was saying. Every once in a while, we did change it up if there was somebody on the other team that used to play for us and knew our signals. We did it before we faced the Carolina Panthers, because Frank Reich had left us to become their quarterback and Bill Polian was their GM.

BILL POLIAN: All week before that game, Frank and I were talking to our defensive coaches. They'd been with New Orleans before joining the Panthers, but they'd never seen the Bills' no-huddle live. We kept saying, "You don't understand how fast they're going to go. Every 15–18 seconds, they run a play. There's no dilly dally at the line of scrimmage. And when Jim gets in a rhythm, they might go every 12 seconds.

They thought we were exaggerating and didn't take our warning seriously. "Nah, nah," they said. "They can't do that."

We actually practiced with two offenses that week. One was specifically designed to try to replicate the no-huddle, but they weren't going anywhere near the pace that the Bills ran.

At halftime, we were leading 6–0 and playing pretty well. We had a good game plan, Frank was playing well, and the Bills were not into it. One of the writers from Carolina said to me at halftime, "This is a big upset in the making."

I said, "Hey, hold on to your hat. They haven't even warmed up yet. You haven't seen anything."

Sure enough, in the second half, the Bills took off like they were in a NASCAR race. *Vroom! Vroom! Vroom!* They outscored us 28–3 in the third quarter on the way to a 31–9 victory. I had a stiff neck watching the red, white, and blue go up and down the field.

After the game, I walked in the locker room and I pulled aside two of the defensive coaches.

"The next time I give you a scouting report, please pay attention to it," I said.

Their eyes were wide.

"Oh, man!" one of them said. "We didn't think anybody could go that fast."

"I told you so."

JIM KELLY: Another time we changed things up with our signals was when we were playing the Patriots and Fred Smerlas, our former nose tackle, was on the other side. Fred knew, "Noah! Noah! Noah!" meant we were snapping on the second hut. So, before we took the line, I said, "Listen, everybody, I'm going to come up to the line of scrimmage, I'm going to go, 'Noah! Noah! Noah!' Fred's going to think it's on two, but we're really going to go on three."

I went to the line, I yelled, "Noah! Noah! Noah!" Then I went, "Set! Hut-HUT!" All of us were standing still and Fred was behind me. He cussed me out like you wouldn't believe.

I just smiled and said, "Got ya!"

BILL POLIAN: The week before "The Greatest Comeback Game," when the Bills rallied from 32 points to beat the Houston Oilers in a wild-card playoff game, we had been soundly defeated and physically roughed up by those same Oilers in Houston.

Jim Kelly and Cornelius Bennett, among others, were hurt in that regular-season finale and would not play in the postseason rematch. Thurman Thomas was also injured the week before. He tried to play that following week but left early and Kenneth Davis replaced him.

There we were, entering a playoff game without two Hall of Famers and one of our two best defensive players. To add insult to injury, we couldn't even sell the game out.

MARV LEVY: We were down 28–3 at halftime. We were in the locker room, sitting glumly. We had several injuries and they were knocking us all over the place. They had beaten us the week before and now they were doing it again. You could tell everyone was thinking our season's over.

I went up to Frank Reich and I told him, "You led the greatest comeback in college football history. You're going to lead the greatest comeback in the history of the NFL." Frank, grim-faced, nodded his head.

As we were walking down the tunnel for the second half, our offensive coordinator, Jim Shofner, said, "Marv, we're down 25 points. The greatest comeback in the history of the league is 28. I know, because I played in that game with Detroit."

"That's okay," I said. "Frank doesn't know that."

FRANK REICH: At halftime, Marv says, "Men, let's just go down fighting. Whatever is going to happen, we're not going to quit. We're going to go out fighting." And then, as we were walking out of the locker room, he said, "Just remember this, Frank, you led the greatest comeback in college football history. Today, you're going to lead the greatest comeback in NFL history."

Bobby Ross was my coach at Maryland, and he had been an assistant on Marv's staff with the Chiefs, so that was a meaningful connection. I didn't take it as coach-speak. Now, did I think it was going to happen? I don't think anybody was thinking that was really going to happen. It was just more of a mindset than anything.

My thought was, "I don't know if that's possible or not, but I know how to do it." It reminded me of how we did it in college, when we were losing 31–0. If you were talking about the quarterback who helped bring the team back from that kind of deficit to win 42–40, you'd say he must have thrown 30 passes in the second half. I threw 15 passes in the second half of the greatest comeback in college football history at the time.

But the whole idea was one play at a time, one series at a time. When Marv said that, it just reminded me of how we did it then: one play at a time, one series at a time, one touchdown at a time.

MARV LEVY: We go out there and on the first series of the second half, Frank throws a touchdown. Unfortunately, it's not to our guy. It's to their cornerback, who intercepts it and goes all the way for a touchdown.

Now we're down 35–3.

FRANK REICH: I throw the pick-six at the start of the second half. We get the ball right back, we drive down, and we score a touchdown to make it 35–10. I'm over on the bench, just talking to the guys. The next thing I know, the coaches are yelling, "Offense! You're up!"

I'm like, "What the heck?"

Without hesitation, Marv had called a surprise onside kick and we recovered. I don't know who does that. That was incredible.

BILL POLIAN: I knew we were going to go for the onside kick. I don't know why. I guess I had been around Marv so much. I was up in our booth with Bob Ferguson, our assistant GM, and John Butler, our player personnel director, and I turned to Fergie and said, "You know, if we get the onside kick here, we're going to win the game."

"You're crazy," he said. "You're smoking something."

"No, no. We're going to do it. I've got that feeling."

FRANK REICH: When we came out, we ran my favorite play, "Nine Calf 47." Don Beebe was running a go route, Pete Metzelaars was running a corner, Andre Reed was coming over on an under route, James Lofton was running a little dig route, and Kenny Davis, the back who had taken over after Thurman Thomas left the game with an injury, was in the flat.

The Oilers busted the coverage. The corner thought they were playing Cover Two, but the free safety was in the middle of the field playing Cover

Three. The corner got a really good jam on Beebe and pushed him out of bounds. But the safety never came over the top.

When I saw the free safety in the middle of the field, I thought it was Cover Three. I saw that the corner was pressed in coverage, but I figured he must be playing press-bail. You're usually not throwing a go route versus that. You're normally throwing a sail to the back in the flat, with Andre coming across the middle.

Sometimes, you don't even look at the corner. I don't know why, but I looked at him and he didn't press-bail. He actually jammed Beebe and then I saw Don running down the sideline. I didn't know he had stepped out of bounds and came back in. The defender saw it and let up. It was an easy call for the official to make, but he didn't because as far as he was concerned, this game was over and he was on to his next playoff game. With the free safety staying in the middle of field, Beebe was wide open for a 38-yard touchdown. That made it 35–17. A 26-yard touchdown pass to Andre cut the margin to 11.

The next time we got the ball, we had a third-and-5. After an incompletion, I instantly knew I wanted to go for it. We knew we had them on the ropes. I looked over at Marv and without hesitation, he said, "Go ahead, you've got it."

The play clock ended up running down and I didn't want to have to rush the snap, so I called timeout. I went over to talk to Marv and Ted.

"Okay, we're going to go for it, right?" I said. "I think I've got the play."

"We're going for it," Marv said, without hesitation.

I was afraid the timeout might have allowed the Oilers to regroup, but I felt good about the play, which would have four receivers running vertical routes.

"I want to run "Bull 65," I said. "And here's why: Earlier in the game, I missed James on the same play because I threw a bad pass. But I saw that the corner was driving hard on the slant. And the nickel, who was supposed to be carrying Andre in the slot, was dropping, he was letting him go. If they play the coverage the same way, Andre is going to be open."

Sure enough, Andre was playing in the slot. He went out and up, they dropped him in coverage, I hit him for his second touchdown. Now it was 35–31.

MARV LEVY: Over a period of seven minutes, we scored four touchdowns. We faced a third-and-13 and I was on the phone with Jim Shofner, our quarterbacks coach.

"We're not punting," I told him. "We're going to use all four downs."

The drive ended with Andre's third touchdown catch to put us up 38–35. The game goes into overtime. Back then, the first score wins the game. We kick off and shortly thereafter, Nate Odomes intercepts a pass to set up Steve Christie's winning field goal.

In the locker room, where we were celebrating like you can't imagine, I go over to congratulate Frank. He said, "Oh, Coach, one thing. I knew we weren't down far enough to have the greatest comeback in NFL history. That's why I threw that interception."

"Thanks, Frank," I said. "And I'll tell you another lie: I believe you."

One of our mantras was play hard, play clean, play to win. But win or lose, dig right back in. They sure did that quite a bit. Yeah, we never won the Super Bowl, but we never gave up, either. As Winston Churchill said, "Never, never, never, never surrender!" They never did.

Another example of that was our third Super Bowl. The final score would hardly suggest as much; we got beat 52–17. But there was a moment that illustrated what our team was about as well as any in my time in Buffalo.

Jim Kelly left the game late with a concussion. Frank was taking us down for what would have been a meaningless touchdown, but he got sacked as he was attempting to throw a long one to Don Beebe and fumbled. Leon Lett, the Cowboys' defensive lineman, picked it up and took off for what would have been yet another touchdown.

But Beebe showed what the Buffalo Bills were all about. From 25–30 yards down the field, he sets sail. And, boy, could he run fast. He sprinted, sprinted, sprinted, sprinted. Leon Lett got 64 yards downfield. Two more yards and he would cross the goal line. At that point, Leon held the football up in the air in triumph. Beebe caught up and slapped it out of his hands. The ball rolled through the end zone and we took over at the 20.

It was one of the things that helped propel us, even to get ready to try to fight our way back to a fourth Super Bowl. We did.

Twenty years after that game, I was at an NFL meeting. As my wife and I were waiting to get into a restaurant at the hotel, we were sitting at the bar. I look over and who's sitting there next to me? Leon Lett. He lifted up a bottle of beer.

"Leon, be careful," I said. "Or I'm going to knock that out of your hand."

I got a chuckle from him.

BILL POLIAN: Marv Levy's unique talents as a motivator, delegator, and innovator are living proof that what it takes to win is simple… but isn't easy.

CHAPTER 8

The Manning/Dungy Colts: Leadership, Innovation, Sustained Excellence

BILL POLIAN: In December of 1997, I became president of the Indianapolis Colts. Owner Jim Irsay had charged me with revamping the entire football operation. We hired former New Orleans Saints head coach Jim Mora. He brought a very organized and highly disciplined approach, which we badly needed. He also hired outstanding assistant coaches such as offensive coordinator Tom Moore, quarterbacks coach Bruce Arians, offensive line coach Howard Mudd, defensive coordinator Vic Fangio, and linebackers coach Mike Murphy.

We also inherited some very good players my predecessor, Bill Tobin, had acquired. Offensive tackle Tarik Glenn and tight end Ken Dilger played key roles in our growth. Running back Marshall Faulk, a star, was traded to St. Louis and replaced by No. 1 draft choice Edgerrin James. Both became Hall of Famers.

Wide receiver Marvin Harrison teamed up with our No. 1 draft choice (and first overall), Peyton Manning. They became one of the most productive quarterback-receiver tandems in pro football history. They, too, are Hall of Famers.

We struggled through a 3–13 inaugural season, but with the program firmly established, we reversed the record in 1999, going 13–3 and winning the AFC East. Prior to the '99 season, we added key veteran free agents, such as Chad Bratzke, Cornelius Bennett, and Chad Cota. Unfortunately, the first of our playoff losses occurred in a 19–16 heartbreaker to Tennessee.

In 1999, we added Jeff Saturday. He played a major role in our no-huddle offense as the center and signal-caller for the O-line. He was a big factor in our rise to championship status. That season brought a 10–6 record and another tough playoff loss, in overtime, to Miami.

In 2001, we regressed to 6–10. Edgerrin James, who had become an All-Pro, was hurt, and Peyton had a rough year trying to carry the team as the defense slipped. We did add Reggie Wayne through the draft and despite the record, most of the key players with whom we would have great success were in place.

We were, however, squeezed under the cap. I felt the way forward, both to deal with the cap and improve the defense, was to go to a simpler, more speed-oriented defensive style. That would allow us to play younger, less-expensive players sooner. That necessitated a change at the defensive coordinator position, which Coach Mora could not agree to. As a result, he left and we were in the market for a new head coach.

I talked with Jim Irsay about potential candidates. He asked, "What if Tony Dungy became available?"

My response was, "All bets are off. He's our man."

Fortunately, Tony agreed to become our new head coach and the rest, as the saying goes, is history. And a remarkable history it is.

Once Peyton Manning arrived and fought through the crucible of his rookie season, the winning commenced. From 1998, when he started as a rookie, through 2010 (he would miss 2011 due to injury), our record with Peyton at the helm was 141–67, a winning percentage of 68 percent.

Tom Moore's no-huddle offense, led by Peyton and featuring Marvin, Edgerrin, Reggie, Dallas Clark, and company, won eight division championships, reached the playoffs 11 times, the conference championship game three times, and two Super Bowls, winning Super Bowl XLI under Tony and finishing as runner-up under Tony's successor, Jim Caldwell, in Super Bowl XLIV.

Peyton was chosen as NFL MVP four times and at the time of his retirement was in the top five in NFL history in every major quarterback statistic.

While our personalities couldn't have been more different—Tony, the epitome of quiet strength; I, full of passion and intensity—we were aligned perfectly when it came to building and sustaining a championship-level organization.

By virtue of our poor 2001 record, we had the 11th pick in the first round of the 2002 draft. We had targeted the defensive line. We had two good candidates. One was a power defensive tackle who would have been the obvious choice in our previous defensive scheme. The other was Dwight Freeney, an outstanding pass-rusher with great speed and sack production, from Syracuse University. At 6'1", he was considered by many experts as "too short" to play defensive end in the NFL.

Just prior to the '02 draft, I asked Tony which player he preferred. He said, "Given a choice between size or speed, I'll take speed every time."

I replied, "Me too!"

Dwight Freeney was our choice. He spent 11 years with the Colts and 16 overall in the NFL. He made first-team All-Pro three times and was named to seven Pro Bowls. He retired with 125.5 sacks, which is 18th in NFL history, and will be a very viable Hall of Fame candidate when eligible.

While Tony was able to rebuild the defense to a Super Bowl level, his background as a quarterback allowed him to help Peyton grow considerably. Tony publicly said, "I'm going to tell Peyton it's okay to punt" as a means of taking away the pressure to score on every possession. What Tony didn't talk publicly about was his ability to work with Peyton on anticipating what defenses would do to counter our no-huddle/up-tempo offensive approach. This helped Peyton greatly to call plays and read defenses at the line of scrimmage, which was the key to our no-huddle offense.

Tony entrusted the offense to Tom Moore, who had been our coordinator under Jim Mora. That trust was engendered by a lifelong relationship. Tom had recruited and coached Tony at the University of Minnesota. He convinced Tony to sign as a free agent with the Pittsburgh Steelers rather than with the Montreal Alouettes of the CFL.

The combination of Tony, Tom, and Peyton led the Colts to a record 115 wins during the decade of 2000 to 2009. In this chapter, you'll hear from Tony, Peyton, Tom, and Dwight.

TONY DUNGY: I was highly recruited as a quarterback at Parkside High School in Jackson, Michigan, which was midway between the University of Michigan and Michigan State. My dad went to Michigan; he bled Maize and Blue. My mom was a Michigan State lady.

I got indoctrinated into University of Michigan sports early, going to football and basketball games. My dad got a chance to do his PhD work at Michigan State, so I spent my third-, fourth-, and fifth-grade years on the campus in East Lansing. Those were the glory years under coach Duffy Daugherty.

In my heart of hearts, I wanted to go to Michigan State and I wanted to be part of that legacy. Duffy had been recruiting me and it was my dream to play for him. But when I was a senior in high school, he announced that he was going to retire after that season.

Duffy's number one assistant was a guy by the name of Cal Stoll, who had gotten the head coaching job at the University of Minnesota. He started recruiting me and said, "Hey, don't go to Michigan State. Come to Minnesota and build your own legacy."

Tom Moore, who was the running backs coach at the University of Minnesota at the time, also recruited me. He was the one who actually got me to visit the campus. I had never been on a plane before and was worried about having to fly, so I called Tom and said, "I don't think I can get on this plane."

He said, "Stay there, and I'll come down and fly back with you." Tom coached me through everything. I ended up going to Minnesota to the dismay of my dad and my mom. I didn't want to divide the house.

The very first meeting Coach Stoll had with us, he talked about looking for uncommon men. He said, "If we want to win a Big 10 championship, if we want to catch Michigan and Ohio State, we're going to need uncommon people. Not people who are content with being okay or average. Not people who are looking for the easy way, but championship mentality. There are two ways you can be uncommon. You can have a talent that nobody else has; that's God-given and you're just blessed. Or you can have a drive or determination that will allow you to do what everybody else could do, but most people won't."

As soon as he said that I wrote it down in my notebook, along with, "That's me!" If all it took was drive and determination and work, that was going to be me. I was in the coaches' offices more than anybody. I watched as much film as I could. I worked out, did everything I could to be that uncommon player. Because of my parents, I was very committed to graduating on time. I just lived in the coaches' offices and in the classrooms.

I played in a few games as a freshman, but I wasn't the full-time starter. I didn't come on the scene with a big bang, but Coach Stoll stuck with me. Fortunately for me, our quarterbacks coach was Tom Moore, who instituted the same no-huddle offense that we used in Indianapolis with Peyton Manning. He put it in my junior year, and we kind of took off. We threw the ball a little more than the Big 10 was used to at that time and I had a lot of fun. My last two years were sensational.

TOM MOORE: One time, we were playing Iowa, which ran the Fifty-three Slant defense. We ran the Veer offense. Knowing they had to make a call at the line of scrimmage before each snap, we just lined up, listened to their call to find out which way they were going to slant, and ran the appropriate play. It was like a handoff drill. We scored four touchdowns in the first half.

At halftime, I told Tony they were going to make some kind of adjustment. I said, "I don't know what it's going to be, but they've got to do something."

When we didn't score on our first drive of the second half, I asked Tony if he noticed anything different. He said, "Yes. The call they're making is different."

"What are they calling?"

"Sometimes they're saying, 'Gee' and sometimes they're saying, 'Haw.'"

I looked at him and said, "You don't know what 'Gee' and 'Haw' is, do you?"

"No, I don't have a clue."

"Well, that's how the farmers used to guide their mules. They'd say, 'Gee' and the mules would turn right, they'd say 'Haw' and mules would turn left."

We went out and got another three touchdowns.

BILL POLIAN: While Tony was playing so well at Minnesota, I was trying to find my way in professional football as a scout with the Montreal Alouettes of the Canadian Football League. I let our personnel director, Bob Windish, know that because of his accuracy, mobility, elusiveness, and leadership, Tony was the ideal CFL quarterback.

Marv Levy, our head coach, felt Tony would be a good fit for the Alouettes. Marv saw those attributes and realized how seamlessly they would fit into the Alouette's multi-faceted offense.

TONY DUNGY: I remember meeting Coach Levy at the East-West College All-Star Game. He said, "We've got your rights, we love you. With your style of play, you wouldn't have to make an adjustment at all. You're just what we're looking for. I think you could play quarterback here for 15 years."

I remember just being so impressed with Marv's knowledge of the game, his personal feel for you. I'd watched a lot of Canadian football when I was growing up in Michigan, so I was familiar with it. But there was something inside me where I just said, "I want to play in the NFL."

At that time, there weren't a lot of African American quarterbacks having success in the NFL. My senior year at Minnesota, we played the University of Washington. Warren Moon was quarterbacking the Huskies and they beat us. At that time, Warren was leading the Pac-8, Washington's conference at the time, in passing. I was leading the Big 10 in passing. Warren ended up going on to become the MVP of the Rose Bowl. He had a tremendous career, but he didn't get drafted by the NFL. I didn't get drafted, either.

Warren went to Edmonton of the CFL and won five Grey Cups up there and the rest is history. I always kind of wonder, in my mind, if I had gone with Coach Levy, maybe we'd have won five Grey Cups. It was a hard decision to pass up the chance to play for Marv, but I went to the Pittsburgh Steelers in 1977 and became a defensive back.

Tom Moore had gone to Pittsburgh to become the receivers coach. He told Coach Noll about me and felt like I would have a chance because I was Coach Noll's type of guy—the kind of athlete who could adjust, who was smart, who would work at things. He said, "Coach Noll's going to love you. You should sign here." I did and, immediately, it became the best thing that happened to me.

BILL POLIAN: I had gotten to know Tony personally through the NFL Competition Committee on which we had both served. I also admired greatly how he had taken the Tampa Bay Buccaneers from the league's worst franchise to the brink of the Super Bowl.

We had to play his teams in Carolina, and I knew, firsthand, how tough they were. Tony's Bucs lost in the playoffs and Tampa ownership decided that he couldn't get them to the "next level" and discharged him.

TONY DUNGY: Tampa had 13 straight losing seasons when I got the job. I brought a philosophy that we were going to build slowly, build through the draft. We were going to develop a defensive team and we were going to win a lot of close, low-scoring games. We were going to do it with good people who were going to make a difference in our community, but we were going to win.

It took a little while for that to take root. I remember our first team in Tampa was 1–8, and people were saying, "Oh, we're worse off than we were before. We're going to have a 14th straight losing season." We did, but staying the course was something that was ingrained in me from my time as a player and assistant coach with the Steelers. One of Coach Chuck Noll's patented philosophies was, "Leaving your game plan is a sign of panic and panic will never be in our game. In staying the course and being a little bit stubborn at times, we let people know that we had a system we believed in and we were not going to leave it."

Everybody who played for us can probably recite these words in their sleep: "Do what we do, don't let anybody define us, don't let anybody tell us how to do it. We know what we're doing and we're going to stay with that and we're going to stay with it together."

We got through that 1–8 period, winning five out of our last seven games, and that kind of got us going. The second year, we started out 5–0 and became a playoff team, and we were rolling. I was feeling good about where we were.

In '99, we had everything in place, but then we had two quarterback injuries and we had to play Shaun King as a rookie. We didn't put too much on Shaun, yet we still won eight of our last nine and got into the playoffs with a lot of momentum. We were kind of this defensive juggernaut going to St. Louis to face the Rams in the NFC Championship Game. The Rams had "the Greatest Show on Turf," but our defense kept them in check and we were winning, 6–5, with four minutes ago. I was thinking, "We're going to shut down the Greatest Show on Turf and we're going to take Shaun King, a rookie quarterback, to the Super Bowl."

Then, Ricky Proehl made a tremendous catch on a 30-yard pass from Kurt Warner in the corner of the end zone. The Rams' two-point try failed and they were up, 11–6, with just under five minutes left. We were driving to try to win the game. With just under a minute to go, Bert Emanuel looked like he caught a ball down at about the 15-yard line. That had been a catch for 100 years in the NFL. The officials ruled it a catch on the field. We took a time out because we wanted to set up for the next play. It was the first year of instant replay and during the timeout, they looked at the play, again and again and again.

Finally, they called it incomplete. We ended up losing. Of course, the league came out the next day and said, "It should have been a completion, we don't know why they reversed it." It became the Bert Emanuel Rule and really set the stage for all this catch/no catch with replay now in the NFL.

We never quite recovered from that game. Our ownership in Tampa got a little frustrated, a little bit impatient, and they didn't think I was the guy that could take them to the Super Bowl. I was fired after four playoff seasons.

Fortunately, that was God taking care of me because eight days later, I was hired by Jim Irsay and Bill Polian as head coach of the Colts.

BILL POLIAN: When Tony and I were meeting in Tampa, at the West Shore Marriott, I asked him a question about how he prepares the team. About two sentences into his answer, he stopped and said to me, "Did I say something funny?"

I said, "No, no, not at all. Why do you ask?"

"Because you're smiling and nodding your head."

"Well, that's because I've heard it all before, from Coach Levy. That's exactly the same philosophy we operated under in Buffalo."

Both Tony and Marv believed in using the off-season to build strength, conditioning, and individual skill. They wanted the preseason to be an opportunity to get the team ready for the regular season without taking undue risk of injury to starters and to find contributors among the new players.

That translated to hard work at training camp and moderate exposure for the starters in preseason games. Once the regular season began, both men believed in relatively short, very fast-paced practices, which related in large measure to situational football with a heavy emphasis on special teams. They also did not want to waste time and/or player energy on drills which had no relation to specific game situations.

As the season wore on, and into the playoffs, practice time on the field was reduced and pads were not worn. The results were tremendous.

Our center, Jeff Saturday, was an influential member of the NFL Players Association negotiating team during the 2011 labor negotiations. These talks resulted in rules that governed how all NFL teams could conduct off-season, training camp, and in-season practices. What was memorialized in the collective bargaining agreement was taken directly from Tony's practice procedures.

PEYTON MANNING: I felt like my game went to a new level when Tony Dungy became the head coach because even though Tony had a defensive background, he was an old quarterback. He knows both sides of it. He and I watched a lot of film together, and he would tell me, "Peyton, this is what the defense is probably going to be trying to do. But this is what you might want to do to counter that."

I think that's an interesting dynamic, to get that defensive perspective and learn what puts pressure on the defense, and therefore, you know what you should hang your hat on, as far as what aspects of the no-huddle were putting pressure on them. Tom Brady benefitted from that same defensive mindset with Bill Belichick.

We didn't do a lot of shifts and motions, because I wanted to see what the defense was in, I wanted to see the finished product. By getting to the line of scrimmage so quickly, mixing in some quick counts, we could get up there, we could have a dummy snap count, see what they were in, and then call some really good plays to take advantage of what that defense was in.

For example, I'd say, "Hey, if the corner presses Marvin Harrison one-on-one, the first chance we get, we want to throw a deep ball to him, a deep go route." So, we called a deep go route in the first quarter and they didn't bump-and-run Marvin. We called it again in the second quarter and they didn't bump-and-run Marvin. Third quarter, same thing. Finally, in the fourth quarter, we had a run play called and I saw they were bump-and-running Marvin. Boom! Now, I'm getting out of the run play and I'm calling the deep go to Marvin to take advantage of something we were trying to do.

The worst thing you can say is, "Well, I wish I would have had that play called when the defense did that." The mental aspect of it was challenging, it was intense. There was no doubt, after the game, I was tired mentally.

I give Jim Caldwell, who was my quarterbacks coach for seven seasons under Tony, a lot of credit for keeping my physical skills sharp—my fundamentals, drops. He was filming every throw I ever made. Every play-action. Every fake. Every handoff. Jim videoed everything and we watched it all together to keep my mechanics from slipping, to keep my delivery the same, my footwork the same. That combination really helped us out.

DWIGHT FREENEY: Tony went beyond the game. To that point, most coaches that I had were your basic coaches. That's kind of how you thought of them. Coach tells you to do something, you go do it. With Tony, you felt like there was something extra, another layer. He wasn't only just trying to be a great coach; he was trying to be a great man. And he wanted you to be a great man.

Before the Colts drafted me in 2002, I had never played for a coach that I would feel so bad when I didn't make the play. I felt bad for my teammates, but until Tony, I never had a moment where I felt bad I didn't make a play for my coach. Letting Tony down would be the worst feeling in the world because of the way he coached you. He treated you like a man.

The way he interacted with you, you felt like, "I'd run through a wall for him." Tony was one of us.

BILL POLIAN: Peyton had three full seasons at Tennessee and excelled. Most draft observers predicted he would be among the top five picks if he chose to declare for the NFL draft, for which he was eligible. Very, very fortunately, he elected to stay at Tennessee and because of our poor record, the Colts had the first choice in the subsequent NFL draft when Peyton made himself available.

PEYTON MANNING: It was certainly a tough decision. I remember my process when I was choosing where to go to college was to write out the pluses and minuses of all the schools I was considering. I did the same thing when I was a junior deciding whether to stay at Tennessee. It always helps me to have a notepad to write it out in front of me.

The tough part was I had my degree. There was a rule that if you were set to graduate that spring that you had up until a month before the draft to declare your eligibility. Most kids decide in January if they're going pro or not. It's right after a bowl game and a lot of kids end up leaving because they make their decision when they're away from campus.

I took 18 hours of classes my junior fall and 22 my junior spring just in case I was willing to leave early so I could have my degree in three years. After we played our bowl game—we had a good win against Northwestern in the Florida Citrus Bowl—I went home to New Orleans and I probably thought that I was leaving. It just seemed like it was a good time to go.

I was still going through off-season workouts, even though coach Phil Fulmer didn't really know if I was going to be back on the team. That created a little bit of an awkward situation, but eventually I just decided I wasn't ready to go. My first three years had been a sprint, always running to class, running to workouts. I wanted one more year to slow things down, to get bigger, to get stronger, to have another 12 games in the SEC.

I went ahead and finished all my classes so I would graduate in my senior year. Let's just say I didn't kill myself academically that year. That gave me extra time to go to meetings with David Cutcliffe, our offensive coordinator and quarterbacks coach, and the other coaches. I really felt like that was the best way to expand my football mind, so that when I got drafted, I would be as prepared as possible.

Basically, it seemed to be pretty clear that the Colts and the Chargers were both going to take quarterbacks with the first and second overall picks. I was still nursing a little bit of a knee injury from my senior year, so I didn't work out at the Scouting Combine at Indianapolis. I wanted to, because I liked the idea of going there and just saying, "Hey, I'm here, I don't have anything to hide." I felt confident, but I just didn't feel like I was maybe 100 percent with that knee injury.

I threw at my Senior Day at Tennessee with some of our other prospects; we had three first-rounders that year, including Marcus Nash, one of my receivers who got drafted by the Broncos. I ended up doing a private workout for the Colts. Bill Polian was there. So were Jim Mora, the head coach at the time; Tom Moore, who was the offensive coordinator; and Bruce Arians, who was the quarterback coach. Bruce was running 12-yard out routes for me.

I remember thinking, "If this team drafts me, I'm really going to like working with Tom and Bruce." I knew what Bill's history was in being able to turn organizations around as he had done in Buffalo and Carolina. There was something about wanting to come to a team and wanting to be a part of the turnaround. There was something exciting about that challenge.

As time went on, I got to the point where I just kind of got tired of all the games, if you will, about whether the Colts were going to take me with the No. 1 pick. I came to Indianapolis for a medical re-check of my knee and I sat down with Bill. I was very honest. I said, "Bill, this is where I'd actually like to come. Knoxville is not far away. New Orleans is not far away. San Diego's a long way away. I'd really like having Marvin Harrison as a receiver. You've got two good tackles, Tarik Glenn and Adam Meadows. I like the tight ends, Ken Dilger and Marcus Pollard. I like the running back, Marshall Faulk. This is where I'd like to go, so I hope you do draft me. But if you don't draft me, I'm just telling you, I'll come back and kick your ass for the next 15 years."

The draft was in New York. I really didn't want to go there and be a part of another reality TV show like I was with the Heisman Trophy. That was not the most fun experience and so I didn't really want to relive it.

I ended up making the trip anyway. The day before the draft, I got a call from Bill. As soon as he told me the Colts were taking me with the first pick, I was glad to be in New York. Draft Day turned out to be a special day, with commissioner Paul Tagliabue calling my name and Jim Irsay, the Colts' owner, there to present the card with my name on it.

A few days later, we had a rookie minicamp. I came in a couple days early. Bruce Arians and Tom Moore holed me up at the Signature Inn, with the blinds down and the doors locked. I wasn't allowed to leave. They felt that was the best way to keep me focused on learning the Colts playbook.

In that first minicamp practice, on a Friday, Jim Mora put me in as the starting quarterback. That's how it all got started.

What a struggle that rookie season was for me. We were 3–13. I think I still hold the NFL rookie record for interceptions with 28. Throwing that many interceptions is actually very hard to do. You have to throw three in your first game, four in your second game, three in your third game. If you get 10 early, boy, you really have a chance to break it. As soon as one of these new rookies wants to break that record, believe me, I'm all for it. I want to get that one off of my résumé.

But I don't think I could have handled that rookie year had I come out as a junior. I think it might have broken me. But I was mentally tough that rookie season, just because I had that extra year of experience in college. Look, it was disappointing, it was frustrating. I had never lost that many games before. I think in my high school and college careers combined, we lost six total games.

But after going 3–13 as a rookie, we went 13–3 in my second season. I give a lot of the credit for that to staying for my senior year, just because it allowed me to be stronger mentally and physically.

TOM MOORE: With Ken Dilger and Marcus Pollard as our tight ends, the whole basis of the offense was to spread them out and attack the outside with our running game and run the slant play. The idea was to make them stop what you like to do best. When they do that, they've got to give up something. Now where do you go? What's your answer?

The Tennessee Titans went to a wide-nine technique when they played us. Jim Washburn, their defensive coordinator, put those ends out there and you weren't getting outside. That was okay because then you just ran up inside. They had to do something to stop your base and everything is based on your answer.

If you've got two tight ends, they can do one of two things. They can go One High and have a safety to one side. If they do that, fine. We'll run away from him. If everybody's over on the other side, you run the opposite way. Our motto was, "Run where they ain't."

If they go Cover Two, then you can run up inside because they've got no safety support. You've got to have two good wide receivers to force that Cover Two. If they go One High and you can't throw one-on-one routes, then they can bring the one guy down to one side and slide the linebackers over to the other side, so you're always going against an eight-man front. But if you have two good wide receivers, you can get them out of that eight-man and get one-on-one coverage you can beat.

The other thing that you have to incorporate in that offense is the ability to establish a good play-action pass scheme. I thought we had one. One thing we did with it was make sure the play-action passes looked exactly like the run. I've seen situations where you have a run, then you put in a play-action pass off it, but your line stands in pass protection. Professional athletes are going to quickly read the difference between the run and the pass.

Howard Mudd, our offensive line coach, did a great job making sure that all our play-action passes looked exactly like runs, and we got a lot of mileage out of that. I remember, after a game against the Pittsburgh Steelers when Marvin Harrison ran right by their ace corner, I was talking with their coach, Bill Cowher. He said, "You know, I told that guy, don't look in the backfield, but he did. That was because of the action." That was where Howard did a great job with the offensive line; the offensive line did a great job of selling the run and Peyton was phenomenal with how he faked the handoff.

After Peyton's first year, he came to me and said, "Hey, Tom, I don't want my legacy to just be that I was known as a play-action pass quarterback."

I said, "Okay."

About four years later, Peyton said, "Hey, Tom, maybe you should put in some more play-action passes this week."

BILL POLIAN: Tom had used the no-huddle extensively in a previous assignment with the Detroit Lions. We had used it to a large degree with the Colts, but at a very slow tempo. The version that became famous and strongly influenced a lot of offensive styles came about almost by accident.

PEYTON MANNING: The no-huddle didn't really start until somewhere around my third or fourth season. We were playing the Jets. We were down 14–0, and the game had barely started. Then Tom Moore just said, "Let's go up-tempo. Let's go 'Lightning.'" That's what we called it.

Sure enough, we took the lead, got back in the game, and won. Somewhere around then, Tom said, "Why are we waiting to get down 14–0 before we go 'Lightning?' Why don't we just come out and start the game that way? Go up-tempo, put pressure on the defense. Peyton, it's going to give you more time at the line of scrimmage to get us out of bad plays."

TOM MOORE: I always tried to give Peyton an idea of what I wanted him to do quick enough, so he had 30 seconds left on the game clock. That gave him 30 seconds up there to manipulate the defense.

Peyton also was good with double cadence. For instance, he might say, "Ice cream!" But "Ice cream" didn't mean anything. Then he'd start the actual cadence. Or he'd say, "Strawberry!" or "Vanilla!" Those first words meant nothing, but the defense didn't know that, and as Peyton went through his first cadence, the defense would kind of have to do away with whatever they were going to do. If they were going to show One High, but with the intention of going back to Cover Two on the snap, Peyton would see that guy's body language, where he was starting to cheat to go back to Cover Two, and he had time to get to the right play.

He also could see the body language of the defensive linemen or linebackers start to give away their intentions. He'd make a "Pink!" call, which told the offensive line that the defense was coming with a dog or was going to slant, whatever was going to transpire at the line of scrimmage.

As Peyton evolved with the double cadence and got more comfortable, he loved it because he could play games with it. He could read defenses better. He didn't have to anticipate as much because he could see the body language of people and have a better idea what they were going to do and where they were going.

His "Omaha!" call became a bigger deal when he was with Denver, and I don't know what, if anything, it meant when he used it there. With the Colts, the original meaning was, if we had a run called to the right, "Omaha!" took it to the left. If we had a pass on and he said "Omaha!" that changed the protection from one side to the other, but the pattern stayed the same.

Peyton's ability to see things at the line of scrimmage would help a lot when he faced quarters coverage, Cover Four, where the defense is four across the board and is reading the number two receiver. If the number two receiver does not go vertical, the safety and the corner double the X or Z receiver. But if you send your number two receiver vertical, the safety has to jump in and that puts the Z one-on-one with the cornerback.

When that happens, you take your backside inside receiver and you send him to the corner. Peyton would see that coverage and he'd go to his audible to get to the pattern, and that was where we would hit Marvin Harrison a lot of times on post patterns. We'd take one of our tight ends, Dallas Clark or Marcus Pollard, and put him on a 14-yard in route, the safety had to drop down and cover him and the corner was out there one-on-one with no safety help because the number two receiver went vertical and we put Marvin on a post.

We got to the point where we didn't see that coverage much, but my last words to Peyton before every game was, "If you see Marvin one-on-one on the post, go for it. And don't worry. If it doesn't work, blame me. Tell them to blame the short, fat, gray-haired guy, and that's okay." I don't think you can ever get into a situation with your quarterback where you give him that latitude and then when something doesn't work he comes off the field and you say, "Why did you do that?" Because then he starts worrying at the line of scrimmage, "Am I making the right audible?"

My feeling was, "You're making the right audible, Peyton, or I've done a horseshit job of coaching you."

PEYTON MANNING: When you're in a one-back offense, the defense can do things to take you out of certain run plays. Tom would just say, "Don't waste any play. If they're all on the left side, don't run in the left. Run to the right or call pass plays."

That second year, we drafted Edgerrin James and became basically a one-back offense. We used two tight ends, trying to create balanced formations, to see which way the defense was going to shift pre-snap and kind of run it the other way.

As Tom and Howard Mudd used to always say: "Run where they ain't." That made sense to me.

TOM MOORE: We wanted to get to a position where we called the best play against what we saw at the line of scrimmage. We wanted to make sure that we had our best players on the field to get that done. We wanted to cause the defense problems, as far as getting substitutes in the game. Since we were going to audible at the line of scrimmage to get to the best play, then why not just line up there?

I was with Jack Faulkner, a former assistant coach and GM in the league, one time and he said, "Coaches amaze me."

I said, "What are you talking about, Jack?"

"I watch a lot of games, and I see all this two-minute offense that you guys run. And I see you just go up the field and the two-minute offense scores. Bang! If that two-minute offense is so good at the end of the game, why isn't it good at the beginning of the game?"

"You may have a point."

Then I started to think, "Why not start out with it?"

But to do it right, you've got to practice it. Your players have to believe in it and your players have to be in shape to do it, because it's taxing.

You can do three versions of the no-huddle. You can do quick-huddle stuff, you can go no-huddle where you're taking your time, and then you can kind of go with a muddle huddle where if they're not squared away, you can go to something right away.

Obviously, when we went no-huddle in that Jets game, our guys had success doing it and said, "Wow! This might be the answer." Then we got to a point where they didn't want to do anything but that because they felt comfortable with it. They were motivated because they had success with it.

In 1994, when I became the Detroit Lions' offensive coordinator, I initiated using the no-huddle. My reason for doing it went back to what I learned from Chuck Noll in Pittsburgh: Make sure you've got your best 11 players on the field. Now your best 11 could be from your best 14 or 13, but make sure you've got your best players on the field. Don't have some guy out there that's less than what you've got standing next to you on the sideline.

In Detroit, our quarterback was Scott Mitchell, who had limitations. I decided that, for Scott, the best thing would be to call all the plays at the line of scrimmage. That way, he could see what the defense was going to do and then get to the right play. We used one pattern—and I got this from Marv Levy—where you release the tight end up the field, you take a receiver down five yards and bring him underneath on a slant. That was the Cover Two audible. And the reason we did it was because Scott Mitchell couldn't throw a slant pattern, but he could throw a short hitch.

Going no-huddle also kept a lot of the defensive substitution packages off the field, because they didn't have enough time to substitute and if they tried, they risked a penalty. I remember we played the Tampa Bay Buccaneers and their defensive coordinator, Monte Kiffin, tried to substitute and got four too-many-guys-on-the-field penalties in one game.

The other thing with the no-huddle is it irritates the defense because they've got to do something they're not used to. Most of the time, those defensive guys are used to huddling up, so you want to keep them lined up and out of the huddle as often as you can. And unless they're on a team that runs the no-huddle, during the week of practice, the offensive service team can't give them the same picture that they're going to see on Sunday.

I was never a great quarterback, but I played the position and I always thought the quarterback sometimes liked to be involved and call his own plays. I know Peyton did. I think we got a lot of mileage out of him because we gave him that flexibility to call plays because we knew he wanted to be in charge.

That's okay if the guy in charge can handle it and do what you have to do to make it succeed. That was Peyton's strength and I think, as a coach, you try to play into your players' strengths. What we did was perfect for Peyton's ability.

DWIGHT FREENEY: I was blessed to be on a team where that offensive juggernaut was rolling. By Bill Polian's design, we put all the money into the offense. Our philosophy was, "Score as many points and surround Peyton with as much talent as possible."

Then we put together a defense with quick, fast guys because now, all of a sudden, opponents had to throw the ball and we had these quick, fast guys that were going to react to the ball and play coverage. And with that Tony Dungy Cover Two, which didn't blitz too often, they weren't going to be able to score as many points because we weren't going to take that many chances.

We did have what I called a "built-in blitz," which was Robert Mathis and me. With us coming off the edge, it would make teams block seven-on-four protection, send fewer guys on routes. Now, all of a sudden, we had more guys available in coverage because we were usually seeing three-man routes or even two-man routes at times.

We were taking teams out of their normal characteristics where they'd release five guys and only keep in a running back to block a blitzer. They couldn't do that against us, because Robert and I would be coming, so they had to devise a game plan they didn't really like.

They couldn't use play-action versus us. I would pray for a play-action pass because I knew I could read the offensive tackle's stance. Why? Because I knew that he knew he couldn't block me. So if he was shaking in his boots before the ball was going to be snapped, it sure wasn't because he had to run-block me. It was because he had to pass-block me. Everywhere else would show run. I would sit there and look at a pass. That would allow me to dial up a sweet pass-rush move in a "running situation," which would then stop their play-action passes. That was our life.

I remember watching film and all there would be was a back in the back-field and that would be the guy who would chip you. I kind of got used to that. I'd say, "Oh, yeah, I could get skinny, I could bull-rush, I could do different things." When they tried to double you, they would leave a tight end on the ball to be the extra blocker. Then we said, "Let's play 'nines' and get outside that guy." All of a sudden, they couldn't double us anymore.

But one day that all changed. We were playing the Patriots. It was third down, Matt Light was across from me at tackle and I thought, "Oh, my God, the stars are aligning. This is going to be perfect. Matt Light can't block me. No one's going to block me." I was running full speed and the next thing I knew I just went flying. And I was like, "Who hit me?"

The Patriots started motioning receivers in from outside the formation to impede our speed and get-off. And that blew my mind. After that, they started putting a tight end two yards outside of me, to where he wasn't on the line and he was wide enough to where I couldn't get outside of him. It was like, "Where do I go? How do I even stop something like this?"

I went up to John Teerlinck, our defensive line coach, after the game and I said, "J.T., can you pull up some film of maybe some people doing this formation or protection?" He said, "Dwight, this has never happened until you and Robert. No one has ever blocked like this. We don't have any film." We had to learn ways to somehow stop what, basically, was a seven-man protection with two guys chipping.

We called it "punt pro," because they were lined up in the same sort of a U-shape type of thing you get in punt protection with guys on the wing. They put these guys a yard or two outside the rushers so that they'd give them a bump, a chip block, to stop their momentum before they got off the ball. That negated the one thing I was, and that was fast. Now, I became a normal guy.

To counter that, we started devising different types of stunts and games inside. We came up with one called the "Ice House" stunt. The name, I think, came from a bar that served a drink where you just throw everything in the jug. With the "Ice House," all the guys kind of wrapped around each other to completely confuse the offensive line. We did the most exotic things we had ever done, just so that we could get our fast guys still going because what the Patriots and other teams started doing to stop us completely changed the game.

When I was with younger edge rushers later in my career and saw what would happen against them, I'd say, "Hey, I'm sorry. I caused this and I apologize, because it is a bitch."

BILL POLIAN: At the combine during Peyton's draft year, we had 20 minutes to interview him personally. He came in, said hello, and told us he had a few questions. We readily agreed to answer them. He took out a yellow legal pad and began to take notes.

Before we knew it, the air horn signaling the end of the interview sounded. Peyton stood up, thanked us, said he hoped we would draft him and left.

We turned to each other and said, "Holy mackerel! He just interviewed us." Little did we know that was an incredible harbinger of things to come.

Peyton's preparation, his dedication to the study of every last detail, was legendary. Being a backup quarterback for Peyton was like being a graduate assistant. He would research blitzes that were used against us two and three seasons before by upcoming opponents or coaches who had changed teams. No detail was too small and no film, regardless of age, was left unwatched.

On the field, there was never a period of practice where he or any of his receivers were not involved directly, where he didn't take them aside and work on routes and adjustments. It's fair to say, for every touchdown pass he threw in a game, he had thrown that same route to that same receiver a hundred times in practice.

Long before the full team's pregame warmup, Peyton would take his receivers out to the field and work on every route in the game plan at its specified location. Within a year, that special warmup became a must-see for opponents' defensive coaches and NFL team advance scouts in the press box. As a result, he had to change the routes and the location but never discarded the practice.

There has never been a more prepared quarterback in pro football history than Peyton Manning.

PEYTON MANNING: The first thing I always did was watch the film of the previous game on my own to really be honest and critical and break down the things that didn't go well, but also the things that did go well. I always made a pretty intense debrief, if you will, of that game.

I liked being coached, I liked being challenged. But I felt like I was very self-critical as well, challenging myself to get better. I probably averaged between 10 to 15 notebooks a season, with just countless pages of notes. I still have all of them.

On Monday morning, you watch the film as a team, as an offense, going through all the coaches' corrections. Monday night was for just kind of processing what had happened, kind of slow down, maybe watch the Monday night game, maybe go out to eat with some buddies.

On Tuesday, my off day, was when it really started. I really liked to watch games on my own. I liked to watch the whole game, and then watch cutups with the coaches in meetings on Wednesday, Thursday, and Friday.

I tried to watch at least four games on Tuesday. It really gave me a good idea of what that defense was trying to do. I tried to watch offenses that were similar to ours, so you could see what happened against common defenses.

We always had a little quarterback game-plan meeting at five o'clock on that Tuesday. It was voluntary, because it was an off day, but everybody was always there. That was where we would get a general feel of what the coaches thought about the upcoming opponent, for the game plan. So when you got to practice on Wednesday, you felt like you had a jump. You knew enough about the game plan to help the receivers and running backs in those first couple days to spread the message about the game plan.

DWIGHT FREENEY: Peyton was part of that veteran leadership that we had in our organization that taught me how to be a vet and how to be a pro. How he prepared for a game was legendary because he would leave no stone unturned. You could see day-in and day-out examples of that in practice— the new ways that he called different plays, the different signals he would use.

You saw him do all of those things throughout the week and throughout so many years. The only way he was able to do that was by being a student of the game and really diving in deep on what was going on. Until that point, I had never seen anybody control the game the way he did. He would know where the blitzer was coming from and he'd tell Marvin Harrison a little something and he'd tell Edgerrin James a little something, and then they would run the play.

The only way you get that way is if you are deep into the film and the studying. Watching that made me want to dive deep into the film and the studying. Therefore, when I got to the game, I was the most prepared individual that you could see as a defensive lineman.

I wasn't a middle 'backer, but I was calling stunts for my defensive line. It was, obviously, a minor thing compared to what Peyton would be doing, but for me, knowing what my guys did best from a defensive-line perspective gave John Teerlinck the confidence to allow me to come up with the pass-rush game plan. Then, as we executed it in the game, I was the one making the calls. If I wanted to run a twist with the defensive tackles or a twist with the defensive ends, I would call that.

That responsibility came with a lot of accountability. I had to put a lot of effort and time into the film work, so that I was putting my guys in the best positions to make plays. I would spend a tremendous amount of time taking notes and I got that from Peyton. Watching Peyton over the years and how he prepared helped my career as an NFL player.

TOM MOORE: Peyton made you a better coach because Peyton would see things and point them out to you. He'd even see things watching college games on Saturday. He'd come to the Saturday night meeting and say, "Alabama did this to Tennessee. If they did that to us, what would be our answer?" That was the right question to ask: What's your answer?

Peyton's recall, and then getting the proper application to what he recalled, was phenomenal.

PEYTON MANNING: Basically, I felt like I got film of every game watched in some way. I would try to watch the majority, but when you get into Week 14, Week 15, now you're talking a lot of games. Our No. 2 and No. 3 quarterbacks, Brock Huard and Jim Sorgi, would watch some games, so would our quality control coach. They knew what I was looking for, like blitzes that we hadn't seen, and they'd give a little summary of each game in a little presentation.

You'd watch coordinators, where they were before, the previous year's film. I was often bringing play numbers into that Tuesday meeting, saying, "Hey, turn on play 40 of the Eagles vs. the Bengals game, I want to talk about this defense." Then, on Wednesday and Thursday, I'd say, "Hey, put on play 20 of the Titans and Jaguars. I want to talk about this defense."

The coaches liked having me bring concepts and could talk it out. I had the freedom to suggest plays. I could say, "Hey, we ran this play last week with Marvin. Let's run the same formation, fake it to Marvin, and throw it to Reggie," or, "We'll have Marvin run an up-and-out this time."

It was fun being able to have some input as a quarterback. You feel some real ownership with that responsibility, but it is a responsibility. It was never something that I took for granted. I tried to earn it.

I always had a fear of getting hit by a blitz and saying after the game that we hadn't seen it before and having their coach come out and say, "Actually, we ran that blitz. It was the third week of the preseason. It was on film."

I said, "That's never going to happen to me. I'm going to watch everything that they show, realizing they can show something new and do something different. But if they put it on film, I'm going to have seen it and feel fully prepared going into that game."

TOM MOORE: Coaches are their own worst enemies at times. Coaches are very, very insecure people by nature. I was one of the worst way back when.

Sometimes, as a coach, you think that if you don't put in four new runs and five new passes, you aren't doing your job. Well, if you put in four runs and five passes, you've got to practice them. And if you put them in, you should run them. All of a sudden, if you're not really careful, around the first of October you aren't doing all that stuff you spent three months practicing in OTAs, minicamps, and training camp.

The biggest thing coaches and players have to fight is boredom. You get bored doing the same thing, but that's also how you get good. Marvin Harrison could run that short-in in his sleep. The year he caught 143 passes, he got 64 on that route. It was almost like a run because it was high percentage, low risk, and you moved the chains. Every time I got in a situation where things were a little stale or something, that's what I'd go to. That was my get-out-of-jail play. I think you've got to have a few get-out-of-jail plays.

Players can't do everything a coach knows. It's impossible. It's too much to practice. You have to be very decisive and very definitive as to what these players do best, and make sure you're continuing to do what they do best.

And don't change. Once players see you're changing, now you've got all these plays that you haven't run, that you haven't practiced back in August and September, and your players are saying, "Well, if these plays were so good in October and November, why the hell weren't we doing them in September?" They lose confidence in you.

I learned that from Chuck Noll. Keep doing what you do best.

PEYTON MANNING: It was an old Tom Moore method to have a right wide receiver and a left wide receiver. That's significant in the no-huddle because the only way to go fast is if you don't have to change the formation all the time and have guys go from one side to the other.

Tom also believed the best way to get timing with your receivers was to have a guy just play on the same side the whole time. If you think about how many out routes I've thrown to Marvin Harrison on the right side, well, if he goes to the left side half the time, that's only half the reps. That's why our timing got so good. In 2001, we got Reggie Wayne and he was on the left side, with Brandon Stokley in the slot.

We were pretty simple on offense. We put players in the same spots and we kind of said, "We don't think you can cover our receivers one-on-one. And if you play double-zone Cover Two coverage, we think we can run the ball with Edgerrin James." It was kind of, whatever the defense wanted to try to take away, we thought we could beat you with the other thing.

Tom would give me three plays in my helmet: a run to the right, a run to the left and then a pass play. Eventually, he just kind of started giving me one play, because he knew that I knew the other plays that went with that play. Sometimes, he would just point at me and say, "Peyton, you've got it."

Everybody says, "Okay, what's the best view to have to call plays? Is it in the press box? Is it on the sidelines?" There is no better view to call plays than at the quarterback position, behind the center. You've got the best view of anybody in that stadium. If your offensive coordinator gives the quarterback the trust to make the calls, knowing he's going to call the plays that are in your system, it really is tough to defend.

But that quarterback has to earn that trust and you've got to have all the right pieces around the quarterback in order to do that. I don't think I ever called a play that surprised Tom Moore or surprised Tony Dungy.

I felt like we were so dialed in. We basically were running the plays that we practiced in training camp, practiced during the week. I wasn't going to call a reverse throwback to the quarterback. I was going to call plays within our system.

TOM MOORE: Keeping receivers on the same sides goes back to Pittsburgh, to Chuck Noll. Lynn Swann was always the right wide receiver and John Stallworth was always the left wide receiver. When I went to Minnesota, Anthony Carter was the right, Cris Carter was left. When I went to Detroit, Herman Moore was always the right, Brett Perriman was always the left. When we came to Indy, Marvin Harrison was right, and Reggie Wayne was left.

That didn't preclude putting them in the slot occasionally. But as a quarterback, are you better off going 100 outs run to the right side and 100 to the left side, or 50 to the right and 50 to the left?

The other thing is, say the defense is going to roll the coverage to Marvin Harrison. If he's always the split end, then they can take away your weak-side running game. But if, sometimes, he's on the strong side, they can't do that. And if they want to roll up strong side, then you can run weak. If you put him weak side and they want to roll up to him, then you can run strong. They can't get you in a situation where they try to take away a receiver and also take away half of your running game.

We had Marvin, but we didn't have the complement until we got Reggie Wayne on the other side. Then the real luck of the draw to me was the addition of Brandon Stokley so we could play him in the slot. Now you've got your three best playmakers on the field. Then Edgerrin James came in and Joseph Addai later replaced him. They were both great runners and good blockers in pass protection.

The other piece of the puzzle that really solidified it was Dallas Clark. Dallas was kind of a man for all seasons from the standpoint that he could play tight end and if Stokley got hurt or anything, we always felt like we could split Dallas out and have our other tight end in there. That eventually gave us a weapon where we could go with two tight ends, with Dallas being one of them.

If the defense stayed with regular people, we could split Dallas out and use him as a wide receiver. If they were afraid of that and wanted to go with nickel people, then Dallas was good enough to come in and play tight and be able to block that nickel back. I don't know if he was going to be able to block a great linebacker, but we didn't ask him to do that.

We had a good offensive line that Howard Mudd did a great job of coaching. The year before we got there, they gave up 62 sacks and we got that number down to 22 our first season.

When I went to Detroit, I replaced Mouse Davis as offensive coordinator. The first quarterback meeting, I told Chuck Long and the other quarterbacks we had, "There's a million pass patterns, but we're going to be protection first, and then we'll put in the pass patterns."

Chuck started to laugh. I asked him what he was laughing about.

"Well, the last guy who was here said, 'All three quarterbacks are going to end up playing because you probably won't make it the full season.'"

"We don't operate that way."

When we came to Indianapolis, I made protecting the quarterback one of my commitments. Howard felt the same way. Because if you hit the quarterback enough, you're going to hurt him. Now I see quarterbacks getting hurt all the time. People design plays where they get hit.

I don't understand it.

BILL POLIAN: When Peyton came into the league, he had a habit of moving his feet in the pocket, which some pundits called "happy feet." They incorrectly thought that he wasn't the most courageous guy in the world because of it.

What Peyton was doing became the standard for the position. Now, every quarterback, from age six on, when they take the snap, move their feet just like he did.

PEYTON MANNING: I was taught in college that your feet and eyes should move together. So if your eyes are going left to right, your feet ought to be moving with you. It's kind of like a boxer, if you will.

The worst thing is to be looking left and you're going to throw left, but your feet are still lined up straight down the middle. By having them move together, it keeps you from being late as you go through your progression.

The key is to get to that second or third receiver as fast as you can, because the defense is going to be reacting.

BILL POLIAN: There are many similarities between how Rich McKay, in Tampa, and I saw the working relationship between the coach and GM. Rich's dad was a coach (the legendary John McKay, who established a dynasty at USC before becoming the first coach of the Bucs) and grew up with the idea that the GM's job was to support the coach and to do it in a collegial manner. Respect, candor, and constant communication are absolutely necessary.

It's a partnership. I was raised in pro football by Marv Levy exactly the same way.

TONY DUNGY: I didn't want to be the guy who did everything. I wanted to coach the team. I wanted to take direction from our general manager and get good players from them. Rich and Bill made it so easy. But the thing that I tell people all the time about working with those two guys is that they were tremendous listeners.

Every system is different. There are some people who want that head coach to be the total package and do everything. But for me, it was the general manager who could look at the long term, set the direction of the team, and understand things and allow me to do my job, which is to coach the players. That's what I wanted and that worked out well.

A great example was our Super Bowl year. We had a situation at running back, where Edgerrin James had been a longtime star for us. He was a great player who would make it to the Hall of Fame, but his contract was coming up and Bill Polian came to me and said, "We can pay Edgerrin what he deserves. It'll be fair, but it's going to hamstring us. If we pay him what he's worth, we're going to end up losing Reggie Wayne, Dwight Freeney, and Dallas Clark down the road, because we won't be able to afford them. Or we can let Edgerrin go, but this is going to be a great year for running backs. We'll have a chance to draft either Joseph Addai or Maurice Jones-Drew and will be a lot better in the long run."

We ended up letting Edgerrin go and drafting Joseph Addai. If I had been making all the decisions, I would not have been prepared to look ahead to the draft and know who was going to come out and what we could do. I would have said, "Let's do the safe route; let's sign Edgerrin. We know what we've got." We might have still won the Super Bowl that year, but we wouldn't have been able to contend for the next five or six years. And that to me is where having that general manager who can look down the road and see things is vital. But you're working together.

Someone asked me one time, "Who controls the 53 in Indianapolis?"

I said, "To be honest, I really don't know." It would make sense that Bill did, and he probably did. But it never came up in our conversations. We'd always talk about what's best for the team: "I like this guy, you like that guy. We'll go home, we'll sleep on it, we'll talk about it, we'll come back, we'll make a decision."

It was never, "I control the 53, so I say we're going to do this. We just never had those kinds of conversations."

With great teams, it starts at the top with your owner, and then flows to the general manager. He kind of sets the tone for things. Everybody's on the same page, everybody's preaching the same message, everybody's getting things across the same way, and it filters down.

But to do that, you've got to have trust, you've got to have good people. The owner has to hire someone that he can tell, "Hey, you run this football operation and I'm not going to second-guess you. I'll be here to give suggestions and to help out, but you're going to run the football operation."

The general manager has the direction and says, "I'm going to hire the coach, I'm going to believe in what he's doing, I'm going to support him, and we're going to filter it down."

The head coach says, "I've got to hire assistant coaches that I trust. Not necessarily everybody who's just like me, but they believe in the same things. They believe in how we're going to win. They believe in getting good people and teaching."

If I have a great staff, then I don't have to micromanage. I don't have to run every drill, I don't have to do everything. And the players sense that. They know they can trust that coach who's coaching them.

That's what we had. That's what we built. I think all championship organizations are that way.

BILL POLIAN: In training camp, I would sit in on the coaches' evaluations after each preseason game. Then I'd go and listen to the scouting evaluations. Then I would come back to Tony and we'd sit together and say, "Okay, here are five players the coaches like and the scouts like and you and I like when we're looking at the tape. So let's make sure we give those guys increased playing time in the second preseason game."

We'd do the same thing after that game and the game after that. When we got to the fourth game, where the starters wouldn't play, we would decide jointly between the two of us, based on what we heard from our respective groups, who would get the playing time.

One that comes to mind is Gary Brackett. He was sort of climbing the charts from the last guy we signed as a free agent after the draft for $2,000 to a guy who convinced Tony to say, "You know, we really ought to give this guy a good dose of it in the last part of the preseason."

I said, "You're right. He's shining out there."

Gary ended up making the team. Tony famously stayed with him when he had to give his brother a bone marrow transplant during his rookie year. He didn't do much because of that. Gary ended up playing nine years and being our defensive signal-caller and middle linebacker.

It's collaboration and setting up a system that allows you to openly share information and respect each other.

PEYTON MANNING: Bill Polian and Tony Dungy just didn't want to put up with selfish guys that didn't like to work. I mean, it just didn't happen a lot. And our best players in games were also our best players in practice.

In a Wednesday practice, Marvin Harrison catches a five-yard hitch and, boom, he's sprinting 45 yards down the field. Reggie Wayne comes in and goes, "Wow! That's how Marvin Harrison practices, that's how I'm going to practice." Then, we draft Anthony Gonzalez, and he sees how Marvin and Reggie practice. Guys saw me taking notes in meetings in my 13th season, so they started taking notes. It was just a trickle-down effect.

I also think we had the right kind of guys setting a good example. Bill was bringing in guys that were wired that way, as opposed to lazy players that were selfish and didn't like to work. A few of them might have come into the building, but I can promise you they didn't last very long because that just wasn't the right place for them.

This was a culture of speed on offense and defense with guys like Dwight Freeney and Robert Mathis. Practice was fast. It was fun to watch if you are a visitor at practice, and I think, as a young player, you caught on pretty quick that, "I'd better practice hard and fast if I want to make this team."

I felt like Bill was drafting guys that loved football. That was one of the top priorities: they had to love football, they had to love to work, but they were also accountable—guys we could count on if we got in tough spots. I felt like he was willing to draft a guy that maybe was not as fast in the 40-yard dash, but was a tough, accountable guy that we could count on.

BILL POLIAN: My feeling was that because of our investment of cap dollars on offense, the only way we would reach the Super Bowl was by implementing a defensive system that was based on speed and simplicity—a system where young, lower-paid players could excel.

That was clearly Cover Two. Fortunately, the modern designer of the scheme—which also become known as "Tampa Two"—Tony Dungy, became our head coach. We struck gold, or rather Lombardi Trophy sterling silver.

TONY DUNGY: In the '70s, people tried to copy the Cover Two a little bit, but they didn't have all the parts. Pittsburgh perfected it, but eventually it kind of died off there.

Fifteen years later, in 1992, I became the defensive coordinator in Minnesota, and we had a lot of those elements in place. We had Chris Doleman and John Randle and some guys who could fire off the defensive line. And then we had some fast linebackers. We got Jack Del Rio from Dallas in Plan B free agency; he was our middle linebacker. Mike Merriweather was another undersized, fast linebacker. We also got some corners who weren't afraid to tackle.

We put the Cover Two defense in, and we ended up leading the league in defense our second year in Minnesota. It really propelled me to my head-coaching job, although it didn't become popularized there.

When Monte Kiffin and I went to Tampa, a lot of the elements for the Cover Two were in place. We had Warren Sapp sitting there to control the inside. Derrick Brooks was Jack Ham. We drafted a couple of corners who could not only run and hit and tackle but could play the ball. Ronde Barber ended up being one of those guys. John Lynch was there as a safety.

By this time, Cover Two had died out, so a lot of the quarterbacks hadn't seen it, a lot of the coaches hadn't prepared for it, and we ended up having some success on defense. All of a sudden, it became the "Tampa Two," like it never existed before. It was only about 30 years old, but we took credit for inventing it.

I thought the Tampa Two would be really great for us in Indianapolis because now we were in the salary cap era, and we had a lot of money invested in the offense. Bill said, "We've got Peyton Manning, the best quarterback in football. We've got to keep feeding him. So our high draft choices, our free agents, they're going to be on offense. We've got to put together a defense that can complement them."

I said, "Bill, this defense will be perfect because we're going to be looking for a number of guys that other people aren't looking for. You don't have to be big to play in this system. We're going to use some speed, we're going to use quickness and striking ability. If guys have that and they're smart, then they can play for us. We'll get some guys that'll play very well that may not be what everybody else is looking for."

We probably sat down for four days, talking about every position. What does it take to be the nose tackle in this defense? What does the three-technique look like? What do the defensive ends look like? What are the linebackers going to be asked to do? What are the corners going to be asked to do? It was different than what Bill was used to.

Bill took notes and he listened. He would ask, "Is this what this means? Is this what you're looking for? Can this type of guy play?" It was exhausting, but it was stimulating at the same time because I was explaining to him what we wanted. Bill would ask, "Who's successful in your system? Who isn't successful? Why not?" We went through every position and talked about quickness and leverage and striking ability, but we never really talked about size. Bill got the idea right away.

I remember our very first draft together, in 2002, Bill and I were on treadmills, talking and walking. Bill said, "We have this dilemma. We've got a big defensive tackle who's a great player and would probably be good for anybody in the league. And then we've got Dwight Freeney, a defensive end from Syracuse. Everything you're describing, that's what this guy does. He plays with leverage, he explodes, he's fast, no one can block him. But he's undersized for what everybody in the league is saying they want. We have the 11th pick in the draft. Can we take a guy who's undersized at that high a pick?"

"Bill, with what you're telling me he can do and what you showed me, he's going to be special in this defense."

We went against the grain and everybody criticized us. "How can you take Dwight Freeney with the 11th pick? He's going to get swallowed up in the NFL."

He went on to be dynamic for us, of course.

DWIGHT FREENEY: I was considered an undersized guy and the people talking to me didn't know where I was going to land in the draft. They were like, "Dwight, you could be projected anywhere from 10 to 30, whatever." I had no idea. I hadn't seen many guys my size drafted in the first round, so I was up for anything. As long as I got drafted, it didn't matter where I went.

I was from a small town, Bloomfield, Connecticut. Not many people make it to the NFL from Connecticut, period, never mind the small town I came from. As long as I got to a place, my mentality was that it would be a dream come true. I was going to go out there and basically do my best and do what I do.

When the 11th pick came up, I got the call from the Colts. My jaw was on the ground. I was expecting to be picked probably somewhere late in the first round. You heard Mel Kiper say, "Oh, this guy's a second-round guy. Situational pass-rusher. Outside linebacker." You hear all of that and you just say, "Oh, well."

But I never had a moment where I let doubt sink in my head, to where I thought I couldn't do something. At no point did I think I was not big enough to make it happen. I also had a defensive line coach in John Teerlinck (who I called "J.T."), God rest his soul, who said, "Hey, you do whatever you need to do to make a play. If you want to do a backflip, do a backflip. You want to do a somersault?" It didn't matter, as long as you made the play.

Now, I will say, playing against Tarik Glenn, our 6'5", 330-pound offensive tackle, in every practice, probably turned me into a man the fastest. He whipped this young guy into knowing what the game was all about because every single day in practice, I had to go against Tarik. And I had to win. We didn't have a mentality of just going through the motions, because you would get called out on it. I had a lot of pressure on me, maybe because I was a first-rounder, but I always put pressure on myself. I had to go out there and win.

Do you know how hard it was to win against a guy like Tarik Glenn, whose biceps were as big as your legs?

When I was a rookie, he was a sixth-year veteran. I had all these college moves. I had this one move where I would take a guy up the field and I would just power him with my left arm and kind of push him by the quarterback. We had this little pass-rush drill that we ran every Wednesday and Thursday, and I would have all these plans, all these moves.

I was feeling pretty good about myself because I had the speed around the corner to beat him, so one day I said, "You know what? I'm going to bring something he hasn't seen yet." He knew I had a spin move, but it's hard because you can't fool somebody you're seeing every day. If you can beat a guy who knows every single move that you're going to do before you do it, then the game becomes much easier. That's how you get so much better.

But when I tried to power him and move him with my left arm, I felt every single bone in my arm crack and it just whimpered down to the ground. I just completely stopped and said, "Okay, I get it. I cannot do that move in the National Football League. I am not big enough. Let me stick to what I know."

I had a spin move that I developed back in high school. I never watched anybody on film of a football game spin. The way it developed for me was, back in the '90s, a big thing was AND1 mixtapes. They were videos of guys playing basketball on the playgrounds, doing all these Harlem Globetrotter moves. I played basketball as a kid and in high school and one day in football practice said, "You know what? I'm going to try to bring AND1 mixtape moves to football. I'm going to do this move, something so exotic, and try to make somebody not just miss, but flat-out miss." Now, where I was from, high school teams didn't pass the ball many times. They would run T-bone and all types of I-formations, so I would do it more against the run block than the pass block because I could just run past guys on pass plays.

When I got to Syracuse, our defensive line coach was Deek Pollard, who had been a defensive back coach with the Rams. He would say, "Dwight, you can spin on pass and run plays. This is what you do well. Go out and do it." And it just kept on going.

When I met J.T., he put the finishing touches on it. He said, "Oh, yes, spin move. But when you use it, I want you to think of having an ice pick in your hand and you want to violently use that to gain momentum and put that ice pick into the back of that offensive tackle's head." I thought that was amazing. I thought that was great. I said, "Oh, yeah, I get to ice pick somebody." From then on, it was known as "the Ice Pick."

J.T. was the most unique individual I've ever met in my life. He didn't B.S. you. He told you exactly what he felt and it was genuine. You get a lot of coaches that do a lot of coach talk. They'll say one thing to you and really mean something else or just say something to hype you up. J.T. would tell you when you stunk, he'd tell you when you did great. I think a lot of what made him so special was that he had played the game, so he could really get into the fibers of a player and how they think.

When it came to playing the Cover Two, J.T. would sit us down and say, "I know what you're thinking. You don't want to be dropping back into coverage and running zone pressures. Let's just stomach that basically until we get to what we really want." Most coaches don't say things like that. That's why you loved him. I got to be coached by a legendary guy who coached Hall of Famers like John Randle. I got to soak up all that knowledge.

There was no other guy on the team like me. I got to sit in a meeting room with guys like Chad Bratzke, Brad Scioli, journeymen. They were all bigger and slower guys, but I got a chance to learn the ropes from them. Watching how Chad and Brad went about their business each day, watching how they worked, it made we realize that was how you were supposed to do it in order to play in the league as long as they did. Chad was in his ninth season when I was drafted.

TONY DUNGY: We treated linebackers the same way we treated defensive linemen. We started looking for quick, fast linebackers, and Bill just came up with guy after guy after guy. Cato June comes to mind. He played great for us in our Super Bowl year. He was a strong safety at Michigan. Bill said, "I don't think he's quite quick enough to play in the secondary, but he can do a lot of the things we talk about." He played weakside linebacker for us and played great.

Our safety, Bob Sanders, was another guy where Bill said, "Oh, gosh! Coach, you're going to love this guy. Now, he's only 5'8"."

When Bill showed me the tape of Bob playing at Iowa, my eyes lit up. I said, "Wow! This is a faster version of Donnie Shell. He's going to be fantastic for us." And he was.

This is how fascinated the rest of the league was in our defense: Bill Parcells was interviewing Leslie Frazier for the head-coaching job in Miami when Bill was the Dolphins' GM and he said, "I don't really want to hire you, you're not my style. But I have to find out how do you guys do it in Indianapolis with all these midgets? How can you win?"

Bill Parcells was intrigued because he had never seen anything like it before. But that was our style, our motto. Speed and striking ability. If guys were competitive, we could win with them.

People tried to take parts of Cover Two, but the people that were really successful with it were people like Lovie Smith, who really believed in it and was our linebackers coach with the Buccaneers. He took it with him to Chicago when he became the Bears' head coach in 2004.

Sometimes people would say, "Well, I want to take parts of it. I want to take Cover Two, but I still want these corners who can play man-to-man and they're fast and small." But then, when they'd have to tackle the fullback in the flat and they'd get run over, those coaches would say, "Oh, Cover Two doesn't work."

You had to buy in to the whole thing. There were very few people that actually bought in to the whole thing and believed in it.

BILL POLIAN: In 2003, we were looking for a running mate for Dwight Freeney who could take some of the double-team pressure off Dwight. Dom Anile, our personnel director, came to me with the workout numbers on Robert Mathis, a 3-4 outside linebacker at Alabama A&M. They were phenomenal.

Robert was a little-known prospect, so we said, "Let's get to the tape." It didn't take long to figure out that Robert was an exceptional pass-rusher. At 6'2" and about 230 pounds, he was on the small side in both height and weight, which would disqualify him from many NFL teams. That, of course, didn't bother us.

The scouting staff raved about Robert's work ethic and character. We had our guy. He finished his career with 123 sacks. Robert and Dwight formed one of the most productive rush combinations in NFL history.

TONY DUNGY: Bill came to me and said, "We've got this young guy, Robert Mathis, who's a great player. He's from Alabama A&M, a small school, nobody knows about him. This is a guy we have to get."

We were in the fourth round of the draft. We made our pick, and Bill said, "We can trade next year's pick and get this guy, Robert Mathis."

I said, "Bill, I love him, he'll be great. But I just hate to give up a pick next year."

I had come up under Coach Noll, where draft choices were so special, so I was always hesitant to make trades. I just didn't like giving away draft choices, even if you're getting something back in return.

Bill looked at me and he said, "Well, what if we said we were going to draft Robert Mathis next year, but we get him a year early? Wouldn't that make sense?" I thought about it and I said, "Yeah, that does make sense."

We traded with the Cleveland Browns for the following year's fifth-round pick and drafted Robert Mathis in the fifth round. We ended up getting a Hall of Fame–caliber player. That was one where Bill had to kind of talk me through it and it was perfect.

BILL POLIAN: Tony loved the draft. He loved to coach and mentor young players. Contrary to his coaching philosophy, he was a gambler. He loved to trade and get extra picks.

There was never a player we wanted more than Bob Sanders. He was going to be the last piece in the puzzle for our defense. The John Lynch of the Colts.

Because he had surgery prior to the 2004 draft for a broken foot, we were sure he wouldn't be taken in Round 1. We traded back into Round 2, where we were confident Bob would be available. Then came another trade-down opportunity. Tony was excited to do it. I, not so much.

In fact, I was a nervous wreck, fearing we'd lose Bob. We decided to stand pat and make the pick. Bob went on to become NFL Defensive Player of the Year and the lynchpin to our Super Bowl victory. Unfortunately, his career ended prematurely because of injury.

TONY DUNGY: We loved Bob Sanders and we knew that he could be the key to this defense. The Iowa coaches told us about how he just energized their whole team. We knew he was going to be perfect for us. He was the guy we wanted in that whole draft. The only thing was, we also understood that he was 5'8", so that was going to take him off a lot of people's boards. He had a foot injury. Our doctor cleared him, but we knew a lot of team doctors weren't going to pass him on their physicals.

We were thinking, "Where do we need to draft him to make sure we get him? We don't have to draft him in the first round. Nobody's going to draft a 5'8" safety with a broken foot in the first round."

Our pick came up and I said, "Bill, we can trade back. Nobody's going to take him. Let's trade back. We'll get some more picks." Bill was okay with that, so we traded down, we got another third-round pick. Our next pick came up, and I said, "Bill, we can trade down again and still get Bob Sanders."

He looked at me and he said, "Pigs get fat, hogs get slaughtered. We don't want to lose this guy and get slaughtered." I was thinking, "We still could trade back one more time, but if we lose him, Bill's going to be so mad and I'll never forgive myself for losing this guy."

We ended up taking him and he was a dynamic player on our Super Bowl team.

BILL POLIAN: From the first trade back until the time we made the pick, I was pacing around the room like I was running a marathon. I was so nervous we'd lose him.

But Tony has a unique knack for knowing who fits in Tampa Two. I think one of the best stories that illustrates it was when I was looking at college tape of Antoine Bethea in 2006. He was a three-deep safety. He played zone defense, but he played in the middle of the field at Howard University.

It looked to me like he had some qualities that would fit for us. Because he was a bigger guy who could tackle, I thought the right fit was maybe at corner. As always, I brought the tape in to Tony and said, "Take a look at this guy. See what you think. I'm not sure he can play corner, but if you think he can, that's where we'll put him. But if he can't, then can he be a safety?"

TONY DUNGY: Antoine wasn't playing in a complex system, but you could see the athleticism and you could see the ball skills and you could see a certain confidence out there.

I told Bill, "I think you're right. I think this guy's got something. I'd love to get him and work with him. I think he can be one of those safeties who can play deep in the middle of the field. But if we have to bring him down and play some man coverage, he can. I think he's going to be perfect for us."

From Day One, Antoine was a leader. He wasn't overwhelmed by anything and he was perfect for us. That was the result of that communication between Bill and me. By that time, it was four or five years of talking back and forth and what guys look like and who could function in this system, and we hit on a lot of those.

You talk about Peyton Manning, Reggie Wayne, Marvin Harrison, Edgerrin James, Bob Sanders, Dwight Freeney, and Gary Brackett. The common thread with each is very good athlete, very productive, all those things, but also the kind of guy you'd want as a son-in-law and the kind of guy that you know is going to make a positive impact not only on the team but in the community.

I used to tell our guys all the time, "When we win, everybody's going to want to be like you. All these 12-year-old kids are going to want to be Indianapolis Colts. I don't want to have to tell their mothers, 'Oh, no, he should pick another guy. You don't want your son to be like him.'"

I didn't have to say that, because the kind of guys we picked were who you would want representing your team. It was not only important, but I think it helped us win.

BILL POLIAN: As we finished our first training camp under Tony, there was a lot of chatter in the media about how other teams were fighting during practice and how it established "toughness." That's what I learned from Coach Levy, who preached, "Don't be dumb and don't be dirty."

Sure enough, a fight broke out during a practice in camp. We got it stopped and Tony brought everyone together. He explained that he learned from Coach Noll that fighting wasn't acceptable and that it wouldn't be to him.

TONY DUNGY: First of all, that was Coach Noll's rule: Practices had to be competitive, but they couldn't be combative, that we were teammates helping each other get better. You got better by competing, but you couldn't build a great team with animosity and fights. You couldn't be a great team if you didn't keep your composure.

You hear a lot of people say, "Oh, well, fights happen in training camp, it's part of football, you just get through it." With Coach Noll, absolutely not. He didn't allow it. We didn't have them. That's how I got trained.

Now, I played in other places that it wasn't necessarily that way, but I believed in Coach Noll's view when it came to fighting. When I became the head coach at Tampa, I gave the players the following rule on fighting: "You can fight, but if you do, you're going to get the same penalties that you would if you fight in a game: a $10,000 fine and you're kicked out. So, if I were you, if you want to fight someone, wait until after practice. Go back in the alley where I can't see it and you can settle it then. But if you fight during practice, you're going to get kicked out of practice and I'm going to fine you as much as the league will allow me to."

We had one fight in Tampa. When the guys got fined and kicked out of practice, everybody knew I was serious.

I gave the players the same speech when I got to Indy. We had a fight take place in practice, I stopped, I explained things, I told them why we couldn't do it, and I sent both the guys to the locker room. I don't think we fined them, but the message came across, and I don't think we ever had another fight there.

Championship teams don't fight. Championship teams work together.

DWIGHT FREENEY: One of the big things with Tony was, "You can't fight in a game, so you don't fight in practice. You guys can't lose your head in a game. It's going to cost you the game. You can't lose it in practice because you want to practice how you play. And if you think it's stressful in practice, what do you think the game's going to be?"

In a lot of organizations and teams, you can fight and coaches will even encourage it. Tony didn't have any patience for that. He'd say, "If you can't keep your cool in practice, then you're going to blow up in a game, and we don't want you here."

One day in practice, I was watching a special-teams period from the sidelines. There was a defensive back running down the field and he got into it with a linebacker. It was a football fight. It wasn't like anybody was throwing any serious punches. It was a whole big wrestling thing, which was a lot for us because we didn't do any of that stuff during practice.

And Tony just went crazy. Now, his crazy was saying, "What are you guys doing? We don't do that here." That was all it was. There was no cursing, none of that.

For anyone else, it was nothing. For Tony, that was losing his cool.

Sure enough, the next day, the linebacker was gone. You couldn't help but think, "Yeah, Tony was mad, but he wasn't as mad as you think for a guy to be gone the next day."

TONY DUNGY: A lot of people didn't think it could be done that way. I remember sitting in interviews and having owners look at me and saying, "That won't work."

But I go back again to my first day on the job with Coach Noll in 1981 when I asked, "What am I supposed to do?"

He said, in one very simple sentence, "Your job as a coach is to help your players play better."

It was so Chuck Noll-ish and it was the truth. As soon as he said that, it clicked in my mind why he was so effective and why I loved playing for him. He didn't look at himself as a genius coming up with great schemes. He didn't look at himself as a dictator. He looked at himself as a guy who was trying to help everybody on the team play the best that they could play.

When he told me that, I asked myself, "Who were the coaches that helped me the most? Who did I enjoy playing for? Who did I get the most out of?" It was the guys on our Steeler staff who were teachers and taught me what to do.

Remember, I switched over from quarterback to safety. I had never tackled a soul in my life until I got to the NFL. It was on-the-job training. I was making mistakes and when I would come off the field after making a mistake, Coach Noll would grab me around the shoulder and say, "What were you thinking out there? Where were your eyes? What were you looking at?"

He'd just walk me through it and that's what helped me. I realized most players want to be coached and they want to be told what to do. Most players don't need to be motivated and yelled at. They want to be good, so teaching and helping them is going to be the way to success. If we can build that mutual respect that we're not going to let each other down, that's how you're going to build that closeness.

That's the way it was on all the good teams I was ever on and that's the way I wanted to coach. In our very first meeting in Tampa, when I took over as head coach, I laid out the format: expectations, execution, no excuses, no explanations, how we're going to do things, make a difference in the community, all those things.

Then I said, "Okay, now, let's get down to winning and performing. I don't believe you guys need to be yelled at to be motivated. I'm not going to yell at you. I'm a Christian, so I'm not going to use a lot of profanity. People tell me that's the only way to get through to you guys. So, let me know now: Is there anybody in this room who needs to be yelled at and cursed at to play well?"

Nobody raised their hand.

"We'll be fine. We understand each other."

Some of the guys, who had been coached the other way their whole life, were wondering, "How do I respond to this guy when he's not really yelling at us?" It took a while to catch on, but once it did, then the veterans went to the young guys and said, "Hey, don't screw this up. We've got a great thing going on here."

That's the way we went for 13 years.

DWIGHT FREENEY: Before that, all I knew was coaches dog-cussing. That was the nature of the game, just very violent. It was similar to how it was, I'm sure, in the Army or whatever. Coaches would yell and scream because that was the old-school way. Tony was not that. It was a quiet strength.

We learned from that and we appreciated that. We found out there was another way to communicate. I think you gain so much more respect coaching that way and relating to players rather than somebody who wants to dog-cuss you. I was blessed to be in that type of scenario.

TONY DUNGY: When we were playing in San Diego, we had a lot of people hurt. I think we only had like 41 guys who could dress that day. So, we had a lot of backup guys playing and it didn't look like we were going to have a chance to win. We ended up falling behind 17–0 at halftime.

I almost lost it with the players. It was one of the few times I ever thought about yelling, but I didn't. I remember saying, "You know what? These guys stink and we're worse. And we need to go out and play better in the second half."

Matt Giordano, one of our safeties then, told one of the rookies beside him, "You don't know it, but you just got cursed out."

DWIGHT FREENEY: It was so funny. That headset would come off, his ears would start to turn a little red. And I'd say, "Uh-oh, Tony's about to raise up a decibel here." It was just one decibel, but when he was upset, we all knew it.

BILL POLIAN: During a game, people described Tony as stoic on the sideline. That wasn't true. He was talking to the coaches and managing the game. But a reporter once asked me, "Did you ever see Coach Dungy lose his cool on the sideline?"

I said, "No, never."

"Well, how does he get through to the players?"

"You'll know when he's somewhat upset with what a player did, and is going to correct him, when he takes the headset off. If you see the headset off, you can be pretty sure somebody made a mistake."

The players would say, "If T.D. takes the headset off, you'd better pay attention."

TONY DUNGY: I was just always talking with the coaches, asking, "What's the next play? What are we going to go to? How are we going to make the situation better?"

When I had to talk to a player, I would take the headset off. It wasn't very often. But that was the signal.

BILL POLIAN: In Tampa, Tony had Hall of Famers Derrick Brooks, Warren Sapp, and John Lynch on one of the league's most dominant defenses. In Indianapolis, he had Hall of Famers Peyton Manning, Marvin Harrison, and Edgerrin James, and strong candidates in Reggie Wayne and Dallas Clark on offense.

You would have thought that he would change his philosophy of coaching, but he really didn't.

TONY DUNGY: Good coaches always play to their strengths. When I got to Tampa, the strength was obviously on defense. Warren Sapp and Derrick Brooks had been drafted the year before I got there. John Lynch was also there. Those are three Hall of Famers that show up right in your lap.

Hardy Nickerson was the captain of the team; he had played for me in Pittsburgh. He was the leader, no question about it. We drafted Ronde Barber and Donnie Abraham, who were a couple more pieces to the puzzle.

We had some tough guys. We were a defensive team and we played that way. We ran the 40-second clock down on offense. We ran the ball a lot and we built around the running game and defense.

I got to Indianapolis and it was just the opposite. We had some Hall of Fame offensive players in place and we were going to build to that and be a scoring team and then put together a defense that could protect the lead and could rush the passer in the fourth quarter when you had the lead.

In terms of strategy, that was different. But in terms of actually cultivating guys and building the philosophy, it was really the same. We had one sign in both of those locker rooms for 13 years. It was simply six words: "Expectations, execution, no excuses, no explanations."

We wanted to expect to win. We wanted to expect ourselves to carry ourselves like champions. And then we had to work at it every day to get that execution, not just dream about it. Excuses and explanations don't really get you anywhere. Let's put our money and value in what we do.

How we did it was really the same in both places, and the leaders carried it on. Having the right type of leaders was one thing that was really important to me. Fortunately, Bill had that same M.O. If we got the right type of player, it didn't matter whether they were offensive stars or defensive stars. They would direct us the right way.

BILL POLIAN: In 2002, Tony's first year with the Colts, we went 10–6, qualifying as a wild-card for the playoffs and went to Giants Stadium to play the Jets. The field was a quagmire because of week-long rains, which certainly didn't help our speed style of play on both sides of the ball. We got blasted by Herm Edwards' team.

TONY DUNGY: Our first playoff game in my first year in Indy was against the Jets. I remember telling the team, "I'm not a betting man, but I would bet my house on us. I think we've got a better team."

And we lost 41–0.

Herm Edwards poured it on us a little bit, I thought, unnecessarily. He was my good friend, so I couldn't get mad at him. Then the media said, "Oh, Tony Dungy can't win the big games, Peyton Manning can't win the big ones."

BILL POLIAN: We had to kind of live through that for a couple of years, but we kept developing the defense and getting better.

In 2003, we had a 12-win team, reached the conference championship game, and lost to the Patriots.

We entered the game on Monday night in Tampa riding a four-game winning streak. Before the game even began, this would be a night of bizarre occurrences.

Legendary Buc Warren Sapp had taken to running through the warmup lines of the opposing team, trying and succeeding in causing a pregame ruckus. As a result, commissioner Paul Tagliabue had ordered the officials to be on the field for the entirety of pregame warmup and to throw a flag for unsportsmanlike conduct if Sapp or anyone else tried this tactic.

We presumed incorrectly that Sapp wouldn't tempt fate or risk a penalty and likely fine. We were wrong. He did. Referee Johnny Grier threw the flag and we were about to start *Monday Night Football* with a 15-yard penalty. Sometime between the end of the warmup and the kickoff, Commissioner Tagliabue changed his mind and told Referee Grier not to enforce the penalty. This was only the beginning of any number of weird moments that night.

The game wasn't a quarter old when it looked certain that our winning streak would come to an end. It wasn't until the fourth quarter that we really got going and, through a number of crazy bounces (and, in the eyes of Tampa fans, bad calls), we were able to pull it out.

PEYTON MANNING: They were loaded. They had won the Super Bowl the year before. It was Tony Dungy's first trip back to Tampa. It was his birthday. We played horrible in the first half and it was 35–14 with three minutes and 50 seconds to go. I threw a pick-six to Ronde Barber. Had he not scored, we probably, mathematically, wouldn't have had enough time to come back.

After the touchdown, they kicked off to us, we ran the kickoff back to the 10, scored, we got an onside kick, and scored again. We stopped them, got the ball back, and went down and scored in overtime to beat them.

It was almost impossible. After you make a comeback in a game like that, boy, it sure does give you a lot of confidence that no matter what situation you're in, the game's not over.

BILL POLIAN: In 2009, we welcomed New England to Indianapolis riding an eight-game winning streak. As often happened, Tom Brady and company got off to a torrid start. The sellout crowd in Lucas Oil Stadium set a fevered pitch before kickoff. By halftime, they were deflated.

But we weren't. As Yogi Berra once said, "It was déjà vu all over again."

As had happened on Monday night in Tampa, we came storming back in the fourth quarter. By that time, the Patriots had lost all of their outside pass-rushers to injury.

PEYTON MANNING: We were behind, 34–28, and the Patriots had a fourth-and-2 from their 28 with a little more than two minutes left. I remember I was standing by Jeff Saturday, and I was saying, "Punt it! Punt it! Punt it! Punt it! Punt it!" Because that was, of course, what I wanted.

All of a sudden, Bill Belichick did something that I thought was the greatest form of flattery. He decided to go for it. I was concerned because I kind of agreed with the decision as well. We were down early, we came back, we were rolling. We just had gotten down so much that we had to play aggressively to come back. I think Bill sensed that they had not stopped us since the end of the second quarter.

But I wanted to have the ball back.

Tom Brady threw to Kevin Faulk and Melvin Bullitt made a great play to hold him to a one-yard gain. It gave us incredible field position. Then, of course, our challenge was, "Hey, let's score, but let's don't score too soon. We don't want to give Brady the ball back."

I would argue that was one of my best drives ever, even though it only started on the 27-yard line. I was able to get 22 yards, but I used the full one minute and 50 seconds. I'm pretty sure the touchdown I threw to Reggie Wayne was with seven seconds remaining, so that was pretty good clock management. There was no chance Brady was going to get back out there on the field.

TONY DUNGY: In 2004, we had another 12-win team, went to the AFC Championship Game and lost again. The media kept after us. *Can't beat Bill Belichick, can't beat the Patriots, and that's the way it's going to be.* We had to live through that and fight through that.

Again, we weren't going to leave our game plan. Then 2005 came and it was probably the best team, other than the Pittsburgh teams when I was a player, I've ever been around as a coach. We had a lot of things in place. We had some dynamic defensive players, and the salary cap was just such that some of our offensive players were still young. We could pay some of our defensive guys and it was perfect.

We won our first 13 games and I was sure that was going to be a Super Bowl team. We ended up having some disappointments. Our son passed away in December that year. A lot of things took place and we didn't get it done.

We lost to Pittsburgh. Pittsburgh ended up going on and winning the Super Bowl. It was the biggest disappointment of my coaching career that we didn't finish off that season.

Once again, all the naysayers were going, "Well, they'll never win the big one."

BILL POLIAN: In 2005, we went 14–2. Most of us felt that, talent-wise, this was our best team. Tragically, Tony's son, James, passed away prior to Game 15.

We never regained our footing and lost to the eventual Super Bowl–champion Pittsburgh Steelers in the divisional round. All we heard was that Tony, Peyton, and the Colts "couldn't win the big one."

A year later, we proved the critics wrong.

TONY DUNGY: In 2006, the salary cap forced us to let some of our defensive players go, so our defense was not as good and we were playing young guys. Antoine Bethea was a starter as a rookie.

And we were winning.

We won our first nine, but it wasn't like the year before when we were dominating. In 2005, we never had a one-score game. We never had a game in those first 13 that came down to the last drive. Well, in 2006, we were winning with Adam Vinatieri making clutch field goals and with a defensive interception in the end zone to seal the game.

Every Monday, I was saying to Bill, "I'm not sure how we're winning these games." Teams began to figure out if they could run the ball and mash us and wear us down a little bit, that was how they were going to be beat the Colts. We went through a stretch where people did run the ball on us. We had some injuries. Bob Sanders only played four games that year for us and the games that he was out, we weren't as good.

I remember, very specifically in December, we were in Jacksonville and they beat us 44–17. They ran the ball for almost 400 yards. I remember coming into Bill's office and saying, "You know what Coach always used to say, 'When you have trouble, when you struggle, don't do more. Do less.' So we're going to cut back a little bit. It's not going to be pretty, but we're going to get our mojo back. And then, when we get Bob Sanders back, we're going to be okay."

We talked through that and we understood it. Nobody else around understood it. The media was asking, "What are you going to do? What changes are you going to make?" I kept saying, "We're not making any changes—no personnel changes, no philosophy changes. We're just going to play better." Gary Brackett, our defensive captain, told me after that season that when I said we weren't making any personnel changes, the guys could relax and just go out there and play. And they played their hearts out.

BILL POLIAN: In 2006, we went 12–4. Again. Without an injured Bob Sanders, we were poor against the run in December. Despite being underdogs in each playoff game, we beat Kansas City at home in a stellar defensive performance and Baltimore on the road, where our defense and kicking game carried the day.

For the first time, we played in a championship game at home against the "Great White Whale," the New England Patriots.

TONY DUNGY: When we got Bob Sanders back for the first game in the playoffs, we were a confident group. We had a nice defensive run. Larry Johnson of the Kansas City Chiefs was the second-leading rusher in the league that year; we held him for 32 yards. Then we went to Baltimore. The Ravens had Jamal Lewis and Steve McNair, and we held them without a touchdown.

All of a sudden, people were saying, "What happened to this defense? Where did this '85 Bears come from?" It was really staying the course and not giving up and not panicking. It was just kind of what our sign said: "Expectations, execution, no excuses, no explanations."

The 2006 AFC Championship Game was against our nemesis, the Patriots. We finally had them at home and we just felt good about it. The night before the game, Jeff Saturday, our center and offensive captain, got up and he compared it to the 1980 U.S. Olympic hockey team. He said, "This is our time. We're playing the Russians and we're going to get them, even though nobody thinks that."

DWIGHT FREENEY: All week, the energy was up. I could barely sleep that whole week. The town was on fire. The RCA Dome was always loud during games, but it was loud in pregame. I was sitting there stretching, trying to get ready. The coaches and Bill came up to shake your hand and give you a little last-minute encouragement, and I couldn't hear a word anyone was saying.

We had this tradition where Peyton threw a deep pass to Marvin at the end of pregame. When Marvin caught it, the crowd went crazy. Over a deep practice throw! That had never happened before. It probably never happened again.

But that was the type of energy that game generated.

TONY DUNGY: In the first half, we kind of had some missed plays. They were gambling, going for it on fourth down, doing uncharacteristic things, and we were down 21–3 right before halftime.

PEYTON MANNING: It's always worse to get down like that in a home game because your fans are disappointed and they're on you. But we started making a comeback.

TONY DUNGY: I remember walking up on the sideline, and we were getting the ball. There was like 1:50 left in the first half and I told the offense, "Go out there. Take this drive down the field. This is still our time."

We ended up going down for a field goal to make it 21–6 at halftime. I remember walking in the locker room and telling the players, "We are going to be fine. Just relax, play our game. We're better than we're playing. If we play our style, we'll have a chance to win this game. We'll have the ball with a chance to win in the fourth quarter and we'll get it done."

BILL POLIAN: As we began that last drive with just over three minutes to go in the half, I was seated with our personnel staff. I turned to Dom Anile, our personnel director, and said, "If we go down here and Vinny kicks a field goal, Tony will take them in at halftime and get everything straightened out and we'll be alright."

Dom was from Brooklyn. He looked at me and in his Brooklyn accent, he said, "You've been smoking something? We're getting our butts kicked."

"No, no, no. Have faith. All we need is a field goal to get us back on track. Tony will take it from there."

TONY DUNGY: I told the team, "We get the ball to start the second half. We don't have to win this game all at once. We don't have to do anything. We're beating ourselves. If we stop beating ourselves, we'll win this game. We need to take the first drive, though, and score. If we get it down to a one-score game, they'll have to keep playing and we'll force them into some mistakes."

DWIGHT FREENEY: Halftime was no different from the perspective that no one was crying. Nobody had to do anything rah-rahish. Our feeling was, "We're going to go out there, we're going to do things that we need to do to win this game." Tony's demeanor was, "We're just going to do the basics of what we do and we'll be in this game before you know it."

That was our mentality. It was no panic. I just knew we were going to do what we needed to do.

TONY DUNGY: That's exactly what happened. Peyton took them down and scored and now it was 21–13. The dome got energized, the fans started screaming again. Even at that point, when we were down eight, I really believed we were going to win it.

PEYTON MANNING: We were able to score, on a short Addai run, with a minute left to give us a 38–34 win.

TONY DUNGY: We scored 32 points in the second half and won 38–34. It had been like six years since a Bill Belichick team had given up 32 points in a game, and we did that in the second half.

BILL POLIAN: Most of the guys I've spoken to—and I agree with this 100 percent—said that the feeling of joy we had in the locker room after that game was better than anything we experienced in all the time there. Including the Super Bowl.

DWIGHT FREENEY: It was the ultimate feeling, beating those guys in that type of game. Part of me feels bad for saying this, because the Super Bowl actually means that you won the big one. But that AFC Championship Game, from an emotional standpoint of what it meant at that moment, of just feeling this 500-pound gorilla off your back, and you finally got an opportunity to go to the big one, there was no feeling like it.

It didn't matter who we played in the Super Bowl, because we were going to win that.

TONY DUNGY: I remember celebrating that night until about four o'clock in the morning. Bill quickly reminded me the next day, "It's not over. We still have one more game to win." That set up our Super Bowl against Chicago in Miami.

Lovie Smith, who was on my staff in Tampa, was the Bears' head coach and he brought the Cover Two to Chicago. It probably was the first time ever that you had Cover Two vs. Cover Two in the Super Bowl.

It was amazing. We didn't even have to script any plays in practice, because that was the defense Peyton saw on a daily basis. That was one reason I was so confident going into the game.

I said to Peyton, "You've played against this defense every day for five years. We should know everything there is to know about it."

BILL POLIAN: The joy of beating New England was still very much alive when we started preparing to meet Chicago in the ultimate game. As we were getting ready to leave for Miami and the Super Bowl, Tony asked me to have the players gather in the indoor facility before we boarded the buses to the airport.

This meeting portrayed the philosophy and motivational genius of Tony Dungy. The Colts "can't win the big one" theme circulated in the media. Tony ignored it. He spoke to the team about all that we had accomplished, symbolized by all of the banners hanging in the practice facility. He told them, "We have one more task, to hang a world championship banner on the wall."

It was the perfect way to begin the trip.

TONY DUNGY: We gathered in our indoor practice facility before boarding the buses to the airport. We saw all the banners that had been up: AFC South Champion, AFC South Champion, AFC Championship Game, all of those banners. But there was one banner missing: Super Bowl Champion. We talked about what it was going to take to put that one up next.

I said, "It won't take anything spectacular, it won't take a superhuman effort. It will take all of us doing what we do, every guy doing their job, and doing just what the sign says: executing those high expectations with no excuses, no explanations. And when we come back, we want to be able to come back and put that banner up in the building."

I think that resonated with everybody.

BILL POLIAN: When we got to Miami, the weather was perfect. The long-range forecast, however, was for rain on Super Bowl Sunday.

Peyton being Peyton, leaving no stone unturned, decided we would practice with a wet ball. As a result, under cloudless skies and 80-degree temperatures all through the week, Jeff Saturday had to snap a soaked football. Jeff was not happy.

It poured rain all day Sunday. It was a monsoon, but we were prepared.

PEYTON MANNING: About once every three weeks, Jeff Saturday and I did a wet ball drill, where we were taking snaps with a ball covered with water. Jeff hated it. He just thought it was annoying and irritating because he got soaking wet. The way it worked was, as Jeff was getting ready to snap the ball to me, our equipment managers would spray the ball with the water bottle. Of course, his hands and arms and pants were also getting wet. I remember one time when Jeff said, "Why are we doing this? We're playing in the RCA Dome this week. There's no chance of it being wet." I said, "You never know. There might be a leak in the dome. We can't take any chances. We've got to keep doing this drill."

Jeff was my center for about seven years and through six years of doing those wet ball drills, I think Jeff always was wondering, "Why the hell are we doing this?"

We got to the Super Bowl, it was an absolute monsoon down there and we had zero fumbled snaps. The Bears had two. David Cutcliffe , our offensive coordinator and quarterbacks coach at Tennessee, taught me as a young player, "One fumbled snap is one to many. You shouldn't have any the entire season. Really, you shouldn't have any your entire career because that is the thing you should do the most, is take snaps from your center, under center and shotgun."

Jeff and I did it every day before practice started. We continued into the full-speed drill, pointing out the Mike, calling audibles, trying to reach an assistant coach who was playing the part of a three-technique defensive tackle. Sometimes we were taking snaps instead of a lazy, jack-around, walk-around period. It was full throttle for us.

During the Super Bowl, Jeff looked at me and said, "Okay, now I know why we did all those wet ball drills." I said, "You know, I'm not crazy happy that it's raining in our first Super Bowl, but at least we were ready for it."

BILL POLIAN: We decided that we were never going to kick off to Chicago's great return man, Devin Hester. For some reason, on the opening kickoff of Super Bowl XLI, we kicked right to him. To no one's surprise, he made us pay for the mistake, going the distance for a touchdown. Talk about shock and awe. The flashing camera lights that are customary for the start of a Super Bowl hadn't stopped and we were behind 7–0.

I, however, was not discouraged. Tony had taught our team, as Marv had taught me, "Accept adversity but expect more to overcome it." We had been through so much adversity in the previous five years that I was sure this wouldn't defeat us.

PEYTON MANNING: I felt like all week we weren't going to kick to them and then somewhere along the way, we changed our mind. I must have missed that meeting.

I remember I always wanted to play in a Super Bowl and see all the flashes from the pictures being taken during the opening kickoff. I always wanted to kind of witness that. So, I'm sitting on the bench and we kick off and I'm looking around seeing all those lights. It really is a powerful moment because it tells you, "Hey, okay, I'm really here, I'm really playing in this game." I was kind of looking around and I hadn't heard a whistle yet. I walked toward the field and Devin Hester was running into the end zone. I said, "That's why I haven't heard a whistle. Because there wasn't one." Not the way you want to start the Super Bowl.

With all that rain, we threw a lot of short passes. The Bears played a lot of zone and Joseph Adai had 10 catches. Every now and then, they'd come up and we'd hit a crossing route to Marvin. Not ideal throwing conditions, but we handled it and, obviously, came away with Indianapolis' first world championship. That's a bond that I'll always have with the players and staff and coaches from that team. It was something very special to be a part of.

BILL POLIAN: On the first day of minicamp after winning the Super Bowl, Tony asked me to make sure, after the meeting and before the players changed for practice, to get everybody together in the indoor facility to take our team picture with the banner.

TONY DUNGY: That was to talk about the journey and what it took and all the people who had gone on it with us—the players, coaches, scouts—and those who were with us in spirit.

I said, "Chad Bratzke, who was our captain in '02 and set the tone for us but didn't get to experience that Super Bowl win. And Edgerrin James, who led the league in rushing twice and overcame knee surgery and didn't get to experience it. But you guys did and here's the banner. And it's a banner that we can be proud of. And now we've got to move forward and see if we can get another one."

BILL POLIAN: Tony had it timed so that when he made the statement, "You guys did it and here's the banner," he had one of the workers roll the banner down.

There was a communal intake of breath. It was just one of those moments that you never forget. I can't speak of it even today without choking up. The symbolism of the banner was so powerful and the use of it as a motivational tool was so Tony.

TONY DUNGY: People don't realize how much those kinds of moments mean. They talk about the inspirational speeches and the fire and brimstone and grabbing guys by the facemask and all that. That's not what does it. It's those kinds of moments that guys never forget. They create the energy that your team needs to be successful.

My son died in 2005. Our defensive captain, Gary Brackett, had his mom, dad, and brother pass away in a 16-month stretch starting in 2003. Gary was giving bone marrow transplants to his brother and missing in a minicamp, missing practices.

Gary didn't want to be absent. He said, "I've got to try to save my brother, but I've got a job here. These guys are depending on me."

Everybody on the team was saying, "Hey, Gary, we'll hold the fort down. You go take care of your brother." And to get that news that his brother didn't make it, all of us were just crushed by that.

A similar situation came up when we were playing Jacksonville early in the season. Reggie Wayne made two or three big catches to take us down in scoring position and win the game. We were celebrating and when we came back in the locker room, Craig Kelly, our PR director, told Bill and I, "We just got a phone call. Reggie's brother just got killed in a car accident in New Orleans." We had to tell Reggie and everybody in the locker room this news after such a high from a big win.

We had a bunch of moments like that. But it brought the team closer together and it made us really fight for each other. That, to me, was the beauty of that 2006 season. We overcame a lot of things and we stuck together.

PEYTON MANNING: I enjoyed every part of my four years in college, my 18 years in pro ball, the relationships that I made, the friendships, the coaches, the support, the confidence by Bill Polian and Jim Irsay to draft me with the first pick; I always felt an obligation to give Bill and Jim a return on the investment they were making in me. And I'll always carry that with me. That's kind of what drove me. I knew a lot of people were counting on me:

teammates, coaches, Bill, Jim, Colts fans. That's what drove me to wanting to get better every year.

There's an old saying you either get better or you get worse every day. You don't stay the same. I was kind of challenged to get better every day. I felt like I improved each year. I felt I got more accurate each year. And continuity was so important to that. What drives me crazy today with some quarterbacks is the constant turnover with coaches. By his third season, Baker Mayfield was on his fourth offensive coordinator in Cleveland. I think Alex Smith had six different offensive coordinators in his first six seasons.

If you really want to screw up a quarterback, go ahead and keep changing his offensive coordinator every year. Bill Polian knew that having the same offensive coordinator for me, Tom Moore, was critical. I loved Tom.

I'm just thankful for so many things that played a role in my development, and thankful for the great players that I got to play with.

Acknowledgments

Aside from the contributions of numerous NFL luminaries that made this book possible, the authors also wish to extend their heartfelt gratitude to Tom Bast, acquisitions at Triumph Books; Jesse Jordan, our editor at Triumph Books; and Noah Amstadter, publisher at Triumph Books. We also wish to thank Fran Levy, Cindy Mangum, Diane Lowe, Tex Watts, Leslie Blount, Eddie Borsilli, Mike Kinahan, and Louie Gold for their invaluable assistance.